The Thorny Gates of
Learning in Sung China

The Thorny Gates of Learning in Sung China

A SOCIAL HISTORY OF EXAMINATIONS

NEW EDITION

JOHN W. CHAFFEE

State University of New York, Binghamton

State University of New York Press

Production by Ruth Fisher
Marketing by Bernadette LaManna

Published by
State University of New York Press, Albany

© 1995 State University of New York

For information, address the State University of New York Press,
State University Plaza, Albany, NY 12246

Library of Congress Cataloging-in-Publication Data
Chaffee, John W.
    The thorny gates of learning in Sung China: a social history of
examinations/John W. Chaffee.
        p. cm.
    Originally published: Cambridge, New York: Cambridge University
Press, 1985. (Cambridge studies in Chinese history, literature, and
institutions)
    Includes bibliographical references and index.
    ISBN 0-7914-2423-5 (acid-free).—ISBN 0-7914-2424-3 (pbk.:acid
free)
    1. Civil service—China—Examination—History. I. Series:
Cambridge studies in Chinese history, literature, and institutions.
354.51003'09—dc20
                                                        94-18315
                                                        CIP

For my parents,
Clifford and Mary Chaffee,
and my late mentor,
Edward A. Kracke, Jr.

CONTENTS

LIST OF ILLUSTRATIONS

LIST OF TABLES

LIST OF ABBREVIATIONS

CCC	Yü Hsi-lu. *Chih-hsun Chen-chiang chih.*
CCCW	Ho Wei. *Ch'in-chu chi-wen*
CKC	Chou Ying-ho. *Ching-ting Chien-k'ang chih*
CWCKC	Chou Pi-ta. *Chou wen-chung kung chi.*
CYLY	Chao Sheng. *Ch'ao-yeh lei-yao.*
CYTC	Li Hsin-ch'uan. *Chien-yen i-lai ch'ao-yeh tsa-chi.*
HCLAC	Ch'ien Yueh-yu. *Hsien-ch'ün Lin-an chih.*
HCP	Li T'ao. *Hsü Tzu-chih t'ung-chien ch'ang-pien.*
HNYL	Li Hsin-ch'uan. *Chien-yen i-lai hsi-nien yao-lu.*
ICC	Hung Mai. *I-chien chih*
MS	Ho Ch'iao-yüan. *Min-shu.*
PCSMC	Lo Chün. *Pao-ch'ing Ssu-ming chih.*
PPTK	*Pai-pu ts'ung-k'an.*
SHY:CJ	*Sung hui-yao chi-kao:* the *Ch'ung-ju* section.
SHY:CK	*Sung hui-yao chi-kao:* the *Chih-kuan* section.
SHY:HC	*Sung hui-yao chi-kao:* the *Hsüan-chü* section.
SKCS	*Ssu-k'u ch'üan-shu.*
SKG	Terada Gō. *Sōdai kyōikushi gaisetsu.*
SKSK	Araki Toshikazu. *Sōdai kakyo seido kenkyū.*
SPPY	*Ssu-pu pei-yao.*
SPTK	*Ssu-pu ts'ung-k'an.*
SS	T'o T'o et al. *Sung shih.*
SSYTL	Wang P'i-chih. *Sheng-shui yen-t'an lu.*
SYKCSL	Hsü Nai-ch'ang, ed. *Sung Yüan k'o-chü san lu.*
TCY	Wang T'ing-pao. *T'ang chih-yen.*
TMH	Lü Pen-chung. *T'ung-meng hsün.*
TS	Yüeh K'o. *T'ing-shih.*
TSCC	*Ts'ung-shu chi-ch'eng.*
WHTK	Ma Tuan-lin. *Wen-hsien t'ung-k'ao.*
YH	Wang Ying-lin. *Yü-hai.*
YHCW	Chang Shih-nan. *Yu-huan chi-wen.*
YYSMC	Yüan Chüeh. *Yen-yu Ssu-ming chih.*

GEOGRAPHICAL NOTE

In order to make the many place-names used in this study as understandable as possible, names and administrative units that changed during the course of the Sung have been standardized. In particular:

1. Circuits (*lu*) that were subdivided during the dynasty are given in their divided forms. Liang-che, for example, is treated as two circuits: Liang-che-tung and Liang-che-hsi.

2. Circuits and prefectures that underwent changes in name are referred to by just one of their names. For prefectures, the change was usually from the status of a normal prefecture (*chou*) to that of a superior prefecture (*fu*). In most cases the *chou* name is used. The alternate name or names are given in Table 26, Appendix 2.

3. There were actually four administrative entities between the circuits and counties (*hsien*): superior prefectures, regular prefectures, industrial prefectures (*chien*), and commandaries (*chün*). For the purposes of the examinations, however, they were functionally indistinguishable, so the term 'prefecture' is used to refer to all of them.

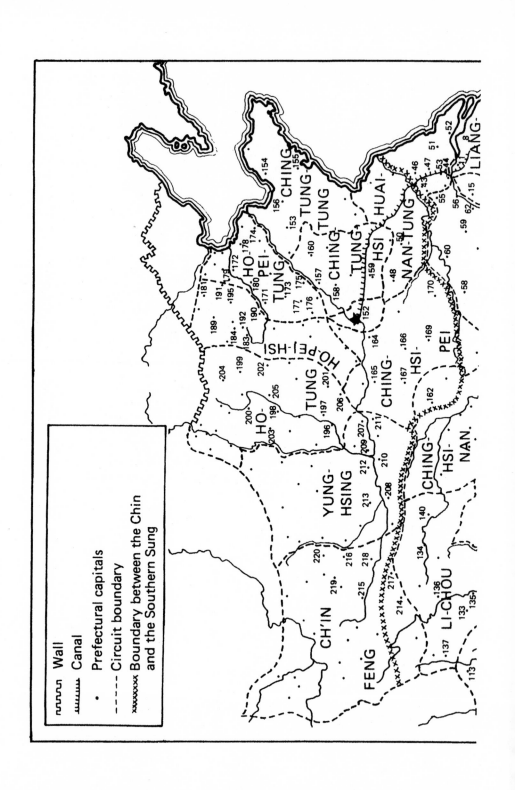

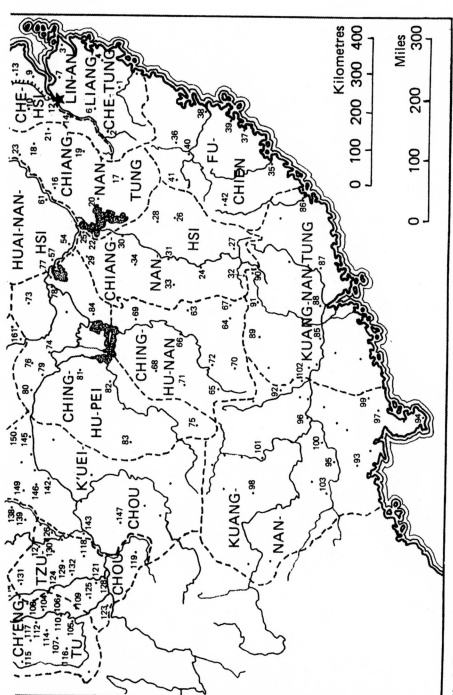

Fig. 1. The circuits and prefectures of Sung China.

PREFACE TO THE SECOND EDITION

On May 2, 1994, the English-language *China Daily* ran an article headlined "Exams are bane of school life." The author, Lin Shiwei, describes the educational problems faced by China today. First, the disparity between ordinary and key high schools, with students from the latter dominating entry into university, creates apathy among students and teachers at the ordinary high schools. Second, the enormous weight given the university entrance examination results in students focusing on examination preparation to the exclusion of other activities, including their regular school work. Third, schools as a result educate students poorly, leaving youths "underdeveloped intellectually, physically and mentally." The article concludes by quoting an educational authority: "The exam-oriented school system needs to find a way to instill these values" (Lin, 1994:5).

Living as we do in a world where examinations are ubiquitous—used not only in education but also as a means of selecting people for jobs and certifying people for job-related skills—these problems are hardly remarkable, for problems of equity and values are commonly associated with systems of competitive selection. What is remarkable is how well they describe the educational problems of Sung China.

It is widely known that the Chinese pioneered in the use of literary examinations for the selection of their officials and political elite, with the beginnings of this practice to be found in the teachings of Confucius and the policies of the Han dynasty, when testing first became a means for the selection of officials. Less well known is the fact that the institutional articulation of the civil service examinations and their development into the premier and preferred means of recruitment occurred largely during the Sung dynasty (960–1279). Thus the Sung Chinese have claim to having history's first examination-oriented society, one that already confronted the problems described in the *China Daily* article.

* * * * *

In *The Thorny Gates of Learning in Sung China*, which was first published in 1985, I attempted to chart both the history and social configuration of that examination-oriented society. Previous treatments of Sung examinations and schools had almost all taken the form of institutional history, and had little to say about the social impact of those institutions, with the notable exception of my late mentor,

E. A. Kracke, Jr., who argued that the examinations had facilitated upward social mobility (Kracke, 1947, 1967).[1] Yet the more I studied Sung examinations, the more convinced I became that they occupied a social and political nexus of great importance. Their functions related to imperial goals, bureaucratic personnel needs, social status, the articulation of local elite society, regional development, and changes in the structure and functions of the family. The book is therefore an attempt to describe the interactions of these multiple functions while also making sense of institutional history.

It takes as its starting point the series of changes undertaken by the founding Sung emperors which effectively remade the system of "classified selection" *(k'o-chü)* that had begun almost four centuries earlier under the Sui. These included dramatically increasing the numbers of degrees given; creating prefectural and palace examinations so that, together with the examination given by the Board of Rites, the system had three levels or tiers; articulating procedures to ensure the anonymity of the written examinations and therefore the utmost impartiality in their grading; and developing a quota system for the prefectural examinations as a means of regulating the flow of prefectural graduates to the capital. These changes succeeded in making the examinations a central feature of the political culture. Candidate numbers grew dramatically, as did the examinations' competitiveness. A system of government schools emerged in the eleventh century, and improving both the schools and examinations became a major goal of reform ministers thereafter. With two further eleventh century changes—establishing a triennial schedule for the examinations and deciding upon the "advanced scholar" *(chin-shih)* degree as the single degree for examination graduates (there had previously been various degrees in different subjects)—the examinations had assumed an institutional form that was to characterize them for the next millennium.

Yet even as the examinations flourished and developed institutionally, the meritocratic aims of the founding emperors were largely subverted. People learned to work the system in order to improve their chances of passing and gaining official status. In addition to outright cheating and corruption, some moved to prefectures where quotas were less stringent. Relatives of officials flocked to special examinations that had been created to reduce the likelihood that they would be unfairly favored by the examiners but which in fact gave them a competitive advantage. As the dynasty progressed, they also made increasing use of the hereditary privilege of protection—or the *yin* privilege—whereby high officials could have one or more of their relatives receive official status upon passing an easy test. Indeed, such was the popularity of protection that in the eleventh and twelfth centuries the proportion of officials recruited via the examinations decreased, even though candidate numbers and examination competition were dramatically increasing.

This failure of fairness, however, did not hinder a number of socio-cultural developments that owed much to the examinations. These included the emergence of the literati as a status group in its own right (by the Southern Sung even partial attainments in the examination process conferred status in local society); the emergence too of local elites involved in examinations and national affairs but actively engaged in local affairs, among which were academies *(shu-yuan)* which flourished in the twelfth and thirteenth centuries, and the articulation of an examination culture with its own rituals, symbols, and lore. The last section of the book is devoted to these phenomena and their regional manifestations.

* * * * *

In the decade since the first publication of *The Thorny Gates*, much new work has appeared dealing with examinations and education and their social significance. With a few exceptions, it has taken the form of articles rather than books and has appeared primarily in Chinese and English. Although a full review of this literature is beyond the scope of this essay (and much of the Chinese and Japanese literature is difficult to get hold of), I would like to offer some reflections on those works I have been able to obtain, and particularly on several attempts at broad synthesis in the form of review articles.

Most of the recent work relating to the Sung examinations specifically has been done by Chinese scholars, with only occasional contributions from Western and Japanese scholars. Much of this has been institutional in focus: meticulous studies sorting out such issues as the curricular requirements of the different degrees that were given in the Northern Sung (Chang, 1991a), the statistics for the number of degrees given (Chang, 1991b), the bureaucratic implications of the high volume of examination graduates (Ho, 1986a), and the institutional development of the examinations (Chin, 1991; Chang, 1986). Thomas H. C. Lee [Li Hung-ch'i], whose erudite and richly detailed book, *Government Education and Examinations in Sung China*, came out at the same time as *The Thorny Gates*, has provided a broad perspective on the examinations in one English and two Chinese articles: the first an attempt to relate the appearance of extraordinarily large families beginning in the ninth century and continuing through the Sung to the demands of the examinations (Lee, 1992); the second an overview of the development of the examinations from the Sui to the Ch'ing (Lee, 1982); and the third a sophisticated analysis of the history, functions, and status of the Sung *chü-jen* ("selected men"—graduates of the prefectural examinations) (Lee, 1988). Also worth brief mention is an intriguing article by the leading Japanese authority on Sung examinations, Araki Toshikazu, relating examination failure to rebellion in twelfth century Fukien (Araki, 1986), and my statistical analysis of the *chin-shih* lists of 1148 and 1256 (Chaffee, 1989b).

For scholars in this country, Sung schools have in recent years proved a far more attractive topic than examinations. The most important development in this regard was the appearance in 1989 of *Neo-Confucian Education: The Formative Stage*, edited by Wm. Theodore de Bary and myself. The nineteen essays in the collection cover a wide range of topics: Buddhist education (Zürcher, Yü), government schools (Lee), pedagogy and the philosophy of education (Tu, Bol, de Bary and Kelleher), education within the family (Ebrey, Wu, Birge), community (Chu, Übelhör), and academies (Chan, Chaffee, Hymes, Walton).

Two foci in the collection are especially noteworthy for they reflect the particular strengths and concerns of the field: the role played by Chu Hsi (1130-1200) and the history of the academies, especially the new and revived academies of the twelfth and thirteenth centuries. The two are related, of course, for Chu's role in the academy movement of the late twelfth century was central. The varied dimensions of that role have been explored by Thomas Lee, not in *Neo-Confucian Education* but in a number of other articles (1984, 1991, 1992, 1993b), as well by Wing-tsit Chan (1989), while my two articles on the White Deer Grotto Academy examined the political dimensions of Chu Hsi's activities (1985, 1989).

Not all treatments of academies work through the filter of Chu, however. Hoyt Tillman has pointed to the important role played by Lü Tsu-ch'ien (1137-1181) (1990), while Robert Hymes' article on Lu Chiu-yuan (1139-1192) and academies develops the intriguing notion that the building and operating of academies can be seen as the development by the local elite of a "middle space" between the government and family (1989). Finally, in a very different vein, Linda Walton has approached Sung and Yuan academies as religious and ceremonial centers, and has thereby offered a useful corrective to a tendency to view them simply as centers of study (1989, 1993).

With the exception of Thomas Lee's article on government education in *Neo-Confucian Education* and Richard Davis' paper on Southern Sung university student activism (1990), recent Western scholarship has paid little attention to Sung government schools. Scholars in China have been much more active, producing, in the last few years, two books and numerous articles treating government schools. Yuan Cheng, in particular, has written extensively on Sung schools; in 1991 he published a book entitled *Sung-tai chiao-yü: Chung-kuo ku-tai chiao-yü ti li-shih-hsing chuan-che (Education Under the Sung Dynasty: A Pivotal Transition in Traditional Chinese Education)*.[2] Yuan's book attaches great significance to the Sung development of graded schools, grading of students, and selection of teachers, and also provides an extensive treatment of the examinations. Most provocatively, he challenges the notion of the academies as private educational institutions, arguing that in the Southern Sung they were incorporated into the empire-wide system of government education, both in terms of their student bodies and the appointment of their teachers (Yuan 1991:231-38, 305-8). Although to my mind this claim stretches the evidence—relying on a couple of well-documented cases where the government's role in academy activities was great—it provides a useful corrective to the simple view of the academies as private that has often prevailed in the past.

Although not specifically focused upon schools or examinations, two important books on the Sung bureaucracy which appeared in the late 1980s also deserve our attention. Umehara Kaoru's massive *Sôdai kanryô seido kenkyû* (*Studies of Sung personnel administration*), while not concerned with the examinations as such, offers the most comprehensive treatment of the various methods of recruitment to date, particularly the *yin* privilege, and also explicates the often confusing rules governing bureaucratic promotion. Winston W. Lo's *An Introduction to the Civil Service of Sung China* covers much of the same ground as Umehara, though in less detail and with a relatively greater emphasis on administrative mechanisms for personnel evaluation and promotion. Both of these books make excellent companions to *The Thorny Gates*, which has little to say about movement through the bureaucracy, whereas all three treat—and for the most part agree on—the varying forms of recruitment into the bureaucracy.

To round out this survey of literature, we should note two works which, though not specifically concerned with examinations and schooling, have nevertheless made important contributions to our conceptions of Sung elite society. Robert Hymes' *Statesmen and Gentlemen: The Elite of Fu-chou, Chiang-hsi, in Northern and Southern Sung* (1986) appeared almost contemporaneously with *The Thorny Gates* and might seem peripheral to our concerns since it employs the approach of local history, yet it has influenced the scholarship on Sung schools and examinations in two important ways. First, following his mentor Robert Hartwell (see especially, Hartwell, 1982), Hymes challenged Kracke's argument that the examinations fostered social mobility and asserted, moreover, that examination candidacy was basically restricted to members of the elite. Since Hymes had also made this argument in his dissertation, my objections to the last point can be found on pp. 40-41 below, but I would at the same time agree that Kracke's view of the examinations fostering the large-scale recruitment of "new blood" is no longer tenable. Second and more important, Hymes argued that a fundamental shift in elite society occurred between Northern and Southern Sung, from domination of a national elite focused on the capital, K'ai-feng, and to a large extent intermarrying, to a large number of local elites with prefectural loci which tended to marry locally within their own circles. Although Hartwell also argued for such a change, the power of Hymes' work lies in his ability to demonstrate this shift for Fu-chou and by his explanatory framework of changing family strategies. For him, education and examination success were dependent variables that helped mark elite status but did not generate it independently.

The second work is a 1991 Berkeley dissertation which specifically takes issue with the Hymes' thesis. Beverly Jo Bossler's "Powerful Relations and Relations of Power: Family and Society in Sung China, 960-1279" is also concerned with the long-term historical changes in the status and power of elite families and the roles played by marriage, education, examinations, and bureaucratic privilege, but approaches them through a detailed and painstaking analysis of two previously unstudied groups: the families of Sung grand councilors and families prominent in

the records of the Chekiang prefecture of Wu-chou. Bossler challenges Hymes'
model of elite change on two counts. First, she argues that the Northern to
Southern Sung change was more apparent than real. While recognizing far-reaching changes in Sung society—especially related to the growing appeal of the examinations—she sees them as gradual and not focused in the early twelfth century.
She sees the apparent rise of local elites in the Southern Sung as an historiographi-
cal anomaly; thanks to the spread of printing and the Southern Sung rise of Neo-
Confucianism *(tao-hsueh)*, far more collected writings were preserved than had
previously been the case. In particular, writings elevating the roles of Neo-
Confucian scholars in the countryside over those of ministers at the capital tended
to be disproportionately preserved, thus giving Southern Sung writings a more local
focus than their Northern Sung counterparts.

Second, Bossler challenges the notion that Sung society was ever dominated by
a homogeneous elite within a highly stratified society. She argues instead for "a
highly integrated continuum of status and prestige, in which wealth, office, social
and kinship connections, personal charisma, and any number of other attributes
could combine to determine an individual's place" (500). In Bossler's view, Sung
society was more fluid and more open to social mobility than many other scholars
believe, though she acknowledges that at times the promise of that mobility was
greater than the reality.

* * * * *

Apart from the varied studies described above, which have collectively
advanced our knowledge of Sung society in many different ways, in recent years
several scholars have attempted through review articles to make broad statements
concerning, among other things, the role of the examinations in Sung and late
imperial Chinese society. Because they represent a new, more synthesizing phase
of scholarship, they are deserving of special attention.

Benjamin Elman's 1991 article, "Political, Social, and Cultural Reproduction
via Civil Service Examinations in Late Imperial China," is one of the most ambitious attempts to date to explain the fundamental nature of the Chinese—as
opposed to the Sung—examination system, though he gives considerable attention
to the Sung examinations, especially the reforms of the early Sung. Elman criti-
cizes two common interpretations of the late imperial examinations—that they promoted high levels of social mobility (Ho, 1962), and that they retarded attempts at
modernization in the nineteenth and twentieth centuries. Instead, he portrays the
examinations as "a brilliant piece of social engineering," an "educational gyro-
scope" that provided a stabilizing center for a system of remarkable longevity. In
making this argument, Elman draws upon the theories of Pierre Bourdieu (1977),
who argues that once a system of degrees, titles, and education has been established, the "dominant class" can use it to control the political, social, and cultural
reproduction of the society. That, says Elman, is precisely the way in which the

examinations worked, even to the point of offering a politically useful but false promise of mobility to non-elites:

> A masterpiece of social, political and cultural reproduction, the civil exami-
> nation system persuaded rulers, elites, and commoners of the viability of the
> Confucian dream of public success and social mobility, thereby inducing
> misrecognition at all levels of its objective consequences. (Elman, 1991:18)

This argument agrees closely with my own finding that "The myth of opportunity was as important for social stability as its lie was to the elite's privileged position" (*The Thorny Gates*, 17). Whether Elman's structuralist approach can serve as
an explanatory framework for the Sung examinations is questionable, however, for
it is not especially good at explaining change: how systems are first put into place,
and how they evolve. This is not a great problem for the Ming and Ch'ing, when
changes in the examinations were few and far between, but it is for the Sung, and I
will have more to say about it below.

In his article, "The Sung Examination System and the *Shih*," Peter Bol draws
upon material from *The Thorny Gates*, not to argue with it so much as to push its
arguments further. What particularly intrigues him is the paradox of rising candidate
numbers in the examinations and decreasing importance of the regular examinations,
which were losing ground to both the *yin* privilege and facilitated examination
degrees (given to elderly, multiple repeaters of the examinations who as a consequence had few career expectations).[3] Why were the literati—he prefers the
Chinese "*shih*"—increasingly attracted to the examinations even as they were
becoming less important as a route of bureaucratic entry? Professor Bol offers
two explanations.

First, that the examinations came to be seen not merely as a route to office but
also as a validation of elite *shih* status. Thus, ever increasing numbers embarked
upon an examination education even though their chances of success were tiny,
and in the process did much to create the civil culture of late imperial China (Bol
1992:166-68). But even accepting this explanation, Bol suggests that it was not as
important as his second explanation, which is that the examinations served as a
mechanism "to preserve *shih* status from generation to generation" (168). In an
argument marked by its painstaking attention to detail, he contends that: a) the vast
majority of those enumerated in the 1213 listing of the civil service (see p. 25 below)
were from bureaucratic families; b) the growing difficulty of the examinations
made it increasingly difficult to count on passing them; c) that most if not all of the
growth in candidate numbers can be explained in terms of the reproduction and natural growth of the eleventh- century bureaucratic families; d) that examination success—including limited degrees of it—came to serve as its own status justification.
Examinations thus became "an institution that allowed local elites to claim the privilege of belonging to a relatively homogeneous national elite" (171).

Although this conclusion is not one that I drew in *The Thorny Gates*, it is consistent with my findings and, in fact, follows logically from a statistical point that I had made but not sufficiently stressed: that Sung elite families were huge (with three to four sons on average), so that their descendants were multiplying from generation (I make the point more forcefully in Chaffee, 1989b). Moreover, if we accept the notion that growing candidates numbers was largely a matter of elite self-propagation, then we might also ask if Robert Hymes' Northern to Southern Sung transformation described above was not, at least in part, another result of large Sung families (Hymes, 1986).[4] At the same time, it is important to note Bol's first, albeit subsidiary point, that the examination candidacy helped to define *shih* status and thereby became a goal for non-elite, upwardly mobile families.

Finally, Patricia Ebrey's review article, "The Dynamics of Elite Domination in Sung China" (1988), analyzes five books that appeared in 1985-86: those by Robert Hymes, Thomas Lee, and Umehara Kaoru which have been discussed above, Richard Davis' study of the Shih family of Ming-chou (1986), and *The Thorny Gates*. Beginning with the debate over the social mobility via the examinations, she agrees with Hartwell and Hymes—as well as Elman and Bol—that the examinations did little to promote social mobility. Like Bol, she also remarks upon the fecundity of the elite, but does so not to explain the quantitative growth of the literati or *shih*, but rather to explain the constant attempts by large elite families to manipulate the system so as to get an *increasing* share of the political pie:

> Established families at both the national and local levels regularly felt pressed to "change the rules" for distribution of prestige and power to give more advantages to people like themselves. Because elite families grew very rapidly, they could not be content simply to hold on to their existing share of the social and political rewards and privileges, but had to expand their share in order to keep their sons at the level of their fathers. (Ebrey, 1988:498)

How was this done? She cites the expansion of the *yin* privilege, uses of the placement system for officials, and the development of special examinations and quotas for the relatives of officials described in *The Thorny Gates*. In doing so she directly challenges Bourdieu's notion of the dominant class passively allowing the system to run for its own benefit: "I am arguing that the elite could not leave the system alone if they wished to continue to dominate it in the terms meaningful to them." (Ebrey, 1988:500)

* * * * *

Although these review articles were each written with different purposes and from different standpoints, their similarities are far more striking than their differences. They point to a growing consensus about the social role of the examinations: first, that the examinations generally served to perpetuate elite domination rather than undermining it; second, that the examinations were of central importance within the social order, providing both hierarchies of status and a shared culture within a vast empire; and third, that the promise of entry into the elite via education and the examinations, while more a mirage than a reality, was nevertheless a politically necessary and potent myth.

This consensus is not without problems, most notably the challenge of Beverly Bossler's work, described above, which calls into question the very notion of discrete social elites, whether national or local. But Bossler's disagreements should not be overdrawn, for she recognizes the importance of the examinations, privilege, and marriage for the status maintenance of powerful families and the dramatic growth of the literate population during the Sung, even while arguing that that growth did not mark a qualitative change. Still, her work ensures that there will be ample discussion and vigorous debate in the future concerning the nature of Sung society.

Many other questions remain. If Ebrey is right concerning elite manipulation of the examinations in the Sung and Elman is also right in saying that the elite were able to benefit from a fairly fixed examination system in the Ming and Ch'ing, then how do we explain the transition from one mode to the other?[5] How do schools fit into this sociopolitical framework? Were government schools and academies both extensions of the examinations, as Yuan Cheng argues, or did the academies, at least, occupy that "middle space" between government and families into which local elites were spreading during the Southern Sung? Finally, how do we interpret the rise toward orthodoxy of Chu Hsi's version of Neo-Confucianism and the role it played by schools and examinations?

As readers approach *The Thorny Gates* today, a certain dated quality is unavoidable, since it was written over a decade ago. It is my hope that the issues and questions raised by recent scholarship will enhance the readers' responses to the book, for to a large extent that scholarship has amplified and clarified my findings, rather than negating them.

Let me close by addressing the general reader who might not be enthralled by the specific issues of historiography and scholarship described above. Of what interest is a book dealing with the schools and examinations of a long-defunct dynasty? My answer is threefold. First, the Sung examinations represent a crucial stage in the development of the Chinese imperial examinations, which lasted into this century (they were abolished in 1905). The palace examination, the use of preliminary examinations outside of the capital, the exclusive conferral of the *chin-shih* degree after the palace examination, the use of the *chü-jen* degree for provincial graduates, the three-year examination cycle, and the development of examination halls—all of these features of the Ming and Ch'ing examinations had Sung origins. Among educational institutions, prefectural schools, county schools, and academies all existed in T'ang times, but in terms of organization, curriculum, finance, campus layout, and, in the case of government schools, formal integration into the examination system, Ming-Ch'ing schools and academies can be viewed as largely Sung creations. Perhaps most important, the overwhelming orientation of the *shih-ta-fu* elite towards education and examination competition characteristic in late imperial China was largely a Sung development. Therefore, the Sung history of examinations and schools are of great significance to Chinese history as a whole.

Second, the importance of the Sung examinations extends beyond China, for the Chinese examinations themselves were of considerable world-historical significance. Many claims are made in Europe and the United States for the centrality of such Western traditions as democracy, human rights, and individualism throughout the world. There is little recognition that another virtually universal characteristic of modern societies—the use of schools and tests not only to educate the young but also to perform the critical functions of occupational selection and status differentiation—originated in China, not the West. Thanks to Jesuits and other Western observers of late Ming and Ch'ing China, the Chinese model of meritocracy served as a powerful model for Enlightenment philosophers, and thereby helped to shape the modern Western world (Teng, 1942-43).

Third, in light of the similarities between the educational problems of the Sung and those described by the *China Daily* article, an analysis of the Sung experience can have contemporary relevance. For example, the remarkable attempt by the early Sung emperors to use examinations to create a meritocracy has many parallels among revolutionaries and reformers of the twentieth century, so the ways in which the attempt was subverted can be instructive for us all. This is not to say that lessons from the past can be simply transplanted into the present, but the very realization that certain problems are not unique to the present may provide valuable perspective and understanding.

John W. Chaffee
Binghamton University

Notes

1. Kracke's studies are often associated with Ping-ti Ho's massive study of social mobility in Ming and Ch'ing China, *The Ladder of Success in Imperial China* (1962), which employs the same methodology to largely the same ends.
2. Described in a detailed review by Bao Weimin (1994).
3. The facilitated degrees, Bol argues, were important socially rather than bureaucratically: they rewarded those willing to spend most of their lives taking the examinations without making them serious competitors for regular bureaucratic posts (161–62).
4. Thomas Lee makes a similar point concerning the impact that huge families with hundreds of members living as a social and legal unit had upon upper-class receptivity to the examinations and the ensuing development of local elite society, but does not adequately demonstrate the representative nature of his large family examples (Lee, 1992).
5. In this regard, see Elman's 1993 article on examinations in the early Ming.

Bibliography

Araki Toshikazu. 1986. "Nung Chih-kao and the *K'o-chü* Examinations," *Acta Asiatica* 50:73-94.

Bao Weimin. 1993. Review of Yuan Zheng's book (see below), *Journal of Sung Yuan Studies* 24:321-25.

Birge, Bettine. 1989. "Chu Hsi and Women's Education," in Wm. Theodore de Bary and John W. Chaffee, *Neo-Confucian Education: The Formative Stage.* Berkeley: University of California Press. Pp. 325-67.

Bol, Peter. 1989. "Chu Hsi's Redefinition of Literati Learning," in Wm. Theodore de Bary and John W. Chaffee, *Neo-Confucian Education: The Formative Stage.* Pp. 151-85.

———. 1992. "The Sung Examination System and the *Shih,*" *Asia Major,* Third Series, 3.2:149-71.

Bossler, Beverly Jo. 1991. "Powerful Relations and Relations of Power: Family and Society in Sung China, 960-1279." Ph.D. Dissertation, University of California, Berkeley.

Chaffee, John W. 1985. "Chu Hsi and the Revival of the White Deer Grotto Academy, 1179-81," *T'oung Pao* 71:40-62.

———. 1989a. "Chu Hsi in Nan-k'ang: *Tao-hsüeh* and the Politics of Education," in Wm. Theodore de Bary and John W. Chaffee, *Neo-Confucian Education: The Formative Stage.* Pp. 414-31.

———. 1989b. "Status, Family and Locale: An Analysis of Sung Examination Lists," in Kinugawa Tsuyoshi, ed., *Collected Studies on Sung History Dedicated to Professor James T. C. Liu in Celebration of His Seventieth Birthday.* Kyoto: Dohosha. 341-56.

Chan, Wing-tsit. 1989. "Chu Hsi and the Academies," in Wm. Theodore de Bary and John W. Chaffee, *Neo-Confucian Education: The Formative Stage.* Pp. 389-413.

Chang Hsi-ch'ing. 1986. "Lun Wang An-shih ti kung-chü kai-ko" (The examination reforms of Wang An-shih), *Pei-ching ta-hsueh hsueh-pao* No. 4:66-77.

———. 1991a. "Nan-Sung kung-chü teng-k'o jen-shu k'ao" (A study of Southern Sung examination degree statistics), *Ku-chi cheng-li yü yen-chiu* No. 5:129-46.

———. 1991b. "Sung-tai kung-chü k'o-mu shu-lun" (A detailed account of the Sung examination curriculum). *Kuo-chi Sung-shih yen-t'ao-hui lun-wen hsuan-chi* (Selected papers from the International Conference on Sung History). Hopei: Hopei University Press. Pp. 320-41.

Chin Chung-shu. 1991. "Pei-Sung k'o-chü cheng hsi jen-yuan jen-yung-chih chih hsing-ch'eng k'ao" (A study of the development of the Northern Sung system of formal personnel employment via the examinations). Paper presented to the International Conference on Sung History. Peking.

Chu Jui-hsi. 1990. "Sung Yuan ti Shih-wen—Pa-ku-wen ti Ch'u-hsing" (The *shih-wen* of the Sung and Yuan—a prototype for the eight-legged essays), *Li-shih yen-chiu* No. 3:29-43.

Chu, Ron-Guey. 1989. "Chu Hsi and Public Instruction," in Wm. Theodore de Bary and John W. Chaffee, *Neo-Confucian Education: The Formative Stage*. Pp. 252-73.

Davis, Richard. 1986. *Court and Family in Sung China, 960-1279: Bureaucratic Success and Kinship Fortunes for the Shih of Ming-chou.* Durham: Duke University Press.

———. 1990. "The Imperial University Leading the Late Sung Bureaucracy: the Ignoble Finale of Ch'en Yi-chung." Paper presented to the Symposium on Confucian Intellectuals: Ideals and Actions. Hong Kong: The Chinese University of Hong Kong.

de Bary, Wm. Theodore. 1989. "Chu Hsi's Aims as an Educator," in Wm. Theodore de Bary and John W. Chaffee, *Neo-Confucian Education: The Formative Stage*. Pp. 186-218.

Ebrey, Patricia. 1988. "The Dynamics of Elite Domination in Sung China," *Harvard Journal of Asiatic Studies* 48.2:493-519.

———. 1989. "Education Through Ritual: Efforts to Formulate Family Rituals During the Sung Period," in Wm. Theodore de Bary and John W. Chaffee, *Neo-Confucian Education: The Formative Stage*. Pp. 277-306.

Elman, Benjamin A. 1991a. "Political, Social, and Cultural Reproduction via Civil Service Examinations in Late Imperial China," *Journal of Asian Studies* 50.1:7-28.

———. 1991b. "Review Article: Education in Sung China," *Journal of the American Oriental Society* 111:83-93.

———. 1993. "'Where Is King Ch'eng?' Civil Examinations and Confucian Ideology during the Early Ming, 1368-1415," *T'oung Pao* 79.1-3:23-68.

Hartwell, Robert. 1982. "Demographic, Political, and Social Transformations of China," *Harvard Journal of Asiatic Studies* 10.2:365-442.

Ho Chung-li. 1986a. "Pei-Sung k'uo-ta k'o-chü ch'ü-shih ti yuan-yin yü jung-kuan jung-li ti kuan-hsi" (The extension of imperial examinations in the Northern Sung dynasty: its causes and its relationship to the emergence of redundant government officials), in Hsu Kuei, ed., *Sung-shih yen-chiu chi-k'an*. Hang-chou: Che-chiang ku-chi ch'u-pan-she. Pp. 87-106.

———. 1986b. "*Sung-shih* li ch'uan jen-wu teng-k'o nien-tai cheng-wu" (The biographies in the *History of the Sung Dynasty*: their dates of passing the highest imperial examinations checked), in Hsu Kuei, ed., *Sung-shih yen-chiu chi-k'an*. Pp. 368-81.

Hymes, Robert. 1986. *Statesmen and Gentlemen: The Elite of Fu-chou, Chiang-hsi, in Northern and Southern Sung*. Cambridge: Cambridge University Press.

———. 1989. "Lu Chiu-yüan, Local Academies, and the Problem of the Local Community," in Wm. Theodore de Bary and John W. Chaffee, *Neo-Confucian Education: The Formative Stage*. Pp. 432-56.

Ihara Hiroshi. 1987. "Chûgoku shomin kyôiku kenkyû no tame no joshô—toku ni Sôdai o chûshin ni shite" (An introduction to research on Chinese popular education, with emphasis on the central role played by the Sung), *Tôyô kyôikushi kenkyû* 11:61-77.

Kelleher, M. Theresa. 1989. "Back to Basics: Chu Hsi's *Elementary Learning (Hsiao-hsüeh)*," in Wm. Theodore de Bary and John W. Chaffee, *Neo-Confucian Education: The Formative Stage*. Pp. 219-51.

Ko Shao-ou. "Sung-tai fu-chou ti kung-yuan" (Examination halls in Sung dynasty prefectures). *Kuo-chi Sung-shih yen-t'ao-hui lun-wen hsuan-chi* (Selected papers from the International Conference on Sung History). Hopei: Hopei University Press. Pp. 304-19.

Kracke, Edward A., Jr. 1947. "Family versus Merit in Chinese Civil Service Examinations under the Empire," *Harvard Journal of Asiatic Studies* 10:103-23.

———. 1967. "Region, Family and Individual in the Chinese Examination System," in John K. Fairbank, ed., *Chinese Thought and Institutions*. Chicago: University of Chicago Press. Pp. 251-68.

Lee, Thomas H. C. [Li Hung-ch'i]. 1982. "K'o-chü—Sui T'ang chih Ming Ch'ing ti k'ao-shih chih-tu" (Examinations: the examination system from the Sui and T'ang to the Ming and Ch'ing), in *Chung-kuo wen-hua hsin-lun,* 259-315.

————. 1984. "Chu Hsi, Academies and the Tradition of Private *Chiang-hsueh,"Chinese Studies* 2.1:301-329.

————. 1985. *Government Education and Examinations in Sung China.* Hong Kong: Chinese University of Hong Kong Press.

————. 1988. "Sung-tai ti chü-jen" (Sung dynasty *chü-jen*), *Kuo-chi Sung-shih yen-t'ao-hui lun-wen chi* (Proceedings of International Symposium on Sung History). Taipei: Chinese Culture University, 1988. Pp. 297-314.

————. 1989. "Sung Schools and Education Before Chu Hsi," in Wm. Theodore de Bary and John W. Chaffee, eds., *Neo-Confucian Education: The Formative Stage.* Pp. 105-36.

————. 1990a. "Chu Hsi, shu-yuan yü ssu-jen chiang-hsueh ti ch'uan-t'ung" (Chu Hsi, academies, and the tradition of private instruction), *Kuo-li pien-i kuan kuan-k'an* 19.2:1-14.

————. 1990b. "Fan Chung-yen yü Pei-Sung ti shu-yuan ch'uan-t'ung" (Fan Chung-yen and the Northern Sung tradition of academies), *Chi-nien Fan Chung-yen i-ch'ien nien yen-ch'en kuo-chi hsueh-shu yen-t'ao hui lun-wen chi,* 1399-1426.

————. 1990c. "The Fulfillment of Education: Social Alienation and Intellectual Dissent in Paradox." Paper delivered to the Symposium on Confucian Intellectuals: Ideals and Actions. Hong Kong, Chinese University of Hong Kong.

————. 1992. " Politics, Examinations and the Chinese Society, 1000-1500: Reflections on the Rise of the Local Elite and the Civil Society in Later Imperial China," in *Family Process and Political Process in Modern Chinese History.* Taipei: Institute of Modern History, Academia Sinica.

————. 1993a. "Ching-she yü shu-yuan" (*Ching-she* and *shu-yuan*), *Chinese Studies* 10.2:307-332.

————. 1993b. "Neo-Confucian Education in Chien-yang, Fu-chien, 1000-1400: Academies, Society and the Development of Local Culture," *Kuo-chi Chu Tzu hsueh-i lun-wen chi (Collected Essays from the International Conference on Chu Hsi).* Taiwan: Chung-yang yen-chiu-yuan Chung-kuo wen-che yen-chiu-suo t'ao-pei-ch'u yin-hang. Pp.945-96.

Lin, Shiwei. 1994. "Exams are bane of school life," *China Daily.* May 2.

Lo, Winston W. 1987. *An Introduction to the Civil Service of Sung China, With Emphasis on Its Personnel Administration.* Honolulu: University of Hawaii Press.

McKnight, Brian. 1989. "Mandarins as Legal Experts: Professional Learning in Sung China," in Wm. Theodore de Bary and John W. Chaffee, *Neo-Confucian Education: The Formative Stage.* Pp. 493-516.

Miao Chunde. 1992. *Sung-tai chiao-yü* (Sung education). Henan University Press.

Tillman, Hoyt. 1990. "Community Action by Intellectuals and Official Action: Some Reflections on Sung Academies and Granaries." Paper delivered to the Symposium on Confucian Intellectuals: Ideals and Actions. Hong Kong, Chinese University of Hong Kong.

Tu, Wei-ming. 1989. "The Sung Confucian Idea of Education: A Background Understanding," in Wm. Theodore de Bary and John W. Chaffee, *Neo-Confucian Education: The Formative Stage.* Pp. 139-50.

Übelhör, Monica. 1989. "The Community Compact (*Hsiang-yüeh*) of the Sung and Its Educational Significance," in Wm. Theodore de Bary and John W. Chaffee, *Neo-Confucian Education: The Formative Stage* Pp., 371-88.

Umehara, Kaoru. 1985. *Sôdai kanryô seido kenkyû* (Studies of Sung governmental institutions). Kyoto: Dohosha.

Walton, Linda. 1989. "The Institutional Context of Neo-Confucianism: Scholars, Schools, and *Shu-yüan* in Sung-Yüan China," in Wm. Theodore de Bary and John W. Chaffee, *Neo-Confucian Education: The Formative Stage.* Pp. 457-92.

———. 1993. "Southern Sung Academies as Sacred Places," in Patricia Buckley Ebrey and Peter N. Gregory, eds., *Religion and Society in T'ang and Sung China.* Honolulu: University of Hawaii Press. Pp. 335-63.

Wu, Pei-yi. 1989. "Education of Children in the Sung," in Wm. Theodore de Bary and John W. Chaffee, *Neo-Confucian Education: The Formative Stage.* Pp. 307-24.

Yang Wei-sheng. 1992. "I-pu chü-yu tu-t'e chien-chieh ti Sung-shih chuan-chu—Ch'a-fei *Chi-wei: Sung-shih k'o-chü yen-chiu* chien-chieh" (A completely unique view on the Sung examinations: an introduction to Chaffee's *Thorny Gates: A Study of the Sung Examinations*), *Sung-shih yen-chiu t'ung-hsun* 21:16-20.

Yü, Chün-fang. 1989. "Ch'an Education in the Sung: Ideals and Procedures,"

in Wm. Theodore de Bary and John W. Chaffee,
Neo-Confucian Education: The Formative Stage. Pp. 57-104.

Yuan Cheng. 1991a. *Sung-tai chiao-yü: Chung-kuo ku-tai ti li-shih-hsing chuan-che* (Education Under the Sung Dynasty: A Pivotal Transition in Traditional Chinese Education). Kuang-chou: Kuang-tung Kao-chiao ch'u-pan-she.

———. 1991b. "Sung-tai hsiao-hsueh ti k'o-ch'eng ho chiao-ts'ai" (On curricula and textbooks in elementary schools of the Sung dynasty). Paper presented to the International Conference on Sung History. Peking.

———. 1991-92. "The Grade System of Schools in Eleventh-to-Thirteenth Century China," *Chinese Studies in History* 25.3:17-52.

ACKNOWLEDGEMENTS

However much the historical enterprise might be extolled — or derided — as a solitary venture, for me at least its social aspects have been much in evidence. Without the flowering of Chinese social history and Sung studies that has occurred in recent decades in China, Japan, Europe and the United States, this book would have been inconceivable, a fact that should be evident in my frequent citations of that scholarship. Without the encouragement and criticism provided by teachers, colleagues and students, this book would probably not have appeared, certainly not in its present form.

My debts are many. The late Edward A. Kracke, Jr, who more than anyone helped to establish Sung studies in this country, spend untold hours reading documents with me, shared his research materials on Sung education, and was enthusiastically guiding me through my dissertation at the time of his death. Michael Dalby then stepped into the breach and not only proved an excellent thesis advisor but has been generous in his counsel and encouragement since then. To Ping-ti Ho I owe not only a good deal of my knowledge of Chinese social history but also the idea of making the empire-wide tabulation of *chin-shih* which became the basis for Chapter 6. Robert Hartwell, whose work I have drawn upon heavily, gave me freely of his time in the early stages of this project and provided valuable critiques of some of my initial results. And Thomas H.C. Lee, whose numerous publications on Sung education have greatly advanced that field, has proved a sympathetic and stimulating correspondent.

My thanks go to Paul Greenough, David Biale, Gerald Kadish, and most particularly Denis Twitchett, the Editor of this series, all of whom read my dissertation and provided invaluable advice on revisions for the book. Among the many who provided help and advice on parts of the book, I should mention Charles Peterson, James T.C. Liu, Thomas Africa, Richard Trexler, Tsing Yuan, William Parish, John Berthrong, Michael Finegan, Paul Ho, James Lee, David Kornbluth, Peter Bol, Robert Hymes, Richard Davis, and the late Robert Somers. The Foundation of the State University of New York provided me with a grant which made possible the research and writing of

Chapter 7. Roger Kose provided the excellent maps for my dissertation which have been used, with minor changes, in the book. Deborah Young provided expert and rapid typing for large portions of the book manuscript. And my editors at Cambridge University Press, Robin Derricourt and Iain White, have been ever helpful and obliging in their dealings with me.

There is, finally, my debt to my family. I had the constant encouragement of my in-laws, Helen and Holland Hunter, and my parents, Clifford and Mary Chaffee, whose missionary service in China was undoubtedly the source of my fascination with that great country. Without the love and support of my wife Barbara during the years of research, writing and revision, this book would have been impossible. Last but not least, I am grateful to my sons Conrad and Philip both for their indulgence at my frequent disappearances to the word processor and for the many welcome interruptions which they provided.

PART I

1

INTRODUCTION: THE EXAMINATION LIFE

Two protests

Ch'en Shu was unpopular in the late spring of 1002. A southerner and
therefore an outsider in the imperial capital of K'ai-feng, which lay on the
North China Plain, Ch'en had a reputation for high principles and incorrupt-
ability, and just months earlier the emperor Chen-tsung (r. 998–1022) had
paid him the singular honor of naming him director of the civil service examinations.[1] The streets of K'ai-feng had filled with over fourteen thousand and
five hundred 'selected men' (*chü-jen*) chosen by their prefectures to take the
examinations in the capital. Their hopes were high, for when the examinations
had last been held, in 1000, over 1500 had received the coveted *chin-shih*
('advanced scholar') and *chu-k'o* ('various fields') degrees, thereby qualifying
for entry into officialdom.[2] When, after the grueling departmental examination (*sheng-shih*), Ch'en and his colleagues passed only 218, the shock and
dismay of the failed candidates swiftly turned to anger, and it was directed
against Ch'en. He became the subject of songs. Effigies of him were daubed
with blood. Placards with his name were hung beside roads where they could
be lashed by passersby.[3]

The abuse heaped upon Ch'en was verbal and symbolic. Some two centuries
later Yang Hung-chung was not as fortunate. A young man who had early
gained renown as a student leader at the Imperial University in the Southern
Sung capital of Lin-an fu, Yang had received his *chin-shih* degree in 1205,
and one of his first official postings was as preceptor (*chiao-shou*) of the
prefectural school of Chang-chou, a coastal prefecture in southern Fu-chien.[4]
One of his duties was to help supervise the triennial prefectural examination
at which Chang-chou's quota of twenty-one *chü-jen* would be selected to
make the trip to the capital.[5] In the fall of 1210 when the examinations
were in progress or being graded (the source does not say which), a group
of 'ruined and lost men' (*p'o-lo* – failed and frustrated candidates?) incited
a riot. Armed with bamboo and wooden sticks, they burst through the
gates of the examination hall, badly beat Yang, and injured the other examination officials. After they had departed, such was the townspeople's fear of

the *p'o-lo* that they refused to divulge their identities. Unable to punish the offenders, the court punished the prefecture instead: the prefect was demoted and Chang-chou *chü-jen* were barred from the upcoming departmental examination in Lin-an.[6]

As these widely separated anecdotes bear witness, the civil service examinations were critical and potentially volatile events during the Sung dynasty (960–1279). The fates of individuals, families, and often entire communities rode on their outcomes. Unlike medieval European society, where the nobility and clergy were sharply distinguished from the slowly emerging bureaucracy, in Chinese society of the imperial period, status, power, and wealth were intimately linked to government service. There were various ways of becoming an official: recommendation, purchase of office, protection (entry by virtue of the high rank of a relative), promotion from clerical status. But examination success conferred the greatest prestige and offered the best chances for bureaucratic advancement. Moreover, the examinations were transformed by the Sung emperors from the numerically minor method of recruitment that they had been since their establishment in 589 A.D.[7] to a major, at times dominant, way of selecting officials. As a result, the promise of learning beckoned broadly, with far-reaching consequences for Chinese society.

The examination life

The Sung literati often described their 'occupation' (*yeh*) as *chin-shih*, that is, preparing for the *chin-shih* examination, and that preparation was an adult as well as adolescent endeavor. In the examinations of 1148 and 1256, the only two for which there are lists of *chin-shih* recipients together with such biographical information as ancestry, marriage connections, and residence, the average ages were 36 and 35 years (Chinese style) respectively, and the age ranges were 19 to 66 years.[8] These were, of course, the fortunate few. The great majority of the literati spent much or most of their lives without achieving success.

Those years of study were spent in mastering a formidable curriculum, which included the dynastic histories, poetry, and the Confucian (*Ju*) classics. For most of the Sung, the last consisted of the *Analects* of Confucius, (*Lun-yü*), the works of Mencius, the classics of History (*Shu-ching*), Poetry (*Shih-ching*), and Changes (*I-ching*), the three classics of Rites (*Li-chi, I-li, Chou-li*), and the *Spring and Autumn Annals* (*Ch'un-ch'iu*) with its three commentaries.[9] Together these were considered to be the ultimate source of political, social, and especially moral wisdom. Writing in 1030, the future chief councilor Fan Chung-yen described their importance in the following manner:

> Now, of those things that improve the country, there is nothing that precedes the education of talent. Among the ways to educate talent,

there is nothing that precedes the encouragement of study. And of the essentials for the encouragement of study, there is nothing that is more esteemed than following the classics. If one follows the classics, the Way will be great; and if the Way is great, then talent will be great; and if talent is great, then achievements will be great. In general, the record of the Sages' regulations is preserved in the Book of History; the methods of pacifying dangers are preserved in the Book of Changes; the mirror [for seeing] gains and losses is preserved in the Book of Poetry; the discrimination of truth and falsehood is preserved in the Spring and Autumn Annals; the ordering of the world is preserved in the Book of Rites; and the feelings of the myriad things are preserved in the Book of Music. Therefore, men of refinement and wisdom gain entry through the Six Classics and thus are able to submit to the record of regulations, investigate the methods of pacifying dangers, set out the mirror [for seeing] gains and losses, analyze the discrimination of truth and falsehood, understand the ordering of the world, [perceive] exhaustively the feelings of the myriad things and cause their followers to help complete the Way of the Kings. What more does one want?[10]

Preparation for the examinations involved more than just the classics, however. During the Southern Sung (1127–1279), when north China was in the hands of the Jurchen, the *chin-shih* candidate took a tripartite examination either in poetry or on a classic. All candidates had to write an abstract discussion (*lun*) on political or philosophical principles and answer three policy questions (*ts'e*), often on complicated, highly technical problems of government. These demanded a broad knowledge of history and the classics. In addition, poetry candidates had to compose a poem (*shih*) and a poetic description (*fu*) on assigned themes using elaborate and precise rules of composition. Each classics candidate had to answer three questions on his classic of specialization and a question each on the *Analects* and the works of Mencius. These required an exact knowledge of the texts and discussions of their meanings.[11]

The lengthy education leading to the examinations began at an early age, either in the home or in small informal family and community schools.[12] Students started with simple primers. The *Three Character Primer* (*San-tzu hsün*, to be distinguished from the early Yüan *San-tzu ching*), the *Hundred Surnames* (*Pai-chia hsing*), and the *Thousand Character Classic* (*Ch'ien-tzu wen*) introduced students to the most commonly used characters in the language. The *Classic of Filial Piety* gave them their first taste of moral and political philosophy. There were also anecdotal works such as the *Admonitions for the Young and Ignorant* (*T'ung-meng hsün*) by Lü Pen-chung (1048–1145), which had stories about famous Sung teachers, admonitions on the proper approach to study, correct deportment within one's family, and so forth.[13]

Once the student had completed this initial stage of education, he began a course of study that included composition, calligraphy, and the recitation and memorization of the classics, histories, and poetry. Without textbooks and with just his teacher's guidance, he plunged forthwith into the texts. One example of what this involved is provided by a stone inscription of school rules for an eleventh century government-run primary school (so-called, for the students had obviously progressed beyond primers):

> The teacher lectures daily on three pages of classics and instructs the students on the pronunciations and meaning of the passages in the classics, on the forms of the characters, on poetry and poetic descriptions, on opposing sentence structures, and on writing stories.
>
> The students are all divided into three levels: In the first level, the students daily draw lots to ask [the teacher] three questions on the meanings of the classics that they have heard, read aloud two to three hundred characters, practice writing ten lines [of text], recite one five or seven-syllable regulated poem [*lü-shih*] and every three days they are examined on one poetic description (or four rhymes of one) and they read one poetic description and read three to five pages of history (memorizing three events contained therein).
>
> In the second level, the students daily read aloud one hundred characters, practice writing ten lines, recite a four-line stanza of a poem and a matching couplet, memorize two themes of poetic description and one item of history.
>
> In the third level, the students read fifty to seventy characters, practice writing ten lines and memorize one poem.[14]

As students progressed, they moved into a world of diverse educational institutions. Many were privately-run, ranging from the humble community schools mentioned above to the grand Neo-Confucian academies (*shu-yüan* or *ching-she*) of the twelfth and thirteenth centuries, which were at times as much centers for philosophical discussion as they were schools. Many others were run by the government. At the height of their development in the early twelfth century, government schools were organized into an empire-wide school system with a combined enrollment of some two hundred thousand students, extending from county schools (*hsien-hsüeh*) up through prefectural schools *(chou-hsüeh)* to the august Imperial University *(T'ai-hsüeh)* with its 3,800 students.[15]

For the more advanced students, study was supposed to be less a matter of memorizing and understanding texts (though these tasks never ceased) than one of applying what they had learned to specific issues and problems. In the words of one thirteenth-century writer: 'The upper school follows principle in order to illumine the affairs of the world; the lower school approaches affairs in order to view the principles of the world.'[16] Using principles to 'illumine the affairs of the world,' we might note, was very much the aim of the examination policy questions.

This connection to the examinations was not accidental, for most education was oriented to the examinations and involved, moreover, frequent testing and evaluation. At the government schools from the late eleventh century on, entrance was competitive and advancement within them was determined largely by tests: monthly, seasonal (at the University), and annual.[17] This was excellent preparation for the civil service examinations; indeed, the annual tests were explicitly modelled on the examinations. But to many critics, it was a perversion of genuine education. To cite just two examples, the rise of the Neo-Confucian academies in the late twelfth century was accompanied by condemnation of examination-oriented education, while in the earlier *Admonitions for the Young and Ignorant* we find the query: 'If examination preparation is used to educate human talent, [the talented] will not know the essentials of action, so how can they be employed [by the government]?'[18]

The life of a student involved more than slavish study and examination preparation, however. By taking a select group of boys and young men away from their families and homes and throwing them together (students usually boarded at school), schools served as powerful socializing forces. This was especially true of the University. Its students studied under famous thinkers (University professorships were prestigious positions within the bureaucracy), had opportunities to meet influential officials, and at times played an important role in court politics.[19] We hardly need mention the worldly pleasure offered by the great metropoli of K'ai-feng and Lin-an.[20] But not the least important were the friendships they made with each other, lifelong friendships in many cases. The noted poet Yang Wan-li (1124–1206), in reminiscing about a former fellow student, Liu Ch'eng-pi, offered a rare glimpse of student life at the University in Lin-an:

> When Yen-ch'un [i.e., Ch'eng-pi] and I were in school together, on every clear night, after studying to the point of exhaustion and when the markets were devoid of human traces, together we would climb into a pavilion, scoop up pond water with our hands, and play under the frosty moon. I think that the happiness of us two was promoting the happiness of the world. How could one change that happiness?[21]

Study and examination preparation were by no means limited to schools. Even apart from those who were educated entirely at home, for most *chin-*

shih there was a considerable gap between the end of formal schooling and examination success.[22] During that interval, young men commonly had other concerns, most notably marriage, and returned to their studies only as the triennial examinations approached. Many took to teaching, in government schools, as tutors (*men-k'o*) in wealthy households, or more humbly, as teachers in village schools. One encounters others serving as merchants, tending to family estates, or active in community affairs. We can only guess at the psychic strains and costs that such a life entailed, with the long three year wait for the examinations and the bitter disappointment which usually attended announcement of the results. But occasionally one can hear the disappointed voices. Liu Nan-fu (1202–ca. 1238), a three-time *chü-jen* from the Chiang-hsi prefecture of Chi-chou, exclaimed to his friend, the famous teacher Ou-yang Shou-tao (b. 1209): 'The examinations have long tired me. If in one's life one can saunter through forests and valleys and fill one's belly with books, that is sufficient. Of what use are other aims, alas!' Liu finally received his *chin-shih* degree in 1238 but he died before he could take any post. 'This can be called drowning in the examination hall,' wrote Ou-yang.[23]

We have talked thus far about the achievers, the rare survivors of the long educational process. Most of those who began their studies with dreams of a *chin-shih* pennant one day flying outside their houses dropped out along the way. Some did so quickly, like the one-time brigand and, later, Sung general, Ma Jen-yü (933–82):

> When he had passed the age of ten, his father ordered him to go to school. He immediately ran away [but then] returned and was sent again to a village school where he studied the *Classic of Filial Piety*. When after more than ten days he had not learned a single character, his teacher whipped him. In the middle of the night Jen-yü went alone and burned down the school hall. The teacher barely escaped with his life.[24]

More typical, one would hope, was the case of Wang T'ing-chen (1088–1142), also of Chi-chou, who was from a well-established scholarly family; one of his brothers became a *chin-shih* and two others were locally noted scholars. T'ing-chen 'did not enjoy the grind of being a section-and-paragraph-writing student' and was even less pleased upon being promoted to the prefectural school. So he quit school and the scholarly life altogether and proved to be very good at making money.[25]

Finally there were those who took the examinations, sometimes repeatedly, only to give up in despair or disgust. Though we have records of only that tiny fraction who made names for themselves, the unsuccessful greatly outnumbered their more successful contemporaries, especially in the Southern

Sung. Some were extolled as exemplars; Wu Shih-jen of Lin-an returned home after failing the examinations and gained renown as a teacher. He 'willing [accepted] poverty and held to the Way, concentrated on mastering the study of sincere righteousness and clear principles, and did not engage in heretical talk.'[26] For others, retirement was intellectually liberating precisely because it freed them from the strictures of the Confucian curriculum. Thus Liu Chi-ming (1059–1131) of Chi-chou turned from the examinations to a broad array of interests which, in addition to the classics, philosophers, and history, included strange and unusual tales, works on astronomy, geography, divination, medical nostrums, Buddhism, and Taoism.[27] And Wang Lo-hsien of T'an-chou (in Ching-hu-nan) upon failing the departmental examination, angrily tore up his (scholar's) cap and became a Taoist monk.[28] In yet other cases retirement led to drink and, occasionally, to ruin. Indeed, in the anecdotal literature popular in Sung elite society one encounters such somber figures as a University student murdered in a brothel and the ghost of an impoverished *chü-jen* haunting a Buddhist monastery.[29]

The examination literature

The voluminous literature dealing with examinations and education in Sung and, more generally, late traditional China has primarily been of two varieties: institutional history and that concerned with the composition and mobility of the ruling elite. The former is the more venerable, with its origins in the treatises of dynastic histories, a genre that was well established by Sung times. When archivists, historians, encyclopedists and local historians dealt with these topics, they usually wrote institutional histories of them, thereby providing us with the bulk of our information about them. In this century this tradition has been very fruitfully continued by such historians as Ch'en Tung-yüan,[30] Terada Gō,[31] Araki Toshikazu,[32] and Thomas H.C. Lee,[33] to cite just a few examples. With discrimination and a sure grasp of the major sources, they have produced detailed histories of the development of government recruitment and examinations, and of schools. Yet informative as they are, these internalist approaches suffer from a certain narrowness, for they do not as a rule relate the institutions to their social contexts.

Such is not the case with the latter approach, which has produced a vigorous debate over the nature of Chinese society. A few decades ago Edward A. Kracke, Jr. and Ping-ti Ho created a stir in the scholarly world by arguing that traditional Chinese society was far more mobile than many scholars had believed was possible for a premodern society.[34] In their studies based upon *chin-shih* lists for the Sung (Kracke) and *chin-shih* and *chü-jen* lists for the Ming and Ch'ing (Ho),[35] they found that a majority had no officials among their paternal great-grandfather, grandfather and father, and thus were upwardly mobile. They concluded that the late traditional Chinese elite was dependent upon office-holding and the examinations for its position and, given the difficulties of examination success, very fluid in its composition.

The lasting achievement of this mobility approach has been its demonstration of the centrality of education and academic achievement in elite and even non-elite society, for the promise of learning did beckon broadly.[36] However, the mobility thesis and its accompanying model of Chinese society has come under challenge in recent years, for it is vulnerable on at least two counts.

First, by making elite membership a function of examination success and/ or government service, it confuses status group with class.[37] While the examination system clearly constituted the preeminent status hierarchy in Chinese society and high status usually (though not always) entailed power and wealth, it does not follow that degree holders (and their families) constituted a ruling class or social elite. Much more persuasive is the concept of upper class membership based upon land ownership which then could lead to education and office.

Second, by its narrow focus upon direct patrilineage, the mobility thesis ignores such critical factors as lineage, marriage relationships, and even siblings and uncles. This is partly a function of the information given by the examination lists, but it is also the result of using a Western model predicated upon the nuclear family as *the* significant social unit. Given the well-known importance of kinship and lineage in Chinese society, such an approach is bound to be misleading.

Even before Kracke and Ho published their studies, there were those whose conceptions of Chinese society were quite different. Karl Wittfogel, in an article on the uses of protection (*yin*) in Liao and Sung times, concluded that the Chinese ruling class was relatively stable in its composition.[38] Hsiao-tung Fei, writing about the rural gentry in the early twentieth century, stressed both its stability and its economic basis in landowning.[39] More recently, Hilary Jane Beattie,[40] Robert M. Hartwell,[41] and his students Robert Hymes[42] and Linda Walton[43] have argued that late traditional China was dominated by a landholding upper class of elite lineages remarkable for their ability to perpetuate themselves and from whose ranks the great majority of officials was drawn. Because of their importance for the present study, Hartwell's findings, which concern the lineages that provided incumbents to the Sung fiscal bureaucracy, demand special consideration.

Hartwell argues that for most of the Northern Sung, the fiscal bureaucracy and, by extension, the government were dominated by a small group of lineages which he calls the professional elite. These lineages, which claimed descent from the great T'ang lineages,[44] maintained their positions by marriage alliances, by optimum use of the examinations and protection, and by factional alliances that gave them control over promotions. Their domination began to weaken in the late eleventh century, however, when the increasing severity of factional disputes resulted in the exclusion of a large number of these lineages from high office. As a consequence, the fiscal bureaucracy from the early twelfth century on was characterized by a larger number of less dominant lineages whose marriages were primarily local in character and whose ability to use protection was relatively limited.[45]

This thesis contributes significantly to our understanding of Sung society. By systematically introducing the variables of lineage, marriage patterns and factionalism, it is able to explain much more than the mobility model, which emphasized the two factors of wealth and examination success for the achievement of status and power. Hartwell, in fact, regards the examinations as a virtual non-factor in social mobility:

> There is not a single documented example, in either Su-chou or in the collective biographical material on policymaking and financial officials, of a family demonstrating upward mobility solely because of success in the civil service examinations. Indeed, in every documented case of upward mobility, passage of the examinations *followed* intermarriage with one of the already established elite gentry lineages.[46]

In other words, marriage, not examinations, was the critical criterion for entrance into a socially-defined elite. Such a position, however, is open to qualification on three counts.

First, even if Hartwell's observation of the temporal priority of intermarriage is borne out by future research, it does not prove that examinations were unimportant, but only that elite intermarriage was a necessary if informal precondition to examination success and office-holding. In fact, most upwardly mobile families also invested in education at an early stage in their rise. A wealthy but uncultured merchant would typically hire teachers for his sons and try to marry them to women from established, respectable families.[47] In the Southern Sung especially, such an academic strategy was socially expected and it provided the most likely means for the achievement of official status. Although members of some rising families may have entered the bureaucracy via the protection privileges of their affinal kin, for most the initial entry had to come via the examinations. Indeed, for many, perhaps most such families, examination success was not achieved. Respectability and local prominence could still be had, but there were clear limits to their potential status and power.[48]

Moreover, it is not clear that examination success was the completely dependent variable that Hartwell makes it out to be. For some young literati

from humble backgrounds, the promise of success was the deciding factor in
making advantageous marriage matches.[49] In other cases, success itself was
the necessary condition for marriage. Chen Ying of Chi-chou, who was from a
'guest' family (*kuan-k'o*) bound to a magistrate's family, was unable to get
the latter's permission to a marriage until after he passed the examinations.[50]
Even more remarkable is the story told by Hung Mai about a county clerk
who learns through a dream that the son of a neighboring doctor (an inferior
occupation) would pass the examinations. Approaching the doctor, who has
already registered his son for the examinations, the clerk promises his daughter
in marriage if the son succeeds. He does and the marriage is concluded.[51]
Therefore even as marriage could aid one in the examinations, so could
examination success be of benefit for social climbing through marriage.

Second, there is an inherent imprecision in speaking of 'elite lineages,' for
Chinese lineages could be extremely heterogeneous bodies, as their common
charity provisions for poor members bear witness.[52] To belong to an elite
lineage did not mean that one was elite, although the connection undoubtedly conferred many benefits upon the poor member unavailable to his un-
connected neighbors. Thus under the umbrella of the lineage and perhaps
concealed by it, there was ample opportunity for individual and family
mobility, both upwards and downwards.

Third, Hartwell's view of the examinations does not take into account the
growing centrality of schools and examinations in Sung society. The changes
underlying the very different conditions of the two protests described earlier
are reflected by many Sung writers. Consider the following entries in the
Sung dynastic history (the *Sung-shih*). Describing the beginnings of the
central government's significant involvement in local education (ca. 1022),
it says:

> In the time of Jen-tsung [r. 1022–63], scholars who pursued Confucian
> learning had been unable to proliferate. So early in his reign he en-
> dowed the Yen-chou school [in Ching-tung-hsi circuit] with school
> fields and also ordered border and capital regions all to establish
> schools.[53]

Two hundred years later, in 1231, we find the observation that 'the scholars
in the examination halls of the time were daily increasing and the rolls of
scrolls were like mountains.'[54] We might note, too, an essay by one Li K'ang
of Ming-chou (in Liang-che-tung) commemorating the building of a library
in 1090:

> Nurtured and nourished by the imperial Sung, the people have increased
> greatly. Those who study esteem the years and months of grinding
> [effort] and scholars daily increase. Good people consider not educating

their sons to be shameful and their posterity consider the lack of renown to be a disgrace.[55]

The change, in short, lay in the greatly increased value accorded education and in the growing predominance of an elite lifestyle that was rooted in education and oriented towards examination success.

The examination system occupied a critical nexus in Sung society. A complex institution, it served many interests and performed many functions, not merely of bureaucratic selection but also of elite advancement and representation, social and intellectual control, and imperial symbolism, to name just a few. Yet none of the studies mentioned above has focused upon that conjunction between institution and society. Such is the aim of this study.[56] thesis While questions of institutional history, social mobility and social structure will not be ignored, the emphasis will be upon the social functions of the examination system and people's perceptions of it, and especially how those changed during the three century span of the Sung.

The plentiful sources that have been used are largely those of past studies – government documents, histories, encyclopedias, the writings of individuals – but they will be used in at least two different ways. First, the sources have been combed for data to make possible quantitative generalizations about the impact of the examinations on Sung society. In particular, the use of over one hundred Sung, Yüan, Ming and Ch'ing local histories has allowed a perspective which emphasizes the humble as well as the exalted and the prefecture as well as the capital. Second, the institutional literature has been read with an eye to its social ramifications. Did certain groups or regions benefit more than others from the examinations' rules, and if so, why? Upon what theory or theories of education were the examinations predicated? And how did China's elite culture adapt to the powerful organizing force of the examinations? It is with such questions that subsequent chapters will be concerned. But first we should consider how society was generally changing during Sung times.

The historical context

The characterization of the Sung as a period of major social and economic change has by now gained widespread acceptance. It was an age of great contrasts, the most remarkable being the coexistence of military (and often political) weakness with economic and cultural vigor. Since the middle of the T'ang, China had been undergoing what some have called the 'medieval economic revolution.' In the countryside, the growth of estates (*chuang-yüan*), the rise of the lower Yangtze region as the empire's economic center and, in the early Sung, advances in techniques of rice cultivation all contributed to a rise in agricultural production. This, together with the growth of a cash economy, the increasingly common payment of taxes in cash, the spread of paper money and the beginnings of industrial development, contributed to a rapid growth in commerce. For the first time fairs and periodic markets appeared in the countryside. In the cities, the walled wards and controlled markets of the early T'ang disappeared. From K'ai-feng south along the Grand Canal and throughout the southeast, sprawling cities emerged, whose size reflected their economic and not necessarily their political importance.[57]

This was an age of great technological advances, not the least being the development and spread of printing. Invented by the Buddhists in the eighth century or before, wood-block printing was first used by the government in the tenth century to produce authoritative versions of the classics.[58] During the Sung it rapidly spread throughout the empire, most especially in the prosperous southeast, as temples, schools and private enterprises set up their own shops (by one count there were some 173 printers during the Southern Sung).[59] The impact of printing on Sung China was profound, and profoundly different from that on Europe in the fifteenth and sixteenth centuries. For where the latter led through the vernacular Bible to the Reformation, the former led through the classics to the examinations.[60] Although this study will be concerned primarily with the institutional factors behind the growth of the literati, that growth would certainly never have happened without printing to make books less expensive and more available.

The social changes of the T'ang—Sung period were equally noteworthy. During the middle and late T'ang, the overwhelming political and social dominance of a small number of aristocratic lineages had given way, at least partially, to the rising power of provincial lineages. According to Denis Twitchett, this was made possible by

> . . . the greatly increased and diversified possibilities for employment in provincial governments of specialized government agencies, which followed the decay of central civil authority and the transfer of effective political and military authority from the central government to the provinces a century or more later.[61]

During the Five Dynasties (907—60), many of the aristocratic lineages disappeared under the repeated onslaught of wars and rebellions, rebellions noteworthy for their expressions of class hatred.[62] Soldiers and wealthy merchants played an unusually prominent role in government,[63] and in general political fragmentation provided opportunities for advancement to many local groups. Thus by the early Sung elite groups were various, including the remnants of the T'ang aristocracy, bureaucratic and military lineages from the north and wealthy southern lineages that had flourished under the relative tranquility of the southern kingdoms.

This diversity was a far cry from the homogeneity of the eleventh century's national elite which, according to Professor Hartwell, dominated the bureaucracy. Why the change? Peace and prosperity, urbanization (especially that of K'ai-feng, the great imperial metropolis), and the increasing availability of books all played a role. So too did the examination system. An old institution even in the tenth century, it was put to new uses by the early Sung emperors who saw it as an instrument for reordering elite society. If the results were complex and often unintended they nevertheless had far-reaching consequences for the development of Chinese society.

The examination system inherited by the Sung had been founded by the Sui in 589 and had changed rather little in the intervening four centuries, when it was characterized by its variety of degrees, its exclusive provisions for candidacy, and its numerically small but prestigious impact upon the bureaucracy. The Sui—T'ang system had six different degrees. Three were specialized, concentrating on law (*ming-fa*), calligraphy (*ming-shu*) and mathematics (*ming-suan*), while the remainder, the *hsiu-ts'ai, ming-ching* and *chin-shih* degrees, tested a broader, more traditional corpus of knowledge. From early on, the degrees were sharply differentiated by their prestige and importance. The *hsiu-ts'ai* ('cultivated talent') degree was so difficult that it never had many graduates and disappeared after the early years of the T'ang. The *ming-ching* ('understanding the classics') degree tested one's knowledge of the classics and had the largest numbers of candidates and graduates. But most important was the *chin-shih* ('advanced scholar') degree, the only one that tested poetic abilities, which eclipsed the classics degree in prestige and all of the others in numbers and prestige.[64]

The T'ang examinations were held annually in the capital. There were two ways to qualify for them: through recommendation from prefectural officials — 'district tribute' (*hsiang-kung*) or 'tribute selection' (*kung-chü*) — and through *hsiao-chü*, attendance at one of several schools in the capital, which with one exception were open only to the relatives of officials. The latter route appears to have accounted for the great majority of the graduates.[65]

The pre-Sung examination system constituted a small and prestigious route of bureaucratic entry. Although its graduates accounted for only six to sixteen percent of the civil service,[66] their career prospects were high and they frequently predominated at the highest levels of government.[67] By introducing literary achievement as a significant factor in political success, the examinations may have helped undermine the position of the great

lineages. But contrary to the assertions of some historians, they did not facilitate social mobility, for the system insured that degree holders would come
either from the great lineages or from locally prominent lineages with traditions of office-holding.[68]

expanding the exams   Beginning in 977, the Sung government began conferring examination
degrees in the hundreds rather than scores; the annual average of degrees
given went from approximately thirty for the preceding three centuries to
192 for the years 997–1272.[69] In expanding the examinations and instituting
other critical reforms, the early Sung emperors were acting upon several concerns. They wanted to fill the civil service of the just reunited empire with
bright and educated men. They wanted to control the military which had
grown dominant in court politics and curb the power of those great lineages
that had survived the wars. And they were not unmindful, if somewhat wary,
of providing opportunities to men from the developing south.[70]

Most of these concerns were met. The government of the mid-Northern
Sung was dominated by an energetic group of men who by and large owed
their positions to examination success. Coming from both established northern families and 'newly risen' families of the southeast,[71] their social stratum
was much broader than that of the T'ang elite but still small enough to be
centered on the imperial capital of K'ai-feng, cosmopolitan in character, and
interlaced by marriage ties. This was possible not only because this elite
group dominated the recruitment process, as Hartwell has argued, but also
because they were relatively unchallenged by others. Many families of means
which could have engaged in education and the examinations chose not to
do so.

During the late Northern Sung, however, a rapid spread in government
schools to most prefectures and counties made education more available and
popular than ever before. Thus as factional struggles eroded the political
position of the eleventh century elite, it began to merge into a larger and
growing stratum of local elites. As a result, Southern Sung elite society was
much larger but more parochial than its Northern Sung predecessor, and
tended to be socially centred at a regional or even prefectural level. Economically based upon landowning and, to some extent, commerce, it nevertheless was deeply involved in education and in the bitterly competitive rigors
of examination life. As will be shown in the next chapter, several hundred
thousand typically took the prefectural examinations in the early thirteenth
century, compared with a few tens of thousands two centuries before.

Given these social changes, one would expect very different relationships
between the examinations and society in early, mid, and late Sung, and
indeed, the subsequent chapters will be devoted to showing how this was the
case. Much of the argument rests upon the numbers presented in Chapter 2,

for the manifold increase in candidates points to an increasingly profound involvement in the examinations by the landowning upper class, and with that
involvement came many attendant problems.

Who took and passed the examinations? In Chapter 3 we shall see how the
institutional developments of the early Sung were shaped largely by an imperial ideal of fairness in support of the earlier mentioned aims of creating
an able civil service and controlling potential rivals. This policy worked fairly
well so long as candidate numbers remained modest, but, as we will see in
Chapter 5, when competition became acute in the Southern Sung, relatives
of officials used their right to take special examinations to subvert the essential fairness of the system. These privileges also served to give the region or
prefecture with many native officials an advantage over others, as we will
see in Chapter 6. With successes breeding success, a few regions such as the
southeastern coast and northern Chiang-hsi were able to gain unparalleled
representation in the civil service.

What should the relationship be between education and the examinations?
It might seem strange that this question arose, for examinations required
years of education to master their Confucian curriculum and they were
justified by the Confucian principle of government by the virtuous and
talented. Yet Confucian critics asked, first, how the virtuous could be selected when the anonymous examination procedures of the Sung made considerations of character impossible, and second, how moral education could
be pursued when students set their sights on examination success and not the
Way. As we shall see in Chapter 4, reform minded statesmen in the Northern
Sung answered the first question by advocating and then creating an empire-
wide school system which, for a time, took over the functions of the examinations, only to see the unwieldy system with its two hundred thousand
students fall under charges of favoritism, cheating and poor education.
Southern Sung Neo-Confucians, by contrast, reacted to the unprecedented
examination competition (caused, in part, by the educational programs of
the Northern Sung) by arguing for disinterested study and moral cultivation,
or in other words, for a separation between education and examinations.

[handwritten marginal note: ① moral ② education for gain not for its own sake]

Finally, as examinations became established in society, they had to be
integrated into culture. As Chapter 7 will show, the examinations spawned
popular stories, portents and myths. With burgeoning numbers of failed
candidates, such social roles as the aging candidate and the wandering literatus were developed and popularized. But most important were the ceremonies, clothing, buildings and community support organizations with
which Southern Sung local leaders created visions of examination honor
even as they subverted the examinations. The myth of opportunity was as
important for social stability as its lie was to the elite's privileged position.

2

THE STRUCTURE OF RECRUITMENT

The Sung bureaucracy

By Sung times the Chinese bureaucracy had come far from its antique beginnings as a household government. Although traces of its patrimonial origins lingered on in such titles as the Left and Right Major-domos, the Sung bureaucracy possessed many of the essential features of a 'modern' bureaucracy: specialization of functions, a hierarchy of authority, a system of formal rules, and an ideal of impersonality.[1] Arrayed beneath the august Emperor, the Son of Heaven, whose power was in theory absolute, were a host of ministries, bureaus, commissions, and other organs whose functions and lines of authority were clearly drawn.[2] Outside of the capital the primary administrative units were prefectures (*chou*) and sub-prefectures or counties (*hsien*), which numbered 306 and 1207 respectively in the year 1100, though there were also some 24 circuits (*lu*) used by various commissioners for tours of inspection. To staff these offices the government employed tens of thousands of officials whose evaluation and promotion were the subject of detailed regulations,[3] and hundreds of thousands of clerks.

As we shall see below, the bureaucracy became bloated as the Sung progressed, as officials increasingly outnumbered the available posts. Nevertheless, what was remarkable was not the bureaucracy's largeness but rather its smallness when set against the vastness of China. The dynasty at its height ruled over one hundred million people in an area of approximately two million square miles.[4] Mountain ranges and forests separated the empire's major regions, each with its own regional economy, dialect groupings, and cultural traditions. Moreover, the communications and transportation systems, though complex and highly organized, were slow and inefficient. Yet despite these constraints, the government managed to maintain relative peace and order for most of three centuries.

That they accomplished this may be attributed to several factors. For the defense of the empire, the Sung depended upon both diplomacy with the various alien dynasties that occupied northeastern, northwestern, and eventually all of northern China, and upon large, closely supervised armies and navies, which consumed a major portion of the government's budget. To manage land and population registration, tax collection, public works, and the maintenance of local order, officials and clerks made use of mandatory unpaid labor and even attempted to organize families into mutual responsibility groups to insure security and the collection of taxes.[5] More germane to our subject, local officials relied upon the local elite for information, support, and philanthropy, and since the elite generally dominated its locality economically and socially and virtually dominated entry into the bureaucracy, its support was generally forthcoming.

A final reason for the government's success at ruling was cultural. The cosmos implicit in the Confucian classics and preached by Sung Neo-Confucians was an interrelated and interdependent whole in which the moral and natural realms were merged. The Son of Heaven was the mediator between Heaven and the world ('all under Heaven') and the capital from which he ruled was an axis mundi, a pivot about which the four quarters revolved.[6] and just as that axis was symbolically recapitulated in every government *yamen* in the empire, so too was the hierarchical pattern of the emperor's dealings with his ministers infinitely repeated as officials dealt with subjects, fathers with sons, husbands with wives, and the elderly with the young. Form and substance overlapped; since a harmonious order could only be created through ritual and etiquette, breaches in them rent its fabric.

This view of a moral universe had two consequences. It certainly contributed to social stability, for while the local elites were its primary exponents and naturally its greatest beneficiaries, it was hardly limited to them. Through laws, lineage rules, educational primers, story tellers and folk lore, it percolated throughout society so that the most divergent local traditions shared a Confucian ethical core, and even among the ubiquitous Buddhist clergy (*sangha*) there was little inclination to mount a cultural or political challenge.

It also insured that the ideal of the specialist familiar to students of Western bureaucracies would not become the norm. A grasp of principles, of the larger picture, was preferred to a command of details, and thus the generalist who knew how to think and act was preferred to the specialist who knew what to do. Principles could be practical, of course, and in the eleventh century men like Wang An-shih (1021–86) argued that the larger picture required a detailed knowledge of institutions and economics, but even they agreed that knowledge of the Kingly Way was essential. And when, following the failure of reform, that Way became more exclusively moral, the ideal of the generalist became more firmly fixed than ever.

Even as social and cultural factors were contributing to the success of

Table 1. *Organization of the bureaucracy*

		Civil service	Military service
Graded:	Administrative	Court officials (*ch'ao-kuan*) Capital officials (*ching-kuan*)	Major officers (*ta-shih-ch'en*)
	Executory:	Selected men (*hsüan-jen*)	Minor officers (*hsiao-shih-ch'en*)
Ungraded:		Various titles	Various titles
		Clerical service	

Sung government, the bureaucracy itself was profoundly shaping society and culture. Since the bureaucracy was the preeminent source of prestige and power, access to it was a pressing concern within elite society. As we shall see below, the structure of recruitment served to mold that society even while political pressures from within the elite worked to modify that structure.

Recruitment of clerks and the military

Like the Chinese cosmos which was divided into Heaven, earth and man, the Sung bureaucracy was tripartite, consisting of civil, military and clerical services. The civil and military services were comparable in size and theoretically equal (although in fact the former was far more highly esteemed), having parallel grading systems and procedures for transfer from one to the other.[7] The clerical service was distinct from them and hierarchically inferior.

Two basic divisions informed the civil and military services. One distinguished graded from ungraded officials. Graded officials comprised the heart of the bureaucracy. In each service they were arranged in a hierarchy of titular offices (*kuan*) which, after 1082, was divided into nine grades.[8] They alone were considered to be proper officials, 'within the stream' (*liu-nei*), and they held virtually every non-clerical position of importance. 'Outside the stream' (*liu-wai*) were the ungraded officials and clerks. The ungraded officials were included in the hierarchy of titular offices and could serve in minor capacities such as assistants in local schools, but being ungraded they lacked the status of officials and could only obtain that through the regular channels of recruitment, such as the examinations.

The second division was between the executory and administrative classes. 'Admission into the administrative class was considered the most important step in the ladder of promotion,' Edward Kracke has noted.[9] All officials began their careers in the executory class and, according to the rules for promotion, could be considered for promotion to the administrative class after a minimum of six to twelve years of active duty.[10] But most never made the step, for as the tables which follow will show, the vast majority of officials were in the executory class.

The executory and administrative classes of the civil and military services were known collectively as the 'four selected [classes]' (*ssu-hsüan*) and Sung statistics for the size of the bureaucracy (such as those in Table 4) almost invariably referred to them and no others. In accordance with this, the terms 'official' and 'bureaucrat', unless otherwise specified, should be taken to refer to them alone.

The focus of this study is on the civil service, its examinations and their social functions. This has been necessary from a practical point of view but regrettable, since the social importance of the military and clerical services was obviously great. But before leaving these two groups entirely, we should consider briefly their personnel and how they were selected.

The clerical service was so large and fragmented institutionally that generalizations about it are fraught with peril. Clerks did not move about like officials but remained permanently in a single *yamen*, office or bureau, each of which was responsible for its own clerical recruitment.[11] At the level of county administration there was considerable variation over time in the degree of professionalism among clerks. Although they were virtually all professional during the late Northern Sung, thanks to the policies of the reformer Wang An-shih, at other times a minor but substantial portion of the clerical work was performed by workers fulfilling service obligations, who were either unpaid or paid by the family which owed the service.[12] Paid or unpaid, the clerical service greatly outnumbered the other services and, by all accounts, it grew throughout the Sung. Although we have no figures for its total size, an idea of its magnitude may be gained from the fact that a proposal in 1001 to reduce its size suggested a reduction of 195,000 positions.[13]

A great gulf separated the clerical service from the other two. Officials looked down upon the clerks, feared them,[14] and kept their promotions into the ranks of officials to a minimum. Although a fair number entered the military service, the civil service was largely closed to them. A handful entered through direct promotion, but this was the only avenue open to them, for in 989 they were barred from the examinations.[15]

Military officials served both as officers and bureaucrats. They provided the officers' corps for the army and navy, staffed the military bureaus and offices in the central government, held posts in the imperial household, and at times even filled civil posts in local administration.[16] The military service,

Table 2. *Classification of the military service in 1213 according to method of entry*

Method of entry	Administrative class Number	%	Executory class Number	%	Total military service Number	%
Protection(a)	1,680	43.5	8,211	52.9	9,891	51.1
Military examination	77	2.0	415	2.7	492	2.5
Imperial clansmen	425	11.0	2,914	18.8	3,339	17.2
Clerks(b)	340	8.8	1,221	7.9	1,561	8.1
Prom. from ranks(c)	1,285	33.2	1,606	10.3	2,891	14.9
Purchase	0	0	508	3.3	508	2.6
Miscellaneous(d)	59	1.5	631	4.1	690	3.6
Total	3,866	100.0	15,506*	100.0	19,372	100.0

Source: Li Hsin-ch'uan, *Chien-yen i-lai Ch'ao-yeh tsa-chi*, 2 pts. (TSCC eds) 2.14:528.
(a) Includes entries for 'admission through recommendation' (*tsou-pu*), a term used to signify protection; 'husbands of imperial princesses' (*tsung-nü-fu*); and 'relatives of imperial concubines' (*hou-chi ch'in-shu*). The great majority were from the first category.
(b) The former clerks of court and capital grade are designated 'non-irregular clerks from miscellaneous services' (*tsa-liu fei-fan li-chih*). The others are merely labeled 'clerks' (*li-chih*).
(c) Includes those listed simply as 'military company' (*chün-pan*) designating troop leaders, perhaps, and those selected for their military accomplishments (*chün-kung*).
(d) Includes those 'returning [from rebel or enemy armies] to serve the Sung' (*kuei-ming kuei-cheng*); 'sons-in-law of those killed in action' (*chen-wang nü-fu*); 'recipients of grace for [relatives of] those killed in action' (*chen-wang en-tse*); and 'managers of tribute' (*chü-kuan chin-feng*).
*The source gives a subtotal of 15,606, but this must be a copying error for the entries add up to 15,506.

like the civil service, had examinations (*wu-chü*) and, in theory, a network of military schools (*wu-hsüeh*) at the capital and in prefectures, though the schools were often just appended to the prefectural schools. But both of these were relatively unimportant avenues to advancement, as we can see from Table 2.

Military examinations aside, this table suggests two important, rather paradoxical characteristics of the military service. First, it was staffed primarily by those entering through some form of kin-based privilege. The imperial clan is particularly noteworthy in this respect, reflecting the considerable political importance and visibility that it was gaining in the late Southern Sung.[17] Second, a sizeable minority (23%) of the military service entered from either the ranks or the clerical service. This suggests significant social mobility, for because these men were promoted from branches of government considered socially inferior, their promotion probably involved substantial inter-class mobility.[18] Indeed, as the great Ming novel, *The Water Margin*, so vividly depicts in its account of the Sung bandit leader Sung Chiang and his fellow 'heroes', the line between rebel and government soldier was a fine one that was frequently traversed.

Finally, civil service recruitment privileges were available to military officials. Both entry to the special preliminary examinations and protection were available to the relatives of appropriately ranked military officials. To determine how many families used this circuitous route into the prestigious civil service would require a separate study, but given the propensity of the literati to employ every competitive advantage available, its use was undoubtedly considerable.

Recruitment of the civil service

There were a number of ways by which men entered the civil service,[19] but two predominated. The imperial grace of protection (*yin-pu, en-yin*) allowed certain capital rank officials to name one or more of their relatives and sometimes even family tutors as officials.[20] The process was not automatic, for those named had to take a placement examination (*ch'üan-shih*). But even at its most competitive, half of those taking it passed.[21] The initial rank of the protected officials varied but was always low.[22] The number one could name depended on one's rank. The proportion of officials with this privilege was small but because it was granted liberally to the highest officials, many entered the bureaucracy by means of it.[23]

Examinations were the alternative. In terms of hierarchical complexity, the Sung examination system falls somewhere between those of the T'ang and the Ming. In the T'ang system, there was only one examination and it was open to recommended prefectural candidates and students in the capital schools.[24] The Ming and Ch'ing systems had three levels of examination – prefectural, provincial, and metropolitan – and the prefectural level was itself divided into three consecutive examinations. The Sung system, by contrast, had just two levels. One first had to pass either the prefectural examination (*chieh-shih*, 'forwarding examination' – a term also used generically for all preliminary examinations), or at one of the less competitive special preliminary examinations.[25] Those who passed were 'presented men' (*chü-jen*) but they were not as a rule qualified to hold office as were Ming and Ch'ing *chü-jen*, who were graduates of the provincial examination. They went to the capital where they took the departmental examination (*sheng-shih*), and those who passed it proceeded to take the palace examination (*tien-shih, yü-shih*), a largely pro forma examination used primarily for ranking individuals.[26] These graduates received either the *chin-shih* ('advanced scholar') degree or, until the 1070s when they were abolished, a degree in one of several fields such as law, history, and rites, known collectively as the *chu-k'o* ('several fields'). Only then were they eligible for office.

There were also special 'facilitated degrees' (*t'e-tsou-ming chin-shih, t'e-tsou-ming chu-k'o*) given to elderly multiple repeaters of the departmental examination, who were given a separate and easier palace examination. These degrees constituted a distinctive and important feature of the Sung examination system. As we shall see, facilitated degree holders constituted a sizeable proportion of the civil service. Because they were usually over 50 years old and their degrees had little prestige, they were a rather insignificant force within the bureaucracy, but socially these degrees were very important, for they conferred official status with its attendant benefits upon many who would never have passed the regular examinations.

Finally, certain special degrees were conferred upon a few select individuals. The degree for youths (*t'ung-tzu-k'o*) was given to boys who displayed precocious talents, usually involving memorization of the classics. There were also decree examinations (*chih-k'o*), extremely prestigious examinations given mainly to active officials for the purpose of promotion, but on occasion to highly recommended non-officials as well.[27] Because these examinations were extraordinary and numerically insignificant, we will not consider them further.

As Table 3 indicates, examinations and protection accounted for 93% of the civil service in 1213. Former clerks and imperial clansmen were both scantily represented, though the absence of the latter may be more apparent than real, for from around the turn of the thirteenth century on, they were receiving *chin-shih* degrees in large numbers and so would have been included under that category.[28] Purchase of office, too, was remarkably unimportant, though this may have changed in the closing decades of the Sung.[29] This table, then, demonstrates the crucial importance of the examinations as virtually the only method of bureaucratic entry for those from nonofficial families. At the same time it points to the great importance of kin-based privilege, which accounted for four-tenths of the civil service and over half of those of administrative grade.

But was this also the case at other times during the Sung? Although there are no data for other periods comparable to those of 1213, it is possible to detect general changes in the relative importance of different methods of civil service recruitment.

Patterns of recruitment

One of the recurring themes in Sung writings on government was that of an oversized bureaucracy: there were too many officials for the available

Table 3. *Classification of the civil service in 1213 according to method of entry*

Method of entry	Administrative class*		Executory class		Total civil service*	
	Number	%	Number	%	Number	%
Chin-shih degrees	975	40.8	4,325	25.4	5,300	27.4
Facilitated degrees	50	2.1	5,065	29.8	5,115	26.4
Degrees for youths	0	0	68	0.4	68	0.3
Protection (a)	1,255	52.5	6,366	37.4	7,621	39.3
Purchase	3	0.1	429	2.5	432	2.2
Imperial clan (b)	24	1.0	560	3.3	584	3.0
Prom. from clerk (c)	8	0.3	165	1.0	173	0.9
Irregular status	2	0.1	28	0.2	30	0.2
Miscellaneous (d)	75	3.1	0	0	75	0.4
	2,392	100.0	17,006	100.0	19,398	100.0

Source: CYTC 2.14:528.

*Includes only administrative officials in grades six through nine. The number of officials in grades one through five was undoubtedly much smaller and their omission, therefore, should not greatly compromise these findings, although at the same time these figures cannot be taken as representative of the highest officials.

(a) Several kinds of protection are specified for the administrative officials: those conferred upon the protector's retirement (529), upon his death (92), on the occasion of the Great Rites (623), and upon tutors (*men-k'o*) (11). Protected executory officials are all grouped under the heading 'recommended' (*tsou-chien*). This term is ambiguous but elsewhere in the same work it is clearly used to mean protection. Ibid. 2.14:532; 15:540.

(b) These appear to have entered through protection privileges specially granted to certain imperial clansmen. The administrative officials are listed as 'admission to office for imperial clansmen who have gone through the [Great] Rites' (*tsung-shih kuo li pu-kuan*), while the executory officials are simply listed as 'imperial clansmen deserving of grace' (*tsung-shih kai en*).

(c) The classification of the 8 administrative officials is problematical. Their entry reads, 'admission to office [through] the Three Departments' (*san-sheng pu-kuan*), that is, the three departments of the Secretariat-Chancellery. My interpretation is that this refers to ex-clerks of those departments. See WHTK 30:285 and HCP 30/12a for an example of a clerk at the Secretariat becoming an official, and SS 169/17b–18a on the promotion procedures for clerks in those departments.

(d) This includes 21 listed as 'admission to office upon the special receipt of the title of literatus' (*t'e shou wen-hsüeh pu-kuan*), 2 admitted because of their families' perpetual right to office (*hsi-feng pu-kuan*), and 52 listed as *feng-piao pu-kuan* ('admission to office for demonstrations of service'). This last term may refer to yet another form of protection (it follows the entry for protection on the occasion of the Great Rites), but I have found no other references to it.

posts. This problem arose throughout China's imperial history, but it was marked during the Sung, particularly as the dynasty progressed. In 1160, the future chief councilor Chou Pi-ta (1126–1204) wrote:

> In general, when posts are first created [at a dynasty's outset], the paths to entering service are few and the vacancies many. After prolonged peace, the paths to service are many and officials then become superfluous.[30]

As for current conditions, which were considerably better than they were to be a generation hence, Chou described the plight of newly qualified officials:

> Lined up at the gate they gather to enter the appointments office. With 'selected men' almost surpassing two thousand [every three years], several score of men vie for each vacancy and five or six years is the wait for each post. A scholar coming to this pass may be said to be 'delayed and impeded, missing official duties.'[31]

In Table 4, a compilation of reports and estimates of the number of those with official status, we can observe this process of bureaucratic accretion. The drop after 1119 was caused by the loss to the Jurchen of northern China, and with it some 35% of the population, but it is interesting to note that by the early thirteenth century the civil service had surpassed its Northern Sung peak. Clearly the problem of supernumerary officials (*jung-kuan*), as they were called, had not been solved.

How were these officials recruited? Except for the year 1213 (see Table 3) we cannot say with any precision. But since there are reliable degree totals for most of the Sung, we can calculate the importance of recruitment by examination at different times in the dynasty. In Table 5, the estimated career length of thirty-six years is based upon the 5,300 degree holders who were officials in 1213.[32] It may be high, but if we are to assume that the average career length for degree-holding officials remained constant throughout the dynasty, and there is little evidence to the contrary,[33] then that makes little difference. Lowering the career length would lower each of the percentages but not change the trend.

The trend is remarkable: the proportion of the civil service recruited via the regular degrees was shrinking progressively during the course of the dynasty, so that in 1213 it was less than half of what it had been in 1046. This does not mean that degree holders were decreasing in number (except for the drop between Northern and Southern Sung the degree numbers were fairly constant), but rather that other channels were becoming more important. Which? The evidence suggests both facilitated degrees and protection.

Table 4. *Estimates of numbers of Sung officials*

Year	Civil service Administrative grade	Executory grade	Military service	Total officials	Sources
997–1022				9,785	a, b
1023–1031	2,000		4,000		a, b
1046	2,700+	10,000	6,000+	18,700+	a, b
1049–1053				17,300	a, b
1064–1067				24,000	b, c
1080				34,000+	a
1119		16,500	31,346		c
1165–1173	3,000–4,000	7,000–8,000			b, c
1191	4,159	12,859	16,488	33,516	b, c
1196	4,159	13,670	24,595	42,000+	b, c
1201	3,133	15,204	19,470	37,800+	b
1213	2,392*	17,006	19,472	38,864*	d

Sources: (a) YH 117/24a, 119/30b–31a; (b) WHTK 47:441; (c) Hung Mai, *Jung-chai sui-pi* 4.4/1a–2a, 5.4/12b–13a; (c) CYTC 2.14:528.
*Does not include officials in grades one through five. See Table 3 note *.

Table 5. *Estimated percentages of regular degree holders* within the civil service assuming an average career length of 36 years*

Year	Civil service qualified officials(a)	Degree holders from the previous 36 years Number(b)	Percent
1046	12,700+	7,207	57%
1119	16,500+	7,494	45%
1170	10,000–12,000	4,805	40–48%
1191	17,018	5,268	31%
1201	18,337	5,396	29%
1213	19,398+	5,256	27%

Sources: (a) See Table 4; (b) WHTK 32; SHY:HC 7–8 or Appendix 2. These are 36 year aggregates of the individual examination totals given in the sources.
*Includes *chin-shih* and *chu-k'o* degrees for 1046 and *chin-shih* degrees alone for other years.

The premier source for Sung governmental institutions, the *Sung hui-yao*, provides facilitated degree totals by examination for most of 1020–1094, and for all but one examination during 1132–1172, and for 1196–1223.[34] During these three periods, the triennial average of facilitated degrees was 498, 374, and 622 respectively. These figures must be used with caution, however, for unlike the *chin-shih* (or *chu-k'o*) degree, the facilitated degree did not automatically carry official status with it.

When a man received a facilitated degree, unless he was one of a small group who had ranked highest in the facilitated departmental examination, he was given a low titular office. Through 1079, the offices conferred were usually those of prefectural associate official (*pieh-chia*), office chief (*ch'ang-shih*), assistant office chief (*ssu-ma*), educational inspector (*wen-hsüeh*), or assistant instructor (*chu-chiao*). Thereafter only the last two were used.[35]

Although these offices could denote actual positions and duties, they were primarily indicators of rank. For most of the Northern Sung, they ranked at the bottom of the graded civil service,[36] but with the Yüan-feng Regulations of 1082, educational inspectorates and assistant instructorships became *ungraded* offices.[37] Whether facilitated degree holders were considered officials prior to 1082 and not thereafter is unclear, however, for the sources do not say.

In 1128, facilitated degree recipients were for the first time grouped into five classes. The first two received various graded offices, the third and fourth were made graded educational inspectors, and the fifth assistant instructors. Hence the critical break came after the fourth class. Fifth class men, although facilitated degree holders and included in the degree totals, were not counted as officials.[38]

While the five class grouping probably increased the representation of facilitated degree holders in the civil service somewhat, the greatest change seems to have come in the late twelfth century. Government discussions from the late 1170s and 1180s betray a concern that facilitated degrees had been conferred too liberally and that too many of the recipients were claiming official status.[39] Hung Mai (1123–1202), an elder statesman whose views on contemporary affairs were widely read and respected, complained in 1196 that three-time *chü-jen* were all receiving special grace in the facilitated examinations, for in the past most recipients had been four- to eight-time *chü-jen*. 'Even assistant instructors,' he wrote, 'are becoming officials and returning [home] as proper men. In every prefecture there are a hundred or more of them.'[40] The impact of facilitated degrees upon patterns of recruitment thus appears to have been substantial in the late twelfth and early thirteenth centuries, as large numbers attained the coveted status of officials.

But facilitated degrees alone cannot explain the declining representation of *chin-shih* in the civil service. Protection was an equally if not more important factor. The evidence relating to its use is less direct than that concerning the examinations, for there are no comparable quantitative data. But what there is strongly suggests that protection was more important in the twelfth century than it had been in the eleventh. While there were few complaints about protection in the earlier period, during the first half of the Southern Sung alone there were not only complaints but also at least two attempts to cut it

back.[41] But the practice was not easily controlled, and yet another attempt
in 1201 to reduce it was just a few years later by a relaxation in its limitations.[42] The problem was simple: protection was a cherished privilege which
mainly benefited the most powerful officials, the very ones who would have
had to lead any successful attempt to curb it. As Chou Pi-ta cautiously noted
in 1160:

> Now it is certain that we should reduce protection and stop the inheri-
> tance of rank, but if we remedy this abuse precipitously, then there
> will be many complaints. If [we act] lightly with regard to set laws,
> then it will be easy to upset [them all].[43]

There are also indications that the *chin-shih* degree was less of a requirement for high office in the twelfth century than it had been previously.
According to the work of that great pioneer of Chinese economic and social
history, Sudō Yoshiyuki, the percentage of *chin-shih* holders among chief
councilors (*tsai-hsiang*) and assistant councilors (*chih-cheng*) dropped sub-
stantially after the reign of Che-tsung (1085–1100), averaging 90% in the
years 997–1100 and just 72% in the succeeding century (1100–1195).[44]
Sudō has also shown that, in six southeastern prefectures, the ratio of *chin-
shih* who reached high office to the total number of *chin-shih* dropped
sharply between the Northern and Southern Sung, which suggests that the
career value of the degree had eroded.[45] Finally, there is the striking fact
that in 1213 (see Table 3) protection accounted for 55% of the administrative officials compared to just 41% for *chin-shih*. Clearly the political
importance of protection grew as the dynasty progressed.

Brian McKnight has recently argued that there was a general trend toward favoritism during the Southern Sung. Chief ministers packed the upper
ranks of the bureaucracy with their protégés and they made great use of
protection.[46] Through imperial acts of grace on occasions like the imperial
suburban sacrifices, there were ample opportunities for favoritism to be
translated into protection.[47] But it should also be noted that more families
received major protection privileges in the Southern Sung than in the Northern Sung. Holding a court-level position was a risky affair in the Southern
Sung. Chief ministers were very powerful but also very transient, as constant
factional struggle took its toll. This made it virtually impossible for a family
to perpetuate itself in high office over several generations, as Robert Hartwell
has noted,[48] but it also meant that more families reached high office and
thus gained, at least momentarily, the great protection privileges that that
entailed. The net effect was therefore to increase protection even though no
single family could have compared with some of the great Northern Sung
families or lineages in their uses of it.

One further factor had a profound impact upon changing patterns of recruitment: the examinations, as we shall shortly see, were becoming increasingly competitive. Protection and the facilitated examinations offered very different paths to office, with one serving the young scions of the powerful and the other the old survivors of the examination halls. They were alike only in being easier than the regular examinations, but in the shifting landscape of twelfth-century society, that was a crucial quality, and many who in earlier times would have taken regular degrees had to settle for something less.

This in turn suggests a different perspective by which to view civil service recruitment. Our attention thus far has been on the effects of sociopolitical changes upon recruitment, but in the remainder of this chapter we shall turn that around and consider how recruitment, specifically the examinations, affected society. For by creating large groups with varying educational status and a huge group of undistinguished literati, the examinations made themselves felt in every corner of elite society and beyond it as well.

Students and *chü-jen*

Among the literati, several groups stood out from their examination-oriented peers by virtue of having achieved some measure of academic success. Most visible of these, and unique in having a degree of political power, were the students of the Imperial University (*T'ai-hsüeh*) and, for the early Northern Sung, of the other schools in K'ai-feng such as the Directorate of Education (*Kuo-tzu-chien*). Initially these schools were restricted to students from official families, but this began to change in the 1040s, and by the reign of the emperor Hui-tsung (1101–25), the majority of students entered through routes open to non-officials, although substantial channels for privileged entry continued to exist for the rest of the dynasty. Entrance procedures varied. The most common method, used for much of the Southern Sung, was an entrance examination (*pu-shih*), which was held shortly after the results of the departmental examination were announced. This gave *chü-jen* who had failed the departmental examination as well as certain non-*chü-jen* an added chance for advancement and, in effect, made the entrance examination an extension of the examination system. Once in the University, the student had great advantages in the examinations, for the University qualifying examination was far less competitive than those in the prefectures, and on occasion large numbers of University students were exempted from passing the preliminary examination.[49]

The University students were a remarkable and highly visible group in K'ai-feng and, later, in Lin-an. Predictably, they had a reputation for conviviality and numerous accounts of their exploits have survived from

contemporary writings.[50] Because they were highly selected and had a history
of producing statesmen from their ranks, their power was considerable if informal. On at least one occasion they took on the local officials. In 1210,
after the prefect of Lin-an fu had, quite rightfully, arrested four students for
profiteering in real estate, both students and educational officials protested
that this was an intrusion into the jurisdiction of the Directorate, which
oversaw the University. In the end the emperor agreed with the students
and the prefect was removed from office.[51] Even more significant was the
active role in advocating state policies which students took during periods
of national crisis. Using petitions and sometimes even marches, they were
on occasion (most notably at the end of the Northern Sung) successful in
getting ministers dismissed and policies changed.[52]

University students also received certain material benefits, including free
room and board when in residence. Under Hui-tsung, exemptions from
service obligations were granted to some students in 1107, and apparently
to all in or by 1117, though these provisions probably did not survive his
reign.[53] In 1149, exemptions were given to all University students who were
the only adult males in their households.[54]

As the quotas in Table 6 indicate, University student numbers grew
dramatically during the Northern Sung and again during the Southern Sung
after the University had been reconstituted in Lin-an in 1142. In the context
of the empire, however, these students were a tiny group, and outside of the
capital their importance was not great.

A second group consisted of the preliminary examination graduates, the
chü-jen or *kung-shih* ('tribute scholars') as they were sometimes called. A
creation of the Sung examination system, they were the most prominent
semi-official group outside of the capital, but their position was ambiguous.
New *chü-jen* were feted by the local officials after the examination results
had been announced and then they journeyed to the capital where they
presented their credentials at the Board of Rites, went through welcoming
ceremonies, and took the departmental examination. There were material
benefits as well. The government sometimes gave travel aids such as postal
station passes and in the Southern Sung many communities established
examination estates to help cover *chü-jen* travel expenses. The government
also gave them the right to convert certain punishments into fines and exempted some, though not all, from the service obligations that families and
individuals owed to the state.[55]

Nor did the benefits cease with the metropolitan examinations. Unsuccessful *chü-jen* kept their *chü-jen* status and had the right to participate with
officials in local feasts and ceremonies. More important, the government
routinely announced exemptions allowing past *chü-jen* (usually those who

Table 6. *University student quotas*

Northern Sung Year	Quota	Southern Sung Year	Quota
975	70*	1142	300
1044	300*	1143	700–900
1050	100	1145	830–916**
1051	200	1148	1,000
1068	900	1200	1,400
1071	1,000	1266	1,636**
1079	2,400		
1093	2,175		
1101	2,400		
1103	3,800		
1120	2,400		
1127	600		

Source: Wang Chien-ch'iu, *Sung-tai T'ai-hsüeh yü T'ai-hsüeh-sheng,* pp. 108-11.

*The entries for 975 and 1044 are actually for the Directorate of Education. Following 1044, the Directorate continued to exist as a school for the children of officials exclusively and had 200 students in 1078. Also, the School of the Four Gates had 450 students in 1058 and 600 in 1062. None of these figures is included in the table above. *Sung hui-yao chi-kao: Ch'ung-ju* section 1/32a–b. This section will be cited hereafter as SHY:CJ.

**Probably represents the actual number of students.

had become *chü-jen* fifteen or more years before) to go to the metropolitan examinations without again qualifying.[56] This, combined with the provisions for the facilitated examinations, meant that a young *chü-jen* had a very good chance of receiving at least a facilitated degree at some future point, even without further success in the regular examinations.

Still, with the exception of *chü-jen* from Kuang-nan in the far south who could hold minor office as 'irregular status officials' (*she-kuan*),[57] *chü-jen* were not officials and indeed had to repass the preliminary examination or gain exemption from it in order to keep what legal privileges they had.[58] Like the Ming and Ch'ing licentiates (*sheng-yüan*) they were a marginal group, esteemed by some but ridiculed by others. At one extreme we find Liu Ch'eng-pi, whose idyllic student days were described earlier.[59] From a famous family of officials in Chi-chou, Liu was a two-time *chü-jen* and retired scholar whom the government honored for his virtue with a banner twelve feet in height. This was in response to a nominating petition from 1,353 of his fellow literati in Chi-chou.[60] But there were others like Lu T'ang of Fu-chien, a *chü-jen* and one-time University student in the late

Northern Sung, who was forced to become a merchant to support himself, thereby incurring the scorn of his acquaintances.[61] In the opinion of at least one official, Ch'en Kung-fu (d. ca. 1140), *chü-jen* were generally an object- ionable lot:

> As soon as they pass the prefectural examination, they begin to search for connections in order to gain a means of livelihood. They are local bullies when they stay at home and roaming vagrants when they wander about in the empire.[62]

The reference to roaming is noteworthy, for in a society that valued im- mobility and distrusted unattached outsiders, the travels of *chü-jen* and scholars generally were viewed with some suspicion.[63]

Because of the complex nature of examination procedures, the data on the size of the *chü-jen* population and changes in it are difficult to interpret. There are two aggregate figures for the prefectural *chü-jen* quotas: 2,334 (or 1,604 for prefectural quotas including K'ai-feng) for 1106[64] and 2,026 for the late Southern Sung.[65] Given the smaller territory and population of the Southern Sung, the latter figure actually represents an increase for the pre- fectures involved. Still, we may reasonably take the figure of two thousand as a rough standard for the number of prefectural *chü-jen* who qualified in each examination in the late Northern and Southern Sung. There were others as well: *chü-jen* from the special qualifying examinations and those exempted from qualifying. In fact, given the figures in Table 7, non-prefectural *chü-jen* must have predominated in the departmental examinations.

Chü-jen numbers did not grow over time. Except for the high figures of the early Sung, a period of institutional flux, the numbers remained remark- ably stable, in the range of five to ten thousand.[66] There was a good reason for this: numbers had to be limited to keep the departmental examination manageable. More speculatively, if we generously assume that for each *chü-jen* at a given departmental examination, there were two who either qualified and did not go[67] or were past *chü-jen*, then the empire's *chü-jen* population would have been in the range of fifteen to thirty thousand after the early Northern Sung. Given a population of roughly one hundred million in the late Northern Sung and sixty million in the Southern Sung, thirty thousand *chü-jen* would have constituted 0.15 and 0.25% of the adult male population respectively, assuming adult males to have constituted twenty percent of the population.

Compared with the Ming and Ch'ing licentiates, who alone constituted an estimated one and two percent of the adult male population respectively,[68] Sung *chü-jen* were a small group. But more relevant is the fact that no lower degree holders at all existed before the Sung. Thus the Sung creation of

Table 7. *Chu-jen taking the departmental examination*

Year	Number of *chü-jen*	Sources
977	5,200	a, b
983	10,260	a
992	17,300	a, c
998	10,000+	a, c
1002	14,500+	a, c
1005	13,000+	a, c
1048	5,000+	c
1086–94	4,732	d
1109	7,000	c
1124	15,000	b, c, e
1211	4,311	c
Late Southern Sung	10,000+	f

Sources: (a) HCP passim; (b) WHTK 30–31; (c) SHY:HC 1–6; (d) Hung Mai, *Jung-chai sui-pi* 4:8/3a; (e) SS 155; (f) Wu Tzu-mu, *Meng-liang lu* 2/3a.

chü-jen, a prominent if marginal semi-official group rivalling the civil service in numbers, was a crucial step in the development of an examination-oriented elite.

Finally there were the students in the government's prefectural and county schools, who numbered around two hundred thousand at their height in the early twelfth century. Although they lacked the status of either the *chü-jen* or University students, they were a selected group, having passed an entrance examination (*pu-shih*), and they received certain financial benefits, chief among which were free room and board. During the late Northern Sung students were also exempted from service obligations, but this seems to have been short-lived.[69]

Government schools were associated with the examinations both through their education, which was geared to the examination curriculum, and through their personnel, who managed much of the examination preparation. On several occasions the government tried to make attendance in the local schools a prerequisite to taking the examinations, and under Hui-tsung it abolished the prefectural examinations altogether, using instead promotion through the school system. In addition, for much of the Southern Sung permission to take the University entrance examination was especially extended to selected prefectural school students. Thus while connections between schools and the examination system were numerous, they tended to be secondary, not directly involving the critical qualifying examinations.

The growth of the literati

In 1184, Tseng Feng, a minor official serving in the southeasternmost circuit of Kuang-nan-tung, bade farewell to an elderly colleague who was departing for the capital in hopes of a promotion:

> Now when men are few, the quest for advancement is easy. When men are numerous, the quest for advancement is difficult. When men are few and the quest is easy, [even if one's talents are] ordinary and mediocre, one can spread one's wings. When men are many and the quest difficult, unless one has greatly surpassing achievements, one will not obtain advancement.[70]

Although Tseng was referring to advancement in business and religion as well as in the examinations and office holding, his concern was clearly with the latter endeavors. And well it should have been, for examination competition was dramatically on the increase.

Candidates attempting the prefectural qualifying examinations numbered approximately twenty to thirty thousand in the early eleventh century and seventy-nine thousand in the examinations of 1099, 1102, and 1105 a century later. By the middle of the thirteenth century, candidates from southern China alone (i.e., the Southern Sung empire) probably numbered four hundred thousand or more.[71]

As candidates increased, so did competition in the examinations. After 1009, when prefectural *chü-jen* quotas were instituted, quota increases (they were seldom decreased) were supposed to be made according to an imperially legislated quota-ratio, that is, a ratio of *chü-jen* to the average number of candidates in recent examinations. There were many exceptions to this practice, but still the fact that the government had to decrease the legislated ratio from 5/10 to 1/200 (see Table 8) in order to limit *chü-jen* numbers as we saw earlier that they did, clearly reflects a manifold increase in examination competition over the course of the dynasty.

In practice, competition could be even worse than these legislated ratios would indicate. The Fu-chien prefecture of Fu-chou, the leading producer of *chin-shih* during the Southern Sung, had some 40 *chü-jen* places for its 3,000 candidates in 1090 (1/75) and just 54 places for 18,000 or more candidates in 1207 (1/333).[72] Yen-chou in Liang-che-hsi had a quota of 18 for 1,781 candidates in 1156 (1/100) and the same quota in 1262 when there were over 7,000 candidates.[73] Further west in modern Anhui, officials from Kuang-chou complained in 1231 that, since the Ch'un-hsi reign period (1174–89), their candidate numbers had increased ten-fold but their quota had only been increased from three to five *chü-jen*.[74]

Figure 2 gives the *chü-jen* to candidate ratios for all of the cases I have

Table 8. *Legislated quota-ratios for prefectural examinations*

Year	Quota-ratio
997	2/10
1005	4/10
1009	5/10*
1023	5/10
1026	4/10
1032	2/10
1045	2/10
1066	1/10
1067	15/100
1093	1/10
1156	1/100
1275†	1/200

Sources: SHY:HC 15–16; SS 156/22a for 1275.
*Empire-wide prefectural quotas first set.
†According to local histories, quotas were also set in 1234.
They do not say what quota-ratio was used, but it must have
been 1/100 or less. Fang Jen-jung, *Yen-chou hsü-chih* 3:33;
Lo Chün, *Pao-ch'ing Ssu-ming chih*, 21 ch. (Sung Yüan Ssu-
ming liu chih ed.) 2/19b. The latter will hereafter be cited as
PCSMC.

found in which both quota and candidate figures are available. Examination
competition was clearly increasing, especially during the Southern Sung.
Indeed, if we look only at the prefectures from the southeast, a region which
dominates the historical records much as it seems to have dominated the
political and intellectual life of the Sung, the rate of increase became ex-
ponential in the late twelfth and early thirteenth centuries. Even in the less
advanced southern and southwestern prefectures, where competition was
less severe, there was without exception greater competition than there had
been in the empire at large in 1106.

These findings are further supported by a comparison of candidate numbers with population figures. In Figure 3, reports of actual candidate numbers
have been used to calculate the candidates' percentage of the adult male
population. The percentages are rough, for prefectural population estimates
have to be used for the Southern Sung.[75] They demonstrate, however, that
the literati were increasing relative to the rest of the population and not
merely keeping pace with Sung population-growth. The increase was most
dramatic in the southeast but is also evident, to a lesser extent, in the central
and upper regions of the Yangtze River Valley. When we consider that these

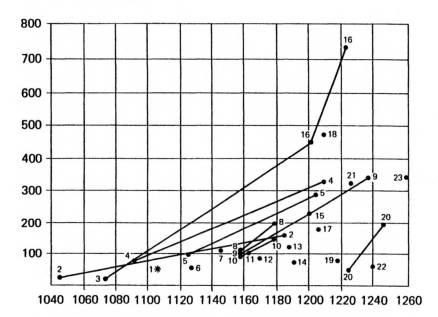

1. Empire
2. Su-chou (Liang-che-hsi)
3. Ming-chou, T'ai-chou and
   Wen-chou (Liang-che-tung)
4. Fu-chou (Fu-chien)
5. Hu-chou (Liang-che-hsi)
6. Ch'ang-chou (Liang-che-hsi)
7. Chi-chou (Chiang-nan-hsi)
8. Chien-chou (Ch'eng-tu fu lu)
9. Yen-chou (Liang-che-hsi)
10. Hui-chou (Chiang-nan-tung)
11. Wan-chou (K'uei-chou lu)
12. Jun-chou (Liang-che-hsi)
13. Chien-chou (Fu-chien)
14. Lung-chou (Li-chou-lu)
15. Chia-chou (Ch'eng-tu fu lu)
16. T'ai-chou (Liang-che-tung)
17. Hsing-chou (Li-chou lu)
18. Wen-chou (Liang-che-tung)
19. Hua-chou (Kuang-nan-hsi)
20. Shou-ch'ang chün (Ching-
    hu-pei)
21. Yüeh-chou (Liang-che-tung)
22. Tao-chou (Ching-hu-nan)
23. T'an-chou (Ching-hu-nan)

Fig. 2. Prefectural examination candidates per *chü-jen* in assorted prefectures for the years 1040–1260.

figures do not include those taking the special preliminary examinations, those who had quit taking the examinations or had already passed them, or those who began their studies with thoughts of the examinations but dropped out along the way, we can begin to appreciate the impact the examinations came to have upon society.

Who were these literati and what are we to make of their appearance in the examination halls? Most simply, they were those who could afford the lengthy education required for the examinations and then pursued it, and that, as we noted earlier, excluded most of the population. Did the literati

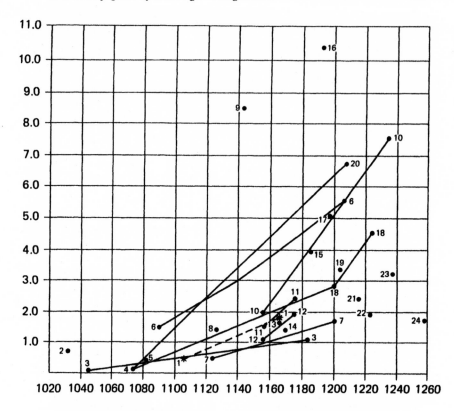

1. Empire
2. K'ai-feng fu
3. Su-chou (Liang-che-hsi)
4. Ming-chou, T'ai-chou and
      Wen-chou (Liang-che-tung)
5. Hsin-chou (Chiang-nan-tung)
6. Fu-chou (Fu-chien)
7. Hu-chou (Liang-che-hsi)
8. Ch'ang-chou (Liang-che-hsi)
9. Chi-chou (Chiang-nan-hsi)
10. Yen-chou (Liang-che-hsi)
11. Chien-chou (Ch'eng-tu fu lu)
12. Hui-chou (Chiang-nan-tung)

13. Wan-chou (K'uei-chou lu)
14. Jun-chou (Liang-che-hsi)
15. Chien-chou (Fu-chien)
16. Lung-chou (Li-chou lu)
17. Chia-chou (Ch'eng-tu fu lu)
18. T'ai-chou (Liang-che-tung)
19. Hsing-chou (Li-chou lu)
20. Wen-chou (Liang-che-tung)
21. Hua-chou (Kuang-nan-hsi)
22. Yüeh-chou (Liang-che-tung)
23. Tao-chou (Ching-hu-nan)
24. T'an-chou (Ching-hu-nan)

Fig. 3. Percent of adult males taking the prefectural examination in the empire and in assorted prefectures, 1020–1260.

then define the elite? In some ways, yes, for education and examinations were preeminently elite activities. In Confucian political culture, the scholar interpreted the will of Heaven for the emperor, and as an official mediated between the emperor and the people. When the elite engaged in unofficial activities, it was its connection with the government that gave it its great authority, and that connection was predicated upon study. Wrote one thirteenth century official:

> Now scholars assuredly constitute the stairway to high office and learning assuredly constitutes the stairway to [becoming] a scholar. Therefore those who are high officials must have [become so] through learning and those beneath officials must persevere in their learning. . . . If the scholars of this town are able to achieve learning, then their stairs will be those to high office.[76]

Strictly speaking, however, scholars were an occupational rather than social group, the first of the four traditional occupations or peoples (*ssu-min*), the others being farmers, artisans, and merchants. As such their relationship to the social elite changed during the Sung.[77] In the early unsettled years of the dynasty when many types of people were active in government, a deliberate attempt was made to constitute scholars as a social elite, for a number of groups (most of them potential rivals to the scholars) were barred from the examinations: government clerks, artisans, merchants, and Buddhist and Taoist monks.[78] These were *not* hereditary prohibitions; there was nothing to stop the son of a merchant or artisan from receiving an education and, assuming that he could obtain the requisite guarantees, taking the examinations. Yet the intent clearly was to create and maintain a purely scholarly group of families to staff the civil service. To quote an edict from 989: 'The examinations were created in order to serve the scholarly classes [literally, 'stream'] ; how can we permit clerks to advance falsely and stealthily take degrees?'[79]

But the attempt was not lasting and by the mid to late eleventh century the prohibitions, with the exception of that against clerks, had lapsed. Even while the very scholarly professional elite was dominating the upper ranks of the bureaucracy, literati from non-scholarly families began appearing in the examinations, spurred at least in part by the government's growing sponsorship of education. 'Why complain that assorted artisans and merchants advance? The scholarly class is mixed and without distinctions, is it not?' queried Ou-yang Hsiu (1007-1072), who was himself from a bureaucratic family of modest means.[80] Slightly later, Su Ch'e (1039-1112), the great poet Su Shih's brother who was known for his political criticism, wrote in an unhappier vein:

In all of today's peasant, artisan, and merchant families, there are those who have forsaken their past [i.e., their family occupations] and became scholars. Those who are scholars daily increase, but the world is increasingly ungoverned. [In the examinations, we] are now selecting those who live at home without managing [their family's] produce. Looking up, they do not support their parents, and facing down, they are inconsiderate of their wives and sons. They wander through the four quarters [of the empire] disturbing the prefectures and counties and fabricating slander. [True] peasants, artisans, and merchants do not take part in this.[81]

By the Southern Sung yet another phenomenon appeared, that of literati families engaging in non-literati activities.

If the sons and younger brothers of an official have no hereditary stipends by which they can be maintained, and no landed property on which they may depend, and they want some way of serving their parents and caring for their dependants, the best thing for them to do is to become Confucian scholars. Those of them who are endowed with outstanding talents and able to pursue the calling of a scholar fitting himself for appointment will, if of the first quality, gain riches and honors through success in the examinations, and, if of the second quality, give instruction to disciples and receive the offering due to a master; while those who are not able to pursue the calling of a scholar fitting himself for appointment will, if of the first quality, be able to fulfill the tasks of writing letters and drawing up documents for others, and if of the second quality, be able to give primary instruction to boys in the arts of punctuating and reading. Those who are not capable of being Confucian scholars may make their living without disgracing their ancestors by working as spirit-mediums, doctors, Buddhists, Taoists, farmers, merchants or experts of some sort. It is the greatest disgrace to the ancestors if sons or younger brothers degenerate into beggars or thieves.[82]

Yüan Ts'ai, a thirteenth century official from Che-tung and author of this remarkable passage, was concerned with the problem of how an elite family could maintain its position or, failing that, decline as respectably as possible, and as Robert Hymes has argued in the case of Fu-chou in Chiang-nan-hsi, his advice to the not-so-talented children of officials was both realistic and heeded. For as access to office became increasingly difficult, elite families diversified occupationally, allowing their less promising (or less bookish) children to pursue occupations that would have been scorned in the past.[83]

If not all elite members were literati, then were all literati from the elite (i.e., from the small group of socially established families that dominated local society)? Hymes believes that they were, that examination candidacy, which required guarantees from the prefectural school preceptor and others as to the respectability of one's family, gave the local elite control over who took the examinations.[84] But such a view overstates the degree of control the elite could exercise in such matters and ignores the masses of Southern Sung literati who crowded the examination halls, especially in those southeastern prefectures where thousands of candidates at a time took the prefectural examinations.[85]

There are other reasons for believing that the great majority of literati may have had elite forebears, however, for Sung literati families were very large. *Chin-shih* had an average of more than three brothers each in 1148 and almost two in 1256, which means that their families were more than doubling in size with each generation.[86] Given such growth, the pressures of downward mobility were intense and produced an abundance of poor cousins of the rich and powerful, of families that had seen better days. Moreover, as we observed in Chapter 1 there is clear evidence of non-elite literati in the Southern Sung who aspired to elite status, adopted its values, invested in education, and tried to marry into its ranks. I would suggest that together, these ex-elite and non-elite families formed a considerable fringe about the edges of elite society. Most of them never succeeded and remain invisible to the historian. But their presence and constant pressure upon the local elites made achievement more important than ever. Unless a family could distinguish itself economically, socially, or educationally — through the examinations or scholarship — it ran the risk of sinking into that fringe.

Recruitment and the social order

The dual trends that we have observed above — of an increasing reliance on facilitated degrees and protection as channels of bureaucratic recruitment on the one hand and of a manifold growth in the literati on the other — present us with an interesting paradox. Even as the examinations were becoming more popular they were becoming less important bureaucratically.

That the use of facilitated degrees and protection was on the rise is understandable. When examination candidates began outnumbering the available *chü-jen* positions by better than one hundred to one, even wealthy and renowned official families could no longer be sure that their sons would pass the examinations. The turn to privileged and/or easier methods of recruitment was thus natural and, as we will see in Chapter 5, occurred within the examination process as well.

But why did the great unsuccessful majority of literati put up with this situation? The conditions appear to have been ripe for a revolution of rising expectations among the literati and for a subsequent frustration of those expectations. And indeed, Sung documents contain ample evidence of social strain engendered by the examinations, especially in the Southern Sung. It is hardly unanimous, for there were those who celebrated the academic climate of the day. Chou Pi-ta wrote in commemorating the renovation of a Chi-chou county school in 1198:

> Now the dynasty has established schools, and the teachings of the Duke of Chou and Confucius have been illumined, the Way of Yao, Shun and King Wen has been met. Although those who are scholars register for examination occupation in order to enter the official class, they still live peacefully, fathers encouraging their sons, elder brothers encouraging their younger brothers. Beginning with sprinkling, sweeping and answering questions [i.e., the earliest stage of education], they are filled with filiality, fraternal love, loyalty and trustworthiness.[87]

And a couple of generations later, the encyclopedist Wang Ying-lin (1223–96) could write of Ming-chou:

> In our town, since Ch'ing-li [1041–8], all of our elders have been pure and cultivated, and since the great Confucian unfolding of orthodox learning in Ch'ien-tao [1165–73] and Ch'un-hsi [1174–89],[88] filiality and brotherly love have been cultivated in families and humanity and obedience have flourished. Age and virtue have been exalted in the villages and customs have been rich. Principle and righteousness have been manifest in the heart and so sagely talent has been abundant.[89]

But such optimistic voices were rare. More common were those like Wang T'ing-chang (1086–41), an unsuccessful examination candidate noted for his lectures at community gatherings:

> In recent generations, customs have decayed. Even among scholars who are related, evil has prospered and wrangling has upset the peace. They can almost be compared with hairs, those who dispute and fight within the [family] courtyard.[90]

As we will see in Chapter 4, the examinations were criticized for having perverted education, for making people study for the wrong reasons. The Hunanese philosopher Chang Shih (1133–80), unlike Chou and Wang Ying-lin, felt that heterodoxy was holding sway in the schools:

> In general, since heretical doctrines became current, scholars have confused basic truths, texts have been selected to study [for the purpose of] excelling, and scholars have been interested in learning the vulgar. And in normal times when they gather and live together, how

much does their work become that of looking for ways to be selected [in the examinations] or scheming for profit?[91]

Not surprisingly, frustrations and anxieties were most evident at the examinations themselves. When candidates were numerous, just getting into the hall and finding a place became an accomplishment in itself, and at times violence could erupt. The examination riot described in Chapter 1 is the most dramatic example,[92] but there are also reports of people being trampled to death in the midst of commotion at the gates in T'an-chou in 1186 and Heng-chou (both in Ching-hu-nan) in 1210,[93] and Wang Yen-wu (1252–1324), who took the Chi-chou examinations as a youth, wrote of them: 'Every year, in the struggle at the gate [as people] pushed and fought to enter, there were those who were trampled to death.'[94]

But despite these disturbances, the many bitter attacks upon examination-oriented education, and complaints about the size of the bureaucracy, the Sung social order does not seem to have been threatened by its institutional tensions. Why this was will be a central concern of the subsequent chapters. Here I would merely suggest that the answer lay in the increasingly elaborate articulation of the examination life. As the *chin-shih* degree became more elusive, lesser successes gained in status and alternative roles became acceptable, from the respected retired scholar down to Yüan Ts'ai's doctors, monks, farmers and merchants. Academic promise, moreover, increased one's marriageability as well as one's chances of obtaining an influential sponsor. When one considers, finally, that the literatus's personal interests were held to be subservient to those of his family, then it is more understandable why individual frustrations were not, as a rule, translated into rebellion or violence.

PART II

3

FOR THE UTMOST GOVERNANCE:
EXAMINATIONS IN THE EARLY SUNG

Sung examinations and the Confucian tradition

Philosophically and culturally, the Sung examination system was a curiously un-Confucian hybrid of Confucianism. It was an imperial creation and therefore reflected imperial interests which, as Joseph Levenson has shown so well, tended to be Legalist.[1] To be sure, Confucianism loomed large within the system, most notably in the curriculum. The aspiring student, once he had worked through the primers, set out to master and memorize the huge corpus of classical Confucianism, and while candidates for the prestigious *chin-shih* degree were also examined on contemporary policy issues and poetry composition, the greatest part of their education was spent with these Confucian texts. Confucian principles also helped to justify the examination system. Confucius (550–479 B.C.) lived at a time when the aristocratic order of the early Chou was breaking down and rulers were increasingly looking to educated commoners and men of noble but humble birth for aid in governing. Although he viewed social hierarchy as natural, he also believed in the natural equality of people and held that rulers should select superior men of virtue and ability as ministers.[2] This idea was most clearly stated by Mencius: 'If a ruler gives honour to men of talents and employs the able, so that offices shall all be filled by individuals of distinction and mark; – then all the scholars of the kingdom will be pleased, and wish to stand in his court.'[3] Thus the examination system's ideal of selecting the best men to serve as officials was thoroughly Confucian.

Un-Confucian, however, were the Sung criteria used for selection: instead of virtue and ability, which required evaluation of an individual's character, memory and the literary skills of argumentation and poesy were used, which did not. Indeed, as we will see, the early Sung emperors' concern for impartiality and fairness (*kung*) meant that character could not be seriously considered in the examinations. Yet the eminent eleventh century Confucian Chang Tsai (1020–77) argued that the truly moral route to government was by the kin-based privilege of protection (*yin*), which had been used by rulers 'to select men of achievement and honor men of virtue, to love them and treat them generously, so as to show that their imperial kindness is unlimited.'[4] Scholars pursuing the examinations, however,

> ... do not realize that selecting an official position is incompatible with moral principles. On the contrary they look down upon those who follow principles as incompetent. They do not realize that hereditary principles are a glory. On the contrary, they consider a hollow fame as a good way to continue the accomplishment of their ancestors.[5]

Although this passage is taken from a famous twelfth century anthology of Neo-Confucian writings, Chang's view was not generally accepted. Still it demonstrates that the examinations were vulnerable to Confucian attack. For in the *impersonality* of the examinations lay the danger of producing alienated and selfish men pursuing 'hollow fame.' Thus the vehicle of Confucian orthodoxy was open to the charge of making men un-Confucian.

Finally, un-Confucian were the political uses to which the examinations were put, for they were made to serve imperial, regional, and elite interests. Quite overt in the opening decades of the Sung when institutional patterns were taking shape, in later times these uses were often disguised as logical, integral parts of the examination system. This is not to deny the impersonal and universalistic norms that have long impressed both Chinese and foreign students of the examination system; in fact, those norms were largely Sung creations. It simply means that politics mattered. As we shall see in this and the following two chapters, the development and evolution of the Sung examination system involved unceasing interaction between it and the social and political forces of the day.

Examinations under the early emperors

The examination system that the Sung founder Chao K'uang-yin (the emperor T'ai-tsu, r. 960–76) inherited from the Latter Chou dynasty (951–60) was a far cry from that which flourished later in his family's reign or, for that matter, from that of its antecedent in the T'ang.[6] In theory it was much like the T'ang system, with annual examinations, a variety of degrees, and small numbers of graduates, but in practice the wars of the tenth century had taken their toll upon both examinations and literati. The lack of standards was such that in one examination candidates were ordered to box each other,[7] while in another, in 975, the lack of *military* prowess among 270 specially recommended *chü-jen* from P'u-chou in Ching-tung-hsi so exasperated T'ai-tsu that he threatened to have them all conscripted into the army. When they tearfully begged for mercy he dismissed them but ordered that the prefectural officials who had recommended them be punished.[8]

T'ai-tsu was well aware of the potential importance of the examinations. In 962 he declared:

> The country has fastened upon examinations to select scholars, choosing men to become officials. Since picking and ranking men in the public court is preferable to [receiving their] thanks for favors in private halls, this will serve to rectify customs that have been lacking.[9]

On another occasion he said, 'For chief councilors one must use men of learning (*tu-shu-jen*).'[10] Most significantly, in 973 he initiated a palace examination (*tien-shih, yü-shih*) under his own personal supervision as the final stage in the examination process, thereby elevating the examinations from a purely internal affair of the civil service to one emanating from the Son of Heaven himself.[11] However, apart from this innovation T'ai-tsu left the examinations unchanged, for he was preoccupied by other matters: the expeditions against the Khitans to the northeast, the conquest of the southern kingdoms, and the problem of controlling the northern generals out of whose ranks he himself had risen.

So it was only after the accession of T'ai-tsu's younger, more bookish brother, T'ai-tsung (r. 976–97), when the reunification of the empire was virtually complete, that the dramatic transformation of the examinations began. Early in 977 T'ai-tsung proclaimed:

> I wish to search broadly for the superior and accomplished within the examination halls. I dare not aspire to select five out of ten, but if only one or two [out of ten] are chosen, even that may be considered preparation for the utmost governance.[12]

In the following days, 109 *chin-shih*, 207 *chu-k'o*, and 184 facilitated degrees were given.[13] Even without counting the facilitated degrees, this was more degrees than had been given during the entire sixteen years of T'ai-tsu's reign.[14] This action did not escape criticism; the scholarly privy councilor Hsüeh Chu-cheng protested that 'If the selection of men is excessive, the employment of men will [increase] too rapidly.'[15] But T'ai-tsung persevered and in subsequent years continued to grant large numbers of degrees. In fact, in retrospect it is clear that the 977 examination marked a major change in government recruitment patterns. During the Five Dynasties, an average of 33.0 degrees were given each year, with 12.5 of them *chin-shih* degrees.[16] Under T'ai-tsu the average fell to 19.2, while 10.2 of them were *chin-shih*.[17] By comparison, during the period 977–1271 an average of 192 regular (i.e., non-facilitated) degrees were given, of which 141 were *chin-shih*.[18] In addition, facilitated degrees, for which we have only incomplete records, accounted for at least another 120 degrees per year.

The initial effect of the expansion in degree numbers was to throw examination practices into disarray. There was an immediate growth in candidate numbers: whereas approximately 5,200 men took the departmental examination (*sheng-shih*) in K'ai-feng in 977,[19] 10,260 took it in 982[20] and 17,300 in 992.[21] Severe stresses were placed upon the now antiquated examination machinery which, with few precedents to rely upon, operated erratically. Examinations were variously held every year, every other year, every third year, and once, from 992 to 998, there was a six-year hiatus.[22] Degree numbers also varied greatly. For example, in A.D. 1000 over 1,500 degrees, 409 of them *chin-shih*, were given, more than in any other year in Chinese history.[23] Two years later, in reaction to this flooding of the bureaucratic pool, only 38 *chin-shih* and 186 *chu-k'o* degrees were given, a drop which met with the popular protest described at the beginning of the book.

Why did T'ai-tsung increase degree numbers so sharply? A century later Ssu-ma Kuang suggested that it was 'to promote civil culture and restrain military affairs.'[24] Wang Yung in the thirteenth century ascribed it to the large number of positions which were vacant in the newly expanded empire.[25] And Ch'en Tung-yüan in this century has argued that T'ai-tsung was attempting to gain the allegiance of the scholarly class.[26] In fact, the need both for control and to provide opportunity were involved.

In the early years of the Sung, when it was still just another northern dynasty attempting to consolidate its position, the issue of control was paramount, for its rivals were legion and powerful: foreign states, generals, and wealthy merchant and military families. To that end, the dynasty's power over office-holding was crucial, its primary carrot to balance its military stick. What is remarkable about the early Sung emperors is that they used that power not so much to selectively employ and coopt their rivals as to win the allegiance of the empire's scholarly families. They were attempting to create a meritocratic elite beholden to the emperor and large enough so that its own most powerful members could not threaten the dynasty. This policy was visible in T'ai-tsu's creation of the palace examination, for as Japanese historians have long pointed out, that served to further imperial power:

> The creation of the palace examination as the final examination, given directly under the emperor's personal supervision, . . . was a necessary step in the strengthening of imperial autocracy.[27]

The policy was perhaps most evident in T'ai-tsung's opening of the examination floodgates in 977, but it did not stop with that. In the succeeding decades as the examination system adapted to cope with the new demands placed upon it, the meritocratic principle of fair impartiality informed its development.[28] And although that impartiality was ultimately compromised and subverted, the attempt to create a meritocratic order was nevertheless remarkable.

Institutional innovations

As *chü-jen* began to flood K'ai-feng and threaten the archaic examination system in the late tenth and early eleventh centuries, the government instituted a number of reforms designed to make the examinations impartial, equitable, and manageable. Most renowned of these were the measures designed to insure the anonymity of the candidate. In 992 the practice of covering up the names on the examination papers (*feng-mi* or *hu-ming*) was initiated for the palace examinations.[29] This was extended to the departmental examination in 1007[30] and to the prefectural examinations in 1033.[31] As an added precaution against the possible recognition of calligraphy, beginning in 1015 clerks copied out the examination papers in the palace and departmental examinations and examiners read only the copies.[32] This practice, known as *t'eng-lu*, was extended to the prefectural examinations in 1037.[33]

These procedures constituted a sharp break with the past. During the T'ang it was deemed not only permissible but desirable for candidates to submit samples of their prose and poetry to examiners before the examinations, so that both reputation and character could be taken into account.[34] During the early Sung this practice had been continued in the form of poetical compositions called 'public essays' (*kung-chüan*) which *chü-jen* had to present to the Board of Rites upon their arrival in K'ai-feng so that the Board could 'pick those with reputations.' But in 1041 the essays were discontinued on the grounds that covered names and copied examinations had made them unnecessary.[35]

Why, apart from providing seasonal employment for thousands of clerks, did the Sung give up such eminently Confucian considerations as an individual's character and reputation? Discussing the use of covered names in 1007, the emperor Chen-tsung (r. 997–1022) declared that 'We must strive for the utmost fairness [*chih-kung*] and select the cultivated amongst the poor landlords [i.e., humble scholars].'[36] A year later he remarked that southern scholars were delighted with the 'complete fairness' of covered names.[37] We shall see in Chapter 4 that these practices were briefly challenged in the late Northern Sung, but thereafter the policy of absolute impartiality in the grading process was maintained.

The problem of scheduling the examinations was also resolved, though slightly later. Through the first half of the eleventh century, two-, three-, and four-year intervals were all tried, until in 1066 a three-year period was decided upon,[38] and this remained the standard up until the examinations were abolished in 1905, providing for Chinese society a distinctive triennial periodicity. One suspects antiquarian motives, for according to the Han dynasty *Classic of Etiquette and Ceremonial*, during the Chou 'district wine-drinking ceremonies' (*hsiang yin-chiu li*) were held every three years,[39] and that, according to later Sung interpretations, was held on the occasion of the triennial 'great comparison' (*ta-pi* – a colloquial Sung term for the examinations), at which the census was taken and tribute men were sent for service to the government.[40] The reasons actually given were more prosaic but instructive.[41] A four-year period was thought too long, providing insufficient incentive for study and encouraging idleness. The two-year period, however, had been tried from 1057 to 1065 and had created difficulty for literati from distant prefectures who had had to spend much of their time in travel. Thus three years was settled upon, with the autumn and winter of one year devoted to qualifying examinations, spring of the next year to the capital examinations, and with no examinations at all in the third year.

During the early Northern Sung, the examinations also underwent a major structural change: the development of the prefectural examination (*chieh-shih*) into a major part of the examination system. At the dynasty's outset, prefectural examination procedures specified that *chin-shih* candidates be tested by the staff supervisor (*p'an-kuan*) and that of *chu-k'o* candidates by the executive inspector (*lu-shih ts'an-chun*). Qualification was determined by the number of questions correctly answered and all candidates who qualified were permitted to go to the capital as *chü-jen*.[42] This alone marked a major break with the past, for in the T'ang the number of 'district tribute' scholars (*hsiang-kung*) a prefecture could send to the capital depended upon its bureaucratic status: superior, middling and inferior prefectures respectively sent three, two and one a year.[43] But further changes followed as the numbers of *chü-jen* escalated in the late tenth century.

In 997, a quota-ratio of two *chü-jen* (who had to have qualified) for every ten candidates was decreed, thereby making the prefectural examination more selective, at least in theory, for it no longer consisted merely of sorting out the qualified from the unqualified.[44] In fact, one finds complaints in subsequent years that unqualified *chü-jen* were being sent to the capital, but these stop after the early decades of the eleventh century.[45] Presumably, advances in education had created a surplus of qualified candidates.

In 1009, direct quotas were substituted for quota-ratios in determining how many *chü-jen* each prefecture was permitted.[46] The quotas were based upon a standard quota-ratio and candidate statistics from recent examinations and, as we saw in Chapter 2, they were readjusted from time to time.[47]

There remained, then, a relationship between *chü-jen* and prefectural candidate numbers, although since special quota increases were granted frequently to individual prefectures, quotas could easily be changed for extraneous reasons, such as rewarding prefectures through which the emperor had passed on a trip[48] or favoring localities that were either backward or strategic militarily.[49] But even with these exceptions, the principle of fairness was not forgotten. In 1037, for example, the emperor ordered a return to the old prefectural quotas because the current ad hoc quotas were 'unfair' or 'unequal' (*pu-chün*).[50]

Two further developments in the prefectural examinations should be mentioned. As early as 972, the government tried to require that *chü-jen* be selected only in their home prefectures (though they could petition for a waiver).[51] A complaint from 992 concerning frequent violations of this rule[52] and a further prohibition in 1015[53] suggest what we shall see below, that the problem of residency was controversial and intractable. But the court's determination to curtail the more lenient T'ang practice is clear.[54] Second, as was noted above the use of covered names and copied examinations was extended to the prefectural examinations during the 1030s, so that they mirrored the capital examinations in their formality and impersonality.

Like the thread that tied Confucius's teachings together, the common theme behind these reforms was the provision of opportunity. If the examinations were truly to select the cultivated and talented, they would have to attract men from throughout the empire and avoid being monopolized by the powerful. One need not ascribe altruistic motives to the emperors, for the control of powerful families and the political integration of the empire that could result from the realization of this policy were quite practical goals. Nor should we think that they were trying to draw from all levels of society, for as we now turn to the question of becoming a candidate, it should become clear that their intentions were somewhat more limited.

Qualifying for candidacy

In 1149 the emperor Kao-tsung (r. 1127–62) issued an edict outlining the steps that local officials were to take in determining who was eligible for the examinations.[55] Prefectural and county officials, operating through the county schools, were to draw up a list with the names of those who would be taking the examinations by the second month of 1150, the year when the qualifying examinations would be held. County officials were to obtain each would-be candidate's family guarantee certificate (*chia-pao-chuang*), which gave such information as the candidate's ancestry and residence, and deliver them to the prefectural officials for forwarding to the prefectural school (*chou-hsüeh*). The school personnel would verify the information in the certificates and report to the preceptor (*chiao-shou*), who would then guarantee the candidates. This would allow them to participate in the district wine drinking ceremony and they could then take the examinations.[56]

It is clear from this edict, the only description of the preparation of candidate lists that has survived, that that process was elaborate and time consuming, involving large numbers of people who would then be responsible for their veracity, and placing great weight upon the respectability of the candidates' families. But this account says nothing about the criteria used for judging families or individuals and for our purposes, that issue is critical. For knowing how 'broadly' the dynasty intended to 'search for the superior and accomplished' is surely essential to any understanding of the social context of the examinations.

In this regard, a proposal from 1044 for reforming the examinations by the Han-lin academician, Sung Ch'i (998–1061), is revealing.[57] It suggested, in part, that candidacy be limited to students who had attended a government school for at least three hundred days and past *chü-jen* with one hundred days of attendance as of the day before autumn taxes were due, though special exceptions were made for only sons and for relatives accompanying officials who were stationed away from their homes.[58] Once the *chü-jen* were selected they were to be grouped into mutual guarantee groups of three men each. If any of the following seven conditions was later discovered, the offender was to be exiled to the border regions and the other two were to be barred from the next two examinations:

1 One was secretly mourning (*yin yu ni fu*).
2 One had a criminal record (*tseng fan hsing-tse*).
3 There were allegations or evidence of unfilial, unfraternal behavior.
4 One had violated regulations either twice with redemptions made or once without having made redemption and having harmed one's community.[59]
5 One was not a resident of the prefecture but had falsified one's household or taken the name of another person.
6 One's father or grandfather had committed any of the first four of the Ten Abominations (*shih-o*).[60]
7 One was an artisan, merchant or clerk[61] or had been a Buddhist or Taoist priest.[62]

Finally, local officials were to investigate the background of each *chü-jen* as well, making sure that none of the above conditions held.

Although Sung Ch'i's full proposal criticized past practices and was only briefly enacted,[63] his approach to candidacy reflects three concerns that were already well developed in the examination regulations. First, the candidate should not have practiced certain undesirable occupations. Second, his residence had to be where he claimed it was and he had to take the examinations in his home prefecture, unless he had some acceptable reason for taking it elsewhere. Third and most important, he had to be of good character.

Occupational prohibitions

The occupational prohibitions had their origin in the years following the expansion of the examinations. In 983, in response to reports that recent *chü-jen* had included many Buddhist and Taoist monks in their ranks, all present and former monks were barred from the examinations.[64] 'They only understand yellow-silk [i.e., religious] doctrines and do not know the meaning of the classics. How could they govern men?' stated the proclamation.[65] In 989, following a report that a clerk in the Secretariat-Chancellery had received a degree, clerks were also barred,[66] and three years later a more sweeping prohibition mentioned artisans, merchants and clerks, as well as the diseased and those with criminal records.[67] There was a loophole in this last prohibition, however:

> If among the artisans, merchants and clerks, there are those whose talent and conduct are unusual, who eminently stand out from the crowd, then they may qualify and be selected.[68]

These prohibitions, which spanned less than a decade, are remarkable when taken together, for the groups involved were all potential rivals to the literati. The monks and clerks constituted two large and predominantly literate groups, the one with a great popular following and the resources of the monastic estates behind it, the other with its bureaucratic expertise and considerable local power. Similarly, the wealthier among the merchants and artisans exercised great economic power. Yet the significance of these prohibitions is not that they denied advancement to the families engaged in these occupations, for they did not. One's social background was irrelevant, at least in the eyes of the government. Rather, the government was insisting that those who wished to take the examinations become literati by receiving the education and assimilating the values of scholars. Its cultural aim was to civilize and unify those diverse and rather uncivil elites that had emerged during the disorders of the preceding century.

Not surprisingly, this process entailed changes in occupational status. As that of the literati rose, those of the prohibited occupations fell. Sung Shee has observed that an official's engaging in commerce, which was socially tolerated at the dynasty's outset, was by the reign of Jen-tsung (1023–64) considered unacceptable.[69] Even more noteworthy was the altered status of clerks, for during the T'ang the clerk/official, *liu-wai/liu-nei* distinction, though important, was blurred, both because many clerks were appointed as minor officials and because officials frequently began their careers in clerical jobs.[70] The result of the Sung prohibitions was to constitute clerks as a separate class, isolated from the officials administratively and socially. To quote Ma Tuan-lin, the thirteenth century encyclopedist:

> Confucian scholars [*Ju*] and clerks have divided into two paths. The scholars take themselves to be cultivated and disparage the clerks as vulgar . . . The clerks take themselves to be knowledgeable and ridicule the scholars as impractical . . . Thus those who cherish and superficial and are unknowledgeable revert to the scholar's [path]; those who are wasteful and without shame revert to the clerk's [path]. Yet both paths are unsatisfactory for obtaining men.[71]

An intriguing feature of the prohibitions is that they ceased after a time. They were restated in the 1044 reform proposal quoted above, but thereafter, except for a passing reference from 1064,[72] the only official mention of the prohibitions that I have found is from 1118, when the 989 prohibition of clerks was cited in a bitter complaint about eunuchs receiving degrees. The complaint was to no avail and the account ends: 'By this time the excellent law of the founding emperors was lost.'[73] This silence may reflect the disuse of the prohibitions or, alternatively, their routine use. But in either case I would submit that their aims had largely been achieved by the late Northern Sung. The examinations had become a focal point of elite culture, schools had multiplied to accommodate the greater demand for education, and the increasing difficulty of the examinations helped to insure that preparing for them was a full-time occupation. Thus the groups in question no longer threatened the literati and the promise, at least, of social mobility through education and the examinations could be countenanced, for these endeavors only reinforced the literati's now dominant position.

Residency requirements

In contrast to the occupational prohibitions, the provisions dealing with residency appeared throughout the dynasty. The basic dilemma they confronted was simple: the government wanted people to take the examinations only in their home prefectures, but many would move and then try to take them in their new prefectures. Although this group probably comprised only a small proportion of all the candidates, they were too numerous to be ignored, especially during the Northern Sung when they congregated very visibly in K'ai-feng. The result was a great deal of vacillation by the government as strict regulations alternated with more lenient ones.

It had long been a practice for prominent families to be associated with specific places, usually counties. From the Six Dynasties to the T'ang, these place-names or choronyms (*chün-wang, pen-wang*) were used to identify the families such as the Lis of Chao-chün or the Changs of Ch'ing-ho. They denoted not where a person lived but his ancestral home, and the two frequently differed. According to David Johnson, however, by the tenth century 'the nature of choronyms had changed from the traditional clan identification to a more purely geographical one.'[74] With this went a change in terminology; the earlier terms, which had connotations of social superiority,[75] gave way to the more value-free 'native place' (*pen-kuan*).

Although this new choronym primarily denoted residence, the older notion of ancestral homes did not disappear entirely. When people moved and settled in a different county, their 'native place' remained the same and they were considered to be temporarily residing (*yü-chi*) in their new homes. Such people worried the examination officials. On the one hand, the officials generally suspected them of moving for selfish reasons (better educational opportunities, easier quotas, etc.) and therefore tried to bar them from the examinations. On the other hand, not only were the temporary residents too numerous (and sometimes too well connected) to be ignored, but it was also recognized that at some point they had to be considered permanent residents, or at least be allowed to take the examinations.

Just where that point lay was a source of frequent contention and contradictory edicts, so we cannot identify a single set of requirements. However, three factors were considered both relevant and important. First was household registration (*hu-chi*), which required the ownership of a house and/or land on which taxes were paid. Its importance, even for those who had not moved, is indicated by an edict from 1041 which provided that those who had not originally had a household but had now purchased taxable property and those who had taxable property but had sold it be allowed to take the examinations, so long as they were guaranteed by a capital-grade official.[76] We should note the assumption that a candidate would normally be a property-owner or from a property-owning family. Since buying property enabled one to register one's household, it was an essential step in establishing temporary residency, and as such concerned examination officials. Yet the government had no consistent policy regarding it. Sometimes aspiring candidates were prohibited from registering their households away from their native places;[77] at other times, the examinations were opened to those who had moved and registered in the past[78] or even to those who had no registration so long as they obtained special guarantees.[79]

Ancestral tombs were a second factor. Their main importance for the examinations lay in demonstrating that a given place was one's ancestral home, that one was a native. Such demonstrations, of course, could be fraudulent. One Southern Sung complaint describes students going to distant prefectures where competition was relatively light and claiming old military graves as the tombs of their ancestors.[80] In another case, bookstores were reported to be selling lists of those buried in lineage cemeteries, enabling the buyers to fabricate genealogies and falsely claim residency.[81] But on at least one occasion, in 1058, ancestral graves were used to help legitimize a change in residency: 'Among those who have had a household residence for seven years, those who own no house or fields and yet have ancestral graves are permitted [to take the examinations].'[82]

The third factor, as this last quotation suggests, was that of time or length of residency. As competition in the examinations increased, concerns were voiced about students opportunistically moving to where they were easier and taking them there. Some argued for a return to the non-mobile conditions of antiquity by requiring that candidates only take the examinations in the prefectures of their native places. In 1222 the Right Policy Monitor Hsi Kai-ch'ing contended that only by insisting that literati not move about could the empire 'nourish the skills of the many literati and enrich the customs.'[83]

But the prevailing opinion was more tolerant of movement, for Sung elite society was quite mobile. Not only were officials constantly moving about, often with family and relatives accompanying them, but as we shall shortly see, Northern Sung K'ai-feng acted as a magnet to literati throughout the empire. And of course the Southern Sung empire was full of refugee scholars from the north who could not possibly return to their native places. We shall see in Chapter 7 that there remained a feeling of considerable disdain towards what was regarded as the needless travel of 'wandering literati' (*yu-shih*), but a family's move from one place to another was more tolerantly regarded. As one official wrote in 1177:

> I would suggest that when the country makes laws it tries to [provide] convenience [for] the people. If there are households that wish to settle in [more] spacious neighborhoods, then they should be permitted to do what is convenient.[84]

Character qualifications

While occupation and residency were matters of concern in Sung Ch'i's reform proposal, his central objective was to keep out any with past histories of criminality or immorality (especially unfiliality). Such a concern with character is neither surprising (most institutions have character qualifications in one form or other) nor was it isolated. In 1000, an edict ordering an investigation into the backgrounds of all K'ai-feng *chü-jen* stated that, 'There are those whose literary skills are acceptable but whose uprightness of character is wanting, [who do things] like writing and sending anonymous and spurious attacks on their superiors.' Any such who were discovered were to be barred forever from the examinations.[85] In a similar proclamation in 1026 which expressed alarm at moral defects among officials, prefectural officials were ordered to examine their *chü-jen* and not send up any who displayed 'manifestations of perversity.'[86] Again in 1057 the court specified that county officials check on the past conduct of candidates and report on it to the officials.[87]

It is possible from the examination records to get some idea as to just what kinds of behavior were considered especially reprehensible. Unfilial or anti-family behavior drew predictably harsh condemnation. A memorial from 1029 describes two cases of literati illicitly attempting to gain K'ai-feng residency by making false kinship claims. One claimed his older brother (a K'ai-feng landowner) as father; the other, a Wang, claimed to be a member of the Chi family with which he was staying and took their ancestral names as his own taboo names. Stated the outraged memorialist: 'I have never seen anything so damaging to filial conduct as this example of changing personal taboos.'[88] Less predictable and thus more interesting was the outcome of the case of thirteen *chü-jen* from K'ai-feng who, after unsuccessfully attempting the departmental examination in 1014, were accused of being only temporary residents of the capital. The men fled the city, were captured and jailed. The Chief Councilor Wang Tan (957–1017) protested, however, saying that having them in jail was damaging to the country's customs. In a personal judgement, the emperor Chen-tsung (r. 998–1022) forgave the thirteen and then sent their accuser Liu Kai, a K'ai-feng native who had passed the examinations, into exile to a distant prefecture where he was to be kept under guard. The reason given, when this decision was itself protested, was that Liu's accusation had occurred only after the examination results were announced and thus had been selfish or un-public spirited (*fei kung-hsin*).[89] This reason, which invoked the same *kung* that we earlier encountered as 'fair', is instructive, for it suggests that disruptions of social harmony for selfish purposes were regarded as worse than fraudulent claims of residency in K'ai-feng.

Curiously, measures for investigating the past conduct of candidates ceased after 1057; at least I have found no later instances of them.[90] It may be that character requirements were difficult to enforce and therefore not stressed in later years, but in all likelihood they remained in effect, for obviously no emperor was going to welcome immoral candidates. Moreover, the most important method of assuring the respectability, at least, of candidates remained in effect, and that was the guarantee.

At least three different kinds of guarantees were used in the examinations at one time or another. One was the mutual guarantee group of *chü-jen*, in which each was responsible for the background and/or behavior of the others. Sung Ch'i's proposed groups of three actually represented a decrease from current practices, for earlier in the eleventh century groups of five were used.[91] In the Southern Sung there was a great latitude in numbers, which ranged from three to twenty. There was also a difference in emphasis, for whereas Sung Ch'i was concerned primarily with the backgrounds of *chü-jen*, twelfth-century officials were more concerned with cheating and rowdy behavior in the examinations.[92] Second were the guarantees required of those given special dispensations in the examinations, such as temporary residents of K'ai-feng who took the K'ai-feng prefectural examination or relatives of officials who took a special avoidance examination, who were typically required to get guarantees from two executory rank officials. But these cases, which did not concern character per se, will be dealt with later, so we will not consider them further here.

The third form of guarantee was the family guarantee certificate (*chia-pao-chuang*) provided by the family and endorsed by the prefectural school preceptor (an official) described in the 1149 provisions cited earlier. As Araki Toshikazu has shown, these commonly involved guarantees or recommendations by community notables as well.[93] Although we have no descriptions of these certificates, it seems that they consisted of biographical data: one's age, marital status, residence (including temporary residence when that were applicable), the names of one's father, grandfather, and great-grandfather and their official ranks, if any, a statement on whether one's father and mother were still living, and the number of brothers that one had.[94] In 1186 complaints about the counterfeiting of kinship and residency information led to the requirement that the branches of one's lineage be identified as well and that the certificate be guaranteed by one's eldest living ancestor (*tseng-tsu*, literally 'great-grandfather').[95] Thus this was designed more to guarantee the respectability of the candidate and his family than to provide assurances of his good character, although in many cases that distinction may have become blurred.

The social and political significance of these guarantees for candidacy is a matter of some interest. Robert Hymes has argued that they served as a mechanism for the political self-perpetuation of the local elite, since the guarantees had to come from the elite which could refuse them to those who were not elite.[96] He presents little evidence, however, to show that the guarantees were actually used in an exclusionary fashion.[97] During the Southern Sung, at least, the huge candidate numbers common to much of the southeast and anecdotal literature describing candidates coming from non-elite families of doctors and nouveaux riches merchants,[98] indicate that qualifying for the examinations was neither an exclusive privilege nor an insurmountable problem for non-elite literati. Although some connection to the elite was undoubtedly necessary in order to obtain a guarantee, elite patronage of promising students as well as plain money could serve as well as ties of kinship or marriage in securing guarantees. The elite indeed used the examinations for their own self-perpetuation, as we shall see, but they did this through privileged movement through the examinations rather than by controlling entrance to them.

The role of K'ai-feng

During the Northern Sung, there was one apparent exception to the early emperors' policy of fairness and impartiality in the examinations: the literati of K'ai-feng were treated differently. Much as it commanded the empire militarily, this sprawling metropolis which was at once the center of a thriving northern Chinese economy and a rapidly growing national economy, dominated the examinations and the bureaucracy.[99] In 998 when fifty-one *chin-shih* degrees were conferred, for example, K'ai-feng residents accounted for thirteen of the first fourteen places and a comparable proportion of the subsequent twenty-five.[100] Even more impressive are the statistics from a 1064 essay by Ssu-ma Kuang (1019–86) in which K'ai-feng accounts for a quarter to a third of all *chin-shih* in the examinations of 1059, 1061 and 1063.[101] And if we include *chü-jen* from the Directorate of Education (*Kuo-tzu-chien*) initial examination, then we find that the capital accounted for as many as one half of all *chin-shih* (see Table 9).

This record of success appears not to have been the result of outstanding accomplishments by K'ai-feng natives, but rather reflects the achievements of those who settled there. Edward Kracke, Jr., has observed that

> In the realms of thought, literature and scholarship the natives of K'ai-feng did not seem outstanding among Sung Chinese. But the Northern Sung capital seems to have drawn outstanding minds to itself rather more than its Southern Sung counterpart would do.[102]

To fully explain why this was the case is beyond the scope of the present study, for it was related to a general decentralization of power from Northern to Southern Sung observable in politics, society, the military and the economy.[103] Our concern, rather, is with the role played by the examinations, and it was substantial.

Northern Sung records make it clear that taking the initial examinations in K'ai-feng was regarded as highly desirable. Lü Pen-chüng (1048–1145) tells a story of Li Chün-hsing (Li Ch'ien, a 1064–7 *chin-shih*), an official from Ch'ien-chou in southern Chiang-nan-hsi who was making a trip to the

Table 9. *Percentages of chin-shih in 1059, 1061 and 1063 who had passed
the K'ai-feng and Directorate of Education examinations*

	1059		1061		1063	
	Number	%	Number	%	Number	%
Total *chin-shih* numbers						
numbers	165		183		193	
K'ai-feng pref.						
examination	44	26.7%	69	37.7%	66	34.2%
Directorate examination	22	13.3%	28	15.3%	30	15.5%
Capital examinations						
total	66	40.0%	97	43.0%	96	49.7%

Sources: Ssu-ma Kuang, *Ssu-ma kung wen-chi*; WHTK 32:306 for degree numbers.

capital. His brothers and sons wanted to go too and their reason was that:
'The examinations are imminent. We want to proceed first to the capital,
establish residence in K'ai-feng, and take them there.' Chün-hsing was scandal-
ized: 'You are men of Ch'ien-chou but would establish residence in K'ai-feng.
Can it be that you seek to serve as rulers yet would first cheat the ruler? I
would rather that you delayed [your success] for several years. You may
not go.'[104] Most literati, however, were not as high minded as Chün-hsing,
who is described elsewhere as 'regarding the avoidance of covetousness to be
the basis of learning,'[105] for again and again one finds complaints and measures dealing with the problem of provincial literati improperly claiming
K'ai-feng residency.[106] Indeed, the problem of defining the meaning of
residency which we discussed above arose because of the desire by literati
to settle in K'ai-feng and take the examinations there.

What made the K'ai-feng examinations so attractive? Su Sung (1019–
1101) explained it in terms of quota differentials:

> In the selection of candidates by the prefectures of the empire, local
> aspirants are many and quotas are small. [Students] frequently go to
> the capital to study and then request residency. There is no greater
> problem with prefectural selection than this. Although the court
> sends out stern warnings, it has not been able to stop them, for the
> aspirants in K'ai-feng are not many [yet] the quota has expanded
> until it has reached one hundred.[107]

But this explanation is not entirely convincing, for while K'ai-feng's quota
dwarfed all others, numbering 335 at its peak in 1075,[108] so too did its
candidate numbers. In fact, the quota ratios used for determining *chü-jen*
quotas were consistently more stringent for K'ai-feng and the Directorate
than they were for the empire at large.[109]

K'ai-feng and the Directorate of Education were, to be sure, the frequent recipients of imperial largess, and this may have had a significant impact on their examination fortunes. In 1008, 1011 and 1014, for example, special initial examinations were held in K'ai-feng and other prefectures through which the emperor Chen-tsung (r. 998–1022) had passed in the course of imperial trips.[110] Much more common were special exemptions from the initial examinations granted to past *chü-jen* from K'ai-feng, allowing them to proceed directly to the departmental examinations.[111] While other places such as Ho-pei (the scene of frequent fighting with the Liao), Ssu-ch'uan and Kuang-nan were also frequently favored in exemption announcements, none could compare with the capital.[112]

Largess aside, the explanation for the capital's success would appear to lie in less tangible factors such as the quality of the education to be had there, particularly the kind of examination preparation that one could only do in a social milieu which included many of the examiners themselves. This is the substance of Ssu-ma Kuang's oft-quoted explanation for K'ai-feng's residency problem:

> In this dynasty's system for employing men, unless one is a *chin-shih* one will not become an outstanding official; unless one is good at poetry, discussions and policy questions, one will not obtain a *chin-shih* degree; and unless one goes and studies in the capital, one will not become good in poetry, discussions and policy questions. For this reason, the scholars of the four quarters are all made to abandon their homes, illegally leave their parents, and grow old in the capital without ever returning again.[113]

Ssu-ma's own figures on the examinations of 1059, 1061 and 1063 lend qualified support to this thesis, for whereas only one in thirty or worse of *chü-jen* from the north, southwest and far south (he provides no figures for the rapidly developing southeast) received *chin-shih* degrees in those examinations, the ratio for K'ai-feng and the Directorate ranged from one in six to one in four.[114] The fact that *chü-jen* from the capital outshone most of their provincial peers goes far towards explaining the allure of K'ai-feng among Sung literati.

K'ai-feng was not equally accessible to all literati, however, for there is reason to believe that the Directorate and K'ai-feng examinations were predominantly patronized by the relatives of officials, especially during the early Northern Sung. Prior to 1042 the Directorate of Education served as a school for the instruction of the sons and grandsons not merely of any officials, but of 'court and capital rank officials of the seventh rank and above.'[115] In 975 when the school's student quota was set at seventy, that rule was breached slightly as *chü-jen* in the capital area were permitted to fill unoccupied places at the school,[116] although it is unlikely that this provided much opportunity for literati from commoner backgrounds. Almost seventy years later, reformers criticized the Directorate as a place where as many as a thousand would appear to enrol at examination time, only to disappear afterwards. Such was the popularity of the Directorate examination, moreover, that many falsely claimed official relatives of the seventh grade or above. To remedy this situation, in 1042 the government established the School of the Four Gates (*Ssu-men-hsüeh*) for those from commoner and low grade official families, with admission determined by an annual entrance examination (*pu-shih*).[117] This was replaced in 1044 by the Imperial University (*T'ai-hsüeh*), and it soon developed into the premier educational institution at the capital.[118] But the 'national youth' (*kuo-tzu*) category remained for children of higher officials, at times as students of the Directorate School usually called the *Kuo-tzu-hsüeh* and at other times as a group with privileged entry into the University.[119]

The K'ai-feng prefectural examination, by contrast, was used by three different groups of literati. First were those whose families were truly native to K'ai-feng, and they undoubtedly contained a fair share of those with commoner backgrounds. But since as we observed above, K'ai-feng natives did not play a prominent role in K'ai-feng's examination successes, those commoner literati could not have been a very significant group. Second were those whose families had come to K'ai-feng for reasons of state and then settled there, thus qualifying them for the K'ai-feng examination. Most notable among them was that group described by Robert Hartwell as the 'professional elite' which dominated the eleventh-century civil service.[120] One suspects that they dominated the K'ai-feng examination as well, but they did not monopolize it, for the third group consisted of literati drawn to K'ai-feng by the examinations. What is interesting about this group, which we have discussed extensively above, is that when they were permitted to stay and take the K'ai-feng examination, they were invariably required to provide a guarantee, and the guarantor usually had to be either an official at their native prefectures or a capital or court grade official. Officials, moreover, were limited to providing one or at most two guarantees per examination.[121] While there were no limitations concerning the status of the candidate, it seems likely that the guarantees would have gone primarily to family, affinal relations, and friends.

If the examinations in K'ai-feng were dominated by literati from official families, as we have argued, then it would appear that this was indeed an exception to the Sung imperial policy of striving for the 'utmost fairness' in the examinations. But it was a limited exception, for although it provided privileged access to the Directorate and, to some extent, the K'ai-feng examinations, we have seen that they were comparably competitive with prefectural examinations elsewhere.

Compared with earlier dynasties, moreover, the Northern Sung is remarkable for the high degree of provincial participation in the civil service. We saw in Chapter 1, for example, how in the T'ang examinations the great majority of graduates came from the schools in the capital. Against that background, the 40–50% accounted for by K'ai-feng and the Directorate in the mid-eleventh century looks modest. It is only when one looks forward to the Southern Sung and subsequent dynasties that one can see the Northern Sung as a pivotal period between the domination of the government by a capital-centered elite which was typical of the early dynasties and the predominance of local elites characteristic of the late dynasties. I would submit that the early Sung emperors' willingness to cast broadly through the examinations was a crucial factor in this change.

Finally, we should point out that as the Northern Sung progressed, privileged access to the Directorate and K'ai-feng examinations was curtailed at least partially. The creation of the Imperial University not only provided literati from humble backgrounds access to capital schools but also heralded a trend towards making a greatly expanded University the preeminent school in the land and the goal of students everywhere. And as the University became more important in the late eleventh century, the K'ai-feng examination became less so; from a peak of 335 in 1075, K'ai-feng's examination quota was reduced to 160 in 1079, so that the Directorate's quota could be increased from 160 to 500.[122] This was the work of the Northern Sung reformers who had their own vision of a fair and moral society, one in which schools rather than examinations played the central role. It is to them that we will now turn.

4

TO BE ROOTED IN SCHOOLS: EXAMINATIONS IN THE LATE NORTHERN SUNG

The Ch'ing-li reforms

In the summer of 1043, the third year of the Ch'ing-li reign period, the Sung empire was in a state of crisis. The long-time Chief Councilor, Lü I-chien, had that spring suffered a stroke, and while he continued to be consulted on affairs of state, he no longer handled the day-to-day affairs of government. More critically, to the northwest the Tangut Hsi-Hsia invasion was being stemmed but only after a major mobilization of military forces, in the northeast the Khitan Liao were threatening to break their peace of forty years, and in central China the rebellion of Wang Lun was posing the first significant internal challenge to Sung rule. According to the draft biography of Ou-yang Hsiu in the Veritable Records,

> While the war in the northwestern border was going on, many groups of bandits rose in the areas to the east and west of the capital. Both externally and internally, the empire felt disturbed. Emperor Jen-tsung, in replacing his leading councilors, wished to see due changes made to cope with various matters.[1]

The men whom Jen-tsung promoted to positions of leadership were an exceptional group. With the prominent exception of Han Ch'i (1008–75), a pragmatic and aristocratic northerner, they were southerners of modest, often local official, background. Their leader, Fan Chung-yen (989–1052), was an exceptional administrator whose bold and moralistic policy criticisms had made him the center of controversy and cost him demotions on more than one occasion in the past.[2] In fact, the distinguishing feature of Fan and such proteges as the brilliant and flamboyant Ou-yang Hsiu, the respected political thinker Li Kou (1009–59), the historian Sun Fu (997–1057), and the acerbic Shih Chieh (1005–45) was their common belief that Confucian principles could be used to reform institutions and improve society.

Thus it is not surprising that when Jen-tsung, on the advice of Ou-yang Hsiu, asked Fan and Han for suggestions on policy, they responded not with ad hoc proposals but by submitting a Ten-Point Memorial outlining a broad series of reforms.[3] Half of the points (6–10) dealt with aspects of local administration such as land reclamation, local militias, corvee labor, and law, but the rest dealt with the recruitment and advancement of officials. Most controversial and significant for our purposes were the second and third items. The second proposed limiting the privilege of protection, cutting back on the number of relatives high officials could name to official rank.[4] The third proposed changes in the examinations.

Complaining that too many literati concentrated either on writing elegant poetry for the *chin-shih* examination or in memorizing passages for the *chu-k'o* examination, which emphasized the elucidation of passages (*mo-i*), Fan and Han suggested changing the emphasis in both examinations. For the *chin-shih*, they proposed reversing the customary order of subjects and putting discussion and policy questions (*lün* and *ts'e*) first and poetry (*shih*) and poetic descriptions (*fu*) last, and in fact not allowing candidates who had not passed the former to take the latter, although candidates who had already sat for three or more examinations were to be exempted from the last requirement. Similarly, *chu-k'o* candidates were to be tested on the meaning of the classics in addition to their elucidations of passages. In support of this change in emphasis, they urged that experts in the classics be appointed as teachers in the local government schools. Finally, in order to insure the selection of the virtuous, they proposed that anonymity be abandoned in the prefectural examinations and that the candidate's moral character be considered in the selection of *chü-jen*.[5]

Five months after the Ten-Point Memorial, in the third month of 1044, another of the reformers, Sung Ch'i (998–1061), submitted a lengthy proposal for reform of the examinations which spelled out the earlier suggestions and then broke new ground.[6] The changes in both the *chin-shih* and *chu-k'o* curriculum were reiterated in a detailed section on the precise content of the examinations, as was the decision to weed out departmental examination candidates after the policy and discussion questions.[7] Along with the abandonment of anonymous grading procedures in the prefectural examinations went the provisions for checking into the backgrounds of all *chü-jen*.[8]

New, however, were the provisions concerning schools. All prefectures without prefectural schools were to establish them and those with over two hundred students were allowed to establish county schools as well. Preceptors (*chiao-shou*) were to be selected by the fiscal intendent and prefect from among the local civil officials to teach in the prefectural schools for terms of three years.[9] Most significantly, in order to take the prefectural examination, the literatus had to have attended the prefectural school for at least three hundred days (or one hundred days for past *chü-jen*), or failing that be guaranteed by an official or three *chü-jen* who had taken the departmental examination.[10] The reason for these measures was clearly stated:

> 'If teaching is not rooted in schools and scholars are not examined in villages, then it is impossible to investigate thoroughly the reality behind reputations. If there are teachers who restrain [students] by proclaiming [their] shortcomings and students concentrate on recitation from memory, then human talent is not fully being realized.' This is the common counsel of the discussants. We have explored the accumulated theories and selected those which are beneficial today. Nothing is better than making all scholars be natives and educating them in schools. But when their prefectures and counties examine their conduct, students will cultivate and prepare [themselves]. Thus we make rules for establishing schools, mutual guarantees and sending [up candidates by] recommendation.[11]

The following month saw one further educational proposal. Citing Han and T'ang precedents, it suggested that the Hsi-ch'ing Hall be converted into an Imperial University (*T'ai-hsüeh*), for the Directorate School was insufficient to the educational demands being made upon it.[12]

Although Jen-tsung expressed agreement with all of these reform memorials and accepted their proposals in full, the reforms proved to be shortlived. Placing their faith in principles and imperial support rather than persuasion, the reformers proved inept politicians, quickly alienating many highly-placed officials. They, by contrast, were adept at arousing Jen-tsung's suspicions as to the reformers' loyalties and intentions. In the summer of 1044, Fan Chung-yen, Ou-yang Hsiu and Fu Pi (1004–83), another leading reformer, were all given assignments outside of the capital, and the following year the reform proposals were repealed.[13] Indeed, the only thing to survive was the University, and even it was taken out of its quarters at the Hsi-ch'ing Hall and placed under the supervision of the Directorate of Education.[14]

Despite this brevity, the Ch'ing-li Reforms as they came to be called marked a major turning point in the history of the examinations. The idea that Confucian principles could and should be invoked to reform society proved attractive to young idealistic literati, who saw in Fan a hero worthy of emulation. As a result, two major and sustained efforts at reform arose in the late Northern Sung, one in the 1070s under the emperor Shen-tsung (r. 1068–86) and the Chief Councilor Wang An-shih (1021–86), the other after 1100 under the emperor Hui-tsung (r. 1101–26) and his Chief Councilor Ts'ai Ching (1046–1126). So too, we must add, arose vigorous reactions to the reform movements thus, making the era one of bitter and increasingly

severe factional struggles. But what is interesting, for our purposes, is the
fact the later reformers agreed with their Ch'ing-li predecessors that the
examinations were the key to producing better officials and thus a more
properly governed empire. And how was this to be accomplished? Through
controlling the curriculum and, even more important, by linking selection to
schools so that the government could nurture as well as choose the talented
of the world.

Curriculum changes

Following the aborted Ch'ing-li reforms the examinations continued
unchanged, but the idea of change had not been stilled. One source of continuing reformist influence came from Hu Yüan (993–1059), a close friend
of Fan Chung-yen's, who after years of teaching in prefectural schools around
Lake T'ai in Liang-che-hsi had been brought by Fan Chung-yen to the capital
to head the newly created university. Hu survived the general demotion of
reformers in 1045 and was a major influence upon young scholars studying
at the University, truncated and weak though it was.[15] Indeed, his pedagogy
is frequently cited as the epitome of reformist education, representing a
marriage between principle and practical application:

> His teaching method was detailed and completely prepared. He estab-
> lished two classes, one on the meaning of the classics and one on the
> management of affairs. In the classics class, he selected those with
> purified moral natures who had the ability and style to handle great
> affairs, and had them elucidate the Six Classics. In the class on affairs,
> each person would manage one topic and assist in another, such as
> governing the people in order to bring peace to their lives, discussing
> the military in order to guard against bandits, damning up water in
> order to improve fields, and calculating the calendar in order to under-
> stand numbers.[16]

Many of those who had participated in the reform such as Ou-yang Hsiu,
Han Ch'i, Sung Ch'i and Fu Pi (but not Fan Chung-yen) eventually returned
to positions of power, although they generally did so with a notable lack of
reforming zeal. Ou-yang was a partial exception for although his policies as a
Chief Councilor in the 1060s were generally conservative, in 1057 he gained
renown and notoriety for his reforming zeal when he served as chief examiner
in the departmental examination. With little forewarning and without permission from the throne, he decided to change the criteria for grading,
putting special emphasis upon the discussion and policy questions and failing
those who engaged in the ornate and eccentric writing style then in vogue
among many literati. Among those who passed were Tseng Kung (1019–83)

and the brothers Su Shih (1036–1101) and Su Ch'e (1039–1112), thus making the examination one of the most famous in Chinese history. The failed candidates were enraged, however. A group of them accosted Ou-yang in the street, bitterly cursing him, and someone wrote up a false obituary notice of him, reviving some scandalous allegations from his past.[17]

Ou-yang's action is credited with resulting in a 'change' in the writing of examinations. Later in the same year, 1057, several more formal though related changes occurred. Additional questions were added to the examinations: policy questions on current affairs for *chin-shih* candidates and discussions on the general meanings of the classics for *chu-k'o* candidates. In addition, a new degree was introduced on 'understanding the classics' (*ming-ching*), after a T'ang degree of the same name.[18] It differed from the other *chu-k'o* degrees with which it was classed in two significant ways. First, while it used elucidations like the others, it gave equal weight to questions on the broad meanings (*ta-i*) of the classics. Second, it divided the classics into major, medium and minor works and allowed the candidate to choose among several combinations of these.[19] Although this new degree hardly constituted a major change, its format was to serve as a model in the future.

In 1067, with the ascension of a new emperor, Shen-tsung (r. 1067–86), and his selection of Wang An-shih to serve as Second Privy Councilor and effectively take over control of the government, a new era of reform began. Wang had received his *chin-shih* in 1042 and had, by his own choice, served almost exclusively in provincial posts, repeatedly turning down invitations to accept offices in K'ai-feng and developing an enviable reputation as a leading proponent of reform in the process. Many of his New Policies, as his substantial and far-reaching reform program was called, dealt with the economy, defense, and local administration, but like the Ch'ing-li reforms, they also placed great weight upon schools and examinations.[20]

At the beginning of 1071, an edict was issued at the urging of Wang An-shih which profoundly altered the form and content of the examinations. Like Fan Chung-yen, Wang believed that the classics and their application to problems of government should be of primary importance in the examinations, but his solutions were more radical. First, the *chu-k'o* degrees were abolished, the *ming-ching* immediately with its candidates entering the ranks of *chin-shih* candidates, and the other degrees following the examination of 1073. Second, poetry (*shih* and *fu*) was eliminated from the *chin-shih* examination. In its place, each candidate was to specialize in one of the five classics (of Poetry, History, Changes, Rites and the Rites of Chou) and all were to master the *Analects* and the works of Mencius.[21]

The scope of this edict was impressive and it affected everyone involved in the examinations. Its effects were uneven, however, for its two provisions met different fates. Even at the outset, they were enacted in different ways. Whereas poetry was simply eliminated from the examinations, special measures were taken to ease the transition for *chu-k'o* candidates. Not only were they given a final chance to take the *chu-k'o* examinations, but they were also considered separately as a special group when they took the *chin-shih* examination. In addition, later in 1071 a new specialized degree, the *hsin-k'o ming-fa* ('new degree in law'), was created for past *chu-k'o* candidates.[22] Its significance was indicated in a later report that 39 such degrees had been given in 1076 and 146 in 1079.[23]

An important regional consideration was involved in this special treatment of *chu-k'o* candidates. By the reign of Shen-tsung, southerners had come to dominate the *chin-shih* examination (see Figure 7) and as a consequence northerners had concentrated on the *chu-k'o* examination. Therefore the elimination of the *chu-k'o* degrees could have been viewed as a threat to the already precarious position of northern officials. If so, then the special provisions mentioned above and also the elimination of poetry may have been, at least in part, compensatory measures, for the southerners' predilection for literature and poetry was proverbial.[24] That such regional balancing in fact took place is suggested by the fact that, included with the past *chu-k'o* candidates taking the *chin-shih* examination who were to be given special consideration were all of the *chin-shih* candidates from the northern circuits of Ching-tung, Shan-hsi, Ho-pei, Ho-tung and Ching-hsi, in short, the entire north.[25]

If the 1071 reforms were aimed at a regional balance, the death of Shen-tsung in 1085 and the ensuing fall of the reform faction quickly upset it. In 1086, poetry was restored to the *chin-shih* examination while the degree numbers for the *hsin-k'o ming-fa* were reduced.[26] In 1089, this was changed, to the advantage of the northerners, by the division of the *chin-shih* into two sub-degrees, one in poetry (*shih-fu chin-shih*) and the other in classics (*ching-i chin-shih*).[27] The latter borrowed from the earlier *ming-ching* degree the notion of major and medium classics and required candidates to prepare two classics instead of the one required by the 1071 edict.

When the reform faction returned to power in 1094, poetry was once again eliminated and it remained so for over thirty years, throughout the period of the Three Hall System.[28] In 1127, citing the need to attract 'truly loyal and unusually talented scholars,' it was reintroduced in accordance with the 1089 provisions.[29] From then until the end of the Sung it not only remained in the examinations but also consistently attracted the most candidates, despite repeated efforts by the government to encourage the classics degree.[30]

What accounted for this remarkable tenacity of poetry as an examination

topic? Few scholars were willing to come to its defense. In 1071 even Wang's
arch-antagonist, Ssu-ma Kuang (1019—86), favored its elimination and its
only noteworthy defender was Su Shih, who with Ou-yang Hsiu, had
earlier advocated emphasizing discussion and policy questions. Su, who as
George Hatch has suggested may have been fearful of the politicization of the
examinations,[31] made an interesting argument for the retention of poetry.
Conceding its irrelevancy, he challenged the relevancy of discussion and
policy questions, since in the final analysis the examinations were nothing
more than a literary exercise.[32] Su's argument, though unheeded at the time,
was prescient, for much to the dismay of later generations of Confucian
critics, the examinations became largely literary exercises in which even
policy questions were graded more on their form than content. Moreover,
in a society where literary skills were the mark of a gentleman, poetry was
extremely popular. Given a choice, a great majority of literati preferred
poetry to the classics as a subject for concentrated study. In 1093, when the
poetry and classics *chin-shih* degrees were supposed to be of equal importance, out of 2,175 University students, 2,093 were studying poetry and
only 83 the classics.[33] Thus practical considerations overrode the objections
of the moralists to insure the survival of poetry in the examinations.

　　The *chu-k'o* degrees lacked any such tenacity. In 1102 the New Degree
in Law was abolished and all of its quota places, which had originally been
chu-k'o quota places, were distributed as *chin-shih* quotas throughout the
empire.[34] This marked the virtual end of degrees for specialized subjects.
Why was this so? Both poetry and the specialized degrees had been attacked
by the reformers, but the crucial difference between them lay in the narrowness of the latter. Ssu-ma Kuang in 1086 remarked of the New Degree in
Law:

> As for laws and regulations, [knowledge of them] all is necessary for
> those who would be officials. [But] if you can get those who are
> scholars to truly understand the meaning of the Way, they will be in
> profound agreement with the laws. Why must we have a single degree
> in law, the preparation for which will be narrow and superficial? This
> is not that which will long cultivate talent and enrich customs.[35]

The generalist ideal of education, always popular, was becoming ever more
dominant, and this worked to the benefit of the *chin-shih* degree, which
had the reputation of attracting the most talented, whereas the *chu-k'o*
degrees were felt merely to select those with voluminous knowledge.

> Burning incense, receive the *chin-shih*; with angry glances await the
> *ming-ching*. When the talented have prepared for the *chin-shih*, at
> examination time they ready the incense altar for rites of worship and

obeisance. When the talented have prepared for the *ming-ching*, at examination time they steel their resolve for the troublesome examinations and fear other commentaries [than those that they have studied].[36]

Add to this the reputation of the *chin-shih* examination as the training ground for future ministers,[37] and it is little wonder that the *chu-k'o* degrees did not survive.

Before leaving this subject, we should acknowledge the human costs of changes in the examination curriculum. Yüeh K'o (1183–1240) tells of an examination held in Ch'eng-tu fu (Szechuan) in the fall of 1180, during which someone pointed out that the written form of one of the characters in the assigned theme for the poetic essay (*fu*) differed from that given in the official rhyme book. When the instructions given by a functionary at the time as to which form to use were unwittingly contradicted by an official the next day, a riot ensued. Angry candidates beat up an examiner and tore down a gate saying: 'The examination officials have carelessly interfered with our three years of fortune and misfortune.'[38] This scene, like that of the candidates cursing Ou-yang Hsiu in 1057, suggests the passions that could be aroused when unfairness in the questions or grading was perceived.

Less dramatic but more poignant are the stories of individuals who, after years of preparation for one kind of examination, could not adjust to new curriculum requirements. Wang T'ing-kuei (1080–1172) of Chi-chou tells how several of his contemporaries reacted to the reintroduction of poetry in 1127. Liu T'ing-chih (1100–60) and his brother Yü-hsi shifted their studies and concentrated on the writing of *fu*, and both received *chin-shih* degrees.[39] Wang Hung-chih (1081–1106), by contrast, decided that his chances were ruined because his style was simple, so he quit the examinations.[40] Most revealing, however, is the case of Liu Tsao (1096–1168), who had been an outstanding student of the classics. When he attempted the examinations with poetry, he 'fell discontented from the examination hall and abruptly decided to quit. He knew that his efforts and his fate were out of harmony and he did not again try for selection.'[41]

Schools and the reformers

When the Ch'ing-li reformers proposed that schools be established in all prefectures (and in some counties as well), they were following a venerable tradition in Chinese history but one which had been curiously ignored during the Sung. From the golden age of the Three Dynasties on down through the great imperial dynasties, the idea of establishing schools had been an integral part of the patrimonial ideology of the Chinese state.[42] Whatever the institutional reality may have been behind these purported school systems, the claim of the ruler to act as moral exemplar and teacher was fundamental to the notion of rule by virtue. As Mencius argued in support of the schools of antiquity, 'The object of them all [the different kinds of schools] is to illustrate the human relations. When those are thus illustrated by the superiors, kindly feeling will prevail among the inferior people below.'[43]

It is tempting to speculate that relative non-involvement of the early Sung government with education represented a retreat from patrimonialism, similar to the transition some two centuries earlier from the equal field system to the two tax system, whereby the state stopped trying to control landownership. Certainly the central government's educational activities, which consisted of running the Directorate of Education school for a handful of officials' children, providing sets of the classics to schools and academies (*shu-yüan*) which had been produced through the revolutionary method of woodblock printing,[44] and controlling the examination curriculum, suggest a willingness to rely upon indirect means of educational and cultural leadership that departed from past practices.

Thus it fell to local officials and literati to establish and run schools. In the late tenth and early eleventh centuries, when the great attraction of the examinations was increasingly felt, students could be found studying in local government schools, academies, Confucian temples (*K'ung-tzu miao, Wen-hsüan wang miao*), and Buddhist schools. By 1022, when the central government increased its involvement in local education by endowing the prefectural school of Yen-chou (in Ching-tung-hsi) with ten *ch'ing* of support land (about 151 acres) and appointing a teacher for it,[45] the spread of schools was already well under way. Table 10, which is based upon references to Sung schools in a variety of sources including more than one hundred local histories, indicates that while the rate of establishing schools peaked under Jen-tsung (1022–63), the increase began under his predecessor Chen-tsung (998–1021) if not before.

What then was the significance of Fan Chung-yen's reforms? Lü Ssu-mien, who is generally skeptical about the existence of government schools on any large scale during most of Chinese history, feels that Fan's residency requirement created an orientation toward office holding which gave government schools a needed *raison d'être*.[46] This, I believe, is an exaggeration given the short duration of the reforms. Moreover, whether his educational program had much of an impact on the spread of local schools is debatable, for the high level of school foundings during Jen-tsung's reign was as much the result of activities before the reforms as after.[47]

Nevertheless, Fan's educational program was important, for it created precedents and initiated an approach to education which was to come to

Table 10. *Sung government schools classified by earliest references per decade*

Period	Prefectural schools		County schools		Total schools	
	References	# per decade	References	# per decade	References	# per decade
Pre-Sung	45		52		97	
960–997	6	1.6	10	2.6	16	4.2
998–1021	10	4.2	22	9.2	32	13.4
1022–1063	80	19.0	89	21.2	169	40.2
1064–1085	32	15.0	36	16.4	68	31.4
1086–1100	5	3.3	32	21.3	37	24.6
1101–1126	17	6.5	51	19.6	68	26.1
N. Sung undated	3		37		40	
N. Sung Total	153	9.2*	277	16.6*	430	25.8*
1127–1162	13	3.6	49	13.6	62	17.2
1163–1189	7	2.6	22	8.1	29	10.7
1190–1224	5	1.4	29	8.3	34	9.7
1225–1264	4	1.0	25	6.2	29	7.2
1265–1279	2	1.3	5	3.3	7	4.6
S. Sung Total	31	2.0	130	8.5	161	10.5
Sung undated	5		57		62	
Sung Total	189	5.9*	464	14.5*	653	20.4*
All schools	234		516		750	

Sources: For a precise listing of sources, see Chaffee, 'Education and Examinations in Sung Society,' Appendix 2.
*These figures include undated schools.

fruition under Ts'ai Ching and Hui-tsung. And here Lü Ssu-mien is quite
correct in emphasizing the link between schools and examinations, for it
constituted the crux of reformist education. The reformers felt that character evaluation should form a part of the selection process and they considered the moral and practical training of future officials to be central
functions for schools. In a memorial from late in 1043, unnamed ministers
memorialized:

> From antiquity the method of selection of scholars has been rooted in
> schools. Since the T'ai-p'ing era (976–1083) schools have prospered.
> [But] we have not yet appointed officials [for them] or regulated
> instruction so as to add weight to their offices. Today we have literati
> vie for the length of a day in the examinations. How can this compare
> with simply nurturing scholars throughout the world?[48]

The organic metaphor of 'rootedness' is significant, for it implies that
the educational inactivity of the early Sung government had resulted in
cultural disunity, a lack of ethical roots among the literati of the empire.
The logical conclusion to such an idea was to delegate the selection function
to the schools, where both character and ability could be evaluated over
long periods of time. In fact this is precisely what occurred and Fan's proposals can be viewed as a first step towards such an end.

During the years of Shen-tsung's reign (1068–85), when first Wang An-
shih and then his followers were in power, the central government was
quite active in education (it was the first period of sustained activity in local
education for the Sung government). The University was greatly expanded
and divided into three halls (*san she*) or grades, thereby introducing the
important notion of advancing by grade through school.[49] Wang felt that
the local schools were too small and understaffed. In 1071, the fiscal intendents (*chüan-yün-shih*) in all circuits were ordered to give each school
ten *ch'ing* of fields.[50] At the same time, schools were told to appoint teaching
officials (*chiao-kuan*) or preceptors (*chiao-shou*) with special emphasis to
be placed upon the appointment of teachers in the northern circuits of
Ching-tung, Shan-hsi, Ho-tung, Ho-pei and Ching-hsi.[51] In 1074 and 1078
there were additional measures providing for the appointment of teachers
and a special examination for teachers was begun in 1076.[52]

In spite of these decrees and Wang's belief that, ideally, officials should
be selected at schools,[53] the educational developments resulting from his
New Policies were not great, at least outside the capital. There is little evidence in local histories to suggest that schools were given additional land at
this time. Also, despite the decrees ordering the appointment of preceptors
in all prefectural schools, there were only 53 of them in 1078 (out of approximately 320 prefectures).[54]

If Wang made any contributions to local education, it was through the appointment of preceptors. This was the first occasion on which the Sung government appointed regular, executory class officials as teachers at local schools, and that in itself was an important step in making the local schools more than just occasionally functioning institutions. Also, despite the relatively small number of prefectures given teachers, they were concentrated heavily in the north, as Terada Gō has observed.[55] Thirty-three were located in northern China and just four in Liang-che and Fu-chien. Whatever the political motivations or consequences of this, it is likely that the educational effects were maximized, since the majority of preceptors were appointed to prefectures outside of the southeast, which had a strong tradition of support for local schools.

The Three Hall System

Sixteen years after the death of Shen-tsung, following a period which saw the central government relatively inactive in local education,[56] a series of far-reaching reforms was implemented. A new emperor, Hui-tsung (r. 1100–26), after a brief period of conciliation towards reformers and anti-reformers alike, had chosen as his Chief Councilor Ts'ai Ching, the most prominent of a third generation of 'reformers', who had received his *chin-shih* degree in 1070 under Shen-tsung. At the suggestion of Ts'ai, who declared that 'making schools flourish is the first order of business today,'[57] the examination system was replaced by a unified, hierarchical school system which was given the dual function of educating students and selecting the outstanding among them for the *chin-shih* degree. Although the triennial departmental examination continued to be held and *chin-shih* degrees given,[58] candidacy was restricted to University students and they, with the exception of the privileged Directorate School students, had been promoted from prefectural schools.

The school hierarchy actually had four levels: primary schools, which were supposed to be established in every county; county schools; prefectural schools; and the University. Each school was divided into three grades or halls (thus the Three Hall System — *San-she-fa* — by which the system was known), following the model used by the University since the time of Wang, and at the University the outer hall was given a separate campus to the south of the city and prosaically named Pi-yung, from a passage in the Classic of Poetry. Promotion from grade to grade and school to school depended upon periodic examinations and required guarantees from the preceptor and local officials.[59] Quotas determined both the number of students allowed in a school and the number who could enter officialdom either by advancing to and through the upper hall or by taking a triennial examination which corresponded to the departmental examination of the examination system.[60] To supervise this system, education intendents (*t'i-chu hsüeh-shih*) were appointed to each circuit.[61]

The Three Hall System was a bold experiment, almost certainly eclipsing in scope the combined schools of the eleventh century. It was, as Table 10 indicates, the last period of wide-scale creation of government schools, resulting in the first true empire-wide system of schools in Sung and possibly Chinese history. The financial resources which the government devoted to education were unprecedented, for local governments were instructed to draw upon land and income from ever-normal granaries (*ch'ang-p'ing-ts'ang*) and heirless land (*hu-chüeh-t'ien*) in order to reach requisite support levels.[62] Overall, the system received income from over 100,000 *ch'ing* of land (over 1.5 million acres) and had roughly 200,000 students, all supplied with room and board by the state.[63] This was in an empire which then numbered around a hundred million people, so the students comprised approximately 0.2% of the total population or 0.4% of the male population.[64]

In 1104, an intriguing and revealing addition was made to the Three Hall System. Provisions were promulgated for the rapid education and promotion of students of outstanding virtue, specifically for those with renown in one of 'eight [kinds of virtuous] conduct' (*pa-hsing*).[65] Such individuals were to be recommended and sent from villages to counties to prefectures, where they were to attend school for a year. They were then to be sent to the University where they were to be admitted without examination to the upper hall, investigated for unorthodox views, and then be given degrees and official rank. Provision was also made for their opposites, those with histories of 'eight punishments' (also *pa-hsing*, but with a different *hsing*), who were to be expelled from the schools.[66]

The edict establishing the 'eight conduct' method of selection was engraved on stelae which were distributed throughout the land,[67] and it remained in use through most of the Three Hall period.[68] In its quest for superior men and sages, it was the most extreme attempt by the reformers to recruit on the basis of virtue rather than ability or talent. Reminiscent of the Nine Rank Arbiter system (*chiu-p'in chung-cheng*) established by Wei Wen-ti (r. 220–7) which attempted to rank people according to their virtue, its subjective criteria and the preferential treatment of its candidates rendered it vulnerable to abuses, although not on the scale of the earlier system, which was swiftly transformed into an hereditary status system.[69]

The references to investigations of orthodoxy and the 'eight punishments' suggest, moreover, that Ts'ai and his followers were as interested in intellectual control as in virtue, and indeed, there is much in their educational program to suggest that this was the case. For while the early reformers like Fan tried to demonstrate the relevancy of their Confucian principles to

the pressing problems of the day, the later reformers insisted that particular
sets of principles and particular applications of them be taught.[70] In 1068,
Wang An-shih had argued that the times demanded orthodoxy:

> At the present talented men are scarce; moreover scholarly skills are
> dissimilar. Each man has an interpretation [of the classics] and for
> ten men there are ten interpretations. When the court wants something
> done, the various arguments are confusing and no one is willing to obey
> instructions. This, in general, is why the court is unable to achieve a
> single morality. To achieve it, we must therefore reform our schools,
> and if we wish to reform our schools, we must change the examina-
> tion regulations.[71]

In the intervening years, the tides of factionalism which Wang had done
much to swell had risen precipitously, and Ts'ai was intent on propagating
the reformers' political vision while chastising his enemies. Most infamous
was his literary inquisition in which 'unorthodox' books and the writings
of some 309 men were proscribed, while in the realm of education, the
teaching of history was banned,[72] private schools were forbidden,[73] and
special 'isolation rooms' (*tzu-sung-chai*) established where students displaying
unorthodox ideas were sent for punishment.[74] How these measures were implemented is open to question. Most of the writings survived, we know of
private schools that were founded while they were in effect, and from Hung
Mai we have a rather benign story involving an 'isolation room' from this
period.[75] But their intent was clear and at least one surviving memorial
testifies to their harmful effects on written examinations:

> Today in all prefectures and counties, there are no entrance examina-
> tions which test the student's ability to write. The first thing the ex-
> aminers look for is whether or not a candidate's essays refer to subjects
> currently tabooed. If the language of a candidate's essays touches on
> such tabooed subjects, then no matter how well he has written, they
> dare not pass him. It is tabooed to say: 'in order to rest the people
> rest the military; to make wealth abundant, regulate expenses; elimi-
> nate the service requirements that are not urgent; incorruptably enter
> officialdom.' All language like this [is tabooed] ;[76]

Even apart from the issue of intellectual control, the Three Hall System
was beset by problems. There were complaints of indifferent and incompe-
tent teaching and of widespread cheating. Declared one critic in a Mencian
vein that was to become common in Southern Sung complaints about examination preparation:

The administrators and professors now in residence at the University all profit by considering ways to nurture their wealth and seeking advancement outside [the University]. The students all profit in the yearly and monthly [tests] and in examination selection. Superiors and inferiors congregate together because of profit. Can they possibly develop and nourish human talent?[77]

The greatest problem, however, was financial. The system taxed the resources of local governments and, in addition, there were numerous charges of corruption. Describing the Chien-chou (Fu-chien) prefectural school, a Southern Sung writer commented, 'The system of selection through halls was exalted and harmonious, but great were the complaints and wasteful the extravagance.'[78] Even more to the point was this memorial from 1112:

> Those who supervise the prefectures and counties do not know that the fundamental aim of the court is specifically the education of great talent. They engage in [obtaining] plentiful food and drink and their abuses extend to converting [grain] from the real price to the market price. They engage in borrowing from students and their abuses extend to breaking laws and damaging culture. Many [cases] reach the courtroom, some [involving] violence against officials and some, encroachments on the people, yet none dare to question [them]. They engage in [buying] superfluous decorations and so have useless expenditures of funds and provisions. They engage in applying for bequests and so there is the evil of quarreling over profits with the people.[79]

Thus when the Three Hall System was abolished in 1121, the move met with little opposition and there were no serious attempts to revive it in the Southern Sung.

The legacy of reform

Had Ts'ai Ching succeeded in gaining acceptance for the Three Hall System, the subsequent history not only of Chinese education but also of Chinese society would have been profoundly different. It would have produced a literati population with much closer ties to the government, with a greater susceptibility to government control, and with perhaps less authority and legitimacy in society at large. It would also have required a government that was far more active, not only in education but also in the activities of the local elites, than was the case in the Southern Sung and subsequent dynasties.

But one might also argue that the Hui-tsung program was unfeasible in the long run. Thomas H. C. Lee has cogently argued that it was premised upon an unresolvable contradiction.[80] On the one hand, the schools were to train and select a small corps of scholar-officials to govern the empire, an inherently elitist goal. To quote Wang An-shih,

> The talent of a person is completed through concentration and destroyed through dispersion, so the former kings' placement of the people's talent was as follows: they placed laborers in government yamens, farmers in the fields, merchants in the market place and scholars in the schools. They had each mind his own occupation and not look on strange things, for it was feared that strange things might harm the occupations.[81]

On the other hand, the reformers looked to the utopian descriptions of the schools of antiquity in such works as the *Rites of the Chou* and appear to have been genuinely interested in pursuing a goal of universal education. Such a goal, of course, was not only contradictory to their goal of training officials but also unfeasible administratively and fiscally for the Sung state as it was constituted.

For these and other reasons (especially the loss of the north, which was blamed upon the reformers), the reform program failed, and henceforth neither was selection rooted in schools nor did the government claim to monopolize education. Yet the legacy of the reformers was profound, for both in what they did and in what was done in reaction to them, they managed to have a lasting impact on later institutions and society.

The institutional impact is perhaps the most evident. In the examinations, Wang An-shih's abolition of the *chu-k'o* degrees made the *chin-shih* degree the goal towards which all literati labored and so it remained until the examinations ended in 1905. We can only speculate as to the effects of this, for while it eliminated an element of educational diversity that had hitherto been present (the *chu-k'o* degrees may have been of lesser prestige but they provided a respectable alternative to those who felt most comfortable with specialized topics or memorization), it may be that this educational uniformity was an essential ingredient of the literati culture that was to dominate Chinese society for the next seven hundred years.

Regarding schools, the reform legacy was one of institutional development. In the early eleventh century, when formal prefectural schools were first appearing, often evolving from Confucian temple-schools,[82] their provisions and regulations were quite fluid. Attendance at them varied greatly, for students would travel considerable distances to study under famous teachers.[83] There were, moreover, no institutional ties between government schools; each was supported and managed by its local government and there was no administrative uniformity.

By the end of the Northern Sung this had all changed. Not only were all government schools connected in a hierarchical empire-wide system, but there was a high degree of organizational uniformity as well. Prefectural school preceptorships became respected posts in local administration which, as far as we can tell, were routinely filled; educational support fields (*hsüeh-t'ien*) and student support provisions became the rule rather than the exception; and to cope with the rising demand for schooling, school entrance examinations (*pu-shih*) became common.[84] In fact, given the formal similarities in organization and physical layout (though not in pedagogy) between the Southern Sung government schools and those of the Ming and Ch'ing, the late Northern Sung can be seen as the key period in the development of the government school as an institution.

There were negative legacies as well. We noted earlier how the reintroduction in the 1120s of poetry, which the reformers had tried to eliminate from the examinations, firmly established it as an integral part of the examination curriculum. Of even greater importance was the failure of the attempt to select students in schools, where character as well as talent could be evaluated, and the return to the principle of anonymity in the examinations. This may well have been an inevitable development, for as literati increased and competition became more intense, anonymous procedures became essential to preserving at least the illusion of fairness. In 1048, an anti-reform official argued for reinstating covered names and copied examinations by stressing the quality of the graduates:

> I have observed the outer prefectures sending up *chü-jen*. Before there were covered names and copied examinations, many with empty reputations were selected and examination officials did not refrain from taking requests on behalf [of candidates]. Also, only old men who had previously been selected were chosen. After covered names and copied examinations [were instituted], the examination officials could not see the names and so had to really judge literary merit, which was more suitable, approaching fairness.[85]

One hundred and fifty years later Hsü Chi-chih (1163 *chin-shih*) a minister of the Board of Rites, also argued for anonymous procedures on the grounds of fairness, but fairness in this case was in the eyes of those who failed:

> Although grading with covered names is still inadequate for obtaining all of the world's eminent talents, the reason why, among them [i.e., the literati], teachers, old scholars, aged and white-haired men are kept from being officials and yet do not complain, is that they submit to the fairness of the examinations.[86]

Given the prominence of schools in the selection of officials in the classics, the idea of linking schools and examinations did not die. Several Southern Sung critics of the examinations, most notably Chu Hsi in his 'Private Opinion on Schools and Examinations,' argued for a return to some sort of linkage.[87] And in the Ming and Ch'ing the two systems were integrated. *Sheng-yüan*, the lowest degree holders, were government school students, and a studentship was in fact the prerequisite for taking the provincial examination.[88] But the reality was far different from what the reformers had envisioned. Except for the early Ming, when attempts were made to employ famous scholars as teachers in the government schools, their primary function was to provide prestige and support to the *sheng-yüan*.[89] Moreover, the examinations continued to be judged solely on the basis of written work. So despite the link, teaching was not rooted in the government schools; education was divorced from the examinations.

There was, finally, a social legacy of reform education, and it was substantial. Much as T'ai-tsung's expansion of the examination system had increased elite participation in the examinations, the reform program focused their attention upon schools and examinations and then, for a time, upon schools alone. As we noted above this resulted in educational abuses, not the least of which was the politicization of the schools as the ideological struggles between reformers and anti-reformers were fought out in curriculum and pedagogy, especially under the Three Hall System.

But there were positive aspects to the Three Hall System as well. With examinations handled by the schools and support given to their students, the prestige, status and benefits that came with attending them were unprecedented. This, I suspect, is the reason why the great majority of biographical accounts that I have read which mention attending government schools describe the Hui-tsung period, for it was then that attendance was considered a noteworthy accomplishment. One also finds in contemporary comments a sense of awe over the resources that were being devoted to education. Chang K'o-ching, an official in Ho-pei, wrote in 1104

> I have heard that the scholars of antiquity took office and only afterwards received a salary. Now these scholars dwelling below [i.e., non-officials] have yet to take office and still they receive support for food and drink, which is regarded as a salary to be given to them . . . This never was the case in the past.[90]

A decade later Hui-tsung declared in an edict raising school support quotas throughout the empire:

> For twelve years, the schools have [followed] the way of improving and nourishing people, establishing teachers and Confucian scholars,

building schools, preparing tasty provisions, and teaching the literati of
the world. Day by day enlightened literati have increased and become a
multitude, approximating antiquity. Yet the quotas for supporting
literati still lag behind past figures . . . and the literati who travel to
schools but are not taught remain numerous. If it is thus, then the
country is neglecting talent.[91]

Though Hui-tsung was hardly a disinterested observer, his statement is percep-
tive and revealing, for the Three Hall System with its two hundred thousand
students had created a multitude of literati such as had never been seen
before, or at least never since the shadowy reaches of antiquity. In addition,
it had served to focus the attention of local elites more than ever before upon
government schools and the training for testing and employment that they
offered, a fact that became evident during the rapid rebuilding of ruined
schools during the early Southern Sung. To a large extent, then, the reform
program in general and the Three Hall System specifically were responsible
both for the dramatic growth of the literati described in Chapter 2 and for
the concomitant failure of fairness in the examinations as bitter competition
led those with privileges to exercise them in whatever way that they could.

Government schools in the Southern Sung

Just five years after the abolition of the Three Hall System, the Sung
lost all of northern China and some thirty-five percent of its population
to the Jurchen invaders. Large areas north of the Yangtze River and even
much of Liang-che became the scenes of protracted warfare between the
truncated Sung and the new Chin empires. For a time, internal rebellions
made Sung government control precarious even in areas completely
unaffected by the war. Even after the immediate crisis passed (peace was
agreed to in 1142), the government's control over the empire was weakened.
It faced the problem of providing for northern refugees who, one modern
scholar has estimated, numbered in the millions,[92] and it had to cope with
widespread destruction caused by war and rebellion.

These events had a devastating impact upon schools, at least initially.
For financial reasons, the government made deep cuts in teaching personnel.[93] But worse, many schools were destroyed in the fighting. Yeh
Meng-te gave the following description of the effects of the Chin invasion
upon Chien-k'ang fu (or Chiang-ning fu) in northern Chiang-nan-tung:

Chien-k'ang commands the eight prefectures on the left [bank] of the
Yangtze and is a great city of the southeast. In other times, its literary
accomplishments were greater than those of other places and it long
had a school in the southeastern corner of the prefecture [i.e., the

Table 11. *Constructive and destructive activities at 64 prefectural and 108 county schools*

Period*	Reports of building, renovation, and endowment increases		Reports of floods, fires, and destruction by troops or rebels	
	Prefectural schools	County schools	Prefectural schools	County schools
960–997	7	2		
998–1021	11	11		
1022–1040	25	9	1	
1041–1063	30	38	1	1
1064–1085	21	29	1	
1086–1100	15	20		
1101–1126	27	43	3	8
N. Sung	136	153	6	9
1127–1162	67	92	14	26
(1127–1140)**	(27)	(35)	(12)	(24)
(1141–1162)**	(30)	(34)	(1)	(1)
1163–1189	52	65	2	6
1190–1207	26	36	1	2
1208–1224	26	43	1	1
1225–1240	24	37	3	3
1241–1264	21	41	2	2
1265–1279	9	6	4	8
S. Sung	225	320	27	48
Total	361	472	33	57

Sources and list of schools used: see Chaffee, 'Education and Examinations,' Appendix 2.

*Periods follow reign periods or, in some cases, combinations of short reign periods.

**These subtotals are given to provide an indication of school activity during the early years of the Southern Sung and to distinguish those years from the years of the school reforms, the 1140s. The subtotals do not add up to the period total because some of the references were insufficiently specific, referring only to the Shao-hsing reign period (1131–62).

city]. Then it suffered soldiers burning the city, reducing it to waste-land. Only the school itself survived. [But even there] falling walls ruined and pressed against each other. The registered students hurriedly scattered and the erudites accordingly did not lecture.[94]

This destruction is also reflected in the figures for the years 1127–62 in Table 11, which shows the record of constructive activity (building, rebuilding, endowment additions) and destructive activity (floods, fires, destruction by troops or rebels) at 64 prefectural and 108 county schools for which there are records of three or more such events.

The effects of these disturbances on schools, however, seem to have been temporary. Accounts of school rebuilding during the 1130s and 1140s are extremely numerous and, as we saw above, the central government began an educational program in 1142, the same year that peace was declared with the Chin. But most remarkable was the role that students played in the recovery. In Liu-ho county of Chen-chou (Huai-nan-tung), students built themselves a ten-room thatched-roof building after their school had been destroyed.[95] Students in Lien-chiang and Ku-t'ien counties of Fu-chou (Fu-chien) and in An-hua county of T'an-chou (Ching-hu-nan) led building drives for the local schools.[96] Most telling is the following account of the conditions in Ming-chou in 1135, where the government school had been destroyed:

> There was no school building to use for educational activities, and there was no millet, meat, water, fire, utensils or plates to use for feeding [the students]. None of the hundred [necessities] was prepared. Yet the students still came with satchels on their backs and sat beneath the ruined rooms. The sounds of singing and recitation did not stop. Because of such customs and love of learning as these, the prefect, Mr Chiu, was induced to submit respectfully a memorial to the emperor extolling Confucianism by the next post leaving town.[97]

By the following year, through donations from the government and local individuals, the money and materials necessary for rebuilding the school had been raised.[98]

During the Southern Sung, the central government was notably uninvolved in local education. The major exception was in the 1140s when the court played an active role in the reconstruction of schools and made repeated efforts to get them all staffed with degree-holding preceptors,[99] for as the emperor Kao-tsung (r. 1127–62) rhetorically asked in 1143, 'If we do not make schools thrive today, how will we be able to obtain talented men for employment in the future?'[100] That same year examination candidates were required either to spend half a year in school or to participate in two district wine drinking ceremonies (*hsiang yin-chiu li*), but there is little evidence to indicate that this was ever enforced.[101] Following this period, the central government's involvement in government schools seems to have ceased. According to contemporary complaints, the schools deteriorated in quality and were subjected to various abuses such as heterodox teaching, no teaching at all, and loss of revenue.[102]

Table 12. *Incidence per decade of constructive activity at 64 prefectural and 108 county schools*

Period	Prefectural schools, incidence per decade	County schools, incidence per decade
960–997	1.8	0.5
998–1021	4.6	4.6
1022–1040	13.2	4.7
1041–1063	13.0	16.5
1064–1085	9.5	13.2
1086–1100	5.8	7.7
1101–1126	10.4	16.5
Northern Sung	8.1	9.1
1127–1162	18.6	25.6
(1127–1140)	(19.3)	(25.0)
(1141–1162)	(13.6)	(15.4)
1163–1189	19.2	24.0
1190–1207	14.4	20.0
1208–1224	15.3	25.2
1225–1240	15.0	23.1
1241–1264	8.8	17.1
1265–1279	6.0	4.0
Southern Sung	14.7	20.9
Total	11.3	14.8

But government schools were hardly defunct. In spite of the complaints and the lack of involvement by the central government, government schools remained active, more active in fact than they had been during the Northern Sung. In Table 12, which shows the net constructive activity (constructive minus destructive incidents) at the schools represented in Table 11, we can see that the levels of activity throughout the Southern Sung were consistently higher than the highest levels during the Northern Sung. Even if we grant a tendency by later sources to provide more information on Southern Sung activities, it is clear that government schools remained vigorous and active throughout the Southern Sung and did not fall into disrepair and disuse as the traditional interpretation would have it.

Government schools were the object of much criticism, however. With unprecedented numbers of literati taking the examinations, it is not surprising that county and prefectural schools came under attack, for although there was no longer a formal connection between them and the examinations, the former remained centers for examination preparation.[103] In 1194 Chu Hsi described the large prefectural school at Fu-chou (Fe-chien) in the following manner:

> The prefectural school of Fu-chou is the largest in southeastern China, with hundreds of students. Yet in recent years its teaching and nourishment [of students] lacked rules. Teachers and students regarded each other indifferently, like men on the highway. Elders were concerned by the daily decline of ancient customs and the disappearance of scholarly spirit, but they were unable to remedy it.[104]

but isn't this always the case?

What most upset educational critics, however, were the corrosive effects of examination preparation and competition. 'A healthy society cannot come about when people study not for the purpose of gaining wisdom and knowledge, but for the purpose of becoming government officials,' wrote Yeh Shih (1150–1223),[105] and in the opinion of many, that is just what people were doing. In 1192, Chao Ju-yü (1140–96), the Minister of Personnel, wrote,

> After the Ch'ing-li period [1041–8], things cultural were refined. Since the restoration [i.e., the beginning of the Southern Sung], the University has been established in the temporary capital and the examinations have been held in all prefectures, but an air of urgent quarreling has dominated and the customs of loyalty and trust have been obscured.[106]

The competitiveness engendered by the examinations, moreover, was associated with the government schools. Chu Hsi described students at the University:

> Those scholars who have set their minds upon righteousness and principle will not seek them at the school. Those who hasten [towards] the hub and arrive are nothing more than the excess of the prefectural quotas, the favorites of class-selection [literally, 'hall selection'] and that is all.[107]

And an early thirteenth-century local historian complained that 'schools are considered to be the business of officials and examinations are considered to be the vocation of scholars, alas!'[108]

Such criticisms were not universal. If anything, the attacks upon examination-oriented education were testimonials to its widespread popularity, and government school activities that succeeded in increasing examination success were lavishly praised.[109] Yet there was an undeniable decline in the prestige of government schools, especially if one contrasts those in the late twelfth century with the more renowned schools of the mid eleventh century. Education itself had bifurcated and the ideal of disinterested intellectual inquiry took many students and scholars elsewhere, to the academies.

The spread of academies

Academies were hardly new to China during the Southern Sung. *Shu-yüan* and *ching-she,* the terms usually translated as 'academy,' both predated the Sung and encompassed a range of functions, serving as schools, studies, and meditation halls.[110] As we can see from Table 13, which lists all Sung academies to which I have found reference, they existed throughout the dynasty. During the Northern Sung, except for a handful of famous, officially recognized academies which functioned much like government schools, most seem to have been either small informal schools or scholars' studies. In the course of the Southern Sung, although informal academies remained common, many others took a form which was to become characteristic of Ming academies, with income-producing endowments, salaried staffs, and campuses with ceremonial temples, lecture halls, dormitories, and kitchens. In this they were much like the government schools. Where they differed was in their educational program: rejecting in large part preparation for the examinations, they advocated instead Neo-Confucian self-cultivation.

The change was of major significance and can be roughly dated to the reign of Hsiao-tsung (1163–89) when three important and related events

Table 13. *Sung academies classified by dates of earliest reference and references per decade*

Period	References	References per 10 years
960–997	12	3.2
998–1021	7	2.9
1022–1063	13	3.1
1064–1085	9	4.1
1086–1100	3	2.0
1101–1126	12	4.6
Northern Sung	56	3.4
1127–1162	33	9.2
1163–1189	45	16.7
1190–1224	78	22.3
1225–1264	75	18.8
1265–1279	30	20.0
Southern Sung	261	17.0
Undated	108	
Total Sung	425	13.3

Sources: See Chaffee, 'Education and Examinations,' Appendix 2.

occurred. First, the establishment of new academies increased dramatically
and continued at a high level for the rest of the dynasty. Geographically, they
appeared in every circuit (see Table 23), but the great majority were in the
fertile and productive southwest, most notably in a broad mountainous swath
extending west from the coastal regions of Liang-che-tung and northern
Fu-chien to the Hsiang River Valley of Ching-hu-nan.

Second, under the leadership of Neo-Confucian local officials, several of
the famous Northern Sung academies were revived. In 1165 the Yüeh-lu
Academy was restored in T'an-chou (Ching-hu-nan) by a pacification official,
Liu Kung (1122–78), who enlisted the young but renowned Neo-Confucian
philosopher Chang Shih (1133–80) to write a commemorative essay for
it.[111] Twenty years later in nearby Heng-chou, the Stone Drum Academy
(Shih-ku Shu-yüan) was rebuilt with an explicitly anti-examination orientation. Its renovator Fan Chih (1126–89) wrote that its purpose was 'to
await and accommodate those scholars of the four quarters who are determined to study but do not consider the business of classes and tests worth-
while.'[112] Most famous, however, was the renovation of the White Deer
Hollow Academy (Pai-lu-tung Shu-yüan) in Nan-k'ang chün in 1179 by the
prefect Chu Hsi, who was even then regarded as a major philosopher. With the
educational program of morality, intellectual inquiry, and self-cultivation that
Chu formulated for it, the academy quickly became the premier symbol of
the academy movement.[113]

Finally, many of these late twelfth century academies demonstrated an
extraordinary intellectual vitality. Such leading thinkers as Chu Hsi, Lu
Chiu-yüan (1129–93), Chang Shih, Lü Tsu-ch'ien (1137–81), and Ch'en
Fu-liang (1137–1203) all taught in academies and had large followings, often
drawn from considerable distances.[114] Many founded their own academies
and it was common to invite famous scholars to come and lecture.

By the end of the twelfth century, critics of the examinations, and there
were many, frequently voiced their distress at the educational and intellectual
climate of the day. Chang Shih wrote in 1169:

> In general, since heretical doctrines became current, scholars have
> confused basic truths, texts have been selected to study [for the
> purpose of] excelling, and scholars have been interested in learning the
> vulgar. In normal times when they gather and live together [i.e.,
> in government schools], how much does their work become that of
> looking for ways to be selected [in the examinations] or scheming for
> profit?[115]

Disgusted by the competitive and philistine character of bureaucratic and
examination life, many scholars withdrew to secluded Neo-Confucian

academies, which were typically located in scenic country spots where they could cultivate their characters and attempt the 'extension of knowledge.' Of course, this very act of withdrawal was somewhat un-Confucian, since it ignored the cardinal principle of service to the ruler and to society.[116] But it was undertaken with great moral fervor; not atypical is a set of school rules written by disciples of Chu Hsi which prescribe in detail how the students were expected to sit, go to bed, walk and stand, see and hear, talk, dress, eat and drink.[117] Similar in character though more marked by its religiosity which stands in striking contrast to the pedagogy of the reformer Hu Yüan which was described earlier, is this description of the teaching of Lu Chiu-yüan at his Ying-t'ien Mountain Academy (Ying-t'ien-shan Ching-she) in Hsin-chou (Chiang-nan-hsi):

> Every morning at the sounding of the academy's drum, he would ascend the mountain and, arriving at the top, meet [the students] with a bow and climb into the lecture seat. His countenance was clear and his spirit severe. The students, using small placards on which they had written their names and ages to make [their age] order known, sat accordingly. At the least, they were several score to a hundred, reverential and not noisy. He would first admonish them to draw together their spirits, nourish a virtuous nature and listen to discourse with an empty mind. The students would all bow their heads and, bowed, listen. He would not only lecture on the classics, but each time would instruct them about the original mind of man. He would select quotations from the classics as evidence — the sound of his voice was clear — and among his listeners there was no one who was not moved.[118]

More important in its political consequences was the claim made by Chu Hsi and his followers that the way of kingly government, lost since the time of Mencius, had been rediscovered by the eleventh century Neo-Confucians and transmitted to them, their twelfth century successors. Such an audacious claim, involving as it did the issue of political legitimacy, provoked strong reactions and was at least partly responsible for the 'False Learning' (*Wei-hsüeh*) controversy of 1195–1200, in which some fifty-nine individuals, mostly but by no means all Neo-Confucians, were banned from office, while examination candidates had to declare that they were not students of 'false learning.'[119]

By the middle of the Southern Sung, the examinations and the academies presented apparently conflicting choices to the literati. The former, which promised prestige and power, were criticized as being morally and socially corrosive, while the latter, with their program of moral cultivation and intellectual inquiry, were criticized for fostering superior airs among their advocates, especially among those who claimed exclusive possession of the kingly way. For the individual, the choice was one which David S. Nivison has perceptively identified as lying between one's filial duty to succeed in the examinations and a personal desire for self-cultivation.[120] But at the level of institutions it is possible to discern a broader conflict, for the academies represented a literati-controlled alternative to the government-controlled examinations (and schools), even though both claimed the authority of the classics. Two factors, however, served to mitigate this conflict and keep it from threatening the socio-political order.

First, the opposition to the examination life was in fact qualified; criticism of the effects of the examinations on education and society seldom extended to condemnation of the examinations as such, which were recognized as necessary. Rather it was how one studied and approached the examinations that was considered important. In a famous lecture which Lu Chiu-yüan delivered, at the invitation of Chu Hsi, at the White Deer Hollow Academy, he said:

> The state examination as an institution for selecting people has existed for a long time. Most well-known scholars and statesmen have been successful candidates at this examination. A student who wants to find a career must submit himself to it . . . Yet students look at the state examination as something to which they aspire. Very few can regard it with contempt. What they read is superficially the books of the sages; but what they aspire to is entirely different from what the sages said . . . Students who perceive that this is not the right attitude for a man, and who make efforts to avoid falling in with mean fellows, must repent and exert themselves strenuously in behalf of righteousness when they enter the examination hall. They will be able to write on their papers what they have learned and what they have determined to do, and they will not deviate from the ways of the sages.[121]

Those who were involved in the academies seldom turned their backs on the bureaucratic world entirely. This is most evident in the many famous academy teachers who also served as officials. For example, all of those teachers mentioned above went back and forth between teaching and official service.[122] It is also likely, though less demonstrable, that students and unsuccessful candidates alternated between the academies and the examination halls. The requirement in 1196 that candidates declare they were not students of false learning implies a belief that many had been, and the logical place for such study would have been at academies. That is, the anti-examination orientation of academy education did not preclude such education from being useful in the examinations. And in some academies compromises were made. For example, at the quasi-official Academy of the Illuminated Way (Ming-tao Shu-yüan) in Chien-k'ang fu, Chu Hsi's rules for the White Deer Hollow Academy were subscribed to but one third of all study time was set aside for examination preparation.[123]

But even if the academy education was of little or no practical value, the triennial periodicity of the examinations made it quite possible for scholars to attend academies and take the examinations. For the mature literatus familiar with the examination curriculum, preparation was probably confined to the year preceding the preliminary examinations, which would have left him ample time for other pursuits. Since the examinations provided a major reason for literati to travel and many academies explicitly welcomed 'travelling scholars from the four quarters,' the year of the capital examinations should have been the busiest for academies. In this regard, it is suggestive that two of the most famous intellectual events of the Southern Sung, the meeting of Chu Hsi, Lu Chiu-yüan, Lü Tsu-ch'ien and others at Goose Lake in Hsin-chou, and Lu Chiu-yüan's lecture at the White Deer Hollow Academy both occurred in such years: 1175 and 1181.[124]

A second factor helping to mute the conflict between academy and examination was that the government attempted to co-opt the academies into the official order. In fact, during the thirteenth century the political challenge represented by the Neo-Confucians was effectively neutralized through official accommodation. The ban on false learning, which had never been very effective, was lifted in 1202, two years after the death of Chu-Hsi. In the following years the court paid great lip service to Neo-Confucian doctrines, promoted Neo-Confucian officials (though seldom to important posts), and encouraged academies. Under the emperor Li-tsung (r. 1225–64), whose reign name itself – 'Ancestor of Principle' – was Neo-Confucian, many academies received imperially-inscribed plaques and a number were actually founded upon imperial command.[125] Even government schools were affected; we find thirteenth-century accounts of sacrificial halls being built and dedicated to Neo-Confucian masters at such schools, and of Neo-Confucian texts being used in them.[126]

But muted though the conflict may have become it did not disappear, for both the dissatisfaction at the kind of education engendered by the examinations and the Neo-Confucian answer to this remained. Neo-Confucian academies were well suited to serve as refuges for frustrated scholars. Rejecting the examination life, they gave prestige and importance to the act of withdrawal and disinterested study. Frederic Wakeman has noted that 'an unbending moral integrity and idealism' which approached 'orthodox intellectual dissent . . . only became a habitual commitment during the Sung period.'[127] The Neo-Confucian belief in the vital importance of moral and

self-cultivation, together with the spread of academies wherein that cultivation could be pursued, served to strengthen the moral authority and
autonomy of the scholar. The many literati who could not succeed in the
examination hall were provided with a rationale for their studies which did
not depend upon government service.

↳ Neo- Confucianism

5

THE FAILURE OF FAIRNESS:
EXAMINATIONS IN THE SOUTHERN SUNG

The examinations at mid-course

For the first fifteen years of the Southern Sung, the dynastic house of
Chao was fighting for its life. The emperor Kao-tsung, who had ascended the
throne at the age of twenty-one after his father Hui-tsung and brother Ch'in-
tsung (r. 1126—7) had been captured by the Jurchen Chin, had to rule with
remnants of the court from a variety of locations in central and southeastern
China. He had to contend, moreover, not only with Chin invasions in 1129,
1134 and 1138, the first of which reached as far as southern Liang-che and
central Chiang-nan-hsi, but also mutinies by troops, popular uprisings,
repeated fiscal crises, and the burden of massive refugee migrations from the
north.[1] The dynasty survived the crisis thanks to local militias and irregular
troops (often rebels who had switched sides), outstanding generals like Yüeh
Fei (1103—41), Han Shih-chung (1089—1151) and Chang Chün (1086—
1164), and a willingness to settle for control of southern China alone. With
the decision in 1138 to name the scenic city of Lin-an fu (Northern Sung
Hang-chou) as the de facto capital and the conclusion in 1142 of peace with
the Chin, a semblance of normality returned to the truncated empire.

Survival came at a price. To marshal the forces necessary to repel the Chin
and restore internal order, the court had to allow a decentralization of
military power. For the remainder of the Sung the empire was divided into
four command systems,[2] and these affected civil as well as military administration, creating regional frameworks within which most officials spent their
entire careers.[3] Moreover, precisely because of the court's weakened position,
Kao-tsung and his principal chief councilor Ch'in Kuei (1090—1155) refused
to concede to the military the preeminence that a truly restorationist policy
would have entailed, and adhered instead to the principle established by Sung
T'ai-tsu of curbing outstanding generals and asserting civil control over the
military. Their purge of generals, most notably Yüeh Fei who was subsequently assassinated in prison, and the unequal terms of the 1142 peace in
which the Sung renounced their claim to all lands north of the Huai River

have drawn the almost unanimous condemnation of Chinese historians ever since, but however one views the outcome one must recognize that the actions were consistent with the commitment to civilism that characterized Sung rule from beginning to end.[4] When the state donated Yüeh Fei's considerable estate to the University for a campus in 1143, it merely underscored that commitment.[5]

Examinations continued to be held throughout this tumultuous period, though usually at four rather than three-year intervals.[6] This is not surprising, for such was their symbolic importance for Sung civilism that their abandonment would certainly have been seen by the elite as an admission of dynastic collapse, but it was impressive, for the obstacles to holding them were formidable. Lost were the past examination records from K'ai-feng and the entire north and even many southern prefectures, thus making it extremely difficult to certify candidates or to verify their eligibility for exemptions or facilitated degrees.[7] Scattered throughout the south were northern literati, often without documents, who had to be provided for. Finally, there were the logistical problems of testing large numbers of literati and arranging for their travel.

The problem of records was addressed by widespread efforts at reconstruction. In prefectures where records were missing, a combination of personal records and guarantees from officials were relied upon, especially in the cases of past *chü-jen*.[8] At the same time the court asked all prefectures to submit lists of past *chü-jen* along with their examination documents and also the prefectural quota authorizations, for virtually all of its records had been lost.[9]

Refugee literati were asked for two guarantees each from officials and were then allowed to sit for the examinations in the prefecture where they were staying, but they were to be examined separately at 'refugee examinations' (*liu-yü-shih*) and not with the native literati. It is unclear whether these examinations, which were discontinued in 1156, were designed to spare refugees from competition with the natives or vice versa. They were intiallly given selection ratios of one *chü-jen* for each twenty candidates,[10] and this was liberalized to one in fifteen in 1136,[11] but evidence from local histories suggests that by the 1150s a quota ratio of one in one hundred was being used, thus making the refugee examinations comparably competitive with the prefectural examinations.[12] Interestingly, the numbers of literati taking the refugee examination were rather small; of the eleven refugee examination quotas to which I have found reference, six were for one *chü-jen*, three for two, and two for three.[13] Thus numerically at least, the northern refugee impact upon Southern Sung examinations appears to have been minimal.

The logistical problems of holding the examinations also entailed extraordinary measures. Late in 1127, Kao-tsung decreed from Yang-chou on the northern bank of the Yangtze River that the departmental examination not be held in K'ai-feng the following spring. Instead, its quota was to be divided up and *chü-jen* examined at the fiscal intendent's office of each circuit.[14] These circuit examinations (*lei-shih*) were also held in 1132,[15] so it was not until 1135 that the departmental examination was resumed, and then it was without the participation of Ssu-ch'uan *chü-jen,* who went to their own examination in Ch'eng-tu from then until the end of the Sung.[16]

The Southern Sung examinations therefore began in a completely decentralized fashion and so they continued after peace was restored, albeit to a lesser degree. Although Lin-an was the jewel of the south and quickly became the undisputed political and economic center of the empire, its examination record of 493 Southern Sung *chin-shih* was only modest, ranking eleventh among all prefectures.[17] Perhaps for the first time the Chinese bureaucracy was dominated not by a metropolitan elite based in the capital, but drew more broadly from a number of flourishing prefectures.[18]

Why did Lin-an not dominate the examinations as K'ai-feng had? The decentralization of power which accompanied the restoration of order was largely responsible. In many parts of the south, elite families had survived the 1120s and 1130s only by asserting their local power, organizing militias, providing sanctuary for northern refugees, and the like. Such security, especially when set against the dangers of serving in high office, undoubtedly lessened the attraction of settling in Lin-an. Moreover, for southern literati Lin-an was much nearer than K'ai-feng had been, so settling one's family in the capital may have been less of a necessity for those appointed to metropolitan offices.

But in part at least, Lin'an's non-domination of the examinations was the result of government policy. Like K'ai-feng, Lin-an attracted large numbers of literati who stayed to take the examinations, but unlike their earlier counterparts, these Southern Sung literati were given a separate, extremely competitive examination. Known both as the *T'ung-wen-kuan shih* ('examination of the T'ung-wen Hall') and the *Liang-che chüan-yün-ssu fu-shih* ('supplemental examination at the Liang-che fiscal intendent's office') or 'supplemental examination' (*fu-shih*) for short, it was started in 1144 as an examination for scholars in the capital whose homes were over 1,000 *li* (roughly 333 miles) away.[19] By the 1170s it had evolved into an examination for provincial students who were studying in the prefectural and county schools of Lin-an fu. The narrowness of its quota (see Table 14), however, meant that it offered no competitive advantage over the prefectural examinations; indeed, it was more difficult than any but a few of them. Nor did the Northern Sung practice of falsifying one's residency offer much hope, for

Table 14. *The supplemental examination (fu-shih) for provincial candidates residing in Lin-an*

Year	Number of candidates	Quota	*Chü-jen*/candidate ratio
1174	87	1	1/87
1177	400	2–3	1/133–1/200
1189	1,311	10	1/131
1195	1,562	10	1/156
1198	1,667	10	1/167
1201	1,449	10	1/145
1204	1,389	10	1/139
1207	1,384	5	1/277
1210	1,069	4	1/267
1213	1,924	7	1/275
1216	1,671	6	1/262
1219	1,993	7	1/285
1222	2,493	10	1/249

Source: SHY:HC 16/19a–b, 21b, 25b, 28b–29a.

Lin-an's prefectural examination quota was a mere 17 in 1156, increasing to 19 in 1234 and 22 in 1264.[20] Since the government could easily have made the quotas to both of these examinations much more generous, we must assume that they were intentionally kept small.

Whatever the reasons behind it, the consequences of this change in the capital's examination role were great. Just when the examinations were becoming much more popular and therefore more competitive, one of the primary routes that official families had used to move their sons through the system — the capital examination — was severely curtailed. In reaction they made increasing use of protection, they engaged in any number of ingenious methods of cheating, and they turned to special preliminary examinations and subverted them to their own ends. As a result the claim to fairness which had undergirded the Northern Sung examinations became increasingly empty.

The special preliminary examinations

Like an old house whose additions jut in odd directions, the examination system acquired a number of special preliminary examinations over the course of the Sung. Some such as the above-mentioned refugee and supplementary examinations, were established for limited and temporary purposes, even though the latter took on a life of its own. Others, however, were created in the early Sung in response to the same concern for fairness and opportunity that informed much of the examination system's development.

The most frequently mentioned worry was that favoritism by the examiners towards family or acquaintances would make success impossible for those without connections. In 997 the censor Wang Chi (952–1010) warned that 'If examination selection is not strict the powerful will struggle to be foremost and the orphans and poor will have difficulty advancing.'[21] His solution was to establish two separate channels of advancement in the examinations, one via the Directorate of Education for the sons, grandsons, nephews and brothers of court-grade officials, the other via the prefectural examinations for relatives of lower officials and commoners. He continued:

> If when they proceed to go up to the Board of Rites, the ranking of their capability also employs two groups, then the powerful will have a separate path and the orphaned and poor will be able to advance themselves.[22]

Wang's proposal, which is reminiscent of the dichotomy between 'school selection' and 'district tribute' candidates in the T'ang examinations, was never implemented as such, but the principle of segregating those with family connections was accepted and became embodied in the examinations for officials and for relatives of certain officials. Unfortunately separate examinations proved conducive to unequal treatment, and so in the long run the policy of segregating the relatives of officials in the interest of equity resulted in pronounced inequities.

This was not the case, however, with the preliminary examination for officials called the 'locked hall examination' (*suo-t'ing-shih*), which originated in the 980s.[23] The government seems to have looked with some disfavor upon officials taking the examinations simply for the prestige or the career advantages that passing them offered. To quote a memorial from 1018: 'If people have official positions, then they should not compete for advancement with the orphaned and poor.'[24]

Unlike the avoidance examination for relatives of officials with which it was often associated,[25] in the locked-hall examination candidates were punished if they did not meet the minimum qualifying standards. This originally entailed loss of office, but it was later reduced to a personal offense (*ssu-tsui*) and then to just a cash fine.[26] In addition, it was felt that officials taking the examinations should not be honored with top places on the examination list. Thus in 1148, Tung Te-yüan, a minor official and *chü-jen* from the locked-hall examination, was moved to the second place on the list even though he was credited with having written the best examination.[27] Finally, there is no evidence to suggest that the locked-hall examination gave its candidates a significant competitive advantage over those taking the prefectural examination and it may in fact have been more competitive.[28]

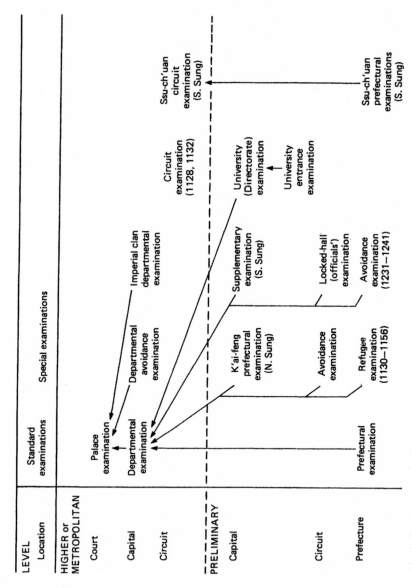

Fig. 4. The Sung examination system.

The avoidance examination appeared just slightly later than the locked-hall examination. In 998 a 'separate examination' (*pieh-shih*) was held for candidates who were related to the examiners at the K'ai-feng and Directorate of Education preliminary examinations.[29] From this simple beginning the avoidance examination, which was called by a variety of names,[30] expanded to include broader and broader categories of candidates. In 1037, three groups were ordered to go to the avoidance examination: the relatives of examination officials; the relatives of prefects serving in their home prefectures; and sons and grandsons accompanying officials who were serving more than 2,000 *li* away from their homes.[31] In 1069, tutors (*men-k'o*) serving in the families of examination officials were included as well.[32]

During the Southern Sung with its unprecedented and ever increasing examination competition, the avoidance examination continued to grow in size, with reports of candidate numbers ranging from 50 and 337 in Liang-che in 1192 and 1195[33] to 3,500 in Ssu-ch'uan in 1153[34] and 5,000 in Liang-che in 1241.[35] As early as the mid twelfth century concerns were repeatedly voiced about the large number of avoidance candidates and the question of eligibility attracted controversy.[36] Complained one memorialist in 1165:

> In the avoidance examination regulations, scholars from Ssu-ch'uan and Kuang-nan may use it, yet [those from] Fu-chien are also being allowed [to take] the avoidance examination; [relatives of] incumbent officials may use it, yet [those of officials] who are awaiting vacancies and who will take office within a year are also being allowed [to take] the avoidance examination; mourning relatives within the same lineage may use it, yet relatives of the fifth degree who are outside the lineage are also being allowed [to take] the avoidance examination.[37]

The last-mentioned problem of affinal kin, an especially critical one in the marriage-conscious world of the local elites, was the subject of no less than four contradictory edicts between 1168 and 1189.[38]

When the avoidance examination regulations were codified in 1168,[39] the list of those eligible was considerably longer than it had been in 1037. Five groups were now included: (1) relatives (both paternal and maternal) accompanying officials who were either from Ssu-ch'uan or Kuang-nan[40] so long as their posts were over 2,000 *li* from their homes; (2) sons and grandsons of ranked military officials either from Ssu-ch'uan or Kuang-nan serving elsewhere or vice versa (as above); (3) relatives of prefects and vice-prefects who were serving in their home prefectures; (4) relatives of circuit officials whose circuits contained their home prefectures, though they had to go to a neighboring circuit for the avoidance examination;[41] and (5) tutors serving in the families of officials holding the office of investigating censor (*chien-ch'a yü-shih,* grade 7B) or higher, though this was limited to one tutor per official.[42] The quota-ratio for the avoidance examination was set at 1/40 and, finally, relatives of the last group of officials who were within the third degree of mourning (*ta-kung*) to them[43] were permitted to take the University preliminary examination, so long as they were guaranteed by two officials of capital grade or higher.

Fraud also played a role in the avoidance examinations, for complaints abounded of literati taking them illegally.[44]

> In the examinations the prefectural quotas are narrow and the candidates numerous, [while] the numbers selected at the circuit offices are rather large. Literati taking the examinations frequently forsake village tribute [i.e., the prefectural examination] and scheme for the [circuit] office list [i.e., the avoidance examination], going so far as to falsely claim [officials as] relatives and to fabricate household registrations

lamented a memorial in 1163.[45] By 1231, so bad had this problem become that the circuit avoidance examinations were abolished and their quotas given to those prefectures with the most restrictive quotas.[46] However, this measure was effectively negated by an accompanying provision which allowed those who had been eligible for the avoidance examination to be examined separately in each prefecture and to be selected under a generous quota-ratio of 1/50.[47] Even as amended, the measure was short-lived, for the avoidance examinations were reestablished by 1241.[48]

At the root of the problem lay quotas and differences in competition, for the avoidance examination quota-ratios, while not easy — they were variously 1/20, 1/40 and 1/50 during the Southern Sung — were very attractive when compared with the 1/100 or worse of the prefectural examinations, and this was in striking contrast to the Northern Sung, when the quota-ratios of the two examinations were kept roughly equal.[49] Accordingly, how to limit entry replaced favoritism by examiners as the dominant concern of memorials and edicts concerning the avoidance examination, and the formal name for it changed from *pieh-shih* ('separate examination') to *tieh-shih* ('official-list examination'). Despite the continuing use of the idea of avoidance to justify the examination, its main function became the provision of an examination *entrée* that was privileged, easier and even honored. Upon the completion of a new hall for the avoidance examination in Chiang-nan-tung in 1213, the respected scholar-official Chen Te-hsiu (1178–1235) wrote that

> The area of Chiang-tung is large, its people numerous and their talent outstanding. In the past several decades, many have been those selected at the fiscal intendent's office examination who received high-placing degrees and had honored careers.[50]

The last of the special preliminary examinations, that of the Directorate of Education or the University (*Kuo-tzu-chien chieh-shih, T'ai-hsüeh chieh-shih*[51]), underwent a different sort of evolution, but in it too privilege played a major role. As we saw in Chapter 3, the early Sung Directorate School was reserved for children of officials of the seventh grade or above, and only after the creation of the School of the Four Gates and the Imperial University in the 1040s were provisions made for accepting the children of low-grade officials and commoners. Later under the reformers' impetus the University became the empire's premier educational institution and open by examination to all literati, although a Directorate School for the children of officials remained as an adjunct to it.

The University offered its students two paths to officialdom. One, established with the creation of the Three Hall System at the University in 1071, lay in advancement within the University. Students in the upper hall (*shang-she*) could take the upper hall examination and, if they passed it, receive degree status directly. This achievement, known as 'shedding rough serge' (*shih-ho*), was extremely prestigious and difficult. Except for Hui-tsung's reign when over three hundred such degrees were given,[52] few received it.[53]

The other path was through the examinations and it was here that the University students received their greatest advantages, at least during the Southern Sung. Through most of the Northern Sung the government managed to keep competition at the Directorate preliminary examination on a rough par with the prefectural and avoidance examinations,[54] but in the Southern Sung its quota-ratio was kept at between 1/4 and 1/5 while prefectural competition rose precipitously.[55] In addition, some students were exempted from the departmental examination altogether. In the early Southern Sung, students in the inner and upper halls who had been to certain numbers of examinations in the past were granted exemptions from the preliminary and departmental examinations.[56] A century later provisions were even more generous, for students who had been enrolled for three years or more in the inner or upper halls, which then had over one hundred students, could skip the departmental examination and so were assured of receiving their *chin-shih* degrees.[57]

These benefits proved a powerful attraction to literati frustrated by the regular examinations. Chu Hsi wrote that

> The reason why literati today are unhappy with prefectural selection and vie to rush to the University [entrance] examination is because the prefectural quotas are narrow and the examinees many, while the University's [*chü-jen*] quota is ample and the examinees few.[58]

But the very attractiveness of the University also made it extremely difficult for most students to gain admission.

The University entrance examination, which was usually held triennially following the departmental examination, underwent considerable change during the Southern Sung as different methods of determining eligibility for the examination were tried.[59] Most of the time the 'mixed entrance' (*hun-pu*) method was used which allowed any literati who fulfilled certain requirements such as residency in or recommendation by their prefectural schools to take the examination. Excessive numbers resulting from this method led to the introduction in 1177 of a more restrictive method called 'awaiting entrance' (*tai-pu*), in which only *chü-jen* and the top 3% (in 1183 it was raised to 6%) of prefectural candidates who had just missed selection as *chü-jen* could take the examination.[60] But it faced administrative problems and complaints of unfairness because of its restricted entry, so in 1202 the 'mixed entrance' method was reintroduced.[61]

Regardless of how eligibility was determined, the University entrance examination proved extremely popular. The number taking it went from 6,000 in 1143[62] to 16,000 in 1175,[63] 28,000 in 1196,[64] and a remarkable 37,000 in 1202.[65] These gatherings, which must have visibly swelled Lin-an for their duration, were so difficult to manage that in 1251 separate entrance examinations were held in each circuit capital, though this experiment was apparently unsatisfactory for it was not repeated.[66] But increasing competitiveness was the most noteworthy consequence of the examination's popularity. With two to three hundred admitted every three years,[67] the selection ratio was 1/100 or worse at the turn of the thirteenth century and thus was on a par with the prefectural examinations.

But not all literati had to make their way through the tortuous entrance examination in order to take the University's preliminary examination, for there, as in the examinations at large, privilege played a critical role. In the avoidance examination regulations of 1168, as we noted above, certain relatives of officials with the office of investigating censor or above were permitted to take the University preliminary examination.[68] This provision was not new, for similar grants allowing the relatives of high officials to take the Directorate's examination had been made in 1130 and 1137 and were to be made in 1192.[69] The specific requirements varied among these acts: in 1130, the relatives of officials with duties (*chih-shih-kuan*) and officials regulating affairs (*li-wu-kuan*) at the capital were declared eligible;[70] while in 1192, though the same types of officials were mentioned, fewer of their relatives were eligible, the *li-wu-kuan* had to be at least of capital grade if civil officials and of court grade if military, and the guarantee provisions of 1160 were repeated.[71]

There were in addition the 'national youth students' (*kuo-tzu-sheng*) of the Directorate School, which had always served the children of officials exclusively. In the mid thirteenth century its two hundred places were reserved for the sons, nephews or brothers of officials serving in court.[72] The Directorate School may even have had its own preliminary examination. One late Southern Sung source describes a 'national youth' *tieh-shih* with a selection ratio of 1/5, which was about the same as the University.[73] This is probably the same examination as the *tieh-shih* for 'eldest sons' (*chou-tzu*) dealt with in a remarkable edict from 1261, which set quotas for the number of relatives different officials could have taking it. These ranged from forty for councilors (*tsai*) down to eight for the vice-prefect of Lin-an and one son or grandson for unnamed others who were eligible.[74] Both the form and size of these quotas are reminiscent of edicts concerning protection. Access to this special examination was clearly a prerogative of high office and had little or nothing to do with either avoidance or one's past accomplishments as a student.

In summary, by the late Southern Sung there were three distinct points of privileged entry to less competitive preliminary examinations: the protection-like 'national youth' *tieh-shih* for large numbers of relatives of the very highest officials and admission to the University preliminary examination for the relatives of high ranking officials serving primarily in the capital, both of which had a very liberal quota-ratio of 1/4–5; and one for the relatives of provincial officials who were, for the most part, of middle rank,[75] in which a quota-ratio of 1/40 was used, still liberal by prefectural standards. Except in the cases of officials from or serving in Ssu-ch'uan, Kuang-nan and, after 1171, Fu-chien, the relatives of low ranking officials, who comprised the great majority of the bureaucracy, had no entree to the special examinations. In social terms, then, the line which separated the prefectural examinations from those that offered competitive advantages lay not at the division between official and commoner but within the bureaucracy itself. The fruits of office were unequal, especially when one considers, as we now shall, the higher examinations where privilege also played a role.

The higher examinations

When a *chü-jen* arrived at the capital from his prefecture, he faced some three months of bureaucratic requirements, ceremonial occasions and, above all, two examinations. The first of these, the departmental examination, was the direct descendant of the T'ang Board of Rites examination and was often called by that name in the Sung. The second, the imperially-administered palace examination, had been created by the Sung founder T'ai-tsu. Shorter and somewhat easier than the departmental examination, it was after 1057 largely a formality, albeit one of great symbolic import, for in that year all departmental graduates were guaranteed a pass at the palace examination, thereby narrowing its role to one of placement of preselected graduates.[76] The departmental examination thus became the only competitive barrier confronting *chü-jen.*

Competition within the departmental examination varied over time and depended on two factors: the number of *chü-jen* taking it and the number of degrees being given. *Chü-jen* numbers, as we have seen, depended themselves upon the numerous qualifying examinations and the ever changing provisions for exemptions. The number of degrees to be given, by contrast, was a matter determined by the emperor or his chief ministers and they determined it using one of two methods.

During the early years of the dynasty, degree numbers were determined anew for each examination and this resulted in large fluctuations between examinations, as we have observed. Gradually this changed. In a report on the examination of 1005, reference was made to 'the unusual procedure of recommending approximately one in ten [for degrees],' but that ratio should probably be taken as a description of past results rather than as a regulation.[77] In 1034, however, a quota-ratio of 2/10 was mandated for the departmental examination.[78] Those who passed of course still had to pass the palace examination. In 1055, quotas of 400 *chin-shih* and 400 *chu-k'o* degrees were substituted for the quota ratio.[79] Thereafter, one or the other of these methods was used to determine the number of degrees to be given.[80] Degree numbers still varied; quotas were changed, sometimes even for specific examinations.[81] But on the whole, the degree numbers remained stable as did the competition in the higher examinations. The ratio of *chü-jen* to degrees was 1/9.5 in 1086–93 and 1/10 in 1109.[82] In the Southern Sung, the quota-ratio was set at 1/14 in 1127, lowered to 1/17 in 1163, then raised to 1/16 in 1175 where it remained.[83] This modest increase in competition contrasted dramatically with that in the prefectural examinations which, as we saw in Chapter 2, went from similar ratios in the Northern Sung to 1/200 or worse in the Southern Sung. Clearly, the locus of the most intense competition had moved from the capital to the prefecture.

To say that competition was worse in the prefectures than in the capital is not to say that odds of one in sixteen were good. There was ample incentive for *chü-jen* to avoid the departmental examination, if at all possible, and in fact that was possible for certain categories of candidates. We noted above that inner and upper hall students at the University could at times go directly to the palace examination and also how Ssu-ch'uan had its own departmental examination during the Southern Sung, although it should be pointed out that the Ssu-ch'uan quota-ratio, 1/14 before 1183 and 1/16 thereafter,[84] was very close to that of the regular departmental examination.

Imperial clansmen (*tsung-tzu*) were also given a special departmental examination, at least during the Southern Sung. In the course of the dynasty, the perennial question of how best to treat the multiplying Chaos, who numbered in the thousands by the end of the Northern Sung,[85] elicited different policies. According to Li Yu, writing at the end of the Northern Sung, in the early Northern Sung when most clansmen were fairly close relatives of the emperor, few were allowed into the civil service and they were limited in how far they could rise.[86] Under Shen-tsung and Hui-tsung, however, they were treated more generously. Those with a mourning relationship to the emperor (i.e., with an imperial ancestor within five generations) could either receive office through protection or take the *chin-shih* examinations.[87] Those more distantly related, who by law were supposed to live outside of the capital, had no protection privileges but could take an examination called the *liang-shih* ('measuring examination'). Candidates were tested by the Board of Rites in either the classics or law and those who passed received facilitated *chin-shih* degrees. Under Hui-tsung this was easier than the *chin-shih* examination and even those who failed it could still obtain official rank after further tutoring at the Board of Rites.[88]

During the early Southern Sung, imperial clansmen advanced both via the *liang-shih* and the *chin-shih* examinations, but when they took the latter they were treated as a special and separate group. In 1145, candidates from the imperial clan living in Lin-an were told to go to the University preliminary examination, where they were to be selected with a quota-ratio of 3/7 if they were officials or 4/7 if they were not; those outside the capital were to take the avoidance examination at the fiscal intendent's office and be selected together with the relatives of officials.[89] This special treatment extended to the departmental examination as well. According to the Sung historian, Li Hsin-ch'uan, quota-ratios of 1/7 were used for imperial clansmen in both the preliminary and departmental examinations, though the departmental ratio was changed to 1/10 during the Ch'un-hsi reign period (1174–89).[90] Thus the imperial clansmen were competing primarily, and often exclusively, among themselves.

Although we have no information about the *liang-shih* for most of the Southern Sung, there is a set of documents describing its workings in the years 1162–72.[91] It was held at about the same time as the palace examination and resembled the regular examinations closely in its curriculum. It produced forty to fifty graduates each time it was held, and they were given low military ranks. Despite their military titular offices, these graduates were called *chin-shih*, though their status was probably that of facilitated *chin-shih* like their Northern Sung predecessors.[92] We noted in Chapter 2 that there was a dramatic increase in the numbers of imperial *chin-shih* beginning from around 1190 and by 1256, 76 of the 572 *chin-shih* were imperial clansmen.[93]

Although I have found no evidence concerning this change, it might well have been caused by making the *liang-shih* graduates regular rather than facilitated *chin-shih.*

There was finally an avoidance examination for relatives of departmental examination officials (*pieh-shih* or *pieh-yüan-shih*). It had its origins in the examination of 1007 when a proctoring official, Chang Shih-sun (964—1049), discovered that some of the examinees were related to examiners and, with the emperor's support, insisted that they be examined separately.[94] For most of the Sung this examination seems to have functioned just to insure avoidance, but in the thirteenth century, when it had a quota-ratio of 1/7 (or less than half that of the departmental examination),[95] attempts were made to include other groups of *chü-jen* in it. After 1190, *chü-jen* who were officials were also examined separately,[96] and around 1230, other groups were included as well. A *Sung shih* entry from 1243 recounts what happened:

> The separate hall examination was generally intended for those scholars who were actually related to examination officials. During Shao-ting [1228—33], those from the 'eldest sons examination'[97] who had no relationships that had to be avoided were also allowed to take it. Some said that this was because of the greed of the children of power-ful officials. In early Tuan-p'ing [1234—7], [such candidates] were sent back to the Great Hall [i.e., the departmental examination] and poor scholars benefited from this. In the first year of Ch'un-yu [1241], they were again sent to the separate hall. This has caused men who should not be subject to avoidance to look forward to it and go. This has caused the scholars of the world to be split without reason and made into two trunks, [thereby] obliterating the original purpose of the separate examination. For this reason, the reform of Tuan-p'ing which made them return to the Great Hall is to be followed.[98]

The comment about the division of the world's scholars is revealing, for nothing compromised the dynasty's concern for fairness and impartiality so much as the special examinations. Because of quota differences the special examinations gave a privileged minority a competitive edge in the examinations, and in effect did create two classes or trunks of scholars.

The extent of privilege
Special examinations, as we have seen, flourished in the Southern Sung and offered those with high ranking relatives comparatively easy paths to the *chin-shih.* But how important were they? What proportion of degree holders did they account for? This question cannot be answered with any precision, for as a rule neither biographies nor examination lists specify the type of examination that people took. Nevertheless the existing records can yield a

good deal of information on this issue, especially if one reverses the question and asks after the importance of the regular examinations.

The most revealing sources for the prefectural examinations consist of three Sung *chü-jen* lists, two for prefectures and one for a county: the prefectures Su-chou in Liang-che-hsi, a rich, populous, cultured prefecture with one of the greatest cities in the empire, and Chi-chou in Chiang-nan-hsi, a prosperous prefecture located on the Kan River and one of the most prolific producers of *chin-shih* during the Sung; the county Shun-ch'ang hsien of Nan-chien chou, situated in the western mountains of Fu-chien. The lists differ in their timespans: 1126–74 for Shun-ch'ang,[99] 1148–1274 for Su-chou,[100] and 1058–1274 for Chi-chou plus 979–1052 for one of its counties.[101] But they are alike in listing only the *chü-jen* selected in the prefectural examinations.[102] By comparing these lists with the *chin-shih* lists for the same places, we can determine the numbers and percentages of *chin-shih* who had passed the prefectural examination rather than one of the special examinations. Table 15 shows the results of such a comparison, using only the Southern Sung portion of the Chi-chou list.

Table 15. *Percentages of* chin-shih *listed in* chü-jen *lists from prefectural examinations*

	Period covered	Total *chü-jen*	Total *chin-shih*	*Chin-shih* who were *chü-jen*	% of all *chin-shih*
Shun-ch'ang hsien (a)	1126–69*	85	14	10	71.4
Chi-chou (b)	1127–1279	2,798**	661	406	61.4
Su-chou (c)	1147–1259	475†	252	57	22.6

Sources: (a) MS 103/16b et seq. (b) T'ao Ch'eng, *Chiang-hsi t'ung-chih* ch. 49–51. The nineteenth century *Chi-an fu chih* by Liu I has lengthier lists of both *chin-shih* and *chü-jen*, but using them yields similar results. Reading across from the *chü-jen* column, its figures are: 3,013; 759; 466; and 58.8%. (c) Fan Ch'eng-ta, *Wu-chün chih* 28 for *chin-shih*, *Chiang-su chin-shih chih* 10/6a–13a for *chü-jen*. Lu Hsiung, *Su-chou fu chih*, 50 ch. (1379 ed.) ch. 12 has more *chin-shih* listed for the same years. Using it, the figures are: 475; 297; 58; 19.5.

*The *chü-jen* list for Shun-ch'ang actually continues on through 1174, but the *chin-shih* list stops at 1169. Thus this cutoff date.

**There are 2,872 names on the *chü-jen* list, but 67 of them were from the University entrance examination, 4 were from the refugee preliminary examination, and 3 were from the avoidance examination. None of these was included.

†Eight *chü-jen* from two undated but pre-1147 Shao-hsing (1131–62) examinations have been included. Because of textual lacunae, only 402 of the 475 *chü-jen* can be identified with certainty. The number of *chin-shih* who were prefectural *chü-jen*, therefore, is undoubtedly greater than the 57 listed, but even if all of the *chü-jen* in question had become *chin-shih*, the percentage would still have only been 51.5%.

Table 16. *Percentages of Southern Sung* chin-shih *listed in the prefectural* chü-jen *lists of Chi-shou and Su-chou*

Period	Chi-chou		Su-chou	
	Chin-shih numbers	Percentages of *chin-shih* who were prefectural *chü-jen*	*Chin-shih* numbers	Percentages of *chin-shih* who were prefectural *chü-jen*
1127–62	72	79.2	33*	9.1
1163–89	44	79.5	79	21.5
1190–1207	55	61.8	61	16.4
1208–25	88	67.0	56	19.6
1226–40	96	74.0	36	22.2
1241–64	172	54.9	32†	28.1
1265–79	130	42.0		

Sources: see Table 15.
*For 1148–62 only, for the *chü-jen* list only begins with the examination of 1148.
†For 1241–59 only, for the *chü-jen* list ends with the examination of 1259.

The variation in the percentages of *chin-shih* appearing on the prefectural lists is large, and there is reason to believe that it was actually even larger. Two of the four Shun-ch'ang *chin-shih* who are not listed as *chü-jen* received their degrees in 1127 and might well have been prefectural *chü-jen* before 1126. Excluding them would yield a percentage of 83.3. The Shun-ch'ang numbers, of course, are too small to be of much significance, but such is not the case with Chi-chou and Su-chou. As we can see in Table 16 which gives their *chin-shih*/prefectural *chü-jen* percentages over time, for much of the twelfth century Chi-chou's was comparable to that of Shun-ch'ang, though it fell dramatically in the late Southern Sung. By contrast, Su-chou's percentage was far lower than Chi-chou's but rose from the late twelfth century on.

The regional character of variations in the importance of the prefectural examinations will be discussed in the next chapter. Here we might simply point out certain sociopolitical differences which lay behind the very different experiences of Su-chou and Chi-chou. Su-chou was not simply an extremely wealthy urban center but was important politically as well, producing no fewer than twelve chief-councilors and assistant-councilors during the Sung.[103] Yet when compared with other southeastern prefectures, its *chin-shih* numbers were not especially large and, more significantly, both its Southern Sung quota of 12–13 and its candidate population — reported at

Table 17. *Prefectural examination* chü-jen *among* chin-shih *classified by patrilineage; Chi-chou and Su-chou, 1148 and 1256*

Patrilineal background	Listed as prefectural examination *chü-jen*	Not so listed
Living court or capital grade officials*	1	5
Chi-chou	(1)	(2)
Su-chou	(0)	(3)
Other officials	8	5
Chi-chou	(6)	(3)
Su-chou	(2)	(2)
Commoner (no officials listed)	13	9
Chi-chou	(13)	(8)**
Su-chou	(0)	(1)†

Sources: SYKCSL passim; T'ao Ch'eng, *Chiang-hsi t'ung-chih* ch. 49–51; *Chiang-su chin-shih chih* 10/6a–13a.

*There were no provisions in the regulations for the relatives of dead officials to take the avoidance examination. In this it differed from protection.

**Two were University students and two imperial clansmen.

†A University student.

2,000 in the thirteenth century – were unusually small.[104] What this would seem to indicate is a small, powerful, highly-placed elite whose members were able, on the whole, to take the special preliminary examinations. Robert Hartwell has argued from the Su-chou example that the power of newly established local elite families was enhanced by the limited prefectural quotas, since they 'controlled access to those slots.'[105] I would submit that the power of the Su-chou elite was most visible in its continued access to the special preliminary examinations, and that in this respect it was unusual. Chi-chou, by contrast, had more than twice as many *chin-shih*, a much larger prefectural quota,[106] and a far larger literati population.[107] Yet it produced only eight chief-councilors and assistant-councilors, and half of them were from the Northern Sung.[108]

In both prefectures relatives of high ranking officials tended to avoid the prefectural examination. Thus in Table 17, which analyses the forty-one *chin-shih* from Su-chou and Chi-chou whose names appear both in the prefectural lists and those of 1148 and 1256, most of the *chin-shih* who were related to high officials did not pass the prefectural examination, while most of the others did. Furthermore, of the nine 'commoners' who do not appear on the prefectural lists, five were University students or imperial clansmen.

Table 18. *Comparison of Sung* chin-shih *and departmental graduate totals*

Period	Departmental graduates	Chin-shih	Triannual difference	Departmental graduates per chin-shih
973–97*	1,641**	1,492	+17	0.91
998–1021	2,672	1,615	+132	0.60
1122–63	5,274	4,255	+73	0.81
1064–85	2,971	2,845	+17	0.96
1086–1100	2,682	2,679	0	1.00
1101–26	5,495	5,495***	0	1.00
1127–62	2,069	3,319†	−138	1.60
1163–89	3,126	4,066	−104	1.30
1190–1207	2,179	2,793	−102	1.28
1208–25††	1,698	2,941	−207	1.73

Sources: See Appendix 2.

*Until the palace examination was begun in 973, the departmental graduates all received degrees.

**Includes no figures for the departmental examinations held in 980, 983, 992. If one omits the *chin-shih* figures for those years, the *chin-shih* would total 779, the triannual difference would be 95, and the ratio 0.46.

***Does not include 336 *chin-shih* who were promoted directly from the University during non-examination years.

†Since no departmental examinations were held in 1128 and 1132, the *chin-shih* totals from those years have not been included. For the years 1135–62, 328 specially designated Ssu-ch'uan *chin-shih* have been included.

††1223 is the last examination for which SHY:HC 1 gives departmental examination figures.

But we should also note that seven of the eight Su-chou *chin-shih* had forefathers who were officials, compared with only twelve out of thirty-three in Chi-chou. Thus the conclusion that Chi-chou's literati population was larger but less privileged than that of Su-chou is not unreasonable.

However we explain the differences between these two prefectures, it should be clear that the special examinations were important throughout the Southern Sung. In the empire's more cultured prefectures they could account for anywhere from twenty to eighty percent of their *chin-shih*. The range is huge and makes it impossible to estimate the aggregate percentage for the empire. But we will see in the next chapter that for many prefectures in the southeast the figure was probably comparable to Su-chou's eighty percent.[109]

Fortunately the evidence on the higher examinations is more informative, for the *Sung hui-yao* provides the number of graduates for every departmental examination from 960 to 1224. When one compares them with the actual *chin-shih* figures (Table 18), an interesting pattern emerges. For the first century, or until the palace examination ceased being used to select individuals in 1057, there were many more departmental graduates than *chin-shih*. From then until the end of the Northern Sung, virtually all departmental graduates and they alone received *chin-shih*. In the Southern Sung, however, *chin-shih* substantially outnumbered the departmental graduates,[110] accounting for roughly one third of all Southern Sung *chin-shih* up to 1225.

Which examinations did that one third pass? For the departmental avoidance examination we have no quantitative information at all. Ssu-ch'uan's circuit examination may have accounted for as much as half of them (18% out of 38%) in 1127–62, but this dropped to less than a third (9% out of 32%) in 1190–1225.[111] Many others came through the University. In addition to the above-mentioned provisions exempting upper and inner hall students from the departmental examinations, an edict from 1169 states that 133 University students 'received titular office' (*shou-kuan*) in the examinations that year, or 22% of the 592 degrees conferred that year.[112] But this certainly included many who took the departmental examination and perhaps even some facilitated degree recipients as well. We also know that imperial clansmen numbered 16 (4.8%) in the examination of 1148 and 76 (13.3%) in 1256.[113] Thus Ssu-ch'uan, the University, the imperial clan and probably also the departmental avoidance graduates were well represented among the *chin-shih* who had not passed the departmental examination.

In summary, during the Southern Sung it was common for *chin-shih* to have passed at least one special examination, and they may indeed have outnumbered those who passed only the regular examinations. This might not seem very different from the 1060s when, as we saw in Chapter 3, K'ai-feng and the Directorate examinations accounted for 40–50% of all *chin-shih*. But the K'ai-feng examination was, technically at least, a regular prefectural examination. What set off the Southern Sung was the proliferation and popularity of the special examinations, for in providing numerous paths for the privileged who could thereby escape the almost impossible odds of the prefectural examinations they served to undermine and degrade the examination system so carefully developed during the early Sung.

The examinations in decline

The quest for advantage did not stop at the special examinations. For many literati the road to success lay through cheating, fraud and bribery, and these appeared in numerous, often ingenious guises. These included having someone else take the examinations for one, smuggling cribs into the examinations, copying other people's answers, bribing clerks and examining officials,[114] and, as we saw in Chapter 3, falsifying residency or family information.[115]

The use of cribs is of special interest because of its connection with books and printing. In 1112 there were complaints about students smuggling 'small basted-together volumes with minute fly's head [sized] characters' into the examinations. These books included Wang An-shih's *New Commentaries on the Three Classics,* the Lao-tzu and Chuang-tzu (Taoist books were then a part of the curriculum) and bookstores were ordered to stop printing and selling them.[116] But the prohibition had no lasting impact, for in 1223 renewed complaints described printed pocket-books with all of the examination topics, designed specifically for smuggling into the examinations, and reportedly fetching high prices among literati.[117]

As with the special examinations, the main beneficiaries of examination corruption were those with money and connections. Hung Mai recounts the story of one Shen Shu, a Hu-chou native who at the invitation of his brother-in-law Fan Yen-hui, an official in Lin-an, went in the fall of 1144 to take the University preliminary examination. Upon his arrival he discovered that he was ineligible because he was of a different lineage than Yen-hui. The Fans then arranged for him to falsely register as a refugee residing in Lin-an and thus eligible for the Lin-an refugee examination, and found an official who, for a mere twenty-five thousand cash, acted as his guarantor. Two nights before the examination, Shen was confronted in a dream by venerable spirits who warned him: 'This is not where you live. Return [home] quickly or we will kill you.' He did and with the active aid of the spirits passed both the Hu-chou and departmental examinations.[118]

However we interpret such divine intercession,[119] a scandal which erupted in 1148 over the previous year's Liang-che avoidance examination suggests that the bribery to which the Fans willingly resorted was not unusual.

> Many powerful families paid bribes and conspired to have those taking the examinations exchange answer sheets and write answers for others [or] write draft answers which would be copied on the real answer sheets. Some assumed the names of others and went to the examinations; some brought in model answers from outside and copied them out after receiving their answer sheets.[120]

Eight years later a case surfaced in which eight virtually illiterate children who were, however, from families of officials, received *chin-shih* degrees. 'Although the examinations still exist, the path of fairness [*kung-tao*] has been terminated,' protested the memorialist, who succeeded in having the degrees of the eight revoked and their places added to the upcoming departmental examination quota.[121]

Professor James T.C. Liu has observed that Sung examination abuses first became a significant problem in the late Northern Sung and only became severe in the Southern Sung.[122] The fact that the majority of complaints about abuses dates from the Southern Sung and the connection that some critics drew between huge literati numbers, competition, and corruption both support this conclusion.[123] But we must not imagine that the examinations were in shambles, for despite all of the problems and corruption, the examinations were held punctually and usually without untoward incident throughout the Southern Sung. Great care, moreover, was taken with examination regulations. One set of prefectural examination rules, which were printed in Lin-an and distributed to all prefectures in 1177, had been drawn up a few years earlier by Shih Hao (1106–94) when he had to supervise the mammoth Fu-chou (in Fu-chien) examination.

> When I was prefect of Fu-chou [in Fu-chien], I worked out several score items [of rules]. The 'evening problem' was eliminated[124] and the examination hall was well ordered. The candidates numbered twenty thousand men, [but] there was no shouting or clamour.[125]

That such careful attention was paid to the prefectural examinations even as imperial clansmen and the relatives of high officials were avoiding them whenever possible illustrates the great distance the examination system had come since the early Sung. The early emperors, we will recall, had directed their policy of 'fairness' (*kung*) at curbing the powerful and attracting the talented, especially from among southern literati. Southern Sung writers also appealed to 'fairness,' but the very different social conditions of that era gave the term a different meaning, one which emphasized the perception of fairness and not necessarily its reality. In 1156 it was decided that the ban against using cribs be enforced even among imperial clansmen, so as to 'demonstrate the utmost fairness in the world.'[126] Yet more telling was Hsü Chi-chih's earlier cited defense of the use of covered names in the examinations, namely that it enabled the 'eminent talents' of the world to 'submit to the fairness of the examinations.'[127] Thus fairness was used to pacify the masses of literati who were threatening to overwhelm the examination system, even as the unfairness of special examinations continued unabated.

PART III

6

THE GEOGRAPHY OF SUCCESS

The rise of the south

In the vast patchwork quilt of local economies and social structures that constituted Sung China, the examination system was one of the hierarchical systems upon which the empire depended. Extending into virtually every prefecture, the examinations played a vital role in promoting political stability and imperial integration. By providing a common educational curriculum and periodically assembling literati in prefectures, circuit offices (for the avoidance examinations) and the capital, they fostered a literati culture that encompassed the empire. Because the rewards of status, wealth, and the power that comes from representation in the bureaucracy benefited not only the men who passed but their families, lineages and regions too, kin and community support for promising students was common, as was local pride in the accomplishments of native scholars, examples of which abound in local histories.

The examinations could also be divisive, for since the degrees were limited in number, one group or region's gain was usually another's loss, and local pride could easily turn to resentment. This problem appeared with particular urgency during the Northern Sung when China's political and cultural center was rapidly shifting to the south.[1] This shift was closely related to a southward economic and demographic movement which began as early as the Han and culminated in the great migrations of the late T'ang and Five Dynasties, when many moved to escape the dynastic struggles in the north, and the early Southern Sung, when people from every walk of life fled the Jurchen.[2] But while this long-term change was undoubtedly the major force behind the political rise of the south, the early Sung emperors' policy of broad and impartial recruitment through the examinations provided its vehicle. Through success in the examinations, southern literati rose from obscurity and by the late eleventh century had come to dominate the civil service.[3] Thus the dynasty's flight from K'ai-feng in 1127 and its reincarnation as a southern dynasty followed and did not cause the southward shift in power.

Not surprisingly, the growing role of the south stirred up feelings of

sectional, north—south antagonism.[4] Not untypical was the following dis-
course by the Northern Sung reformer and K'ai-feng native Sung Ch'i of the
differences between the northwest and southeast, the traditional and
emerging centers of power and culture:

> In the southeast, heaven and earth are mysterious and hidden, yielding,
> soft and base; in the northwest, heaven and earth are strong and up-
> right, brave, honorable and majestic. Thus the flourishing of emperors
> and kings has always occurred in the northwest, which is the way of
> heaven, and the southeast is the way of earth. What is to be done about
> the southeast? It is said, 'Its soil is thin and its water shallow. Its living
> things are nourished, its resources are rich. Its men rob and do not con-
> sider that important. They waste food and dishonesty is produced.
> Scholars are timid and few are constant; if you press them they will
> yield.' And what of the northwest? It is said, 'Its soil is thick and its
> water cold. Its living things are few, its resources are unproductive. Its
> men are resolute and simple. What they eat is tasteless but diligence is
> produced. Scholars are extremely profound but few are clever; if you
> pressure them they will not yield.'[5]

Apart from such stereotyping, the growing prominence of southern literati
raised a fundamental question concerning examination policy: should the
locus of the examinations' fairness be the region or the individual? If one
took as a goal a fundamental regional balance within the bureaucracy, then
regional quotas were necessary, for without them those from backward
regions would be unable to compete with those from the most advanced
regions, who had far greater economic and educational resources on which to
draw. If, however, one operated solely from the principle of selecting the
most talented men, then, given regional disparities in development, regional
quotas would be both counterproductive and unfair to those from the more
advanced regions.

   The clearest statements of these opposing arguments occurred in a famous
debate in 1064 between Ssu-ma Kuang, a scion of a venerable northwestern
family, and Ou-yang Hsiu, born of a minor bureaucratic family from Chiang-
hsi. The date is significant for at that time there was considerable discussion
and activity concerning the examinations. Empire-wide prefectural quotas
had been set in 1058, adjusted for certain areas in 1060, and were to be reset
in 1066.[6] Also in 1066, the examination period was to be lengthened from
two to three years, so as to give scholars from distant prefectures more time
between examinations.[7] The debate furthermore came at the end of a half
century during which, as we shall see, the number of degree-holders from
southern China increased dramatically, thereby challenging the age-old

Table 19. Chü-jen to chin-shih ratios for selected circuits in the examinations of 1059, 1061, and 1063

	1059			1061			1063		
	CS	CJ	CS/CJ	CS	CJ	CS/CJ	CS	CJ	CS/CJ
Directorate	22	118	1/5	28	108	1/4	30	111	1/4
K'ai-feng fu	44	278	1/6	69	266	1/4	66	307	1/5
Ho-pei	5	152	1/30	–	–		1	154	1/154
Ho-tung	0	44	0	0	41	0	1	45	1/45
Ching-tung	5	157	1/31	5	150	1/30	–	–	
Shan-hsi	–	–		1	123	1/123	2	124	1/62
Tzu-chou	2	63	1/32	–	–		–	–	
Li-chou	2	26	0	–	–		0	28	0
K'uei-chou	1	28	1/28	0	32	0	–	–	
Ching-hu-nan	2	69	1/35	2	69	1/35	2	68	1/34
Ching-hu-pei	–	–		0	24	0	1	23	1/23
Kuang-nan-tung	3	97	1/32	2	84	1/42	0	77	0
Kuang-nan-hsi	0	38	0	0	63	0	0	63	0

Source: Ssu-ma Kuang, *Ssu-ma kung wen-chi* 30/2a–3b.

Note: The *chü-jen* figures include all *chü-jen* (those from the preliminary examinations and those with exemptions) who took the departmental examination. They do not include *chü-jen* selected by their prefectures who did not make the trip to the capital.

domination of bureaucracy by the north. Finally, we should note that both men spoke (or actually wrote, since the 'debate' consisted of a memorial by Ssu-ma Kuang, which was in fact written in support of another memorial that is no longer extant[8] and an answering memorial by Ou-yang Hsiu) from the authority of experience. Ou-yang had been Director of the Examinations in 1057 and Ssu-ma the Acting Associate Director in 1063.[9]

In his memorial, Ssu-ma Kuang contended that the examination system discriminated unfairly against candidates from distant and less developed regions, particularly the northwest and southwest. Lacking the educational opportunities of the capital and southeastern regions and enduring great hardships to travel to the capital, they were at a disadvantage in the departmental examination and did poorly. In support of this thesis, he gave statistics from the departmental examinations of 1059, 1061, and 1063 demonstrating the poor performance of candidates from the north and west compared with those from the capital (see Table 19). To rectify this unfair situation, he proposed establishing quotas by circuit in the departmental examination, set by a quota-ratio (he suggested one in ten) as in the qualifying examinations. Thus he would have modified the merit criterion to insure a more equitable geographical distribution of *chin-shih* degrees.[10]

Ou-yang Hsiu made several points in response.[11] First, he argued that a comparison of *chin-shih* results was misleading when considering the northwest and southeast. The former had always been strong in classical studies, so its candidates tended to excel in the *chu-k'o* examinations, while the latter was strong in literary studies and produced many *chin-shih*. Second, he disparaged the educational level of some of the distant regions such as the Kuang-nan circuits in the far south: 'These circuits rely only upon numbers in sending up [*chü-jen*]. The *chü-jen*, too, know that they lack literary skills. They merely go once to the metropolitan examination and then return to become irregular officials.'[12] Third, Ou-yang pointed out that the southeastern *chü-jen* had already been through much greater competition in the prefectural examinations than those from other areas, and so were already being discriminated against. In his view, further restrictions of southeastern candidates through geographical quotas would be extremely unfair.

Finally, Ou-yang heatedly rebutted a point raised not by Ssu-ma but by other supporters of regional quotas, that unless the northwest was treated more generously in the examinations, its scholars might rebel. He pointed out that the northwest had no monopoly on rebels, the southeast having produced such famous examples as Hsiang Yü, the rival to the Han founder Liu Pang, Hsiao Hsien in the Sui, and Huang Ch'ao and Wang Hsien-chih in the late T'ang. But his central point was that containing potential rebels was an inappropriate use of the examinations: 'The examinations were established basically to await those of sagely ability. For winning over lawless men there should be other methods which do not involve the examination hall.'[13]

This last assertion is noteworthy more for its frank statement of the issue than for its validity as a normative statement, for one of the essential functions of the examinations was clearly to maintain the support of potentially rebellious elites.[14] And however principled Ou-yang's arguments may have been, they resulted in enormous benefits for his native region, the southeast. Ssu-ma's protests and proposals went unheeded, for despite certain exceptions that we will shortly consider, the departmental examinations remained without geographical quotas, and as a result the southeast was able to dominate the examinations and bureaucracy in a manner unparalleled in Chinese history. For in subsequent dynasties, regional and, under the Mongols and Manchus, even racial quotas were used in the allocation of *chin-shih* degrees.[15]

This conclusion, while important, is vague, for the term 'southeast' covered a variety of regional economies and local cultures during the Sung. To even begin to understand the geographical dimensions of the examinations – the reasons for the success of a locality or region and the patterns of success – a much more detailed analysis is necessary. Unfortunately, few of the studies that have been made on the subject discuss regional differences or offer hypotheses to explain them. In part, this inattention has stemmed from insufficient data. The data bases used by studies thus far have ranged from a few hundred to almost fifteen hundred individuals. These are considerable numbers, but when spread over an entire dynasty or even half of it, they are insufficient to allow for very detailed analysis. Furthermore, since most of these studies have been based upon biographical collections, the possibility of geographical biases in the selection of biographies cannot be avoided or resolved.[16] Examination lists are fortunate in this regard, for they reflect a selection process which had relatively objective and ascertainable criteria. Kracke's short but excellent study of regionalism in the examinations of 1148 and 1256 therefore avoids many of the problems inherent in the other studies.[17] Yet he in turn was confronted by another problem, that of generalizing from the results of just two examinations, particularly for those regions that did poorly in those examinations, since places could and did have exceptionally good and bad years.

The data to be used in this chapter circumvent most of these problems. They consist of numerical listings of *chin-shih* degrees by prefecture and examination for all prefectures under Sung control (Chin examination results will not be considered) for all of the Sung. These data have been gathered from prefectural and provincial local histories dating from the Sung through the Ch'ing using, as a rule, the earliest extant list for each prefecture. The results of this compilation are uneven. In north China, successive waves of destructive warfare subsequent to the Northern Sung made examination lists so fragmentary as to be almost useless. There is also a question concerning the reliability of Ming and Ch'ing lists. This is discussed at length in Appendix 4 and the following conclusions are reached: the degree numbers for north China and especially for K'ai-feng are far too low; those for the southeast, especially for the two Chiang-nan circuits, are somewhat high; and those for certain peripheral regions of south China are somewhat low. Even with these reservations, however, the data for south China appear to be generally reliable.

Two factors make this body of data particularly attractive to the historian. One is its comprehensiveness and scope. Since it covers some thirty-five thousand individuals, its very size should permit a higher level of generalization about the regional distribution of degree holders and changes in that distribution than has hitherto been possible. Second is its use of the prefectural unit. Ideally the county unit should have been used, but the labor and problems associated with compiling separate lists for over eleven hundred counties made that unfeasible for this study. Nevertheless, the use of the prefecture as the basic unit, as it was in the examinations, should not only facilitate comparisons with other studies using larger units but also enable us to test hypotheses regarding the role of regions in examination success.

Geographical biases

Even though the Sung examinations never employed a system of regional quotas, they were far from blind to geographical considerations. The ideal of all candidates competing under uniform conditions was qualified in two important respects.

The first concerns the setting of prefectural quotas. The reader may have noticed that Ou-yang Hsiu's statement about the several prefectural examination competitions in the southeast is at variance with the description in Chapter 2 of how prefectural quotas were set according to uniform quota-ratios after 1009. The existence of large discrepancies in prefectural competition may be explained in part by the fact that, in the sometimes lengthy periods between the empire-wide adjustments in prefectural quotas, differences in educational development produced differences in examination competition. At the time Ou-yang was writing, it had been almost twenty years since quotas had last been set on the basis of candidate numbers and a uniform quota-ratio;[18] the 1058 setting of quotas mentioned above was in fact a halving of the existing quotas and not a recomputation using new statistics of candidate numbers. But this is at best a partial explanation, for there is evidence suggesting that there was a consistent policy of restricting the quotas of advanced prefectures and allowing more backward ones larger quotas than the legislated quota-ratio would have permitted.

The redetermination of quotas that occurred in 1045 provides perhaps the best example of such restrictions. The new prefectural quotas were to be two tenths of the number of candidates taking the examinations in 1037 or 1041, whichever was greater, but a prefecture's new quota could not be more than 50% larger than its old quota.[19] This prevented the more developed prefectures from increasing their quotas inordinately but it also meant that differences in competition remained. Later, in 1156 when quotas were set based on a quota-ratio of 1/100, 'three prefectures', probably Wen-chou, T'ai-chou and Wu-chou (all in Liang-che-tung), were told to use a ratio of 1/200.[20] Again, the apparent aim was to prevent large quota increases, for as we shall see, Liang-che-tung was, educationally, the most rapidly developing circuit in the Southern Sung. Without such quota restrictions, its success in the examinations would certainly have been more spectacular than it was.

The more lenient treatment given to the less advanced regions is evident mainly in edicts that set new quotas for specific places. Although there were such edicts for southeastern prefectures, they tended to have as a rationale the narrowness or restrictiveness of existing quotas.[21] By contrast, the edicts for the northern and southwestern prefectures evince more concern with the smallness of their quotas. Competition, or the lack of it, was not a factor. In 1020, for example, the circuits of Shan-hsi (i.e., Yung-hsing and Ch'in-feng), Ssu-ch'uan and Kuang-nan were given permission to send as *chü-jen* all qualified candidates, regardless of previous quota limitations.[22] This was rescinded in 1024 after complaints of numerous cases of forged residency,[23] but in 1026 quota increases were granted to these same regions and in 1029 additional increases were given to prefectures in Ssu-ch'uan and Shan-hsi.[24] Such edicts are not as numerous for later periods, though one can still find instances such as that of the circuit of Ching-hsi-nan (or that part of it still under Sung control) in 1126, which was allowed to use a quota-ratio of 1/20 instead of the prevailing 1/100.[25] However, the numerous complaints in the Southern Sung about people going to 'distant places and falsifying residency there where the examinations were less competitive indicate that the quota differences described by Ou-yang Hsiu continued.[26]

Secondly, at times during the Southern Sung certain regions had their own departmental examinations. In those cases, interregional competition was of course impossible, for the candidates taking them were competing only against each other for some predetermined number of degrees. We saw in Chapter 5 how in 1128 and 1132 the critical military situation necessitated holding departmental examinations at each circuit capital. Similarly, the protracted war against the Mongols during the last decades of the Sung

Table 20. *Ssu-ch'uan* chin-shih *and their representation in south China and in the empire*

Period	Ssu-ch'uan chin-shih*	Percentage of all chin-shih	Percentage of south China chin-shih**
960–97	46	2.9%	18.2%
998–1021	45	2.9%	8.9%
1022–63	333	7.8%	15.6%
1064–85	220	7.7%	12.8%
1086–1100	197	7.4%	14.6%
1101–26	495	8.5%	15.5%
Northern Sung	1,336	7.1%	14.6%
1127–62	748	17.6%	17.6%
1163–89	524	14.9%	14.9%
1190–1224	508	8.9%	8.9%
1225–56†	598	10.3%	10.3%
Southern Sung*	2,378	13.2%	13.2%

Sources: See Chaffee, 'Education and Examinations,' Appendix 2.
*Includes Ch'eng-tu fu lu, Tzu-chou lu, Li-chou lu, and K'uei-chou lu.
**Includes all of the Southern Sung territory except for those parts of Ch'in-feng lu and Ching-hsi-nan lu that remained under Sung control.
†After being invaded in 1258 by the Mongols, Ssu-ch'uan's representation in the examinations virtually ended. The Southern Sung *chin-shih* are therefore calculated for the years 1127–1258.

resulted in Huai-nan, Ching-hsi, Ching-hu-pei and Kuang-nan-hsi holding their own departmental examinations.[27] Most important was the Ssu-ch'uan departmental examination (*Ssu-ch'uan lei-sheng-shih*) which began in 1134 and continued for most, perhaps all, of the Southern Sung.[28]

What were the effects of the special departmental examinations? If we look at the examination performances of the regions in question before and after their special examinations were instituted, changes in their proportion of all *chin-shih* should tell us whether or not they benefitted from being examined separately.

Because the separate departmental examination of Ssu-ch'uan *chü-jen* began in 1128 and thus coincided with the loss of the north, Ssu-ch'uan's percentage of southern China *chin-shih* is a better measure of the examination's effects than is its percentage of all *chin-shih*, which includes the north for the Northern Sung. In Table 20, we can see that Ssu-ch'uan's percentage of south China *chin-shih* actually declined slightly lower from the Northern to Southern Sung.

It would be a mistake, however, to conclude that Ssu'ch'uan did not benefit from this special departmental examination. For despite its lack of increased success *vis à vis* the rest of south China in the Southern Sung, it probably fared better than it would otherwise have done. As in the regular departmental examination, the numbers passing the Ssu-ch'uan examination were determined by a quota-ratio. For most of the Southern Sung, the two quota-ratios were identical, but for twenty years in the twelfth century, Ssu-ch'uan's was actually more generous, 1/14 compared with 1/17 (during 1163–1175) and 1/16 (during 1175–83).[29]

This favored treatment was a result of Ssu-ch'uan's unique role in the Southern Sung. Its four circuits were distant, isolated, and vital to the defense of the empire, whose western flank it constituted. Throughout that period it functioned as a semi-autonomous territory under the rule of a Pacification Commissioner (*An-ch'a-shih*), whose authority extended to the civil service and the examinations.[30] In 1157 an attempt was made to abolish the Ssu-ch'uan departmental examination. It was thwarted by the argument that forcing the *chü-jen* to make the long trip to the capital caused great hardship for the many poor scholars of Ssu-ch'uan.[31] While undoubtedly true, this could hardly have been persuasive, for the trip to Lin-an was far easier than had been the trip to K'ai-feng and it was easier, or at least no more difficult, than the trip from Kuang-nan. However, Ssu-ch'uan's defender happened to be Yang Ch'un (1094–1166), a native of Mei-chou (Ch'eng-tu fu lu) and an 1124 *chin-shih* who had placed first in the departmental examination, who was then Acting Minister of War, and he carried the day. Clearly, those from Ssu-ch'uan felt that the examination served their interests.[32]

In the relatively backward circuits of Huai-nan, Ching-hsi, Ching-hu-pei and Kuang-nan-hsi, the separate departmental examinations had a marked effect on examination results. While the combined *chin-shih* of these circuits accounted for 1.1% of all *chin-shih* in the period 1190–1224, from 1251 to 1271, after they began their separate departmental examinations, they accounted for 2.9%.[33] This change is also reflected in the lists of 1148 and 1256, in which they account for 1.2% and 8.5%, respectively, of all *chin-shih*.[34] This was, in fact, what the officials of Kuang-nan-hsi had hoped for. Unlike the other circuits, Kuang-nan-hsi had not been involved in fighting the Mongols, and while its officials used the other circuits as precedents, their reason for requesting a special departmental examination was to improve their examination success, for 'in general, our mountains and forests are of a rustic nature [and our scholars] cannot compete with the scholars of the central region.'[35]

In conclusion, these circuit departmental examinations provided tangible benefits to the circuits involved, dramatically in the cases of Huai-nan *et alii,* more modestly for Ssu-ch'uan. Also, with the exception of Ssu-ch'uan (or at least the very successful circuits of Ch'eng-tu fu and Tzu-chou), these examinations together with the government's prefectural quota policy discussed above helped to improve the examination lot of the least successful regions.

The problem of regional units

The analysis in the sections below will employ both circuits (*lu*) and physiographic regions, based respectively upon hierarchies of administrative and economic activity, for both were consequential in the Sung examinations and neither, I would submit, is sufficient to explain the examination results.

The bureaucratic circuit (*lu*) has obvious attractions. It conforms by definition to groupings of prefectures, our primary statistical unit, and it is important statistically since certain Sung data are broken down only by circuit.[36] The avoidance examinations and the extraordinary departmental examinations of the Southern Sung were held at circuit capitals and a variety of measures intended to encourage backward regions defined those regions by circuit. However Sung circuits had very weak geopolitical identities. In contrast to the provinces of other dynasties, Sung circuits supervised prefectural administration but did not control it, for that was done directly by the capital.[37] Moreover, circuits were bypassed in the regular examinations, which were held in prefectures and at the capital.

Physiographic regions, by contrast, delineate integrated market systems bounded by topography. According to G. William Skinner, whose regionalization model we will be using with modifications,[38] small regions or subregions were the first to develop, through the growth of markets and commerce, into integrated economic systems. These eventually gave way to regional systems and finally to macroregional systems, of which he has identified nine.[39] These macroregions had two salient features. First, 'each region was characterized by the concentration of resources of all kinds — arable land, population, capital investments — in a central area and a thinning out of resources toward the periphery.'[40] These regional cores were, for the most part, 'river-valley lowlands, which almost by definition enjoyed higher levels of agricultural productivity and crucial transport advantages.'[41] Second, each macroregion was the locus of a distinctive departmental cycle:

> I am prepared to argue . . . that much of the flux of economic and social history in imperial China, urban phenomena included, falls into meaningful temporal patterns when the data are first specified by physiographic region. In a word, it seems to me that the economic

development, demographic history, and sociopolitical dynamics of each region have displayed a distinctive rhythm. These regional cycles were associated in medieval and late imperial times with the buildup of an urban system centered on a particular apex city and with its subsequent (at least partial) breakdown.[42]

The attractiveness of this regional theory for examination analysis lies in the relationships it suggests between macroregional development and examination success, and with their lack of circuit or provincial quotas, the Sung examinations are well suited to test them. Skinner himself has used Ch'ing data to show that regional cores were far more successful than peripheries, and that urban centers, particularly the higher-level cities in the economic hierarchy, were also disproportionately successful.[43] Although we will examine the Sung data for similar distributions, we will pay more attention to the proposition that the physiographic regions themselves constitute meaningful units for examination analysis so that patterns of success gain coherence by their use.

But while this approach is well suited to those regions where a high level of economic integration existed, questions arise as to its applicability to the more backward reaches of the empire, for Skinner has argued that by the late Sung macroregional integration had occurred in North China, Northwest China, the Lower Yangtze and the Southeast Coast, but not elsewhere.[44] Where the level of economic integration was low, might not the very use of macroregions or even, in such areas as western Kuang-nan and Ching-hu-pei, of regions suggest a regional unity that did not exist during the Sung? In such places, moreover, the social and economic roles of the administrative hierarchy were probably more pronounced, especially with regard to the examinations where, as we have seen, circuits from backward regions frequently received special consideration.

Thus our analysis will employ both circuits and physiographic regions. We shall use the former in empire-wide comparisons, where the need for standard, comparable units is greatest, and also in our discussion of the least successful regions. But when we examine examination patterns in the most successful parts of the empire, namely Ssu-ch'uan and the southeast, we shall use the physiographic regions.

The distribution of *chin-shih*

In Table 21 and Figures 5 and 6, the empire-wide distribution of Sung *chin-shih* is shown in two different ways. The table gives the distribution by circuit using a periodization of reign periods and combinations of reign periods. The figures present the data visually, showing the Northern and Southern Sung aggregates for prefectures and circuits.

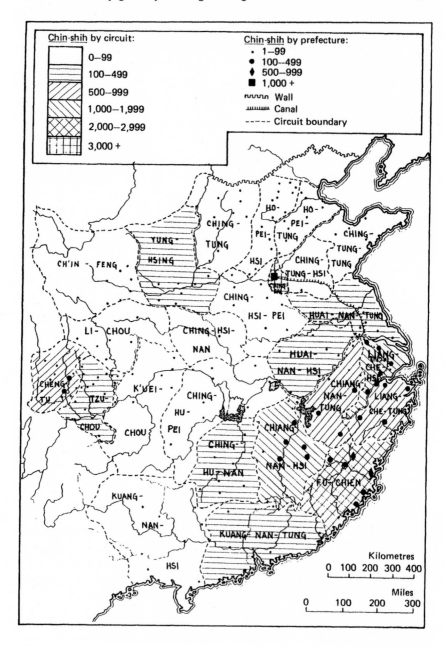

Fig. 5. Northern Sung distribution of *chin-shih* degrees.

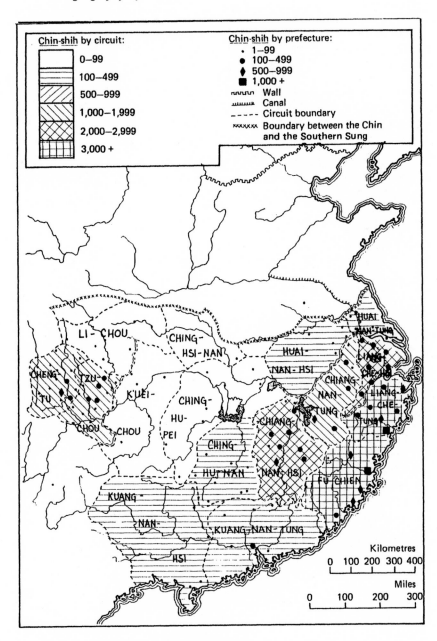

Fig. 6. Southern Sung distribution of *chin-shih* degrees.

Table 21. *Sung* chin-shih *by circuit based upon lists in local histories*

Circuit	960– 997	998– 1020	1021– 1063	1064– 1085	1086– 1100	1101– 1126
Southeast China						
Liang-che-tung	10	33	198	173	144	353
Liang-che-hsi	12	61	297	351	210	513
Chiang-nan-tung	21	34	161	124	130	388
Chiang-nan-hsi	53	92	325	218	180	357
Fu-chien	67	183	623	497	370	860
Central China						
Huai-nan-tung	6	7	52	44	21	58
Huai-nan-hsi	7	3	35	15	17	47
Ching-hu-nan	19	27	29	35	47	43
Ching-hu-pei	4	7	30	15	3	22
Ling-nan						
Kuang-nan-tung	4	8	35	20	18	39
Kuang-nan-hsi	5	6	24	9	7	20
Ssu-ch'uan						
Ch'eng-tu fu	25	24	197	128	131	283
Tsu-chou	16	12	111	87	49	172
Li-chou	5	6	22	5	10	25
K'uei-chou	0	3	3	2	7	15
North China						
Ching-chi	15	12	23	13	3	7
Ching-tung-tung	2	3	0	0	0	0
Ching-tung-hsi	7	8	12	3	3	2
Ching-hsi-nan	1	0	6	0	0	0
Ching-hsi-pei	17	11	17	18	5	5
Ho-pei-tung	21	8	7	5	3	1
Ho-pei-hsi	4	5	8	2	9	4
Northwest China						
Ho-tung	14	10	16	8	9	10
Yung-hsing	27	20	33	40	4	2
Ch'in-feng	0	1	2	0	0	0
Local History Totals	362	584	2,266	1,812	1,380	3,226
Degrees Conferred	1,587	1,615	4,255	2,845	2,679	5,831

Sources: For local histories, see Appendix 4 or Chaffee, 'Education and Examinations,' Appendix 2. For degrees conferred, see Appendix 2.

Table 21. (*cont.*)

Northern Sung	1127–1162	1163–1189	1190–1224	1225–1279	Southern Sung	Undated	Total Sung
911	587	660	1,029	1,624	3,900	47	4,858
1,444	517	497	533	655	2,202	0	3,646
858	399	240	399	700	1,738	49	2,645
1,225	422	303	525	1,386	2,636	0	3,861
2,600	743	869	1,367	1,546	4,525	19	7,144
188	45	20	20	21	106	14	308
124	14	10	17	62	103	43	270
200	55	48	96	217	416	48	664
81	8	6	7	59	80	32	193
124	50	20	37	152	259	0	383
71	57	15	19	84	175	0	246
788	479	227	127	300	1,133	91	2,012
447	316	315	334	273	1,238	19	1,704
73	15	13	29	38	95	14	182
30	19	9	18	27	73	0	103
73	0	0	0	0	0	0	73
5	0	0	0	0	0	27	32
35	0	0	0	0	0	16	51
7	0	0	0	2	2	7	16
73	1	0	0	0	1	2	76
45	1	1	0	0	2	43	90
32	1	0	0	0	1	47	80
67	0	0	0	0	0	62	129
126	0	0	7	1	8	22	156
3	0	0	1	0	1	7	11
9,630	3,729	3,253	4,565	7,147	18,694	609	28,933
18,812	4,238	3,525	5,680	9,102*	20,793*		39,605*

*Includes estimates of 500 each for the years 1253, 1265, and 1271.

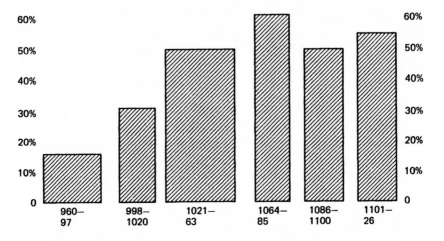

Fig. 7. Representation of south China *chin-shih** in the Northern Sung examinations.
(Bar widths vary according to the lengths of the periods, which are reign periods
or combinations of reign periods.)
*Includes the circuits of Liang-che-tung and -hsi, Chiang-nan-tung and -hsi,
Fu-chien, Huai-nan-tung and -hsi, Ching-hu-nan and -pei, Kuang-nan-tung and -hsi,
Ch'eng-tu fu, Tzu-chou, Li-chou, and K'uei-chou.

We should reiterate that there are biases in these data, the most serious
being the underrepresentation of northern China. For the Northern Sung,
records exist for only half of the *chin-shih* degrees that we know to have been
given. If, as it is argued in Appendix 4, the figures for southern China are
fairly reliable, then most of the missing degrees would be from the north,
making it far more successful than it appears either in the table or on the
maps. In one case I have tried to rectify this; the evidence of K'ai-feng's
dominance in the Northern Sung examinations is so overwhelming that, in
Figure 5, I have estimated its *chin-shih* numbers to have been in excess of
three thousand.[45]

Turning now to the table and maps, several observations can be made about
general trends in examination success. First, the north—south distribution of
chin-shih, presented graphically in Figure 7, corroborates our earlier generalization about the growing political dominance of southerners during the
Northern Sung. Not only does this accord with the assertion by Lu Yu
(1125–1209) that Jen-tsung's reign was the first in which southerners were
admitted to the bureaucracy freely and without discrimination,[46] but it also
agrees with Robert Hartwell's finding that only during the reign of Shen-tsung
(1067–85) did the south's proportion of policy-making officials equal the
south's proportion of the population, for we would expect a lag of roughly a

generation before changes in recruitment patterns were reflected at the highest levels of government.[47]

Second, the series of wars which the Southern Sung waged against the Jurchen and later the Mongols, had a measurably deleterious effect upon the examination performances of the territories involved in the fighting. Whereas the Southern Sung circuits as a whole had over twice as many *chin-shih* as they had had during the Northern Sung, the four border circuits of Huai-nan-tung, Huai-nan-hsi, Ching-hu-pei and Ching-hsi-nan did more poorly in the Southern Sung, while the only other border circuit, Li-chou lu, had the smallest percentage increase of any of the other circuits. This is hardly surprising, for not only did these wars cause disruption and southward migration, but we might also presume that they turned the attention of the local elites from education to military affairs.

Finally, and most important, so great was the range in the examination performances of the circuits of southern China that we can divide them into two groups: successful and unsuccessful. The successful circuits, each of which had over fifteen hundred *chin-shih,* were centered primarily in the southeast (Fu-chien and the Liang-che and Chiang-nan circuits) and secondarily in Ssu-ch'uan (Ch'eng-tu and Tzu-chou). So great was their domination that they accounted for 84% of all *chin-shih* in the Southern Sung, which had sixteen circuits in all.[48] The unsuccessful circuits were those in south and central China (Ching-hsi-nan and the Kuang-nan and Ching-hu circuits), those in the Ssu-ch'uan periphery (Li-chou and K'uei-chou) and the Huai-nan circuits to the north of the lower Yangtze. With the exception of Ching-hu-nan, none of these had more than four hundred *chin-shih.*

Before proceeding to separate considerations of these successful and unsuccessful regions, and then to a discussion of the factors behind success, it might be helpful to examine the geographical distribution of Sung schools. Tables 22 and 23 give the distributions of government and private schools respectively, schools whose chronological development was discussed in Chapter 4. Again, we must acknowledge geographical biases. Like the examination data, the school data for northern China are fragmentary, as are those for Ssu-ch'uan. Also, Sung local histories did not, as a rule, make note of academies, so many probably vanished without a trace, though what geographical biases resulted from this is impossible to say.[49]

In a general way these tables reflect the same dichotomy that we noticed in the examinations. The successful circuits (at least in the southeast) had prefectural schools in all prefectures, county schools in the great majority of counties, and large numbers of academies and other private schools. Although the unsuccessful circuits had prefectural schools in most prefectures, many,

Table 22. *Geographical distribution of government schools*

Circuit	Prefectures		Counties		Examination rank†	
	Pref. schools	% with schools*	County schools	% with schools*	N. Sung	S. Sung
Southeast China						
Liang-che-tung	8	100+%	38	90%	5	2
Liang-che-hsi	8	100+%	37	97%	3	4
Chiang-nan-tung	9	100%	31	82%	6	5
Chiang-nan-hsi	11	100%	57.	100+%	4	3
Fu-chien	8	100%	48	100+%	2	1
Central China						
Huai-nan-tung	11	92%	10	26%	10	11
Huai-nan-hsi	8	80%	11	33%	13	12
Ching-hu-nan	10	100%	36	92%	9	8
Ching-hu-pei	13	93%	29	52%	16	14
Ling-nan						
Kuang-nan-tung	15	100%	25	58%	13	9
Kuang-nan-hsi	23	82%	26	40%	20	10
Ssu-ch'uan						
Ch'eng-tu fu	11	69%	26	45%	7	7
Tzu-chou	13	87%	18	33%	8	6
Li-chou	8	80%	9	24%	18	13
K'uei-chou	5	36%	7	22%	23	15
North China						
Ching-chi	0	0%	3	19%	1	
Ching-tung-tung	8	89%	11	29%	22	
Ching-tung-hsi	7	70%	12	28%	21	
Ching-hsi-nan	8	89%	7	23%	25	16
Ching-hsi-pei	6	60%	10	16%	17	
Ho-pei-tung	7	37%	7	12%	15	
Ho-pei-hsi	9	47%	24	37%	19	
Northwest China						
Ho-tung	11	41%	18	22%	12	
Yung-hsing	8	44%	12	14%	11	
Ch'in-feng	9	56%	4	14%	24	
Totals	234	72%	516	44%		

Sources: See Chaffee, 'Education and Examinations,' Appendix 2.

*Percentages based on the prefectures and counties that existed ca. 1080. Later changes in both account for the percentages greater than one hundred.

†For rank ordering, undated *chin-shih* for all Northern and Northwestern circuits except for Ching-hsi-nan were added to their Northern Sung totals. Also, for reasons explained in the text the capital district of Ching-chi is ranked in the Northern Sung examinations.

Table 23. *Geographical distribution of private schools*

Circuit	Academies*			Other private schools	All private schools
	Shu-yuan	Ching-she	Acad. per prefecture		
Southeast China					
Liang-che-tung	43	3	6.6	5	51
Liang-che-hsi	20	0	2.9	6	26
Chiang-nan-tung	46	3	5.1	4	53
Chiang-nan-hsi	90	3	9.0	2	95
Fu-chien	52	15	8.4	18	85
Central China					
Huai-nan-hsi	7	0	0.7	1	8
Ching-hu-nan	36	0	3.6	0	36
Ching-hu-pei	17	0	1.2	0	17
Ling-nan					
Kuang-nan-tung	34	0	2.3	1	35
Kuang-nan-hsi	14	0	0.5	0	14
Ssu-ch'uan					
Ch'eng-tu fu	10	0	0.6	0	10
Tzu-chou	8	0	0.6	0	8
Li-chou	2	0	0.2	0	2
K'uei-chou	3	0	0.2	0	3
North China					
Ching-tung-tung	2	0	0.2	0	2
Ching-tung-hsi	3	0	0.3	2	5
Ching-hsi-pei	6	0	0.6	0	6
Ho-pei-hsi	3	0	0.2	0	3
Northwest China					
Ho-tung	1	0	0.04	0	1
Yung-hsing	4	0	0.2	0	4
Totals	401	24	1.2[†]	39	464

Sources: See Chaffee, 'Education and Examinations,' Appendix 2.

*Schools that began as *ching-she* but subsequently became *shu-yüan* have been classified as the former.

[†]Includes all Sung prefectures, not just those in the circuits for which we have records of private schools.

often most, of their counties had no county schools and they had few academies or other private schools. The magnitude of these differences, however, was far smaller than it was in the examinations in which, for example, Fu-chien had nineteen times as many *chin-shih* as its neighbor, Kuang-nan-tung. This is partly because government school numbers were limited by the number of prefectures and counties in a circuit, but it also suggests that the spread of schools during the Sung was a truly empire-wide phenomenon. Also, there were exceptions to this general correlation between examination success and school development, the most notable being Ching-hu-nan, whose school figures were indistinguishable from those of the southeastern circuits. Clearly, a high level of formal educational development did not, of itself, ensure great examination success.

The unsuccessful regions

The existence of two groups of south China regions sharply demarcated by their degree of success in the examinations raises an important question about many of the basic findings of this study. Were such developments as the great and sustained expansion of both government and private education and the manifold growth of the literati truly empire-wide in scope, or have we in effect written an educational history of just a few advanced regions? I would argue that these developments in fact extended to all regions, or at least all circuits, of southern China and probably northern China as well, though our evidence for the latter is extremely fragmentary. But this does not mean that they extended to all counties or even prefectures; patterns of examination results in the least successful circuits almost suggest islands of Confucian learning in an uncultured, often non-Han sea.

In some ways, the most compelling evidence for the widespread influence of the examinations is the fact that all circuits produced *chin-shih* and, in fact, except for Ching-hsi-nan whose *chin-shih* figures are incomplete, all of the southern circuits produced over a hundred. The *chin-shih* degree was, after all, a very considerable achievement, not only for the individuals involved but also for their localities or lineages, which had made long-term educational investments to make it possible, and for those from cultural backwaters who lacked both family connections, plentiful books (since most of the printers were located in the southeast), and first-rate teachers, the achievement was especially impressive.

Schools, too, could be found in every part of the empire. While the distribution of schools, as we noted above, reflects the successful/unsuccessful dichotomy found in the examinations, the differences are far less marked. Except for K'uei-chou and, ironically, Ch'eng-tu, all southern circuits had schools in 80% or more of their prefectures. Although the numbers of academies and county schools in the unsuccessful circuits were considerably less impressive than this, their percentages of counties with county schools ranged from 22% to a remarkable 92% and, with the exception of Huai-nan-tung, all of them had at least a few academies.

These figures are very abstract and may reflect the availability of sources more than anything else. For a concrete view of educational development in an unsuccessful circuit, we are fortunate to have an anonymous late Southern Sung local history for Shou-ch'ang chün (Ching-hu-pei), a commandary created in 1222 from Wu-ch'ang county in E-chou and located on the Yangtze downriver from modern Wuhan.[50] As a county, it had had a school as early as the Ch'ing-li reforms of 1045, which was moved twice in later years (1106 and 1174–89). When the county became a commandary, the school was enlarged and it subsequently underwent further enlargements or renovations in 1227, 1237, 1250 and 1253. In the 1250s, it had fifty rooms (*chien*) worth of buildings, a large endowment, six dormitories, a staff of twelve, a library with well over two hundred and fifty volumes (*ts'e*) of books, and it managed an examination estate.[51] Shou-ch'ang also boasted the Nan-hu Academy, which was built in 1242 with fifty rooms and had a separate endowment and a library almost as large as the commandary school's.[52] This educational activity in the thirteenth century had a dramatic effect on the literati population; the examinations which had drawn a hundred candidates in 1222 were attracting some four hundred in 1252.[53] Yet for all this activity, there were only five *chin-shih* during that thirty-year period.[54]

How representative was Shou-ch'ang chün? We cannot say with any certainty since we lack comparable information for other places, but it seems likely that it was typical of at least the most successful prefectures in the unsuccessful circuits. As a commandary, its prefectural examination quota was two, so its selection ratio went from one in fifty to one in two hundred. Comparing these figures with those that we have for other prefectures such as Lung-chou and Hsing-chou in Li-chou lu, Wen-chou (which produced no *chin-shih* at all) in K'uei-chou lu and Hua-chou in Kuang-nan-hsi as shown in Figure 2, we see that all of the figures from the unsuccessful circuits either fell within this range of competition or were more competitive. If we further compare their competitive levels and the sizes of their scholarly populations (Figure 3) with those of the successful circuits, we can see that although they lagged behind the successful circuits during the Southern Sung, their Southern Sung levels were substantially higher than those of the successful circuits during the Northern Sung, though this does not mean that their educational standards were at all comparable.

This activity was not demonstrably universal. If we look at where the more successful prefectures in the unsuccessful circuits were (in Figures 5 and 6 or, more precisely, using Appendix 3 and Figure 1), we find some most interesting distributions. In the central Yangtze success was distinctly subregionalized and restricted to core areas. Excepting the Kan River Valley which we will consider later, prefectures in the Hsiang River Valley were the most successful (though far less so than those in the Kan Basin). Then came the Yangtze corridor, including the lowlands around Tung-t'ing Lake. Finally, the Yüan and Han River Valleys were almost unrepresented.

Elsewhere we find that all prefectures with even a moderate degree of examination success were located either in core areas or along major trade routes or both. In Kuang-nan, of the seven prefectures with thirty or more *chin-shih* during the entire Sung, Ch'ao-chou, Hui-chou, Kuang-chou and Liu-chou all had important river locations, either at their mouths or at important junctures, while Shao-chou was on the extremely important trade route into the Yüan River Valley. In Huai-nan, too, 69% of the *chin-shih* for whom we have records were from prefectures located along the Yangtze or the Grand Canal.[55]

Forty-odd prefectures in southern China produced no *chin-shih* at all. Predictably, most were located in regional peripheries away from major rivers or trade routes. They were also concentrated in certain circuits: Kuang-nan-tung (8), Kuang-nan-hsi (16), Li-chou lu (3), K'uei-chou lu (3) and Ching-hsi-nan (7), although this last may reflect just poor examination records. Moreover, of these prefectures, five from Kuang-nan-hsi, two from Li-chou lu, three from K'uei-chou lu and two from Ching-hsi-nan had no schools of which we have record, suggesting a lack of educational development.[56]

It is no coincidence that all of these circuits, save Ching-hsi-nan, were in frontier regions. The Chinese presence in the south and southwest during the Sung, as in virtually every other imperial dynasty, was in part a colonizing one, with Han and non-Han peoples living side by side and not always in peace. For example, a Man rebellion in 1051 forced the government to hold special qualifying examinations for candidates from Kuang-nan-tung and -hsi in Chiang-nan-hsi and Ching-hu-nan respectively.[57] The literati in these frontier regions constituted at most a thin stratum in local society. Even the southernmost Chiang-nan-hsi prefecture of Kan-chou which produced a respectable 163 Sung *chin-shih* was described by one Southern Sung official as a poor and isolated place close to Kuang-nan and with customs similar to those of the Man.[58] Kuang-nan itself was evocatively described by Chang Tz'u-hsien (1193 *chin-shih*) in 1222:

> [There is] a single climate [of] constant heat [and] the four seasons are like summer. Grass and trees last through the depth of winter and

poisonous snakes roam about during [the time] of hibernation.
People's risk of malaria [is such that], of those who become ill, few
survive. Since their entire environment is similarly strange, the reeds
and rushes are boundless and the people who live there few. Families
with Confucian vocations are thus spread out. [As for] the numbers
of scholars with literary capabilities, in entire prefectures examination
candidates at the most number three to four hundred, and at the least,
not even a hundred.[59]

The smallness of their numbers, however, does not mean that literati or
the examinations were unimportant. We noted earlier how special provisions
allowed Kuang-nan *chü-jen* to become irregular officials (*she-kuan*).[60] This
had the dual effect of making office much more attainable and of giving the
Kuang-nan elites a significant role in local government.

Schools and the examinations may also have played an important role in
the sinicization of the non-Han inhabitants of these regions. The anthro-
pologist Barbara Ward has argued persuasively that this was the case during
the Ch'ing:

> By limiting power to officeholders, by insisting upon educational
> qualifications for office and standardizing them in such a way that all
> aspirants to administrative position had to spend many years studying
> the same texts, the system insured the rapid spread of a powerful and
> most prestigious stratum of fully sinicized persons over even the most
> barbarous of the Chinese territories . . . The fact that the examinations
> were competitive and open to all comers would have given ambitious
> men in the newly administered areas the strongest possible motivation
> to see their sons and grandsons educated in the Chinese way, whatever
> their ethnic origin.[61]

Our evidence is too meager to determine whether or not this process was
occurring during the Sung, but the little that we have is suggestive. In 1105
newly established frontier prefectures in Shan-hsi were permitted to open
'barbarian schools' (*Fan-hsüeh*), which would use foreign languages to instruct
students in the classics, statutes, Chinese language and even Buddhist writings
with the aim of 'gradually changing customs.'[62] There is also an intriguing
memorial from officials in Ch'eng-tu fu in 1171 indicating non-Han participation in the examinations on a regular basis. The memorial asked for a quota
increase because of the many candidates who were refugees from the northwest and also because '*chü-jen* from great barbarian [*ta Fan*] [families] of the
southwest are generally increasing.'[63]

Whether or not the examinations aided the process of sinicization and

however thin the stratum of literati may have been in places, our findings that
schools were widespread and that candidate numbers were increasing in even
the least successful parts of the empire indicate that the educational developments with which we have been concerned were truly empire-wide phenomena. This is of consequence to more than just this study, for it suggests
that the integration of local elites into a national elite culture was proceeding
apace. It has been argued that the lack of any sustained political disunity in
China after the Sung was due to the growing economic integration of the
country.[64] While this was undoubtedly the case, our findings here suggest that
the cultural unity created, in large part, by schools and examinations was an
important contributing factor to the political unity of late imperial China.

Patterns of success

The success of Ssu-ch'uan and southeastern China in the examinations
is hardly surprising, for economically they were among the most advanced
regions in Sung China, rivalled only by the regional system of the North
China plain which was centered on K'ai-feng. Not only were they leading
producers of such primary commodities as rice, tea, salt and timber,[65] but
they also led the empire in producing such scholarly essentials as paper, ink,
inkstones, brushes and printed books.[66] In the southeast, a high level of trade
(both internal and overseas) had created a remarkable urban network which
was most articulated in the Yangtze Delta but extended up the Yangtze into
Chiang-nan and down the coast as far as Kuang-chou (Canton).[67] Ssu-ch'uan
was somewhat less developed, but the fertility of the Red Basin made it one
of the richest, most populous and most cultured parts of the country. Noteworthy among its accomplishments were two pioneering enterprises in
printing during the tenth century: the first printing of the Buddhist *Tripitaka*
and one of the first two printings of the Confucian classics.[68]

   To say that there was a general correspondence between levels of economic development and examination success tells us nothing, however, about
the complex process of translating wealth into useful learning or about how
inevitable that process was. Such a general explanation also does not take into
account the considerable variations in wealth, commercial activity, educational development and examination success within Ssu-ch'uan and the
southeast. Thus we need a more discriminating form of analysis.

   The physiographic regions which we shall be using (see Figures 8 and 9)
correspond, on the whole, to those proposed by Skinner, but there are several
differences. First, because *chü-jen* from the four circuits that comprised Sung
Ssu-ch'uan had a separate departmental examination during the Southern
Sung, I have kept them together as a group, even though Skinner's Upper
Yangtze macroregion is slightly smaller. But since the prefectures in question

were virtually unrepresented in the examinations, the practical difference is minimal. Second, the Kan Basin will be treated as a separate region comparable in size and importance to the Lower Yangtze and the Southeast Coast, rather than as a subregion of the Central Yangtze. Third, I have followed Yoshinobu Shiba in not including territory north of the Yangtze in the Lower Yangtze macroregion.[69] Even if the southern parts of Huai-nan-tung and Huai-nan-hsi were integrated economically into the Lower Yangtze, the loss of records and the educational disruption caused by the Chin wars would make comparisons of them with the rest of the Lower Yangtze misleading. Fourth, Ming-chou (Ningpo) has been assigned to the Southeast Coast rather than the Lower Yangtze. As a center of inter-regional and international trade, its regional orientation was ambiguous. Its principal counties were on the coastal plain which circled Hang-chou Bay and formed the Yangtze Delta to the north, and it was connected by canal to Lin-an to the west.[70] But its capital was also an important port,[71] its rivers were small and its hinterland limited, all of which were characteristics of the Southeast Coast. Given the great importance of maritime commerce during the Sung, the coastal character of Ming-chou seems to have been dominant at that time.

In Figures 8 and 9, two of the physiographic regions (or macroregions) are subregionalized and two are not. I would suggest that regions can be characterized as naturally unitary or segmented. Unitary regions have either a single dominant river system or a single valley or basin forms a relatively undifferentiated core bordered by an upland periphery. The Kan Basin and, to a lesser extent, Ssu-ch'uan are examples of such regions. The latter is problematical, for the Red Basin is somewhat subregionalized by its rivers and, as we shall see, this made a difference in the examinations. But Ssu-ch'uan's dominant physiographic characteristic is that of a unitary core, the Red Basin, sharply set off from a mountainous periphery, and I have therefore classified it as unitary. Segmented regions, by contrast, are composed of discrete subregions, usually small river systems, each of which usually had its own core and periphery. The Southeast Coast is an archetypical segmented region.

Our fourth region, the Lower Yangtze, is more difficult to classify, for since much of it consists of delta-land, 'physiographic constraints on the development of socioeconomic subregions were weak,' to quote Skinner.[72] I would argue, however, that even weak constraints produced three discernible subregions: a natural subregion corresponding to the watershed of the Ch'ien-t'ang River; the Yangtze Delta, a rather unnatural subregion in that its unifying waterway was the man-made Grand Canal; and Chiang-tso, the northern section of Chiang-nan-tung which had a northwestern drainage into the Yangtze and was centered economically on the city of Chien-k'ang fu

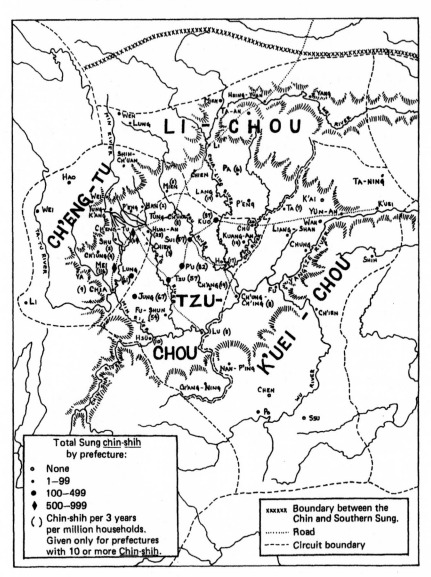

Fig. 8. Sung Ssu-ch'uan (the Upper Yangtze Region).

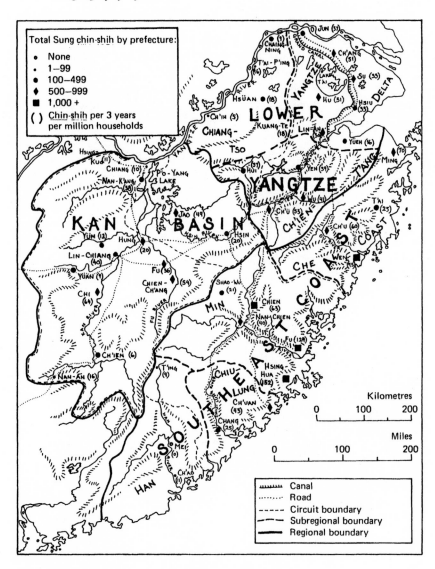

Fig. 9. Regions and subregions of southeastern China.

(Nanking). Thus even though the Lower Yangtze does not fit the criteria for segmented regions precisely, I would still classify it as such.

Turning now to the examination data for the prefectures in these regions, we can distinguish different patterns of success. In the Kan Basin, the success of the core and periphery are hard to discern because many prefectures spanned the two. But it is noteworthy that seven of the eight prefectures with over twenty *chin-shih* per three years per million households were either right around Lake P'o-yang or in the prosperous rice-growing country along the lower to middle reaches of the Kan and Fu Rivers.[73] The temporal pattern of the Kan Basin's success is also noteworthy (Figure 10), for its increases came in three phases: a steady increase to around ten percent during the first century of the Sung; a jump at the beginning of the Southern Sung which probably reflects the loss of northern China more than anything else; and a dramatic increase at the dynasty's end to twenty percent. This last increase, which was balanced by relative declines in the Lower Yangtze and the Southeast Coast, began a period educational and political vitality which continued for another two centuries, for in the first century of the Ming Kiangsi produced more *chin-shih* than any other province in China.[74]

Domination by the core is even more evident in Ssu-ch'uan where not one of the prefectures in its periphery (i.e., outside the Red Basin) received more than nine *chin-shih* degrees during the entire Sung, compared with the vast majority of core prefectures that did. One can also observe that the most successful prefectures were concentrated in the western part of the Red Basin, which for centuries had been the economic and cultural center of Ssu-ch'uan.

In the Lower Yangtze and the Southeast Coast, the patterns were different. Most of the prefectures were extremely successful, but the significant

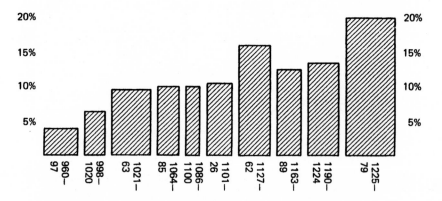

Fig. 10. Examination record of the Kan Basin: percentages of all *chin-shih*.

Table 24. *Distribution of prefectures in the Lower Yangtze and Southeast Coast by their three-year averages of* chin-shih *per million households*

Region/subregion	0–19	20–39	40+
Lower Yangtze			
Chiang-tso	5		
Yangtze Delta	1	5	1
Ch'ien-t'ang		2	2
Regional total	6	7	3
Southeast Coast			
Che Coast		1	3
Min		1	4
Chiu-ling		1	1
Han	3		
Regional total	3	3	8

Sources: Appendix 3; Chao Hui-jen, 'Sung-shih ti-li chih hu-k'ou piao,' pp. 19–30 for prefectural populations ca. 1102.

variations in the degree of success tended to divide along subregional lines and not according to cores and peripheries. This last point must be qualified, for in the Min subregion, Fu-chou and Hsing-hua chün were much more successful than the still very successful inland prefectures. Also, so small are the other coastal subregions that only a county-level analysis could reveal the presence or absence of core/periphery distinctions. In the Lower Yangtze, however, the peripheries (southern Chiang-tso and all of Ch'ien-t'ang) did as well if not better than the core area.

As to subregional differences, we can see from Table 24 that the two subregions with examination levels dramatically different from the others were Han and Chiang-tso. In view of the fact that the former was sparsely populated and the latter was rather poor agriculturally,[75] and neither was centrally located within its region, it may be that they were only minimally integrated into their regions. If we disregard them, we find a high degree of consistency in levels of success within each region; 64% of the Lower Yangtze prefectures had between 20 and 39 *chin-shih* per three years per million households, while 73% of the Southeast Coast prefectures had over 40.

In terms of this measure of *chin-shih* per examination controlled for population, we find significant variations at both the subregional and regional

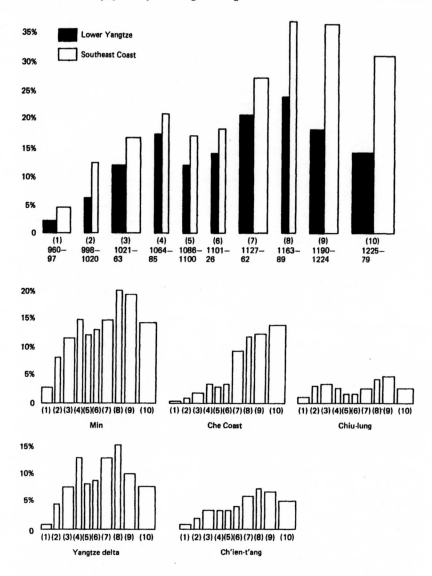

Fig. 11. Examination successes of the Lower Yangtze, the Southeast Coast, and their principal subregions.

levels. Of course this is just one of several possible measures and it is also static, a three-century average. Figure 11 compares their examination records over time and reveals striking similarities as well as differences. The greatest similarity lies in the parallel shifts in the examination fortunes of the two regions: rapid growth in degree numbers for the first century of the Sung, a drop in the late eleventh century followed by increases culminating in a peak in the late twelfth century, and finally a long decline in the thirteenth century. This pattern is also evident in each region's dominant subregion (Min and the Yangtze Delta) and, to a lesser extent, in Chiu-ling and Ch'ien-t'ang. But the differences are also striking. Not only did the Southeast Coast's fourteen prefectures consistently outproduce the Lower Yangtze's sixteen, but the gap between them widened greatly during the last century of the Sung. Likewise, Min's late Sung drop was later and more moderate than that of the Yangtze Delta. Most remarkable, however, is the record of the Che Coast. Only minimally represented in the Northern Sung examinations, the subregion's proportion of *chin-shih* tripled in the early Southern Sung and continued growing thereafter.

Of the many questions raised by these findings, we shall concentrate on two. First, how did the initial examination successes of both the Lower Yangtze and the Southeast Coast occur, coming as they did from a history of almost no representation in the imperial bureaucracy? Second, how can one account for the extraordinary success of the Che Coast in the Southern Sung?

Although the examinations in the early Northern Sung attracted successful candidates from all parts of the south, a few prefectures produced far more than their share of *chin-shih*. For the first century of the Sung (960–1063), Chien-chou in Fu-chien led all other southern prefectures with 282 *chin-shih*, followed by its Fu-chien neighbors Ch'üan-chou (194), Hsing-hua chün (152), and Fu-chou (142). The other six of the top ten were Ch'ang-chou (108), Su-chou (75), and Ch'ü-chou (73) in the Lower Yangtze, Chi-chou (115) in the Kan Basin, and Ch'eng-tu fu (121) and Mei-chou (88) in Ssu-ch'uan.[76]

Fu-chien's record is especially remarkable, for during the T'ang it had been a backward frontier region and played little if any role in imperial affairs.[77] But during the late T'ang and then as the kingdom of Min (879–978), it wad benefitted from sustained immigration, become an important agricultural region, and, thanks to Ch'üan-chou, emerged as a major center of overseas trade.[78] Hugh Clark has argued that the autonomy which accompanied the T'ang-Sung 'interregnum' allowed Ch'üan-chou to develop unhindered as a port and provided its local elite with the opportunity to serve in government and skim off commercial profits, an activity which had previously been the prerogative of non-native officials. Thus the Ch'üan-chou elite was well prepared to flourish in the Sung.[79] This is persuasive, and I would amend the argument only to say that the extremely early success of Ch'üan-chou in the examinations (they began producing *chin-shih* within a year of joining the Sung) betokened not merely a tradition of government service but also an unusual commitment to classical education during the Min period, a widespread willingness to assume literati lifestyles and values.[80] One Yüan writer ascribed to the Ch'üan-chou elite just such a pioneering role:

> The esteem with which the *chin-shih* degree is held by men of Min began with the men of Ch'üan. From this [beginning] literary creations overflowed and rippled outwards until by the end of the Sung, the Confucian air [i.e., customs] of Min were unexcelled in the southeast.[81]

Although we lack the space to consider them individually, it seems likely most of the prefectures which early excelled in the examinations shared these characteristics of economic prosperity, a history of official service in the southern kingdoms as well as, in cases, the T'ang, and an early commitment to education. Most were in regional cores and those from Ssu-ch'uan and the Yangtze Delta had venerable traditions of learning. Most also gained enormously by their precocity, for these were precisely the places most heavily represented in the professional elite described by Robert Hartwell, that group of lineages which dominated the eleventh century bureaucracy.[82] Thus until later years of the Northern Sung, these prefectures were well and powerfully represented in K'ai-feng.

It was in this context of longstanding examination success by the neighboring subregions of Min and the Yangtze Delta that the remarkable rise of the Che Coast occurred. Undoubtedly the Che Coast elites, like local elites elsewhere, benefited from the increased opportunities for advancement that resulted from the disintegration of the professional elite. They surely also benefited from the booming economy of the Southeast Coast, for its prosperity was more coastal in locus during the Southern Sung, aided by the continuing commercial ascendancy of Ch'üan-chou[83] and the supremacy of the Southern Sung navy which improved the security of shipping conditions.[84] In 1227 Hu Chü, then prefect of Ming-chou, was to write that:

> This prefecture is in an out-of-the-way place on the seacoast and completely depends on seaships that stop and anchor here. Civil authorities depend on the profits from taxes returned and residents have an abundance from trade.[85]

Thirty-three years later, in 1260, another prefect financed much of a rebuilding project for the Ming-chou prefectural school with proceeds from a

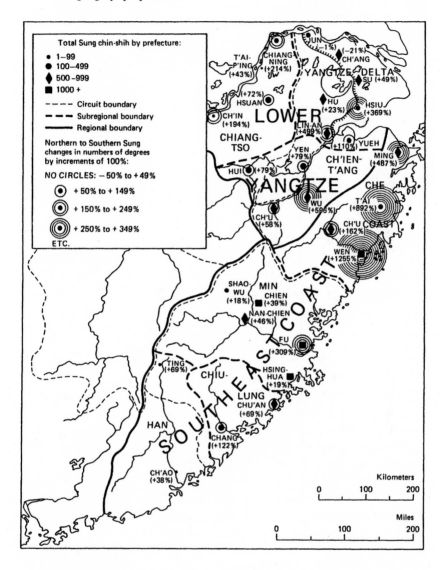

Fig. 12. Northern to Southern Sung changes in the examination success of Southeastern prefectures.

tax on junks.[86] The most persuasive evidence of coastal prosperity in the Southern Sung, however, comes from the examinations themselves, for as we can see in Figure 12, most of the prefectures in the Lower Yangtze and the Southeast Coast whose *chin-shih* numbers increased by 150% or more were situated on the coast and usually had an important port. In fact, the seven coastal prefectures of the Southeast Coast alone had a cumulative increase of 239% and accounted for 28% of Southern Sung *chin-shih*. This compares with 23% of Ming *chin-shih* and 16% of Ch'ing *chin-shih* who came from the entire provinces of Chekiang and Fukien.[87]

But coastal prosperity alone cannot explain the Che Coast's Southern Sung success, which overshadowed that of other coastal prefectures and included Ch'u-chou, a non-coastal prefecture. Much of the credit must be given to the region's extraordinary educational culture that became noteworthy in the mid-Northern Sung and flourished through the Southern Sung. In the thirteenth century Wang Ying-lin began his discussion of the cultural history of Ming-chou with the Ch'ing-li period (1041–8), 'since which time all of our elders have been pure and cultivated.'[88] It was then that the prefecture's first famous teachers, the 'Five Masters of Ch'ing-li' became active[89] and it was also around this time that we first find references to local officials promoting education at the county level.[90] By 1090 a Ming-chou writer was describing an atmosphere in which literati flourished and 'good people consider not educating their sons to be shameful.'[91]

Although we lack comparable information for the other Che Coast prefectures, it seems likely that they underwent the same kind of educational development, for in the Southern Sung they shared not only great success in the examinations but also a remarkable intellectual vitality. In the 1160s four students from Ming-chou – Yang Chien (1140–1226), Yüan Hsieh (1144–1224), Shu Lin (1136–99) and Shen Huan (1139–91) – studied with Lu Chiu-yüan's brother, Chiu-ling (1131–80), at the University in Lin-an. They became leading proponents of Chiu-yüan's 'school of mind' and through their teaching at academies which they founded they made Ming-chou one of the main centers of that school.[92] Even more concentrated geographically were the utilitarian or pragmatist thinkers led by Yeh Shih (1150–1223) from Wen-chou and Ch'en Liang (1143–94) from Wu-chou.[93] Indeed, so many of this group came from the Wen-chou county of Yung-chia that they came to be known as the Yung-chia school. Finally, Chang Chia-chü has tabulated the geographical origins of those with biographies in the Neo-Confucian (*Tao-hsüeh*) and Confucian (*Ju-lin*) sections of the *Sung shih*. In the Northern Sung, seven out of forty-four came from the modern provinces of Chekiang and Fukien; in the Southern Sung, it was twenty-five out of forty-five.[94] Inconclusive as these figures are, since much of Chekiang is in the Lower

Yangtze region, they still reflect an intellectual vitality that was certainly
a fundamental cause of its great success in the Southern Sung examinations.

There is other evidence as well. The Che Coast was home to some 30
academies, or 7.5 per prefecture, and while this was excelled by Min's 56
academies (11.2 per prefecture), it easily surpassed the 19 prefectures of the
Yangtze Delta (2.7 per prefecture). Even more dramatic are the comparative
reports of prefectural examination candidate numbers. While Min again led
with figures of ten thousand in Chien-chou and twenty thousand in Fu-
chou,[95] the eight thousand reported in both T'ai-chou and Wen-chou[96] were
far greater than the one to three thousand reported in Jun-chou, Su-chou and
Hui-chou of the Yangtze Delta.[97] In a more impressionistic vein, contemporary discussions of local culture also suggest that learning or an 'academic
strategy' for success had a broader appeal in Min and the Che Coast than it
did in the Yangtze Delta. Ch'en Hsiang (1017--1080), an eleventh century
prefect of Hang-chou (Lin-an), blamed the poor examination record of that
prefecture on the influence of coastal trade and the desire for profit:

> How could it not be that the people living on the seacoast propagate
> the teachings of sages rarely, practice frivolous customs, follow profit
> and select the inferior? Therefore, although they have excellent youths,
> some of them are lost to the professions of artisans, merchants, Bud-
> dhists and Taoists. They have not known that if the way of Confucian
> teaching is honored, then the art of humanheartedness and righteous-
> ness will triumph.[98]

By contrast, Tseng Feng in 1184 described his native Fu-chien as a place
where competition drove men to succeed both as literati and in more humble
occupations:

> Everywhere these days there are people leaving agriculture to become
> literati, Taoists, Buddhists or professional entertainers; but those from
> Fu-chien are the most numerous. The land of Fu-chien is cramped, and
> inadequate to feed and clothe them, so they scatter to all the four
> quarters.[99] For this reason wherever studying goes on, there Fukienese
> literati will be found. Wherever there are Buddhist or Taoist halls there
> will be Fukienese Taoists and Buddhists. Wherever there are markets
> there will be Fukienese professional entertainers.[100]

As the Che Coast prefectures became increasingly successful in the
Southern Sung examinations, a change occurred which had important ramifications both for their future success and for their elite societies: the proportion of their *chin-shih* who had taken the prefectural examination
shrank. Figure 13 plots the ratios over time of *chin-shih* per examination to

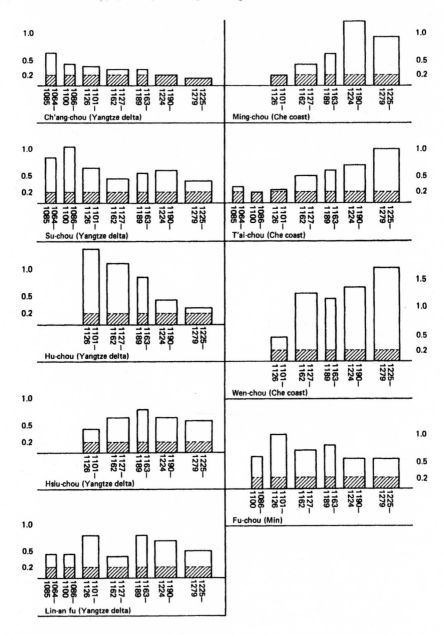

Fig. 13. Ratios of the average number of *chin-shih* per examination to the prefectural *chü-jen* quota in various prefectures of the Lower Yangtze and the Southeast Coast. (Shaded area = *chin-shih* who passed the prefectural examination.)

prefectural quota for a number of southeastern prefectures. In the extant Sung *chü-jen* lists the percentages of prefectural examination *chü-jen* who became *chin-shih* are all within the range of 13–20%.[101] Thus it seems reasonable to assume that *chin-shih* in excess of 20% of the quota (or 0.2 in the graphs) had passed a special preliminary examination. In all three Che Coast prefectures the ratio went from at or near the 0.2 level in the late Northern Sung to in excess of 1.0, meaning that the majority of *chin-shih* had passed the special examinations. Many of these were literati discouraged by the extreme competition in the prefectural examinations who took and passed the University entrance examination in Lin-an. Chu Hsi, in fact, wrote of that examination:

> Today most of those who extol the mixed entrance examination are men from Wen, Fu [in Fu-chien], Ch'u, and Wu, and not from other prefectures. It is not that only the men from these prefectures fiercely contend while all men from other prefectures modestly retire, but rather that the circumstances [i.e., prefectural competition] drive them to it.[102]

Apart from these University *chin-shih*, however, the others must have been imperial clansmen or those who through family or personal connections were able to take the avoidance examination or gain privileged entrance to the University.

This is a classic case of success spawning success, for the more officials the Che Coast produced, the more high officials there would be with recruitment privileges for their kin. Thus use of the special examinations must be added to the causes of the Che Coast's success. At the same time their use must have contributed to a widening social gap between the thousands who battled very long odds in the prefectural examinations and those who took the special examinations as a matter of course.

Turning to the other subregions represented in Figure 13, the Yangtze Delta prefectures all indicate significant access to special examinations in the Northern Sung, which then held roughly steady (Hsiu-chou, Lin-an fu) or declined (Ch'ang-chou, Su-chou, Hu-chou) in the Southern Sung. This is generally consistent with our characterization of Su-chou in Chapter 5 as having a relatively small literati population but a powerful elite with continued if declining access to the special examinations. It also suggests that the social lines between literati and wealthy but non-literati families were more closely drawn in the Yangtze Delta than on the Southeast Coast, perhaps because of the continuing influence of the descendants of the Northern Sung professional elite.

In the Min example of Fu-chou, another center of the professional elite, a different pattern appears. Thanks in part to two Southern Sung quota increases that tripled its prefectural quota to ninety, by far the largest in the empire, recourse to the special examinations declined from a late Northern Sung peak of 1.0 to 0.6. But that was still high compared to the Yangtze Delta, suggesting that even in the thirteenth century as many as two thirds of its triennial average of fifty-plus *chin-shih* had passed a special preliminary examination. This, however, is what one would expect from a prefecture whose bureaucratic position was among the most eminent in the Northern Sung and yet which also boasted the largest and most varied literati population in the Southern Sung, for in this it differed both from the Che Coast and Yangtze Delta prefectures.

From the above analysis, it should be clear that examination success was patterned both regionally and subregionally, and also that no one variable is sufficient to explain those patterns. Economic development, the particularities of local elite history, educational traditions, and the special examinations were all critical factors, and each had its own geographical dimensions. Thus while the profits of maritime commerce probably aided all coastal prefectures in the examinations, the differing social structures and educational traditions of the Southeast Coast together with the early development of Fu-chien and the Yangtze Delta all helped to shape the unique examination histories of each of the southeastern subregions.

But most interesting is the revelation of the degree to which certain regions were able to dominate the examinations, given the minimal constraints the Sung placed upon them. The academic strategy of wealth, education, and special examinations worked, and it is little wonder that subsequent dynasties governing from the north attempted to curb the southeasterners who had perfected it.

7

THROUGH THE THORNY GATES:
THE CULTURE OF EXAMINATIONS

The terminology of testing

One of the most intriguing features of the Sung examination system is
the colorful vocabulary which was frequently used in place of the drier
institutional terms. At times it emphasized ancient precedents and the
imperial role in selection. The examinations themselves were often called the
'great comparison' (*ta-pi*), a reputedly Chou dynasty term for the triennial
census when districts would select local worthies to be sent to the court.[1]
Similarly, 'tribute halls' (*kung-yüan*) referred to the halls where candidates sat
for the examinations and 'district tribute' (*hsiang-kung*) or 'tribute scholars'
(*kung-shih*) to the 'selected men' (*chü-jen*) chosen in them. At other times ↗ *kang*
popular terminology emphasized the glory of success: the *chuang-yüan* ('first *nguyen*
in appearance'), the highest graduate of the palace examination, was sometimes called the 'great eminence' (*ta-k'uei*) or the 'dragon's head' (*lung-shou*),
and the tablet (*p'ang*) on which the graduates' names were listed was also
known as the 'cassia register' (*kuei-chi*). Yet other terms emphasized the
difficulty of passing the examinations, as when the examination hall was
called the 'thorny gate' (*chi-wei*).

These examples of linguistic inventiveness, which could easily be multiplied, are evidence of the cultural importance of the examinations in Sung
elite society. As a central factor in the lives of many, perhaps most upper
class men, the examinations became a preoccupation and came to influence
the ways in which people acted and thought. Of course that influence both
predated and postdated the Sung, but it was during the Sung that two critical
developments occurred. First were the unmistakable beginnings of a public
examination culture, embedded of course in the prevailing elite culture but
with its own ceremonies, symbols, buildings, and support organizations.
These were not confined to the capital as they had been previously, but
were spread throughout the empire, most visibly in the successful regions
of the south. Secondly, more than ever before the examination endeavor,
with all of its uncertainties and attendant insecurities, engaged the attention

of writers and story-tellers, thus enabling us to chart at least some of the relationships between the examinations and elite culture. It is with these two largely neglected topics that this chapter is concerned.

The spread of ceremony

The examinations at the capital had always been replete with cere- mony. Indeed, when Sui Wen-ti created the examination system in 587 A.D., he placed it under the Board of Rites (*Li-pu*) rather than that of Personnel, thus indicating that its ritual functions were to be considered central. From the candidates' presentation of documents upon their arrival at the capital through the departmental examination, the listing of its results, the palace examination, the hanging of the final placement list, congratulatory feasts, and an imperial audience, one occasion followed another. By their con- clusion the successful commoner had made the transition from commoner to official and had received, however fleetingly, the attention of the Son of Heaven. In the words of a twelfth century description,

> He entered the Bureau of Great Officials and stood at the foot of the court with several hundred of his fellow students. They were all wearing white robes and occupied the western side [of the court]. The emperor sat above. One by one the clerk called every name, and each was con- ducted to the east side . . . [Kung] P'i-hsien followed the calling [of his name] and went to the east.[2]

While elaborate ceremonies at the capital were well developed as early as the T'ang,[3] there are almost no accounts of local examination ceremonies from the Northern Sung or before. The one exception was the 'district wine drinking ceremony' (*hsiang yin-chiu li*), a reputedly Chou dynasty ritual in which men of a district (*hsiang*) gathered to drink, eat, and listen to music, all with the utmost gravity.[4] According to later commentators, there were several variants of this ceremony,[5] but the T'ang adopted one which was associated with the selection of local worthies at the time of the 'great com- parison' (see above) for use when prefectures submitted their annual tribute of goods and scholars: 'On the day that the tribute should be sent, perform a district drinking ceremony and sacrifice sheep so that the [sending of] official goods may be complete.'[6]

For a brief period during the Sung, the district drinking ceremony served as an integral part of the examination system. In 1143, with a humiliating peace with the Jurchen just concluded and the government eager to secure the support of the southern elites, all examination candidates were required either to have attended a government school for half a year or to have partici- pated in two district wine drinking ceremonies.[7] Thirteen years later, in

1156, the rule was repealed, perhaps because of the difficulty.of making the ceremony universal.[8]

In Ming-chou and possibly elsewhere, however, the ceremony had a much longer history. According to a late Southern Sung account, during the Northern Sung it had been an annual affair held during the new year period at which thé prefect led the educated elite (*shih-ta-fu*), arranged by order of age, in presenting food offerings to the Former Sages and Teachers (*hsien-sheng hsien-shih*).[9] Halted when the prefectural school was destroyed in the fighting of the late 1120s, the ceremony was revived in 1137, received 106 *mou* of fields to provide for expenses in 1140, and in 1143 served as the model and inspiration for the edict of 1143 mentioned above.[10] Thereafter a pattern developed of the ceremony falling into disuse only to be revived by prefects with help from members of the elite. Of the known revivals in 1165–73, 1214, 1227, and 1246, the last two were noteworthy for having involved in excess of fifteen hundred and three thousand participants respectively.[11]

Ming-chou cannot be considered typical, for with its outstanding success in the examinations (as we saw in Chapter 6) and its vibrant elite culture, it was more leader than follower in cultural developments.[12] Still its example is instructive both in illustrating the Sung trend towards public ritual and in suggesting the important role played by the government schools in that trend. Indeed, the schools with their ancient and thoroughly Confucian goal of 'spreading culture' (*chiao-hua*) to a great extent provided the context in which the examination culture developed. But as the most visible symbols of literati life, they had a problematical relationship to the examinations, which demanded a different role of them: preparing students to pass the examinations. Particularly after the Three Halls experiment under the emperor Hui-tsung, when schools and examinations were merged, the government schools tended to be viewed as a preparatory step for the examinations. (The logical end of this tendency was reached during the Ming when they became pure appendages of the examinations, places for the support of lower degree holders.) But the debate over the proper role of the schools continued, with Neo-Confucians especially arguing that acculturation and the teaching of the *tao* were their proper roles. It is in this light that the Ming-chou drinking ceremony should be viewed, for despite the exemplary role that it played in the examination regulations of 1143, its stated purpose was 'to make flourish the practices of the literati and the spirit of the people.'[13]

Other Southern Sung ceremonies, however, focused specifically upon the examinations. The most intriguing, though unusual, again was found in Ming-chou as well as in Ssu-ch'uan in the late Southern Sung and involved the announcement of prefectural examination graduates.[14] On the appointed day, the candidates and others would gather outside the examination hall and an official would come down to uncover the names. When the first-place name was uncovered, that individual would be led into the hall where his name, residence, and the names of his father, grandfather and great-grandfather were inscribed on a green, wooden, gold-flowered placard (*chin-hua p'ang-tzu*) about twenty-one by eight inches in size, which was then given to him.[15] Leaving the hall, he would present the placard to his followers, who could then go out with bells and announce the news. This signified the official announcement of the examination results.

In the Chiang-hsi prefecture of Chi-chou there was a 'hopeful gathering' (*ch'i-chi*) at which *chü-jen* congregated after the announcement of the prefectural examination results in celebration and expectation of the departmental examination. The eminent Chou Pi-ta, a native of Chi-chou, wrote of it in 1198 with delight, for an unprecedented 50 *chü-jen* had attended it that year:

> Foremost [in the process] of selecting scholars in villages and elevating their names to the storehouse of Heaven is the ceremony of the gathering of hope. Lu-ling [Chi-chou's metropolitan county] is called a scholarly district, so this ceremony has greatly flourished, but this year it was especially flourishing.[16]

Unfortunately Chou does not describe the ceremony, except to say that poems written by the guests had been collected. It seems likely that it was, in fact, a local variant of the most famous and widespread of local examination ceremonies, the congratulatory banquet for successful *chü-jen* called the Feast of the Barking Deer (*Lu-ming yen*).[17] This was attended by local and retired officials, past *chü-jen,* and new *chü-jen* from both the prefectural and the special qualifying examinations, which made it a large affair in the more successful prefectures. It featured the presentation of gifts to the new *chü-jen,* most importantly stipends for the trip to the capital but in at least one place also including quantities of writing brushes, rolls of paper, and bottles of wine.[18]

Hung Mai, in his twelfth century collection of marvellous tales, the *I-chien chih,* tells of a literatus from the very academic prefecture of Fu-chou in Fu-chien, who dreamed one night of arriving in a great hall for a group audience, and in the hall there was a tablet which read: 'When rank and office are first approached, court etiquette is still unfamiliar.' Ch'en Mao-lin, the literatus, awoke convinced that this dream of an imperial audience, as he interpreted it, foretold not only his passing the examinations, but that he would place first as well, and he indeed placed first in the 1147 prefectural examination. Come the Barking Deer Feast, at which the *chü-jen* were to have an audience with the prefect in the Hall of Great Completion, Ch'en challenged the established precedent by which they were supposed to line up according to age, saying, 'I was the first selected and I should lead all of the scholars.' No one argued and he led, but at the ceremony's end when the incense was burned and all were supposed to bow twice, the inexperienced Ch'en mistakenly bowed thrice. Those who knew of his dream laughed and said that its meaning was now clear. Ch'en was disconcerted, also doubting his interpretation of it, and in the end did not receive a *chin-shih* degree.[19]

Brief as this vignette is, it nevertheless suggests the importance of public ritual in the lives of examination candidates. Examination dreams, as we shall see, were thought to work in many different ways. In this case the dream pointed to Ch'en's tendency to behave improperly, not only in his bowing but more importantly in his discordant insistence that he be first.

The support of *chü-jen*

The rewarding of stipends, which could be substantial, raises the question of how examination life was financed. It was expensive and while some literati managed by attending government schools which provided room and board, or by relying on the beneficence of a rich patron, the primary source of support was usually the individual's family. Hung Mai tells of one mother who responded to her son's request to try for the examinations by saying, 'You seem simple and unlettered, and students have expenses for travelling. You may not [attempt them].'[20] In another story, we learn of a young man's feelings of guilt because he was preparing for the examinations in leisure while his family was suffering from extreme poverty.[21]

While the costs of study were long-term and substantial, the examinations themselves exacted the greatest financial burdens. The candidate first had to make his way to the prefectural capital and if he succeeded there, he faced the much longer and more difficult trip to the imperial capital in K'ai-feng or Lin-an. The prefectural examinations were usually held during the eighth month, the departmental examination in the second month of the following year, the palace examination in the third month, and the final results in the fourth month. Thus successful passage through a cycle of examinations virtually took a year, if one includes the journey home, and a great deal of travel.[22] That travel was expensive and could be harrowing; we shall see later how it drove some *chü-jen* to resort to unusual stratagems. But because of those expenses, both lineages and localities began during the Sung to make formal provisions for their members.

The lineage provisions for the examinations were actually a part of a broader revolution in kinship organization which had its origins in the Northern Sung. In 1050, the statesman and reformer Fan Chung-yen (989–1052) donated some 3,000 *mou* of land to his patrilineage in Su-chou. This land, which was

officially registered and corporately owned by the lineage, was organized
into a 'charitable estate' (*i-chuang*) with the purpose of providing financial aid
to lineage members, especially for the great expenses of weddings and
funerals.[23] Provisions for travel stipends to lineage *chü-jen* were added in
1073, increased in 1196, and in the late thirteenth century a lineage school
(*i-hsüeh*) was established as well.[24] The Fan example was influential.
References to charitable estates from the late Northern and Southern Sung
are numerous for southeastern China and can be found elsewhere as well.
Still, it seems likely that they remained the exception rather than the rule,
even among the elite lineages of the southeast,[25] and moreover, even those
that cited the Fan example rarely if ever seem to have adopted a comparatively complex lineage structure.

While examination support was not an initial motivation behind the
charitable estates, problems posed by the Sung recruitment system contributed to their spread. Elite families correctly perceived that the task of
maintaining their positions over generations had been exacerbated by the
dynasty's uncommonly heavy reliance on examinations and by the spread
of education, which made the examinations more competitive. While some
advocated a return to a system of primogeniture as a way of maintaining the
position of the family or lineage,[26] the cornerstone of lineages' success
strategies increasingly became the charitable estate.

Ch'en Te-kao, an early thirteenth century literatus from Tung-yang county
in Wu-chou (Liang-che-tung), was exemplary in this regard. When the death
of his father required that he quit his study for the examinations and take up
his family responsibilities, Te-kao stated that because he could not fulfill his
father's wish that he pass the examinations, he would act to nourish his
lineage by establishing a charitable estate modelled upon that of the Fans.
The estate, which had 1,000 *mou* of land and a lineage school, was praised
by his former teacher, the famous poet Lu Yu (1125–1210), who wrote:

> The kinship system should be like this: if you consider the hearts of
> your ancestors, you will love their sons and grandsons and want them
> to be given sufficient clothing and food. When they marry, you will
> want them to become scholars and not want them to drift as artisans
> and merchants, to descend to become runners, or to leave and become
> Buddhist or Taoist monks.[27]

While Lu was intent upon showing how one's responsibility to distant
relatives was based upon filiality, obviously a lineage which encouraged its
men to 'become scholars' and prepare for the examinations would have an
easier time producing officials and maintaining its high status than would
an individual family. And as lineages came to cast their nets widely, so too

did whole localities, or at least the elites within them. At the end of the twelfth century county and prefectural examination estates began to appear.[28] These were usually called 'estates for tribute scholars' (*kung-shih-chuang*) but more fanciful names such as 'estate for the flourishing of worthies' (*hsing-hsien-chuang*) and 'myriad cassias estate' (*wan-kuei-chuang*) were used as well. They typically consisted of endowed landholdings, the income from which was managed by the government school officials and exclusively designated for stipends for *chü-jen* and, sometimes, for those who passed the departmental examination.

The earliest known reference to examination estates comes from Ching-hu-pei in 1184: 'All of the prefectures [in Ching-hu-pei] bought fields and delegated prefectural educational inspectors [*wen-hsüeh*] to manage the income that was given to *chü-jen*'.[29] The first reference that I have found to an actual estate is slightly later, 1197,[30] but from then until the end of the dynasty they are common in most of central and southeastern China.[31]

From what we can tell, the examination estates were typically joint ventures of elite families and local officials; the central government played no role whatsoever. Prefects or magistrates were almost invariably credited with founding them, though we should recognize the tendency of local historians to credit presiding officials with any positive activities that occurred during their tenures. In some cases the official role is obvious, as when the local government donated the land for the estate.[32] In other cases both officials and the local elite were involved. For example in 1270, the Chi-chou prefectural school preceptor called a meeting to discuss enlarging the endowment of the examination estate, and the result was large donations of land from two local families.[33]

Regardless of the initiative for the estates, the response of local elites to them was very positive, and well it should have been, for the aid that they provided to local *chü-jen* was substantial. In Chen-chiang fu (or Jun-chou of Liang-che-hsi) in 1197, new *chü-jen* received 100 strings of cash and another 150 if they passed the departmental examination.[34] In Chiang-ning fu (or Chien-k'ang fu) the amounts were 50 strings for prefectural *chü-jen* and 200 for the departmental examination graduates.[35] According to figures given by Chu Hsi in 1190 for student boarding allowances at the Yüeh-lu Academy in Ching-hu-nan, 50 strings would have supported a student for 250 days,[36] so such an amount would probably have paid for much though by no means all of a trip to and from the capital.

Essays dealing with the examination estates also betray a strong element of local pride. The competition and divisiveness of prefectural selection were forgotten as the locality prepared to send off its *chü-jen*. Panegyrics to its advanced culture abounded. One writer, for example, gave several reasons for

Ming-chou having produced more *chin-shih* than any other Liang-che prefecture: 'It has been able to restore the spirit of antiquity; it has made its villages
beautiful in appearance; it has been able to prevent the noisy disorders of
successful candidates.'[37]

We shall return shortly to this sense of community solidarity as it related
to the evolving examination culture of the Sung. But first we must consider
the visible signs of that culture.

The signs of selection

While examination ceremonies and the fruits of examination estates
made their appearances only trienially during the activities associated with
the qualifying examinations, other features of the examination culture had a
more enduring visibility. One was clothing, which played an important role in
the status-conscious society of the Sung, for sumptuary laws, though often
violated, were numerous.[38] Most elaborate, of course, were the prescriptions
for the court dress of high officials with their caps, robes, belts, boots, and
audience-tablets, the materials and colors of which were all minutely prescribed according to rank. For the local elites, however, less exalted distinctions were crucial. The 'long robes' (*shen-fu*) or 'Confucian robes' (*Ju-fu*) of
the literati set them off from their unlearned contemporaries. And while the
dress distinctions between the *chü-jen* and literati were relatively minor,[39]
with the *chin-shih* degree came the graduate's robes (*lan-shan*) which marked
one as an official.[40] As a deceased literatus turned underworld administrator
puts it in one of Hung Mai's stories:

> In my lifetime I studied painstakingly, hoping for blue gowns, but to no
> avail, for I was overshadowed by the efforts of Ch'en Te-kuang [who
> had passed the examinations]. But now I have been made the City
> God's vice-administrator and wear fine clothes . . . I have exceeded my
> place in my life on earth.[41]

In Sung biographical accounts one also finds the term 'time of cotton cloth'
(*pu-i chih shih*) used to describe the period before the individual passed the
examinations.[42]

The most visible and impressive symbol of the examinations was the
examination hall, the 'thorny gates' through which the aspiring candidate had
to pass. This Sung addition to the urban landscape of traditional China made
its appearance in the twelfth century. For most of the Northern Sung, examinations were usually held at a temple, at the prefectural school (another
symbol of Confucian learning), or even at the *yamen*. In 1112, all prefectures
were ordered to build examination halls,[44] but judging from accounts in local
histories, most were built during the Southern Sung,[44] when the general rule

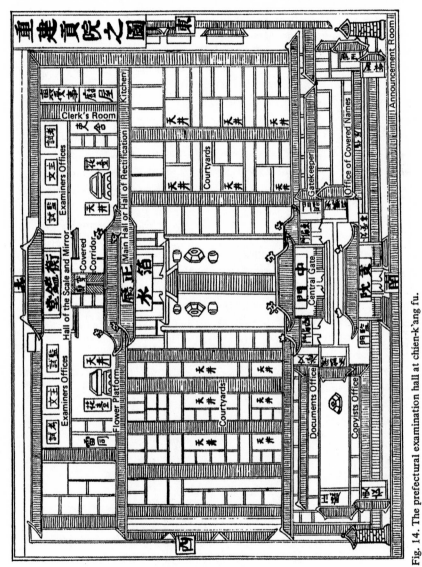

Fig. 14. The prefectural examination hall at chien-k'ang fu.

was that any prefecture with more than one hundred candidates was to build one.[45]

The halls could be quite elaborate. Chien-k'ang fu's rebuilt hall of 1261, the only Sung examination hall for which we have a drawing, was first built in the 1130s and underwent renovations in 1168, 1192, and 1223.[46] It was located in the cultured easternmost portion of the walled city, near to both the prefectural school, the Ming-tao Academy, and a sacrificial hall to former worthies (*hsien-hsien tz'u*).[47] The drawing (see Figure 14) depicts a large walled compound with offices for the registrars, proctors and clerk-copyists at the front, innumerable examination cubicles in the center, and the examiners' offices together with a kitchen and a building for clerks to the rear. Most striking is the commanding south to north axis which took one from the outside gate past a courtyard and through a great Central Gate (*Chung-men*), then up a long walk (shortened by the artist) flanked by the cubicles, through a Main Hall or Hall of Rectification (*Cheng-t'ing*), and up a covered corridor to arrive finally at the Justitia-like Hall of the Scale and Mirror.

The halls were built primarily because of the swelling ranks of candidates, for when candidate numbers increased from the hundreds to the thousands, as they did in many places, the temporary transformation of temples and schools became inadequate.[48] But we should be mindful of their visual impact as well. To outsiders who saw only the walls and exterior gates, they must have been slightly mysterious but permanent reminders of the promise of the examinations, a mystery that was probably deepened by the fact that they were only used for three days of testing every three years.[49] To those who entered, the complexity of the compound and the imposing central axis (itself a reflection of the imperial axis mundi) undoubtedly served to rein-force their feelings of high seriousness.

The beginnings of an examination culture

The evidence presented above is admittedly sparse. Not only does it come overwhelmingly from the prosperous southeast, but even if one general-izes from the examples given, the 'examination culture' of the Sung is still a far cry from that of the late imperial period when the examinations were supported by a vast array of schools, academies and provincial hostels, and degree holding offered a way of life to over a million men at a time.[50] What seems clear, however, is that in the southeast at the very least, a public examination culture with its own symbols, ceremonies and institutions was in the making.

Why did this happen? There were obvious practical reasons. The local elites, larger in size and more powerful in the Southern Sung than they had been before, needed to tie themselves to the imperium, for as a civil ruling class they were utterly dependent upon the imperial order. Given the great social, political and economic benefits the successful candidate-turned-official could confer upon his family, his affinal kin, his neighborhood, and the local elite in general, the attempt to maximize success through such institutions as the examination estates made eminent sense. It also made sense to increase the prestige of the examinations through symbols and ceremonies, to impress upon commoners, especially the masses of literati, the strength and glory of the prefecture's ties to the empire.[51] Thus local pride is a common element in writings on the examinations. Like the boast about Ming-chou culture cited earlier, Chou Pi-ta's essay on the 'hopeful gathering' ceremony in Chi-chou, after describing some of the great officials who earlier emerged from the prefecture, exhorted the *chü-jen* to continue the local tradition of national service: 'You gentlemen must exert yourselves to follow in the high footsteps of these earlier worthies and increase the abundant undertakings of our country.'[52]

Desirable for their prestige, examination ceremonies and symbols were also useful in controlling literati. Not only was it important for unsuccessful candidates to accept the results, despite their competitiveness and unfairness, but it was also necessary to keep disturbances from breaking out as they sometimes did. One twelfth-century writer wrote concerning the enlargement of the Chien-k'ang examination hall:

> Ever since the edicts encouraging participation in the triennial examinations, candidates have usually numbered in the hundreds and thousands. Fighting and a hundred other things abruptly occur and the officials must ceaselessly keep order in the rooms.[53]

Implicit is the assumption that more ample and impressive premises would result in greater order and decorum.[54]

The aim of control was also furthered by a downward spread of rewards, for the whole thrust of the evolving examination culture was to increase the status and prestige of *chü-jen* and even candidates. This did not hinder derisive reactions against arrogant and presumptuous *chü-jen*, but on the whole it probably made more palatable the long years and meager results that were the lot of so many.

Cultural considerations were, if anything, even more important, for the examinations formed a part of a broader culture of learning which included government schools, private academies, and sacrificial temples (*tz'u*) to honor past sages, which were frequently erected on school campuses. One of the distinguishing features of the Sung literati was the exalted view they had of their cultural role. Living under a dynasty which had raised the cultural,

literary, and civil values of *wen* over the martial values of *wu,* seeing themselves raised, via the examinations, to positions of unprecedented power,
Sung scholars saw themselves as Confucius's superior men, transmitters of
civilization, and in the process of transmission they realized the remarkable
Confucian revival of the eleventh century. There were of course disagreements over the form Confucianism should take. Was the received literary and
cultural tradition embodied in *wen* and evident in the poetry sections of the
chin-shih examination the best means of approaching the *tao,* as men like
Su Shih argued?[55] Or could the *tao* only be apprehended by discovering the
truths in the classical canons and acting upon them? This latter view was
particularly popular among Southern Sung Neo-Confucians who saw it as
an answer to the political and cultural crisis posed by the loss of the north.
They emphasized the notion of ritual or customary behavior (*li*) as that which
civilizes. One thirteenth-century scholar described the importance of sacrificial halls in this manner:

> *Li,* alas! If for one day we lack it, then we will be lost among the
> barbarians. This is greatly to be feared. Thus, in beginning to build
> sacrificial halls comes the knowledge of *li,* and following the removal of
> sacrificial halls comes the destruction of *li.*[56]

The examinations partook of both *wen* and *li,* but also subverted them.
Poetry and the classics formed the basis of the curriculum, and yet consideration of one's literary reputation or virtuous conduct was impossible given
the anonymous grading procedures which placed a premium upon the
mastery of written forms. According to one thirteenth-century critique,

> The emperor must use examinations in the selection of literati, [but]
> literati should not look only to the examinations. From the literati's
> absorption in advancing through selection comes the destruction of the
> study of the *tao.* From advancing through selection not being located in
> the prefectural schools comes the decline of local schools.[57]

But the solution implied here, that selection should be rooted in schools as
the Northern Sung reformers had advocated, was unrealistic, for the perceived
failure of just such a policy under Hui-tsung and its association with the loss
of the north made it politically unfeasible. One answer, as we saw in Chapter
4, was to establish academies for the pursuit of genuine learning. Yet another
was to give the examinations as much order, ceremony, and seriousness as
possible, to invest them, in short, with *li,* and this, I submit, was a major force
behind the emergence of an examination culture.

Important as the examinations were to the literati, their influence had
clear limits. Occurring as they did only once every three years, they were the

means to an end – the status, wealth and power that could come with degree holding and officialdom – and not an end in themselves. They were often described as 'gates' (*wei*),[58] for they constituted barriers through which the ambitious had to pass, unless they could somehow qualify for protection. Most literati, moreover, never made it through those gates and never participated in the ceremonies described above, and even most of those who passed did so only after years of waiting. How did the public examination culture affect that majority who remained on the outside? To answer this we must consider a different kind of evidence, one which considers popular views of the examination life.

Examination stories

Much as a local examination culture seems to have made its appearance during the Sung, the examination life as a common topic in anecdotal literature appears to have been primarily a Sung development. The pioneer in this regard was Wang Ting-pao (870–ca. 955), whose 'Collected Stories Concerning the T'ang' (*T'ang chih-yen*) present an unparalleled view of T'ang examination life.[59] Wang's primary concern, however, was with the examinations in Ch'ang-an, and while he was interested in local selection,[60] his occasional story on the subject cannot begin to match in quantity, detail, or social depth the examination stories of the Sung.

Whether because of greater elite participation in the examinations, or simply because with economic growth and the spread of printing, more literati were writing than ever before, Sung stories about the examination life abound. Some, like the *T'ung-meng hsün* ('Admonitions for the young and ignorant') by Lü Pen-chung (1084–1145),[61] draw primarily from the lives of the author and his family. More often, as for example in the cases of Wang P'i-chih (d. after 1096),[62] Ho Wei (1077–1145),[63] Yüeh K'o (1183–after 1240),[64] and Chang Shih-nan (d. after 1230),[65] the stories have been gathered from other books and acquaintances, and often the source is noted. The preeminent work in this genre, however, is the voluminous *I-chien chih* ('The collection of I-chien') which Hung Mai (1123–1202) compiled over a forty-year period in the late twelfth century.[66] Although none of these works is devoted to the examinations, the examinations and schooling figure prominently in them all.

Anecdotal stories are not the historian's traditional sources and they must be used with care. Their hearsay nature means that their assertions must be treated with skepticism. Since most of the stories were selected because they were unusual, they obviously cannot be taken as typical. And the appearance of such 'supernatural' elements as gods and ghosts in many of them might raise the question of whether they can be used at all. It should be noted, however, that these stories are presented as fact and not fiction and that most Sung Chinese had no difficulty with accepting ghosts as part of everyday life.[67] More generally, the great utility of these stories lies in the values and attitudes that they portray, in their material and behavioral detail, and in the range of activities they describe. In this way we will use them here.

We should also recognize that these stories do not come from the common people. Rather they are invariably by and primarily about the elite, and if they at times portray attitudes and concerns which we might label 'popular,' it is not enough to explain this as the influence of the lower classes. In part the problem lies with out overly narrow view of elite culture, a view propagated by orthodox Confucian scholars though not by our sources. Indeed, except for Lü Pen-chung who once studied under Ch'eng I,[68] none of our story collectors were identified with the Neo-Confucians. Wang P'i-chih, Chang Shih-nan and Yüeh K'o were known primarily as competent local officials.[69] Ho Wei's father had been a protege of Su Shih's and Su's influence is evident in Wei's diverse investigations into music, poetry and inkstones, not to mention strange stories.[70] Even Hung Mai, who enjoyed high office and was renowned as one of the great polymaths of his day, wrote little on philosophy and had few dealings with his contemporary Chu Hsi.[71] It may be that these writers represented an alternative tradition to that of the Neo-Confucians, one that emphasized the diversity of culture over the unifying demands of principle and the Way.[72] But whatever their significance, their accounts of the literati as active participants in the local cultures in which they lived provide a vital dimension to our emerging portrait of the literati life.

Two themes stand out in these stories. One concerns the proper and improper behavior of examination candidates. With large numbers of often elderly literati living in a highly visible state of limbo, traditional age-based roles were frequently violated. Second is the very prominent part played by gods, ghosts, portents and prophecies. It is to these two aspects of examination life that we now turn.

The problems of youth

One of the common characteristics of Sung examination stories is a sense of something amiss. If we were to take them as representative, we would almost have to conclude that licentious young men, conniving and libelous scoundrels, cheaters, and pitiably thick-headed old men were as common in the ranks of candidates as the sincere and upright scholars. Of course we can do no such thing, but the very presence of these types in the stories suggests a considerable behavioral diversity among the literati and

reflects, moreover, a concern for the life stages that a literatus was supposed
to undergo.

In a recent article on 'The Confucian Perception of Adulthood,' Professor
Wei-ming Tu has persuasively argued that the Confucian tradition conceived
of adulthood not as a state that one suddenly attained through some initi-
ation rite, but rather as an ideal towards which grown men worked throughout their lives.[73] The 'capping ceremony' (*kuan-li*), which according to the
Classic of Rites was performed at the age of twenty, marked the division
between child and adult, but only the beginning of the moral journey towards
'becoming a person' (*ch'eng-jen*). That journey could be expressed in terms of
moral progress, as in Confucius' famous formulation:[74]

> At fifteen I set my heart upon learning.
> At thirty I established myself [in accordance with ritual].
> At forty I no longer had perplexities.
> At fifty I knew the Mandate of Heaven.
> At sixty I was at ease with whatever I heard.
> At seventy I could follow my heart's desire without transgressing the
> boundaries of right.

But one could also speak in terms of a sequence of roles. Thus in the *Book of
Rites* the capping ceremony was followed by marriage and fatherhood at
around thirty, the beginning of one's official career at forty, the peak of one's
public service after fifty, and retirement after seventy.[75]

This Han dynasty career prescription must have seemed remarkably
germane to Sung readers, for it closely conformed to the typical Sung pattern
of literati success. Marriage and the examinations were the preeminent
concerns of literati in their twenties, but while most married then,[76] the
average age for receiving one's *chin-shih* degree was thirty-six,[77] and the
standard age for retirement from the civil service was seventy.[78] Such a career
had never been universal (any official career was the exception among
Southern Sung literati) and no one argued that it was necessary for realizing
one's humanity, for had not Confucius been a political failure? In fact much
of the *Analects* is devoted to showing how the superior man can overcome
adversity and maintain his commitment to the *tao*.

Yet there is reason to believe that the career and age expectations described above were deeply held by Sung literati. Examination success brought
with it the key change from commoner to official and, at a more personal
level, could be seen as marking the transition from early- to mid-adulthood,
from youth (*shao*) to manhood (*chuang*). By extension, then, the examination life was viewed as a typically youthful (or early adult) endeavor.
Conversely, the failure to advance when and as expected was often regarded
as a failure to develop as an adult. There were alternatives, of course; most

unsuccessful literati at some point quit the examinations and turned to other learned or not so learned careers.[79] But those who failed yet persevered lived almost as if in a delayed state of adolescence or early adulthood.

Nothing set examination candidates off from the rest of society so much as their mobility. They were constantly on the move visiting each other, requesting instruction from well known scholars, attending schools and academies, and taking examinations. Other groups such as merchants, transport workers, and officials were also very mobile. But unlike the first two, the literati were leisured, elite, and often well connected. Unlike the last, they were relatively young, free from responsibilities, and tended to gather in large groups.

This is not to say that the candidate's life was easy and free from cares. In a world where parents could not be wired for emergency funds, distant travel could be a hazardous undertaking. This was particularly true for *chü-jen,* since they had to leave their prefectures where they and their families were known and make the trip to the capital, braving bandits, thieves, and government underlings collecting transit taxes. Ho Wei tells of Wu Wei-tao, a *chü-jen* from Nan-chien chou (in Fu-chien) who was brought before Su Shih in 1090 when he was prefect of Hang-chou. He had been caught smuggling two hundred pieces of silk in two trunks labelled with Su's own brevet and K'ai-feng address. Confessing all, Wu told how he had bought the silk, which he was using to pay for his travel expenses, with cash gifts that people in his community (*hsiang-jen*) had given him. Because he feared losing the better part of it to transit taxes, he decided 'to use the name of a great official known for encouraging young scholars.' His mistake was to choose Su, who had recently arrived in Hang-chou, for it was right on the way from Nan-chien to K'ai-feng. Su's response was to laugh and send Wu on to the capital with his trunks protected by Su's genuine papers. The following year Wu passed the examinations and returned to thank Su, who spent several days with him in celebration.[80]

Hung Mai tells a similar story of a *chü-jen* named Li from the Kuang-nan prefecture of Ch'iung-chou, who left a bag containing his travel capital of gold, silver, and gold hairpins at an inn in Chiang-nan where he had spent the night on his way to the departmental examination. Fortunately a kind and honest innkeeper had stored the bag unopened, so Li was able to collect it and continue on his way. But for a time he thought the bag stolen and was 'black in the face, dumbfounded with mouth agape.' To the innkeeper's query he said,

> My home is beyond the ocean. For a trip of five thousand *li,* I could only take a few things to use for travel expenses. In one night I have lost them and now I will die on the road, unable to return my bones.[81]

Not all accounts were so sympathetic. What some saw as the legitimate peddling of goods to pay for travel expenses others saw as smuggling, and there undoubtedly were literati who were smugglers on the side. Witness the damning by Mei Yao-ch'en (1002—62) in his poem, 'On Hearing that *Chin-shih* Are Dealing in Tea':[82]

> The fourth and fifth months are when the tea is best in mountain
>   groves;
> then southern traders like wolves and jackals sell it secretly.
> Foolish youths risk crossing the dangerous peaks
> and work at night in teams, like soldiers with swords or spears.
> The vagrant students also lust for profit,
> their book bags are turned into smugglers' sacks!
> Officers may apprehend them at the fords,
> but the judges let them off, out of pity for their scholars' robes.
> And then they come to the cities, where they prate of Confucius and
>   Mencius,
> not hesitating to criticize Yao and T'ang in their speeches.
> If there are three days of summer rain, they rant about drowning
>   floods;
> after five days of hot weather, they complain of a drought.
> They make money in a hundred ways, dining on roast meat and wine
>   while their hungry wives at home lack dry provisions.
> — If you end up in a ditch, you're only getting your deserts:
> the *chin-shih* degree of generals and ministers are not for the likes of
>   you.

Clearly more was involved for Mei than a simple worry about smuggling. His target was the 'wandering literati' (*yu-shih*), men who left their homes ostensibly to study but in fact to make mischief, or so claimed many Sung writers.[83] We saw in Chapter 3 how they were accused of going to prefectures with more liberal prefectural quotas than their own and fabricating family backgrounds so as to claim residency there.

A more common claim was that they engaged in malicious slander and lawsuits. Liu Tsai (1166—1239) devoted a lengthy memorial to the problem of 'wandering literati who gather in the capital and scatter to the four quarters [of the city].'[84] They come to the capital with schemes of advancing through the avoidance examinations, or through entry into the prefectural school or University. 'For a long time now their numbers have been increasing daily. These students are truly troublesome and they are, moreover, suffering from hunger and cold [yet] are led on by music and pleasure.' His catalogue of their sins includes colluding in improper litigation, public slander in the marketplace or through songs and writings, and writing essays to gain the ear of officials. Most interesting, though, is Liu's explanation for how the literati got away with their activities in his description of the government's sources of information:

> The ears and eyes of the court are entrusted on the outside [of the
> bureaucracy] to circuit officials and prefects and on the inside to
> censors. But circuit officials and prefects cannot know all of the affairs
> of every circuit and prefecture and censors cannot know all of the
> affairs of the empire. So they make inquiries and make use of rumors
> [*feng-wen*, literally the 'news of the wind'] and the wandering literati
> know this. Thus when [the literati] choose to treat individuals well
> they have many ways of inviting praise, and when they [choose to]
> oppose them, they defame them in the marketplace.[85]

Liu's proposed solutions involved examination reforms to reduce the attractiveness of coming to the capital; he had no recommendations concerning
their activities as such, which frequently involved the connivance of
officials.[86]

The music and pleasure which attracted Liu's wandering literati raise one
further subject common in examination stories, that of licentiousness. As we
noted above, most literati were either married or betrothed. But even when
married, their mobile lifestyle frequently separated them from their wives and
families. It was then that they were most vulnerable, for in examination
stories with sexual themes, the literatus is almost invariably living away from
home, without social ties to help rein in his passions.

Most of these stories end unhappily, in a moralistic manner. We find young
literati seduced by a ghost in the guise of a prostitute,[87] by the spirit of a
drowned ewe in human form who claimed to be a widow,[88] and by the ghost
of the woman who was the man's wife three incarnations earlier and whom he
deserted for a prostitute.[89] In each case the man dies as a result. A University
student disappears from his dormitory in K'ai-feng and is found to have been
murdered in a brothel, one especially popular among Chiang-nan-tung
literati.[90] Liu Yao-chü's punishment is longer in coming. Having bought a
boat to travel from Hsiu-chou to Lin-an for the examinations in the fall of
1147,[91] Yao-chü is attracted by the boatman's daughter who, however, is
zealously guarded by her parents. On the examination's second day, Yao-chü
finishes his answers early, rushes back to the boat on which he is staying and
seduces the girl. That night his parents are told in a dream: 'Your son has
committed an immoral act and Heaven has suspended him for an examination.' But even though passing three years later, he dies before taking
office.[92]

The few stories with happy endings are equally instructive. A University
student becomes so caught up in the pleasures of the flesh that he develops
consumption and almost dies, but is saved by a Taoist priest who gives him

medicine and converts him to a life of total abstinence.[93] In another, a Ssu-ch'uan literatus who is living with a family in Ch'eng-tu while preparing for the examinations spurns the advances of his host's concubine. In his village his wife is immediately informed through a dream:

> Your husband is living alone in another district but has been able to maintain his resolution and has not taken advantage of a darkened room. The gods all know this and are ordering that he be set before all other scholars to be a reward.

The following year he placed first in the Ssu-ch'uan examinations.[94]

What is noteworthy in these stories is less their moralistic tone than their view of the literati as prey to their own lustfulness and vulnerable to seduction. Why is this theme so prominent? In the rootlessness of the literatus away from home we can find part of the explanation, but part too lay in the literati's presumed youth. Confucius observed that in his youth when his blood and vital humors (*hsüeh ch'i*) are not yet settled, the superior man guards against lust.[95] Obviously many literati were not 'superior men', but their very susceptibility to lust suggests that the examination life was indeed regarded as a youthful endeavor.

The problem of age

But what, then, of age? Were those who failed to pass regarded as somehow stunted, as continuing on in an untimely youth as we suggested earlier?

From accounts of elderly candidates, who were often the objects of pity and derision, one would have to answer yes. Thus one Liu Shih, who had 'grown old in the examination hall,' finally received a facilitated *chin-shih* degree in 1142.[96] His kinsmen were not impressed, calling him 'Liu the unsalaried minister' as he waited to fill a minor post. When word of its vacancy arrived he said to them: 'All my life you said I wouldn't obtain an office, but now in old age it has arrived.' They made their apologies. As he left home he said, 'If only I can receive a salary, I will not again speak of fate.' But fate remained unkind to him and he died *en route* to his post.[97]

Of greater interest are the complaints associated with elderly candidates that they had not 'accomplished' (*ch'eng*) anything. This is the same *ch'eng* as in *ch'eng-jen* ('becoming a person') which, as we saw above, is central to the Confucian concept of adulthood, and its use in fact contains a sense of arrested development. One individual who entered the Imperial University (*T'ai-hsüeh*) at the ripe age of fifty, was soon discouraged by his age: 'I have no accomplishments. I wish to quit the examinations and return [home].' But he stayed, encouraged by two propitious dreams, and not only won a *chin-shih* degree but had a moderately successful career as well.[98] Even more revealing is the story of Shen Wei-fu, a native of Wen-chou in the early twelfth century, who had studied for a long time at the University without 'establishing his name' (*pu-ch'eng-ming*). Returning home, he made his living in a way familiar to students of Ch'ing social history, by living off the gifts given to him for interceding with officials. He continued to take the prefectural examinations but always without success, and one day in despair he said:

> Wei-fu is an unlucky failure without accomplishments. [I am] the object of satirical songs in the district and my five viscera are split apart [*wu-nei fen-lieh*]. Does Heaven know me?[99]

However self-pitying this remark, the complaint of physical distress suggests a profound sense of disharmony; lack of accomplishment had led to personal disintegration and not merely to arrested development, or so he is claiming.

Another indication of the special character of the examination life is its association with the feminine principle of *yin*. Hung Mai tells of one Hsü Shu-wei, a poor scholar who was told in a dream one night: 'If you want to rise in the examinations, you must store up your *yin* virtue. But if your efforts are unsuccessful then you should become a doctor,' for as he was later told in a second dream, 'medicine has secret merits [*yin-kung*].'[100] Such an association may seem surprising in light of the stress placed upon literati virility in the preceding section, but we must distinguish between the literati's lifestyle and their occupational role. The student's task was essentially passive, concerned with acquiring knowledge and preparing for the active, *yang* life of the official, and indeed, one might argue that the passiveness of his life created an imbalance of *yin* and *yang* which contributed to his reputed licentiousness. And since *yin* was the female principle, this may help to explain the cryptic remark of one Chang Hsien-t'u who, after years of attempting the examinations, finally became an official through protection and said to his wife, 'I have now received office. You can no longer complain about my being the orphan of the Luan bird.'[101] As Luan was the fabulous female bird of Chinese mythology, the counterpart to the male P'eng bird, Chang appears to be saying that his prolonged (thus the 'orphan') *yin* life had come to an end.

Also revealing is the story of Ch'en Hsiu-kung of Chien-yang county in Fu-chien, an impoverished literatus who was debating whether or not to take the examinations. Entering a country temple one day, he prayed to the temple's god for guidance, threw three bamboo strips which all fell *yin*, and returned despondently to town. That night he was summoned in a dream to an audience with the goddess of the temple, who explained that she had been off at a banquet at the time of his prayer and her husband had improperly investigated Ch'en's case. The *yin* strips were in fact mistaken, for Ch'en would not only pass the examinations but would even become a chief councilor. Needless to say, the goddess was right.[102]

While the problem of untimeliness was most evident among elderly examination candidates, unusual precocity was also considered to be a problem. The Neo-Confucian philosopher Ch'eng I (1033–1107) once said that attaining a high degree at a very young age was one of the three things that are unlucky for men.[103] In a similar vein, Wang P'i-chih tells of a youth who received his *chin-shih* at nineteen and was told by a physiognomist:

> Your appearance is very noble, but you have passed the examinations at too young an age and I am afraid that your end will be unfortunate. If you [wish to] succeed, you should retire young in order to avoid great calamity.[104]

Such views were not universal, and in fact the Sung continued the T'ang practice of holding special examinations for young prodigies (*t'ung-tzu-k'o*).[105] But these examinations were controversial. Banned on several occasions during the Sung, they were abolished for good in 1266.[106]

It is important to remember that the cultural patternings presented here represent only one of several systems that gave life to Sung culture. Military power, wealth, religion, and above all the family and lineage all had their own ways of organizing society and of creating expectations and handling their fulfillment or the lack thereof, so that failure in the examinations by no means insured that one would be or see oneself a failure in life. But it helped, given the influence of office on wealth and kinship and the ever-increasing popularity of the examinations. Indeed, such were the rewards and uncertainties of the examination life that an appeal for divine aid became yet another common feature of the examination life.

With help from the spirits

Judging from the examination stories, Sung literati lived in a world full of gods, ghosts, omens, prophecies, fortune tellers, dragons and the like. Indeed, such is the wealth and diversity of the material on these subjects that it is sometimes difficult to do much more than catalogue their uses. Yet the material is revealing, so revealing in fact, that to ignore it as writers on the examinations have almost always done is to miss a major aspect of literati culture.

The phenomena which concern us here fall roughly under the headings of omens, prophecies, and dreams and apparitions. Of the three, omens are perhaps the most familiar to students of Chinese history, for ever since Tung Chung-shu's cosmological Confucianism with its theory of correspondences in

the Western Han and probably well before, omens had had an accepted place
in orthodox cosmology. Indeed, Chu Hsi wrote that 'There is no harm if one
dreams of something which is an omen,' and his thirteenth century com-
mentator elaborated that 'When they [omens] are revealed in dreams, it
means that the mind is acting according to the principle of influences and
response. There is no harm in this.'[107] Most of the Sung examination omens
concerned unusual natural phenomena which foretokened someone's
success in the examinations: the splitting apart of a treetrunk with the
resulting cracks forming characters,[108] a tiger breaking down a wall and
carrying away a pig,[109] the falling of a large rock or the appearance of an
unusual flower,[110] or even something as insignificant as finding a piece of
paper whose characters contained some hidden meaning.[111] Even more
auspicious were the appearances of dragons in school ponds, which augured
well for all local literati in the examinations.[112] We should note that where
traditional omenology was concerned primarily with imperial conduct and
the state of the empire, these omens were given far more particular readings.

We might also include here the effects that *feng-shui*, that is the placement of buildings or tombs in relation to the winds and waters, had upon
the examinations. This was seen most commonly in the building or moving
of local government schools,[113] but it could involve other buildings as
well.[114] The most interesting case that I have found involved an official
family in the northern prefecture of Cheng-chou. They became so frightened
at a scholar's comment that the *feng-shui* of their tombs was so good that the
family would one day produce an emperor, a treasonous prophecy to Sung
dynastic ears, that they intentionally damaged the *feng-shui* by flattening out
the site. As a result the family stopped producing *chin-shih.* But then after a
great flood a stream appeared beside the tombs and within seven years they
produced two *chin-shih,* though both had modest careers.[115]

Like the omens, examination prophecies by the living did not usually
involve recourse to the spirit world. They most frequently occurred as
unexplained and often unsolicited pronouncements about someone's future,
but could also be based upon such practices as physiognomy[116] or divination
with hexagrams.[117] The practitioners of prophecy were a diverse lot, coming
from all levels of society. They included officials and their kin,[118] recluses
(*shan-jen*),[119] magicians (*shu-shih*),[120] professional fortune tellers,[121]
shamans,[122] monks (the most numerous category),[123] and madmen,[124] all of
whom shared a gift for clairvoyance. There is even an account of an ugly and
illiterate farmer who, after eating half a bitter peach given to him by an
immortal, is filled with a divine madness which makes him clairvoyant, a
master of the brush, and adept at chanting hymns. Becoming a monk, he is
popular with the local elite and known for his examination prophecies.[125]

This social diversity helps to explain the movement of ideas, beliefs, and customs between elite and non-elite which we noted in our discussion of the examination stories. More to the point, this involvement of many non-elite individuals in the examination life adds credence to our thesis that the promise of examination success was one of the great myths underlying the Sung social order, for such a promise would have been of little moment had the non-elite not been aware of it.

The combination of dreams and apparitions may seem strange, but in fact both involve communication with the spirit world, the major difference being whether that is accomplished in a sleeping or a waking state. But in contrast to a multitude of dream stories, I have found only a handful of stories about apparitions. Three of them feature literati encounters with ghosts; in two, the literatus returns home in a fright, ails, and dies,[126] while in the third the ghost (the literatus' late brother-in-law) foretells his success in the examinations, which occurs, but only after a violent and debilitating illness.[127] Clearly ghosts were dangerous creatures. Three other cases involve examination halls, in one of which a spirit in the guise of a proctor helps a virtuous candidate pass.[128] One wonders whether the normal emptiness of the halls punctuated by the stressfulness of the examinations might not have made them appear particularly conducive to encounters with ghosts and spirits.

The great majority of contacts with the spirit world, however, come through dreams, and as with the omens and prophecies, the dreams take all forms. Most common are those that simply involve 'dream people' (*meng-jen*) who utter a prophecy and disappear. Deceased relatives are also well represented, not merely ancestors returning to help their descendants on their way or to urge them to observe the ancestral rites,[129] as one would predict, but also dead children returning to console their grieving parents and announce examination successes that they will achieve in future incarnations.[130] We also see emperors (including Wen-ti of the Wei dynasty),[131] and famous characters from history. For example, there is a story about the annual examination of the Hu-chou prefectural school, where it was the custom to award five bottles of wine to the first place student, three each to those placing second and third, and two each for those fourth and fifth. In 1151, one student named Ch'en Yen dreamed that he was called to the head of the hall and given five bottles by Confucius, but that Confucius's disciple Tzu-hsia angrily kicked away two of them. When the results were announced, Ch'en was second. The preceptor told him that he had originally placed first but that a mistake had been found in his treatment of an incident involving Tzu-hsia, so he had been dropped to second.[132]

Special mention should be made of the god (*shen*) of Tzu-t'ung. Ts'ai T'ao

(d. after 1147) tells of a temple to this god on the road from Ch'ang-an to Ssu-ch'uan which rewarded officials who passed in stormy weather with the post of Chief Councilor and similarly *chin-shih* candidates with first place (*k'uei-shou*) in the examinations.[133] Hung Mai likewise tells of a Ch'eng-tu official who successfully prayed to the Tzu-t'ung-shen in 1134 to learn who would succeed in that year's provincial examinations.[134] Tzu-t'ung-shen appears to have begun as a local thunder deity of very ancient origin.[135] At some point he became associated with a Szechuanese general, Chang Ya-tzu, who died in battle during the Chin (265–420) and who, according to myth, was 'charged by the Jade Emperor with keeping the registers of the titles and dignities of men, and distinguishing between good and bad literati, rewarding and advancing the first and punishing the second.[136] Most interesting, however, is the fact that by Yüan times, Tzu-t'ung was identified with the God of Literature (Wen-ch'ang ti-chün) who with his associated deities was worshipped in Ming and Ch'ing times by literati throughout the empire who were hoping for examination success.[137] These twelfth century references suggest, therefore, Sung origins for the examination-centered God of Literature cult.

There are, finally, dreams involving gods or spirits (*shen*), though usually these are deities of a lower order; temple gods like the one whose husband mishandled the supplicant's stick-throwing or beneficent but unnamed spirits.[138] The august gods do not appear nor should they, we might speculate, given the parochial nature of the literati's hopes, but occasionally their pronouncements are reported, as in the punishment of the adulterer mentioned earlier. However, the bureaucrats and functionaries of the underworld appear in force, and with good reason. They are frequently deceased friends or relatives of the literati who naturally occupy the official posts in the underworld since that is what they had trained for in life. As officials, moreover, they have access to the registers where not only times of birth and death but also details of examination results are recorded, and they are thus able to sneak this information out to the living.[139]

Despite the diversity of these stories of omens, prophecies, and dreams, there is a remarkable unity of purpose: they are overwhelmingly concerned with foretelling examination success. For example, when one dead literatus who is toiling unhappily in the service of the City God (*Ch'eng-huang*) gets the chance to appear to an old friend in a dream and, with tears streaming down his face, asks after his family, his friend replies:

> Since you are the City God's retainer, you should know who from our district will pass this fall's examination and the names of those who will receive degrees in the spring.[140]

The main interest in many of the stories therefore lies in the examinations themselves, in conditions that are required for success or in the misinterpretations that men make of their prophecies. Some are given advice on how to prepare for the examinations: which classics to specialize in, poems to write on, or biographies to study.[141] Others are told to change their names.[142] Another poor soul was told that he would become an official only after meeting the 'three Hans'. After years of seeking out men named Han, he accompanied an envoy to Korea and only then did he learn that Korea was known as the 'land of the three Hans.' He subsequently passed.[143] Far less lucky was Hsü Kuo-hua, a University student during the Hsüan-ho period (1119–25), who had a dream in which a gold-armored man struck a large golden bell and made a cryptic remark which Hsü interpreted to mean that he would place first in the examinations. In fact the remark gave the location of the grave where he was buried after dying of beriberi when K'ai-feng was under seige by the Jurchen in 1126.[144]

Hsü's fate illustrates the pitfalls which could await one when interpreting dreams. But why, might we ask, was there such great interest in examination dreams and prophecies as to give rise to this literature? After all, whatever prophecies one might have received, one still had to pass the examinations. First, the great majority of the stories date from the late Northern Sung or later, just when the examinations were becoming extremely competitive and increasingly arbitrary; there was no guarantee that talent or virtue would be rewarded. Against the feelings of insecurity and powerlessness to which the examinations gave rise, omens and prophecies offered reassurance and some certitude.

But even more important, dreams and prophecies were popular because the literati believed that they helped. Although they often talked of their 'fate' (*ming*) being fixed,[145] that did not mean predestined, for with knowledge and perhaps some help from the spirits, one could improve one's lot. Communication with the spirits could therefore be considered yet one more success strategy to be employed by ambitious but frustrated literati. Nowhere is that clearer than in the common literati practice of praying for a dream. With an examination approaching, candidates would enter a Buddhist or Taoist temple and pray for a dream or ask the gods a question, which would then be answered in a dream.[146]

This, I submit, was another examination ritual, a private one in contrast to the public rituals discussed earlier. Both had a place in the examination sequence and both were integrative — tying the literatus to the imperium and elite order in the one case and to the spirit world in the other. But while the public ceremonies were primarily celebratory in nature, the prayers were invocatory, a plea for a sign that the thorny gates would, in fact, be surpassed.

8

CONCLUSION

The attempt at meritocracy

It might seem presumptuous to claim a special Sung role for the Confucian literati, scholar-officials, examinations, and schools which have engaged our attention in this book, so central were all of them in the Chinese tradition. None was a Sung creation and all flourished to the end of the imperial age. Yet the Sung role was special, for it was then that the constellation of values, institutions, and social structures centering on the examinations assumed much of the shape that it was to have throughout the late imperial period.

Much of the praise — or blame — for this may be levelled at the Sung emperors themselves. As one thirteenth-century writer observed: 'The founding emperors used Confucian scholars to establish the dynasty and the examinations to obtain the scholars.'[1] By expanding degree numbers, adding a formal prefectural examination, introducing such procedures as covered names and copied examinations, and, under Jen-tsung, promoting education, the early emperors were clearly trying to create a meritocratic state. Reacting against the T'ang example of great families among which the imperial Lis were merely *primus inter pares* and the military domination of the Five Dynasties, the Sung Chaos were determined to create a civil state in which selection for office was made with the utmost fairness, in which achievement was rewarded, by the emperor, with advancement. The result was to greatly enhance the emperor's power, though whether this should be seen as an essential step in the growth of Chinese autocracy, as some have argued, is open to question.[2]

In many respects this policy was a great success. Civil officials dominated the government even in times of military peril; witness the fate of Yüeh Fei.[3] Although quite a few Northern Sung families or lineages succeeded in producing high officials over several generations, none could begin to rival the great families of the Six Dynasties and T'ang in longevity, prestige, or perhaps even power. Most important, the promise of the examinations transformed learning from an elite concern to a preoccupation. Education became less the domain of scholarly families comprising one portion of elite society and more an activity urged upon academically promising boys and young men throughout elite society.

With the spread of learning, however, came the subversion of its meritocratic principle. That principle had always been qualified, for even in the early Sung past precedent had been followed in restricting the Directorate of Education to 'sons of the state' (*kuo-tzu*), that is the sons of officials. But only in the Southern Sung do we find avoidance examinations, which were designed to promote fairness, becoming a privileged means of advancement. In the proliferation of such special examinations and in the increasing use of protection, we can see both the considerable power of the bureaucratic families and the imperial clan, the chief recipients of privilege, and their reaction to the competitive rigors of the regular examinations. As was the case in early modern England, when the educational revolution of the seventeenth century led to the more aristocratic society of the eighteenth,[4] the Sung expansion of education resulted in the contraction of opportunity and the growth of privilege.

The examinations also allowed certain regions and localities a degree of political influence that they never again matched, for the Sung's lack of regional quotas allowed for relatively unbridled competition between places. The debate between Ssu-ma Kuang and Ou-yang Hsiu in 1064 over regional quotas articulated the ambiguities inherent in the notion of fairness,[5] for fairness to individuals entailed unfairness to certain regions, and vice versa. A century later the ambiguities were, if anything, heightened. In the empire's most successful region, the Southeast Coast, prefectural candidate numbers were higher and quotas narrower — by policy — than anywhere else. Yet such was the size and power of its privileged groups that the use of special examinations was enormous. So while unprivileged literati faced the most competitive of examinations, for the elites in general success bred success. By contrast, localities without past histories of success had only the regular examinations and the University's entrance examination by which to achieve it.

A millennium earlier Confucian principles had been used to justify the Nine Rank Arbiter System of recruitment, in which individuals were ranked according to their virtue, and it quickly became a system of hereditary ranks. The meritocratic principles of the examination system were far more tenacious. Even amidst the special examinations and widespread allegations of abuse in the Southern Sung, the examinations were held as scheduled and their elaborate procedures were generally followed. And in later dynasties their meritocratic features actually increased. The use of protection was virtually eliminated in the early Ming,[6] and so were the avoidance examinations, for candidates with relatives among the examination officials were simply barred from the examinations.[7] This was in large part a result of the despotic government of the late dynasties, for the examinations were an excellent way to secure talented but dependent and therefore unthreatening officials. But the examinations also owed much of their longevity to the cultural values which had developed about them, and to the social importance and utility which they came to assume for local elites, and these were, in large measure, a legacy of the Sung.

Learning and authority

Over the long history of the examinations, one of the things that most distinguished the Sung and other dynasties was its predilection for change. At no other time were the examinations challenged so fundamentally or experimented with so drastically as in the Northern Sung.

Foremost among the challengers were the Northern Sung reformers. For them the issue was not meritocracy, which they favored, but rather the relationship between training and choosing, or education and recruitment. Their demand that selection be rooted in government schools meant, of course, a broadening of criteria for selecting officials to include character and academic record. It also meant that the purpose of those schools was to train students morally and practically to become officials. The result, as manifested in the Three Hall System of the early twelfth century with its recruitment functions as well as its specialized schools for law, medicine, mathematics, calligraphy, painting, and the military,[8] was an incipient professionalism that stands in striking contrast to the generalist ideal that dominated most of Chinese educational history.[9]

This was also a period of institutional developments. The standardization of teaching personnel, school finances, entrance examinations, and grades through which students advanced were all products of reform. It was just such developments that Philippe Ariès has argued underlay the European transition from church school to *collegium* in the fourteenth and fifteenth centuries, a change which he regards as critical for the emergence of modern education.[10] But where in Europe these changes led to institutions that long were to hold a virtual monopoly on formal education, the Three Hall System did not outlast its founders. Because of abuses, expenses, and the excesses of the reformers, the system was abandoned after just twenty years, and the ensuing loss of the north, which many blamed upon the reformers, insured against its resurrection. Despite its impressive legacy of institutional development and educational expansion, the separation of examinations from the government schools deprived the latter of their brief educational monopoly. Henceforth what really mattered was how well one could write examinations and not where one had studied, and examination preparation became a primary educational task whether one studied with a tutor, in a community or lineage school, or in a government school. Thus the innovations of the Three Hall System never played the catalytic role that similar innovations later did in Europe.

In intellectual and cultural histories of China, the Sung is remembered largely as the age of Confucian revival. Thanks to protracted peace in most of the empire, economic prosperity, the spread of printing, and the stimulus of the examinations, the Northern Sung witnessed a remarkable and diverse flowering of thought and literature which drew heavily from the Confucian canon for its vocabulary and concerns. The reform movement was one fruit of this revival. Another was the attempt by Su Shih, most notably, to make the civil and literary value of *wen* the guiding principle of civilized life.[11] A third was the development of Neo-Confucian thought, the School of the Way or of Principle (*Tao-hsüeh, Li-hsüeh*), as it was known in the Sung. Though most famous for its philosophical accomplishments, Neo-Confucianism's educational influence was enormous and was closely related to the examinations.

Much, perhaps most of the epistemology and metaphysics developed by the Neo-Confucians was the work of the Northern Sung masters, particularly the Ch'eng brothers, but the popularization of Neo-Confucianism among the literati was a late twelfth-century phenomenon. It owed much to the teachings and writings of Chu Hsi and others, and to the spread of academies where literati gathered for self-cultivation and philosophical discussion. It is hardly surprising that this occurred in the first half of the Southern Sung, for the loss of the cultural heartland of the north together with the persuasive influence of Buddhism, especially the intellectually attractive Ch'an, had created a sense of crisis among twelfth-century thinkers, a feeling that something fundamental was amiss. As the Hunanese Neo-Confucian Hu Hung (1100–55) put it, 'When the Central Plain is without the Way [*Tao*] of the Central Plain, the barbarians enter; when it restores the Way of the Central Plain, the barbarians return to their territory.'[12] There was thus a large and receptive audience for the claims of the Neo-Confucians that truth was revealed in the texts of the classics, that learning and self-cultivation could lead to sagehood, that the Way of the Former Kings had been transmitted from Confucius and Mencius down to them, the Neo-Confucian masters, and that moral education was essential for the restoration of the empire. These claims were at once conservative, in their reliance on tradition, and radical, in their assertion of the autonomous authority of the true scholar. They were also controversial, leading to the short-lived ban on 'false learning' at the close of the twelfth century.

An instructive parallel to Neo-Confucianism can be found in the Jewish approach to learning, for they shared a belief in the authority of canonical texts, a veneration of learning, and an esteem for scholars. Just as rabbis were both teachers and priests, so in a way were the Sung Neo-Confucians, for their concern with ritual, moral cultivation, and transcendence gave them at least a semi-priestly role.[13] One can even find similarities between the Neo-Confucian academy and the Jewish yeshiva in early modern Europe, for however striking their differences — the academies had nothing comparable to the yeshiva's training in casuistry — both were centered about a scholar-teacher, attracted students from afar, and had as their goal the rearing of mature scholars.[14]

In one respect, however, the Jewish and Neo-Confucian approaches to learning could not have been more different. Whereas the former was securely nested at the center of Jewish culture, the latter arose and flourished in uneasy opposition to examination-centered education. One took the examinations in order to advance in life; one went to the academies in search of philosophical understanding and moral self-improvement. The examinations were an imperial institution controlled by the emperor and his officials. Neo-Confucian education, by contrast, appealed directly to the classics and to interpretations of them by contemporary masters, thus bypassing the emperor entirely.

The opposition was qualified, to be sure. Not only did the two forms of education share the same Confucian texts, but after the Yüan adopted Chu Hsi's commentaries on the Four Books and Five Classics as examination texts, they even shared Neo-Confucian texts. Moreover, even as the state depended on Confucian political theory for its legitimacy, so the literatus had to take the examinations if he wished to advance. But the opposition proved incapable of resolution, for the scholar's claim to autonomy remained and so did the examination system, degrading and aggravating to its critics but indispensable nevertheless. The result, then, was a continuing sense of tension, a dialectic underlying the cultural and political life which functioned up until both state and culture began to disintegrate at the end of the Ch'ing.

Examinations and society
Hung Mai tells a story of a wealthy family named Tsai that lived in Wu-hsi County (Ch'ang-chou) on the Yangtze delta in the late Northern Sung. The Tsais were blessed with two sons and a large productive estate that was worked by thirteen men. One night a 'cultivated talent' (*hsiu-ts'ai*) named Li Mo appeared to the father in a dream and a few years later a townsman and *chin-shih* by that name married his daughter. When the father was about to die he summoned his sons and told them: 'You are plain and unestablished

[*ju-tsao su pu li*] and certainly cannot protect your inheritance.' He urged them therefore to give the estate to Li rather than letting others take it. This they did and in the disorders of the early Southern Sung, Li's was the only estate in the area to escape destruction by 'bandits.'[15]

This is hardly a typical story, for it was highly unusual for a prosperous family with sons to give its land to a son-in-law and must reflect the extremely hazardous conditions of the time. But it is revealing, both for the clear view it provides of the concerns about which elite lives revolved — family, land, marriage, and the examinations — and for the father's belief that wealth without office offered little security. One might speculate that it was Li Mo's family, with military resources of its own, that really protected the estate, but if so Hung Mai, an official himself living in a more secure age, chose to ignore that fact and stress instead the role of the examinations in 'establishing' a family.

It has been a contention of this book that the examinations were a critical factor in the changes that elite society underwent during the Sung. Obviously other factors were also at work. As Robert Hartwell has argued so persuasively, the demographic and economic development of southern China produced a.landholding elite stratum which became politically prominent in the late Northern Sung and exhibited a remarkable longevity from that time onwards.[16] Kinship structure, marriage, occupational diversification, and at times the ability to command military power, all must be considered to understand these local elites. What set the examinations apart was not merely the rewards that flowed from success but also the influence they exerted on every facet of elite life.

The rewards were obvious. Office-holding offered prestige, wealth, especially if one had no compunction about accepting gifts and bribes, and fiscal and legal privileges, while high office held out power and recruitment privileges for one's relatives. Moreover, while there are examples of elite families that never produced officials,[17] doing so nevertheless constituted an essential step in establishing a family and one which most Sung elite families achieved at some point in their history.[18]

The examinations' influence, while less obvious, is no less striking. The ever-increasing numbers of people who took to the examinations following their tenth-century expansion and the eleventh-century spread of schools was a social fact of major consequence. It meant that when the eleventh-century professional elite — itself an early product of the expanded examinations — disintegrated through factional struggle, into its place would step a far larger group of local elites bitterly competing for office. It meant that the chances for an individual elite family to obtain office worsened, thus increasing the importance of the lineage and contributing to the development of lineage organizations. It meant an even stronger tie between learning and marriage than had existed before. On the one hand academic promise and examination success made a man highly desirable as a marriage partner; on the other hand a wife with high ranking relatives could be of great benefit in the examinations.

Paradoxically, the growth of the literati also contributed to occupational diversity within the elite. As competition in the examinations increased, families with scholarly traditions were less likely to encourage all of their sons to prepare for them, even while wealthy landlord and merchant families on the fringes of the elite were more likely to educate their brightest sons in hopes of social advancement through marriage and the examinations. This occupational diversity is illustrated in a story, again from Hung Mai, about a student from Fu-chien attending the University in the Ta-kuan period (1107–10). Reproached by a spirit in a dream for not having buried his deceased parents and ordered to go home and do so, he protested that he had brothers at home, so why should the guilt be solely his? The spirit answered: 'Because you are a Confucian who practices the rites and righteousness, the fault is yours. The other sons are rough and irregular. They are not up to the responsibility.'[19]

In this story we can discern an audacious literati claim to sole moral authority, for the brothers are rendered almost inhuman by the spirit's dismissal of their filial obligations. This helps to explain why occupational diversity was accompanied not by cultural diversity but rather by the growing dominance of literati values within elite society. If the spread of Neo-Confucianism and academies represented a growing literati claim to autonomous authority, the emergence of an examination culture can be seen as a claim to derived imperial authority. The institutions, ceremonies, symbols, and stories surrounding the examinations set off officials from commoners, literati from non-literati, and to the literati engaged in the examination life they offered the elusive, at times illusory, hope of success.

APPENDIX 1

METHODS OF ENTRY INTO THE CIVIL SERVICE

Examinations (*K'o-chü*)

Two kinds of degrees were given by examination: *chin-shih* and *chu-k'o* degrees, which usually required the passage of a preliminary examination (*chieh-shih*), the departmental examination (*sheng-shih*), and the palace examination (*tien-shih* or *yü-shih*) (see Figure 4); and special examinations for small numbers of recommended individuals.

–– *Chin-shih-k'o*: 'Advanced scholar degree.' From the beginning of the dynasty to 1071, candidates were tested on discussions on the classics (*lun*), policy questions (*ts'e*), and poetry (both poems, *shih*, and poetical descriptions, *fu*). From 1071 to 1089 and 1094 to the end of the Northern Sung, candidates were required to write expositions on the classics rather than poetry. From 1089 to 1094 and during the Southern Sung they had the option of writing expositions on a single classic or poetry. The preliminary and departmental examinations took three days each, the palace examination, which was primarily a placement examination, one day.

–– *Chu-k'o*: 'Various fields.' Consisted of a number of examinations on specialized topics, with an emphasis on memory passages (*t'ieh*) and written elucidations (*mo-i*) on the meaning of passages. The *chu-k'o* were abolished in 1071 and replaced by a 'new degree in law' (*hsin-k'o ming-fa*) but it was abolished in 1089. In the early Sung the following *chu-k'o* examinations were offered:

Ming-fa: law

San-chuan: the three commentaries, which tested one on the *Tso*, *Kung-yang*, and *Ku-liang* commentaries of the *Spring and Autumn Annals*.

San-shih: the three standard histories (*Shih-chi, Ch'ien Han Shu*, and *Hou Han Shu*) covering the history of China from the beginning to 221 A.D.

San-li: the three classic works on ritual (*Chou-li, Li-chi*, and *I-li*).

K'ai-yüan-li: the *Ritual of 732*.

Chiu-ching: the Nine Classics or the classics of Changes (*I-ching*), Documents (*Shu-ching*), Poetry (*Shih-ching*), the three classics of ritual and the three commentaries on the *Spring and Autumn Annals*.

Wu-ching: the Five Classics or the classics of Changes, Documents, and Poetry, the *Li-chi*, and the Kung-yang commentary on the *Spring and Autumn Annals*.

Hsüeh-chiu Mao Shih: the Mao version of the classic of Poetry.

— *T'e-tsou-ming chin-shih; T'e-tsou-ming chu-k'o*: 'Facilitated *chin-shih*' and 'facilitated *chu-k'o* degrees.' Given to elderly, multiple repeaters of the capital-level examinations who passed a special, relatively easy departmental examination. Graduates received very low grade or ungraded offices.

— *T'ung-tzu-k'o*: 'Degrees for youths.' For precocious youths recommended by their prefectures and examined by the Emperor or the Secretariat. They had to be under 15 years of age (Chinese style) during the Northern Sung and 10 during the Southern Sung.

— *Chih-k'o*: 'Decree examinations degrees.' Prestigious degrees given to those who passed an extremely difficult examination. Candidates could be officials or non-officials but had to be recommended to the examination.

Protection (*Yin-pu, En-yin*)
A privilege conferred upon mid- and high-grade officials allowing them to have official rank conferred upon their relatives and, occasionally, their family tutors. The individuals still had to take a placement examination (*ch'üan-shih*) and their initial ranks were quite low.

— *Chih-shih pu-kuan*: 'Admission to office [upon the] retirement [of the protector].' The most exclusive form of protection, limited to the highest civil and military officials.

— *I-piao pu-kuan*: 'Admission to office [upon the] death [of the protector].'

— *Ta-li chien-tsou pu-kuan*: 'Admission to office [upon] recommendation [at the] Great Rites.' The Great Rites were imperial ceremonies usually performed on the outskirts of the capital every three years, the year after the examinations at the capital. Numerically, this was the most important form of protection.

Purchase (*Chin-na pu-kuan*)
Grants of low official rank were sometimes given to individuals making substantial contributions of grain or cash during times of war or famine. Small in number, their career opportunities were severely limited.

Irregular status (*She-kuan pu-kuan*)
Irregular status officials (*she-kuan*) were Kuang-nan *chü-jen* who were permitted to hold minor offices in Kuang-nan. They could, after a certain period of service, obtain regular status.

Clerical promotion (*Liu-wai pu-kuan*)

Clerks with twenty years of service who passed a special examination could enter from 'outside the stream' (*liu-wai*) and receive official rank. In 998, however, their numbers were limited to 20 per year.

APPENDIX 2

TABLE 25. DEPARTMENTAL GRADUATES AND DEGREES CONFERRED BY YEAR

Examination year	Departmental chin-shih graduates	Chin-shih	Chu-k'o	Facilitated chin-shih	Facil. chu-k'o
960	19	(19)*			
961	11	(11)			
962	15	(15)			
963	8	(8)			
964	8	(8)			
965	7	(7)			
966	6	(6)			
967	10	(10)			
968	11	(11)			
969	7	(7)			
970	8	(8)			
971	10	(10)			
972	11	(11)			
973	11	26**	96		
975	290	31	24		
977		109	207		
978		74	82		
980		121	534		
983		239	285		
985	485	259	699		
988	120	59	700		
989	363	186	478		
992		353	774		
998	50	50	150		
999	71	71	180		
1000	547	409	1,129		
1002	78	38	180		
1005	492	247	570		
1008	891	207	320		
1009		31	54†		
1011		31	50†		

Examination year	Departmental chin-shih graduates	Chin-shih	Chu-k'o	Facilitated chin-shih	Facil. chu-k'o
1012	190	126	377		
1014		21	21[†]		
1015	89	280	65	78	72
1019	264	140	154		
1024	200	200	354	43	77
1027	498	377[†]	894	109	234
1030	401	249	573		
1034	661	499	481	857 comb.	
1038	499	310	617	26	587
1042	577	435		332	
1046	715	538	415	223	1,655
1049	637	498	550		
1053	683	520	522	166	430
1057	373	388	389	122	102
1059	200	165	184	29	16
1061	200	183	102	44	41
1063	200	193	147[†]	72	28
1065	213	200	18		
1067	306	250	36		
1070	300	295	355	474 comb.	
1073	408	400	40	475	217
1076	426	422	194	447	197
1079	348	348		778 comb.	
1082	485	445		836 comb.	
1085	485	485			
1088	523	523		533 comb.	
1091	519	519		323 comb.	
1094	513	512		346 comb.	
1097	569	564			
1100	558	561			
1103	538	538			
1104		16[‡]			
1105		35[‡]			
1106	671	671			
1107		40[‡]			
1108		51[‡]			
1109	685	685			
1110		15[‡]			
1112	713	713			
1113		19[‡]			
1114		17[‡]			
1115	670	670			
1116		11[‡]			
1117		12[‡]			

Examination year	Departmental chin-shih graduates	Chin-shih	Ssu-ch'uan chin-shih	Facilitated chin-shih	Facil. chu-k'o
1118	783	783			
1119		54‡			
1120		66‡			
1121	630	630			
1124	805	805			
1128		451	87		
1132		259	120	158	
1135	201	220	137	272	
1138	212	293			
1142	254	254		514	
1145	230	300	73	247	
1148	232	330	23	457	
1151	237	404	18	531	
1154	206	348	63	434	
1157	243	426		392	
1160	254	412	16	513	
1163	560	541		277	
1166	492	492		295	
1169	390	592		418	
1172	389	389			
1175	244	426			
1178	226	417			
1181	300	379			
1184	246	395			
1187	279	435			
1190	557	557			
1193	396	396			
1196	288	506		778	
1199	254	412		789	
1202	325	435		497	
1205	259	433†		611	
1208	273	426		411	
1211	255	465		679	
1214	270	502		669	
1217	269	523		663	
1220	270	475		647	
1223	361	550		679	
1226		987			
1229		557			
1232		493			
1235		466			
1238		422			
1241		367		637	
1244		424			

Examination year	Departmental chin-shih graduates	Chin-shih	Ssu-ch'uan chin-shih	Facilitated chin-shih	Facil. chu-k'o
1247		527		750	
1250		513		615	
1256		569		660	
1259		442		309	
1262		637		743	
1268		664			
1271		502			

Sources: WHTK 32: 304–7 for all *chin-shih* and *chu-k'o* figures for 960–1223 except where otherwise noted; SHY: HC 1 for the departmental graduate figures; Ibid. 7–8 for the facilitated *chin-shih* and *chu-k'o* figures, for *chin-shih* in 1027, 1104, 1105, 1107, 1108, 1110, 1113, 1114, 1116, 1117, 1119, 1120, and 1205, and for *chu-k'o* for 1009, 1011, 1014 and 1063; and Aoyama Sadao, *Sōdaishi nempyō*, 2: 217–60 for 1241–71. Aoyama's major source for these figures is the *Sung-shih ch'üan-wen hsü tzu-chih t'ung-chien* 33–36, though he uses the 1256 examination lists from SYKCSL for that year. Examination figures comparable though not identical to that in WHTK 32 may be found in SHY: HC 7–8 and, for the Northern Sung, in HCP and Chen Chün, *Huang-ch'ao pien-nien kang-mu pei-yao*.

*The palace examination was begun in 973. Prior to that graduates of the departmental (or Board of Rites) examination all received degrees.

**In 973, 11 *chin-shih* degrees were given initially but subsequently 15 more were given upon reexamination.

†SHY: HC figures were used for *chin-shih* and *chu-k'o* totals in instances where the WHTK either did not have any figures for that year or when the WHTK figure was suspect. For example, in 1205, WHTK gives 38 *chin-shih* and SHY: HC 8 gives 433, which is very close to the number in neighboring examinations, so the latter was used.

‡From 1104 to 1120, a number of degrees were given in non-examination years to University students promoted from the upper hall.

APPENDIX 3

TABLE 26. SUNG *CHIN-SHIH* TOTALS BY PREFECTURE BASED UPON LISTS IN LOCAL HISTORIES

Fig. 1 Map ref.	Northern Sung	Southern Sung	Undated	Total Sung
LIANG-CHE-TUNG LU:				
1 Ch'u-chou	193	506		699
2 Ch'ü-chou	250	359		609
3 Ming-chou (Ch'ing-yüan fu)	127	746		873
4 T'ai-chou	38	377		415
5 Wen-chou (Jui-an fu)	83	1,125		1,208
6 Wu-chou	67	466	47	580
7 Yüeh-chou (Shao-hsing fu)	153	321		474
Circuit Total:	911	3,900	47	4,858
LIANG-CHE-HSI LU:				
8 Ch'ang-chou	498	394		892
9 Hsiu-chou (Chia-hsing fu)	75	352		427
10 Hu-chou (An-chi chou)	242	298		540
11 Jun-chou (Chen-chiang fu)	137	126		253
12 Lin-an (Hang-chou)	165	493		658
13 Su-chou (P'ing-chiang fu)	213	317		530
14 Yen-chou (Mu-chou)	124	222		346
Circuit Total:	1,444	2,202		3,646
CHIANG-NAN-TUNG LU:				
15 Chiang-ning fu (Chien k'ang fu)	28	88		116
16 Ch'ih-chou	17	50	5	72
17 Hsin-chou	120	217		337
18 Hsüan-chou (Ning-kuo fu)	90	155	40	285
19 Hui-chou (Hsi-chou)	155	278		433
20 Jao-chou	329	621		950
21 Kuang-te chün	22	53	2	77
22 Nan-k'ang chün	60	223		283
23 T'ai-p'ing chou	37	53	2	92
Circuit Total:	958	1,738	49	2,645

Fig. 1 Map ref.	Northern Sung	Southern Sung	Undated	Total Sung
CHIANG-NAN-HSI LU:				
24 Chi-chou	266	643		909
25 Chiang-chou	54	38		92
26 Chien-ch'ang chün	195	452		647
27 Ch'ien-chou (Kan-chou)	76	87		163
28 Fu-chou	179	445		624
29 Hsing-kuo chün	22	52		74
30 Hung-chou (Lung-hsing fu)	174	375		549
31 Lin-chiang chün	156	234		390
32 Nan-an chün	13	50		63
33 Yüan-chou	57	66		123
34 Yün-chou	33	114		147
Chiang-hsi Imperial Clan*		80		80
Circuit Total:	1,225	2,636		3,861
FU-CHIEN LU:				
35 Chang-chou	83	185		268
36 Chien-chou (Chien-ning fu)	809	509		1,318
37 Ch'üan-chou	344	582		926
38 Fu-chou	550	2,249		2,799
39 Hsing-hua chün	468	558		1,026
40 Nan-chien chou	216	315	1	532
41 Shao-wu chün	107	88		195
42 T'ing-chou	23	39	18	80
Circuit Total:	2,600	4,525	19	7,144
HUAI-NAN-TUNG LU:				
43 Chao-hsin chün		1		1
44 Chen-chou	57	35		92
45 Ch'u-chou (1)	17		2	19
46 Ch'u-chou (2)	3	1	1	5
47 Kao-yu chün	19	10		29
48 Po-chou			9	9
49 Ssu-chou			2	2
50 Su-chou		2		2
51 T'ai-chou	72	38		110
52 T'ung-chou	6	13		19
53 Yang-chou	14	6		20
Circuit Total:	188	106	14	308
HUAI-NAN-HSI LU:				
54 Ch'i-chou	1	11	26	38
55 Hao-chou		2		2
56 Ho-chou	47	45		92
57 Huang-chou	1		6	7
58 Kuang-chou	3			3

Fig. 1 Map ref.	Northern Sung	Southern Sung	Undated	Total Sung
Huai-nan-hsi lu (*cont.*)				
59 Lu-chou	14	17		31
60 Shou-chou (Shou-ch'un fu)	5	4	9	18
61 Shu-chou (An-ch'ing fu)	13	1	2	16
62 Wu-wei chün	40	24		64
Circuit Total:	124	104	43	271
CHING-HU-NAN LU:				
63 Ch'a-ling chün		49	4	53
64 Ch'en-chou	25	53	11	89
65 Ch'üan-chou	9	22		31
66 Heng-chou	19	24	24	67
67 Kuei-yang chün		17		17
68 Shao-chou	6	20		26
69 T'an-chou	46	98		144
70 Tao-chou	59	75	9	143
71 Wu-kang chün		6		6
72 Yung-chou	36	52		88
Circuit Total:	200	416	48	664
CHING-HU-PEI LU:				
73 An-chou (Te-an fu)	18	6	4	28
74 Chiang-ling fu	5	1	3	9
75 Ching-chou (Ch'eng-chou)		1	2	3
76 Ching-men chün	7		1	8
77 E-chou	5	23	12	40
78 Han-yang chün		1	1	2
79 Hsia-chou		1	1	2
80 Kuei-chou	1			1
81 Li-chou	6	2	2	10
82 Ting-chou (Ch'ang-te fu)	8	18	2	28
83 Yüan-chou	6	7		13
84 Yüeh-chou	25	20	4	49
Circuit Total:	81	80	32	193
KUANG-NAN-TUNG LU:				
85 Chao-ch'ing fu (Tuan-chou)	7	16		23
86 Ch'ao-chou	37	51		88
87 Hui-chou	15	43		58
88 Kuang-chou	29	105		134
89 Lien-chou	4	3		7
90 Nan-hsiung chün	7	19		26
91 Shao-chou	25	22		47
Circuit Total:	124	259		383

Fig. 1 Map ref.	Northern Sung	Southern Sung	Undated	Total Sung
KUANG-NAN-HSI LU:				
92 Chao-chou	22	22		44
93 Ch'in-chou	1	1		2
94 Ch'iung-chou		5		5
95 Heng-chou		7		7
96 Hsün-chou	2	5		7
97 Hua-chou	1	2		3
98 I-chou (Ch'ing-yüan fu)	5	16		21
99 Kao-chou	1	3		4
100 Kuei-chou (Ching-chiang fu)	17	83		100
101 Liu-chou	18	19		37
102 Wu-chou	3	4		7
103 Yung-chou	1	8		9
Circuit Total:	71	175		246
CH'ENG-TU FU LU:				
104 Ch'eng-tu fu	330	251	78	659
105 Chia-chou (Chia-ting fu)	11	59		70
106 Chien-chou	5	8		13
107 Ch'iung-chou	8	20	6	34
108 Han-chou	11	22		33
109 Lung-chou (Hsien-ching chien, Ling-chou, Ling-ching chien)	66	146		212
110 Mei-chou	328	567	3	898
111 Mien-chou	23	31		54
112 P'eng-chou	1	2		3
113 Chih-ch'uan chün		14		14
114 Shu-chou (Ch'un-ch'ing fu)	2	6	3	11
115 Wei-chou		2		2
116 Ya-chou	2	4		6
117 Yung-k'ang chün	1	1	1	3
Circuit Total:	788	1,133	91	2,012
TZU-CHOU LU (or T'UNG CH'UAN FU LU):				
118 Ch'ang-chou	12	44		56
119 Ch'ang-ning chün	4		1	5
120 Chü-chou	38	34		72
121 Fu-shun chien	7	58		65
122 Ho-chou	21	66		87
123 Hsu-chou	3	15		18
124 Huai-an chün	35	43		78
125 Jung-chou	21	81	18	120
126 Kuan-te chün (Ning-hsi chün)	31	41		72

Fig. 1 Map ref.	Northern Sung	Southern Sung	Undated	Total Sung
Tzu-chou lu (*cont.*)				
127 Kuo-chou	65	152		217
128 Lu-chou	2	36		38
129 P'u-chou	86	195		281
130 Sui-chou (Sui-ning fu)	46	255		301
131 T'ung-ch'uan fu (Tzu-chou)	28	61		89
132 Tzu-chou	48	147		195
Circuit Total:	445	1,228	19	1,694
LI-CHOU LU:				
133 Chien-chou (Lung-ch'ing fu)	7	32		39
134 Hsing-yüan fu	1	2		3
135 Lang-chou	47	26	14	87
136 Li-chou	2	2		4
137 Lung-chou (Cheng-chou)	5	3		8
138 Pa-chou	1	13		14
139 P'eng-chou	10	13		23
140 Yang-chou		4		4
Circuit Total:	73	95	14	182
K'UEI-CHOU LU:				
141 Ch'ien-chou (Shao-ch'ing fu)		4		4
142 Chung-chou (Hsien-ch'un fu)		3		3
143 Ch'ung-ch'ing fu (Kung-chou)	9	27		36
144 Fu-chou	1	5		6
145 K'uei-chou	4			4
146 Liang-shan chün		3		3
147 Nan-p'ing chün		8		8
148 Shih-chou	1			1
149 Ta-chou	10	20		30
150 Ta-ning fu	2			2
151 Yün-an chün	3	3		6
Circuit Total:	30	73		103
CHING-CHI LU:				
152 K'ai-feng fu	73			73
CHING-TUNG-TUNG LU:				
153 Ch'ing-chou	5		18	23
154 Lai-chou			5	5
155 Mi-chou			2	2
156 Wei-chou			2	2
Circuit Total:	5		27	32
CHING-TUNG-HSI LU:				
157 P'u-chou	7		7	14
158 Ts'ao-chou (Hsing-jen fu)	1			1

Fig. 1 Map ref.	Northern Sung	Southern Sung	Undated	Total Sung
159 Ying-t'ien fu (Sung-chou)	24		9	33
160 Yün-chou (Tung-p'ing fu)	3			3
Circuit Total:	35		16	51
CHING-HSI-NAN LU:				
161 Sui-chou	6	2		8
162 Teng-chou	1		7	8
Circuit Total:	7	2	7	16
CHING-HSI-PEI LU:				
163 Ch'en-chou (Huai-ning fu)	4			4
164 Cheng-chou	9			9
165 Ho-nan fu	42	1		43
166 Hsü-chou (Ying-ch'ang fu)	3			3
167 Ju-chou	2			2
168 Meng-chou	6			6
169 Ts'ai-chou	6			6
170 Ying-chou (Shun-ch'ang fu)	1		2	3
Circuit Total:	73	1	2	76
HO-PEI-TUNG LU:				
171 Chi-chou	2		4	6
172 Ch'ing-chou (Ch'ien-ning chün)			1	1
173 En-chou	2			2
174 Pin-chou			1	1
175 Po-chou	2		1	3
176 Shan-chou (K'ai-te fu)	8		4	12
177 Ta-ming fu	11		14	25
178 Ts'ang-chou	4		3	7
179 Ying-chou (Ho-chien fu)	3		2	5
180 Yung-ching chün	3	1		4
Liao territory	10	1	13	24
Circuit Total:	45	2	43	90
HO-PEI-HSI LU:				
181 An-su chün			1	1
182 Chao-chou (Ch'ing-yüan fu)	6		6	12
183 Chen-ting fu	2		15	17
184 Ch'i-chou	7	1		8
185 Hsiang-chou	2			2
186 Hsing-chou (Hsin-te fu)	1		6	7
187 Huai-chou	4			4
188 Ming-chou	3			3
189 Pao-chou			7	7
190 Shen-chou			5	5

Fig. 1 Map ref.	Northern Sung	Southern Sung	Undated	Total Sung
191 Shun-an chün			3	3
192 Ting-chou (Chung-shan fu)			2	2
193 Tz'u-chou	1			1
194 Wei-chou	4			4
195 Yung-ning chün	2		2	4
Circuit Total:	32	1	47	80
HO-TUNG LU:				
196 Chiang-chou	6		7	13
197 Chin-chou (P'ing-yang fu)	6		2	5
198 Fen-chou	6		5	11
199 Hsin-chou	1		1	2
200 Lan-chou	1		3	4
201 Lu-chou (Lung-te fu)	4		5	9
202 P'ing-ting chün			2	2
203 Shih-chou			1	1
204 Tai-chou			1	1
205 T'ai-yüan fu	22		27	49
206 Tse-chou	24		8	32
Circuit Total:	67		62	129
YUNG-HSING LU:				
207 Chieh-chou	3		1	4
208 Ching-chao fu	19		4	23
209 Ho-chung fu	4		4	8
210 Hua-chou	4			4
211 Shan-chou	2		7	9
212 T'ung-chou	13	8	6	27
213 Yao-chou	81			81
Circuit Total:	126	8	22	156
CH'IN-FENG LU:				
214 Ch'eng-chou			1	1
215 Ch'in-chou			2	2
216 Ching-chou			1	1
217 Feng-chou			1	1
218 Feng-hsiang fu	3	1		4
219 Wei-chou			1	1
220 Yüan-chou			1	1
Circuit Total	3	1	7	11
Total for all Circuits:	9,630	18,694	609	28,933

Sources: See Local History Bibliography or, for greater specificity, Chaffee, 'Education and Examinations,' Appendix 2.

*These imperial clansmen were listed without prefecture in T'ao Ch'eng, *Chiang-hsi t'ung-chih.*

APPENDIX 4

AN EVALUATION OF LOCAL HISTORIES
AS SOURCES FOR SUNG *CHIN-SHIH* DATA

The attempt to reconstitute Sung *chin-shih* lists from an assortment of local histories dating from the Southern Sung through the Ch'ing raises questions of methodology and veracity. Using sources that differ greatly in age and quality, how can one distinguish between alternative versions of a given list? More importantly, once one has made these choices, how can one determine the accuracy of the results? In this appendix I shall try to answer these questions, first by describing the methodology used, and second by considering evidence which bears upon the validity of the results.

The following methodology was used in the survey:

1. The local histories consulted were the provincial and prefectural histories at the University of Chicago collection. County histories were avoided, both for practical reasons since there are so many of them and also to minimize the possibilities for double counting.[1]

2. The local history *chin-shih* lists employ varying degrees of chronological specificity. Wherever possible, I took down prefectural totals for each examination. Some sources list the *chin-shih* only by reign-periods, reigns, or dynasty. Except for the last, these made relatively little difference for the aggregated tables, since they are divided chronologically by reigns.

3. When confronted by two or more histories for a prefecture, each with slightly differing lists, I generally opted for the earliest. There were some exceptions, however:

—   In several cases a later history was used when it was more detailed and appeared to be more complete or more accurate than earlier histories. This was done for Ch'u-chou in Liang-che-tung; Ch'i-chou and Huang-chou in Huai-nan-hsi; Hsüan-chou, Kuang-te chün and T'ai-p'ing chou in Chiang-nan-tung; and for most of Ssu-ch'uan, where the coverage of the Ch'ing *Ssu-ch'uan t'ung-chih* by Yang Fang-ts'an was far more detailed than that of the Ming *Ssu-ch'uan tsung-chih* by Tu Ying-fang.

—   In the case of Ch'ü-chou (Liang-che-tung), there were three sources dating between 1662 and 1736. Their lists were very similar but not identical, so all of them were used.[2]

—   The Sung *chin-shih* lists in the local histories for northern China are fragmentary and incomplete. This is clearest in the case of K'ai-feng, which other sources describe as the greatest producer of *chin-shih* in the Northern Sung, and is evident for the rest of the north as well, given the remarkably small numbers in the local histories. Because of this, for each prefecture in northern China the source with the most names listed was used, regardless of its date.

4. Lacunae from the major sources were filled with data from alternative sources when possible.

Sources that give comprehensive quantitative data on Sung examinations are relatively rare and it is therefore difficult to check and evaluate the *chin-shih* lists. Nevertheless, the data that we have, if properly used, are sufficient to support qualified conclusions about the veracity of these lists.

Three types of error are most likely to be found in the local history lists. The first is omission and would be indicated by list totals being smaller than expected. A second is the inclusion of non-*chin-shih* who received other kinds of degrees: *chu-k'o* or, more probably, facilitated degrees. Such inclusions are specifically mentioned in the 1277 *Pao-ch'ing Ssu-ming chih* by Lo Chün with regard to the *chin-shih* in the 1169 *Ch'ien-tao Ssu-ming t'u-ching* by Chang Chin.[3] Third is the problem of double-listing, in which an individual was claimed by different prefectures, often because his familial and actual residences differed. Two other possible errors should be mentioned, though I do not believe that they are significant. One is that of fabricated names on the lists, which seems unlikely since there would have been no reason for later historians to have made up names. The other is that of incorrect dating. This certainly occurred; I found a number of ambiguous dates such as incorrect reign periods in the course of this survey. However, because the analysis uses relatively large blocks of time and also aggregate comparisons between circuits, regions and prefectures, these chronological errors should not be of great importance.

An idea as to the completeness of the local history data as a whole may be gained from the two bottom rows of Table 21, which compare the local history totals with the aggregate figures for the empire given by the *Wen-hsien t'ung-k'ao* (hereafter the WHTK) and other sources.[4] Omissions are indeed a problem in the local history lists, for no local history total exceeds that of the WHTK or the other sources. This problem appears to be relatively minor for the Southern Sung but serious for the Northern Sung. How are we to explain this difference? Is it because the Northern Sung data are generally unreliable, or is it that most of the missing *chin-shih* were from northern China and their records largely lost or destroyed? I tend towards the latter explanation. There are a few cases in south China where *chin-shih* records begin only well into the Northern Sung,[5] but in general the southern lists give the appearance of being complete and sometimes even cite their sources, such as stone inscriptions at prefectural schools. The north China lists for the Northern Sung, by contrast, are very poor when they exist at all. They often lack examination dates and seem to contain an overproportion of famous graduates such as *chuang-yüan* — the top graduates in the palace examination — suggesting that they may have been recreated from biographies. The educational sections of these same histories are similarly full of omissions, so it would appear that little information was available to Ming and Ch'ing local historians in northern China concerning the Sung.

This was particularly true of K'ai-feng and its vicinity; indeed, it may be that the loss of the K'ai-feng lists alone account for most of the Northern Sung omissions. In the examinations of 1059, 1061, and 1063, K'ai-feng

Table 27. *Comparison of* chin-shih *listed in the SYKCSL and in local histories for the examinations of 1148 and 1256*

	A	B	C	D	E	F	G
				In A & B same pref.	In A, not B	In A & B diff. pref.	In B, not A
	LH	SYKCSL	A/B				
1148:							
Liang-che-tung	52	52	1.00	48	2	2	4
Liang-che-hsi	43	38	1.13	35	3	5	3
Chiang-nan-tung	41	30	1.37	29	8	4	1
Chiang-nan-hsi	37	23	1.61	22	13	2	1
Fu-chien	77	66	1.17	65	4	8	1
Huai-nan-tung	3	4	0.75	2	–	1	2
Huai-nan-hsi	–	–	–	–	–	–	–
Ching-hu-nan	1	1	1.00	1	–	–	–
Ching-hu-pei	1	1	1.00	1	–	–	–
Kuang-nan-tung	5	5	1.00	5	–	–	–
Kuang-nan-hsi	–	–	–	–	–	–	–
Ch'eng-tu fu	34	35	0.97	31	1	2	4
Tzu-chou	24	27	0.89	21	1	2	6
Li-chou	3	2	1.50	2	–	1	–
K'uei-chou	4	4	1.00	4	–	–	–
Subtotal:	325	288	1.13	266	32	27	22
North China		26					26
Imperial clan (no residence given)		16					16
1148 Total:	325	330	0.98	266	32	27	64
1256:							
Liang-che-tung	127	99	1.28	86	31	10	13
Liang-che-hsi	36	29	1.24	25	3	8	4
Chiang-nan-tung	53	39	1.36	29	21	3	10
Chiang-nan-hsi	81	58	1.40	55	20	6	3
Fu-chien	121	124	0.98	100	14	7	24
Huai-nan-tung	6	8	0.75	4	2	–	4
Huai-nan-hsi	8	7	1.14	2	5	1	5
Ching-hu-nan	15	9	1.67	7	6	2	2
Ching-hu-pei	12	16	0.75	9	2	1	7
Kuang-nan-tung	14	17	0.82	8	3	3	9
Kuang-nan-hsi	15	22	0.71	12	–	3	10
Ch'eng-tu fu	37	36	1.02	34	–	3	2
Tzu-chou	44	50	0.88	43	–	1	7
Li-chou	9	15	0.60	5	1	3	10
K'uei-chou	3	5	0.60	3	–	–	2
Ching-hsi-nan	–	3	0.00	–	–	–	3

Table 27. (*cont.*)

	A	B	C	D	E	F	G
				In A & B same	In A,	In A & B diff.	In B,
	LH	SYKCSL	A/B	pref.	not B	pref.	not A
1256 (*cont.*)							
Sub-total:	581	537	1.08	422	108	51	115
Imperial clan		29					29
Residence							
missing		35					35
1156 Total:	581	601	0.97	422	108	51	179

accounted for 44, 69, and 66 *chin-shih* respectively, or 27%, 38%, and 34% of the degrees given. If we add in the figures for the Directorate of Education, we get 66, 97, and 96 degrees, or 40%, 53%, and 50%.[6] Some of these capital *chin-shih* were undoubtedly claimed by other localities as well.[7] For example there was a complaint in 998 that as many as 38 of the 50 *chin-shih* that year were from K'ai-feng.[8] Yet the local histories claim some 40 non-K'ai-feng *chin-shih* for the same year, which suggests that many of the K'ai-feng *chin-shih* had ties, probably ancestral or family homes, in other prefectures. But even if one adjusts for such double-counting, K'ai-feng *chin-shih* clearly represent the single greatest gap in the local history lists.

Although the examination totals found in the WHTK and other sources provide us with the only evidence against which the local history lists can be checked as a whole, other sources allow us to check specific years or regions. Most important are the examination lists for 1148 and 1526, the first two lists in the *Sung Yüan k'o-chü san lu* (hereafter SYKCSL).[9] These allow us to check the local history lists by name for those two years and to verify residences as well. Table 27 gives the results of such a check.

In purely numerical terms, and that is our main concern here, since tables and not lists of names are being compiled, the agreement is remarkably close for both years, whether one uses the SYKCSL total of all degrees or just those for which residence is given.

Looking at the actual agreement on names or residency (Columns D–G), the results are less satisfactory, especially for 1256. Column D shows the numbers where there is agreement on both names and residences. Column F represents those where the names but not residences are in agreement. It is subdivided further in Table 28.

The last three rows in Table 28 actually provide information missing in the SYKCSL, filling in lacunae. Also, those listed in the second row, where residences differ but there is no double listing, are also listed in Column G of Table 27. Thus if one were concerned with just the number of correct names that the local histories contain for the two years, they would be 282 and 459 respectively (i.e., adding Column D in Table 27 to Rows 2–5 in Table 28, but subtracting two of those in 1256 because of the double listings in Rows 4 and 5).

Table 28. *Subdivision of column F from Table 27*

	1148	1256
Double-listed in local histories	11	12
LH residence different from that in SYKCSL*	5	23
North China residence in SYKCSL	8	–
Imperial clan – no residence in SYKCSL	3	10[†]
Residence missing in SYKCSL	–	6[†]
Total:	27	51

*In some cases in the SYKCSL, two residences are given for an individual, an official residence (*pen-kuan*), and the place where he is or has been living (*yü-chi*). In most such cases, the candidate is claimed by the local history for the latter and not the former, and it is the latter that I have taken to be the residence for the purposes of these tables.

[†]One imperial *chin-shih* who has no residence listed in SYKCSL is claimed by two prefectures in the local histories. The same is true of one non-imperial *chin-shih*.

We can only speculate about the origin of those names in Column E. My guess is that they were recipients of the facilitated *chin-shih* degree (459 were given in 1148 and 660 in 1256), but it is impossible to tell. Luckily, in both years Columns E and G roughly balance each other out, so that the numerical agreement between the two lists is very close. In fact, compared to the degree of agreement shown in Table 21, the 98% and 97% agreement shown in Column C are so close as to be suspicious; perhaps the authors of the local histories used these lists in making their own lists. In the case of Ssu-ch'uan (Ch'eng-tu through K'uei-chou in Table 27), this may well have been the case, for the entries for those two years in their major source, the *Ssu-ch'uan t'ung-chih,* list more *chin-shih* and attribute them to more prefectures than they do for other years. And these attributions are highly accurate, as we can see from Table 27. But Ssu-ch'uan seems to have been unique in this respect. Certainly the authors of the Chiang-nan and, for 1256, the Liang-che local histories could not have made much use of the lists, considering the size of the Column D entries for those circuits. In fact, the table suggests that those circuits are overrepresented in the local history tables while the Ssu-ch'uan circuits are underrepresented.

While the SYKCSL gives us a pretty good idea of the accuracy of the lists for the Southern Sung, the Northern Sung presents a problem. Without similar checks, how can we have any confidence at all in the data? There is no good answer to this question. However, there are at least two partial checks which one can make for the earlier period.

To determine the degree of the duplication of names among the local histories, I arbitrarily chose three Northern Sung examinations and recorded all of the names given for those years in the histories consulted. Table 29 shows the incidence of duplication for those years and also for 1148 and 1256. Except for the 992 examination, duplication appears to have been minimal.

A second possible check comes from the statistics given by Ssu-ma Kuang in his debate with Ou-yang Hsiu over examination quota policy. To support his argument that candidates from the north and west were discriminated

Table 29. Chin-shih *duplication in local histories*

Year	Total chin-shih	Duplications*	Percentage
992	97	10	10.3%
1061	110	3	2.7%
1109	435	5	1.1%
1148	325	11	3.4%
1256	578	12	2.1%

*This represents the number of repetitions of names already listed. Thus a name listed twice counts as one duplication and one listed three times (which occurred only once, in 992), as two.

against in the examinations at the capital, he gave a number of *chin-shih* figures for northern and western circuits, plus those for K'ai-feng and the Directorate of Education for the years of 1059, 1061, and 1063. Table 30 shows those figures and the comparable figures from the local histories. Because some Chia-yu (1056—1063) *chin-shih* are undated in the local histories, figures for all four Chia-yu examinations are given.

The main impression one gets from this table is of disagreement between Ssu-ma Kuang and the local histories. However, such are the unknowns that even negative conclusions would be difficult to draw. Between the lacunae in Ssu-ma's data and the undated Chia-yu *chin-shih*, not to mention the possibilities of slight misdatings, none of the circuit comparisons are trustworthy. Also, while there may be few duplications among the *chin-shih* in the local histories, we have no way of telling how many of Ssu-ma Kuang's K'ai-feng and Directorate *chin-shih* might have been listed in the local histories. Indeed, it is probable that quite a few were, for Ssu-ma's circuit data pertain specifically to the *chü-jen* advancing through the prefectural examinations and not to provincial students studying in K'ai-feng and taking preliminary examinations there who would still have been claimed by their local communities upon receiving degrees. Such a conclusion is supported by Table 31, which gives the local history *chin-shih* totals for the same three examinations plus Ssu-ma's figures for K'ai-feng and the Directorate and compares them with the examination totals from the WHTK.

Considering that there are probably many omissions in the local history lists, the fact that the combined local history and Ssu-ma Kuang totals in two cases out of the three exceed the WHTK totals certainly suggests considerable duplication of names between the capital and the rest of the empire. At the same time the closeness of the two sets of totals gives us at least some assurance that the local histories lists approximate the actual record.

However rough and unsystematic these checks might be, they demonstrate the general validity of the local history lists. The low incidence of name duplications and the substantial agreement between these lists and the lists of 1148 and 1256 testify to the care taken in the compilation of the former. But if these lists are to be of any value, we must be clear about their limitations. Here I would mention four.

First, the Northern Sung data are very incomplete and must be used with

Table 30. *Comparison of 11th Century chin-shih data from Ssu-ma kuang and local histories*

Circuit	1057 LH	1059 SMK	1059 LH	1061 SMK	1061 LH	1063 SMK	1063 LH	Undated 1056–63	Total SMK	LH 1059–63	LH 1056–63
Kuang-nan-tung	6	3	0	2	0	0	0	0	5	0	6
Kuang-nan-hsi	1	1	3	0	0	0	0	0	1	3	4
Ching-hu-nan	0	3	2	2	0	2	0	1	7	2	3
Ching-hu-pei	0	–	1	0	0	1	0	2	1	1	3
Tzu-chou lu	7	2	5	–	2	–	3	5	2	10	22
K'uei-chou lu	1	1	0	0	0	–	0	1	1	0	2
Li-chou lu	0	1	0	–	0	0	0	7	1	0	7
Ho-pei	2	5	3	–	0	1	0	0	6	4	6
Ho-tung	1	0	0	1	0	1	0	3	2	1	5
Ching-tung	0	5	0	5	0	–	0	7	10	0	7
K'ai-feng	–	44	–	69	–	66	–	–	179	–	–
Directorate	–	22	–	28	–	30	–	–	80	–	–

Sources: Ssu-ma Kuang, *Ssu-ma kung wen-chi* 30/1a–5b; Local History Bibliography or Chaffee, 'Education and Examinations,' Appendix 2, for local histories.

Table 31. Chin-shih *for 1059–1063: Ssu-ma Kuang's K'ai-feng and Direc-*
torate figures plus local history totals compared with WHTK totals

	1059	1061	1063	Undated Chia-yu
Local history totals	87	110	106	49
K'ai-feng	44	69	66	
Directorate	22	28	30	
	153	207	202	49
WHTK Totals	165	183	193	

great care if at all. Even if all of the information that we have is accurate, it still represents only half of all Northern Sung *chin-shih* and less than a quarter of the *chin-shih* from the late tenth century. The largest known omissions are from K'ai-feng and the Directorate of Education and it could be that these alone account for most of the missing *chin-shih*. Such appears to have been the case in 1059, 1061, and 1063. The low rates of duplication that we found for 1061 and 1109 are encouraging, however, for they help to rule out an obvious and important source of error. We have no reason, therefore, to exclude Northern Sung data as such, although they are certainly subject to the limitations mentioned below.

Second, the records for northern China and for the peripheral regions of southern China tend to be poor in quality and lacking in detail; they almost certainly underreport examination results. Fortunately for us, these were the least successful regions in the empire, so that even a large error in under-reporting would be small in absolute numbers and would not affect sub-stantially the overall pattern of regional distribution.

Third, even as the more backward regions seem to have been under-represented, so some of the more advanced regions appear to have inflated figures. A prime example is Chiang-nan, where the local history figures exceeded those of the SYKCSL in both 1148 and 1256 by over one third. Also notable is Liang-che in 1256. Such errors are important, for the numbers involved are quite large, and for certain kinds of comparisons adjustments might have to be made. But most regional differences were still of sufficient magnitude so that the adjustments would not alter the basic distribution.

Fourth, the quality of the local history lists seems relatively poor for the late Southern Sung. This is most apparent in Table 27 where in 1256 the numbers of additions (Column E) and omissions (Column G) are both far higher than the comparable figures in 1148. In Table 21, too, the percentage of all *chin-shih* accounted for by the local histories drops from 90% in the twelfth century to 76% in the mid-thirteenth. By both of these measures, the data for the Southern Sung before 1190 appear to be optimal in both coverage and accuracy.

Finally, I would add that a major value of this *chin-shih* survey derives from its size and scope. So long as one is aware of its major biases and accounts for them, it can be used beneficially to study academic, political and socioeconomic changes in Sung China. But it must be borne in mind that inaccuracies exist and that the sources used vary in quality. Thus any detailed use of it must be made with caution and with consideration for the particular sources used.

NOTES

Notes to Chapter 1

1. T'o T'o et al., *Sung-shih,* 495 ch. (Taipei: I-wen yin-shu-kuan, 1962) 267/6b. This will be cited hereafter as SS.

2. *Sung hui-yao chi-kao*: Hsüan-chü section (Taipei: Shih-chieh shu-chü 1964) 7/8a; Ma Tuan-lin, *Wen-hsien t'ung-k'ao,* 348 ch. (Taipei: Hsin-hsing shu-chü, 1964) 32:305. These works will be cited hereafter as SHY:HC and WHTK.

3. Li T'ao, *Hsü tzu-chih t-ung-chien ch'ang-pien,* 520 ch. (Taipei: Shih-chieh shu-chü, 1967) 51/13a. This will be cited hereafter as HCP.

4. SS 455/14b; *Sung-shih hsin-pien* (Shanghai: Commercial Press, 1974) 148:47.

5. The quota figure is from a list of prefectural examination quotas which appears on an anonymous and undated Southern Sung map found in a Japanese monastary. A facsimile of the map is appended to Aoyama Sadao's *Tō Sō jidai no Kōtsū to chishi chizu no kenkyū* (Tokyo: Yoshikawa Kobunkan, 1963).

6. SHY:HC 16/31a–b.

7. As early as the Western Han, examinations (*k'ao-shih*) were sometimes used by the emperor to test men who had been recommended for office. But the *k'o-chü* system of the Sui and T'ang was far more complex and formal.

8. Hsü Nai-chiang, ed., *Sung Yüan k'o-chü san-lu* (1923 ed.) This will hereafter be cited as SYKCSL.

9. That is, the works of Confucius and Mencius plus what were known as the Nine Classics (*Chiu-ching*). Sometimes the Classic of Filial Piety (*Hsiao-ching*) and the early dictionary, the *Er-ya*, were also included.

10. Fan Chung-yen, *Fan Wen-cheng kung chi,* 20 ch. plus appendices (Taipei: Commercial Press, 1965) 10:121.

11. SHY:HC 4/12b–22a.

12. The age at which schooling began was usually given as eight or ten (Chinese style), but at that point they had probably had considerable instruction at home. The twelfth century philosopher Chu Hsi, in his widely read *Hsiao-hsüeh* ('Elementary Learning'), wrote that children should learn numbers and place names at six, that boys and girls should be separated at seven, that they work on manners and deportment at eight, that they be taught the calendar at nine, and be sent out to school at ten. *Hsiao-hsüeh chi-chu,* 6 ch. (Ssu-pu pei-yao ed. This will hereafter be referred to as SPPY) 1/1b–2a.

13. Most of this information is from Ch'en Tung-yüan, *Chung-kuo chiao-yü shih* (Shanghai: Commercial Press, 1936), pp. 311–17. See also Sidney O. Fosdick, 'Chinese Book Publishing during the Sung Dynasty: a Partial Translation of *Isotoriia Kitaiskoi Pechatnoi Knigi Sunskoi Epokhi* by Konstantin Konstantinovich Flug with Added Notes and an Introduction' (M.A. Thesis, University of Chicago, 1968), and Thomas H.C. Lee, 'The Schools of Sung China', *Journal of Asian Studies* 37 (1977):48–49.

14. Wang Ch'ang, comp., *Chin-shih ts'ui-pien*, 160 ch. (1805 ed.) 134/22b–23b.
15. See Chapter 4 for a description and discussion of the system.
16. Chou Ying-ho, *Ching-ting Chien-k'ang chih*, 50 ch. (1261 ed.) 30/17a. This will hereafter be cited as CKC.
17. SS 165/12a–b; Chao Sheng, *Ch'ao-yeh lei-yao*, 5 ch. (Ts'ung-shu chi-ch'eng ed. This will hereafter be cited as TSCC.) 2:22–3.
18. Lü Pen-chung, *T'ung-meng hsün*, 3 ch. (Wan-yu wen-k'u ed.) 3/30. This will hereafter be cited as TMH.
19. The literature on the political activities of Sung University students is considerable. See especially, Huang Hsien-fan, *Sung-tai T'ai-hsüeh-sheng chiu-kuo yüntung* (Shanghai: Commercial Press, 1936).
20. These are vividly described in contemporary accounts of the two cities: Meng Yüan-lao, *Tung-ching meng-hua lu*, 10 ch. (Peking, 1959), and Wu Tzu-mu, *Meng-liang lu*, 20 ch. (Pai-pu ts'ung-k'an ed. This will hereafter be cited as PPTK.) In English, see Jacques Gernet, *Daily Life in China on the Eve of the Mongol Invasion*, trans. H.M. Wright (Stanford: Stanford University Press, 1962).
21. Yang Wan-li, *Ch'eng-chai chi*, 132 ch. (Ssu-pu ts'ung-k'an ed. This will hereafter be cited as SPTK.) 71/9a–10a.
22. For a discussion of marriage and the examinations as the twin concerns for the young scholar in his early twenties, see Thomas H.C. Lee, 'The Schools of Sung China,' p. 52.
23. Ou-yang Shou-tao, *Sun-chai wen-chi*, 27 ch. (Ssu-k'u ch'üan-shu ed. This collection will hereafter be cited as SKCS.) 7/14b.
24. SS 273/21b–22a.
25. Wang T'ing-kuei, *Lu-ch'i wen-chi*, 50 ch. (SKCS ed.) 46/7a–8a.
26. Shi O, *Ch'un-yu Lin-an chih*, ch. 5–10 extant (Wu-lin chang ts'ung-pien ed.) 6/5a.
27. Liu Ts'ai-shao, *Shan-ch'i chü-shih chi*, 12 ch. (SKCS ed.) 12/14a–16b.
28. Ho Wei, *Ch'in-chu chi-wen*, 10 ch. (Sung-jen pai-chia hsiao-shuo ed.) 3:28–30. This will hereafter be cited as CCCW.
29. Hung Mai, *I-chien chih*, 4 vols., 80 ch. (TSCC ed.; Shanghai: Commercial Press, 1937) 4.11:85; 4.18:140. I have used the 80 ch. edition from the TSCC rather than the full 420 ch. edition. This work will be cited hereafter as ICC.
30. *Chung-kuo chiao-yü shih*; *Chung-kuo k'o-chü shih-tai chih chiao-yü* (Shanghai: Commercial Press, 1933).
31. *Sōdai kyōikushi gaisetsu* (Tokyo: Hakubunsha, 1965). This will hereafter be cited as SKG.
32. *Sōdai kakyo seido kenkyū* (Kyoto: Dobosha Press Co., 1969). This will hereafter be cited as SKSK.
33. 'Education in Sung China' (Ph.D. Dissertation, Yale University, 1974); 'The Schools of Sung China'; *Sung-tai chiao-yü kai-lun* (Taipei: Tung-sheng ch'u-pan shih-yeh yu-hsien kung-shih, 1980). While Lee's excellent work has been primarily institutional, it displays an acute sensitivity to the social context of education.
34. Edward A. Kracke, Jr., 'Family vs. Merit in Chinese Civil Service Examinations Under the Empire', *Harvard Journal of Asiatic Studies* 10 (1947): 103–23; 'Region, Family and Individual in the Chinese Examination System,' in *Chinese Thought and Institutions*, ed. John K. Fairbank (Chicago: University of Chicago Press, 1961), pp. 251–68. Ping-ti Ho, *The Ladder of Success in Imperial China: Aspects of Social Mobility, 1368–1911* (New York: Columbia University Press, 1962).
35. Ming and Ch'ing *chü-jen* were eligible to hold office, unlike their Sung counterparts.
36. See Evelyn Sakakida Rawski, *Education and Popular Literary in Ch'ing China* (Ann Arbor: University of Michigan Press, 1979).

37. This point was first made by D.C. Twitchett in 'A Critique of Some Recent Studies of Modern Chinese Social-Economic History,' *Transactions of the International Conference of Orientalists in Japan* 10 (1965):28–41, and since then by Hilary Jane Beattie in *Land and Lineage in China: A Study of T'ung-Ch'eng County, Anhwei, in the Ming and Ch'ing Dynasties* (Cambridge and New York: Cambridge University Press, 1979), p. 19.

38. 'Public Office in the Liao and the Chinese Examination System,' *Harvard Journal of Asiatic Studies* 10 (1947):13–40.

39. 'Peasantry and Gentry: An Interpretation of Chinese Social Structure and its Changes,' *American Journal of Sociology* 52 (1946):1–17; *China's Gentry* (Chicago: University of Chicago Press, 1953).

40. *Land and Lineage in China.*

41. 'Demographic, Political, and Social Transformations of China, 750–1550,' *Harvard Journal of Asiatic Studies* 42 (1982):365–442; 'Community Elites, Economic Policy-making and Material Progress in Sung China (960–1279),' paper presented for the CISS–CSNA Workshop on the Sources of Asian History and the Generation of Quantifiable Historical Indicators, Toronto, February 1976; and 'Kinship, Status and Region in the Formal and Informal Organization of the Chinese Fiscal Bureaucracy, 960–1165 A.D.,' paper presented at the Annual Meeting of the Social Science History Association, Ann Arbor, October 1977.

42. 'Prominence and Power in Sung China' (Ph.D. Dissertation, University of Pennsylvania, 1979).

43. Linda Walton-Vargo, 'Education, Social Change, and Neo Confucianism in Sung Yuan China' (Ph.D. Dissertation, University of Pennsylvania, 1978).

44. Hartwell does not say whether he accepts these claims. David Johnson, however, has persuasively argued that the great majority of them were probably fictitious. 'The Last Years of a Great Clan: the Li Family of Chao-chung in the Late T'ang and Early Sung,' *Harvard Journal of Asiatic Studies* 37 (1977):51–9.

45. Hartwell, 'Transformations of China,' pp. 420–5.

46. Ibid., p. 419.

47. This generalization is based upon a study of mine on prominent lineages in Chi-chou (Chiang-nan-hsi). For examples of upwardly mobile families pursuing joint strategies of elite intermarriage and investment in education, see Wang T'ing-keui, *Lu-ch'i wen-chi* 44/5b–6b, 46/3b–5a; and Liu Ts'ai-shao, *Shan-ch'i chü-shih chi* 12/23a–26a.

48. For examples of Chi-chou families or lineages that can be traced for three generations or more whose members tried but never succeeded in the examinations, see Chou Pi-ta, *Chou wen-chung kung chi*, 200 ch. (SKCS ed.) 31/1a–3a (this will be cited hereafter as CWCKC); Wen T'ien-hsiang, *Wen-shan hsien-sheng ch'üan-chi*, 21. ch. (Taipei: Commercial Press, 1965) 11:389–91; and Yang Wan-li, *Ch'eng-chai chi* 130/2b–4b.

49. See, for example, Chang Shih-nan, *Yu-huan chi-wen*, 10 ch. (TSCC ed.) 4/6a–7a, in which an 'extremely poor' young candidate so impresses a prefectural examining official by his demeanor that the official betroths his daughter to him. This work will hereafter be cited as YHCW.

50. Yü Chih-chen, *Chi-an fu chih*, 36 ch. (1585 ed.) 29/2b–3a. Before passing, he left home and received the patronage of a wealthy woman.

51. ICC 3.11:83–4. See also Ibid. 4.3:25 for a marriage which did not occur because the man did not pass the examinations, and Chu Yü, *P'ing-chou k'o-t'an*, 3 ch. (TSCC ed.) 2:16 on the high dowries fetched by *chin-shih* recipients in Northern Sung Kuang-chou (Canton). This last is cited in Thomas Lee, 'Schools of Sung China,' p. 52.

52. For such provisions in the prototypical lineage organization, the eleventh century Fan lineage, see D.C. Twitchett, 'The Fan Clan's Charitable Estate, 1050–1760,'

in *Confucianism in Action*, eds. David Nivison and Arthur Wright (Stanford: Stanford University Press, 1959), pp. 97–133. Chinese lineages were characterized by their large and corporate organizations, as exemplified by the Fans. Because in most Sung cases the presence or absence of such an organization cannot be determined, 'lineage' will be used more loosely here to refer to a large group of kin from the same locality (usually county) while 'family' will refer primarily to nuclear and stem families.

53. SS 157/2a.
54. Ibid. 156/15a–b.
55. Chang Chin, *Ch'ien-tao Ssu-ming t'u-ch'ing*, 12 ch. (Sung Yüan Ssu-ming liu chih ed.) 9/16a–18a.
56. For a brief treatment of some aspects of that conjunction, see John W.Chaffee, 'To Spread One's Wings: Examinations and the Social Order in Southeastern China During the Southern Sung,' *Historical Reflections/Réflexions Historiques* 9 (1982):305–22.
57. These generalizations are based upon a large body of scholarship on T'ang and Sung economic change. For useful introductions to the subject in English, see Yoshinobu Shiba, *Commerce and Society in Sung China*, trans. Mark Elvin (Ann Arbor: Center for Chinese Studies, The University of Michigan, 1970) and Mark Elvin, *The Pattern of the Chinese Past* (Stanford: Stanford University Press, 1973), Part II.
58. Thomas F. Carter, *The Invention of Printing in China and Its Spread Westward*, revised by L. Carrington Goodrich (New York: Ronald Press Co., 1955), pp. 56–62.
59. Chang Hsiu-min, 'Nan-Sung (1127–1279) K'o-shu ti-chu k'ao,' *T'u-shu-kuan* 1961, no. 3, p. 54.
60. The argument is Joseph Needham's, who believes that the bureaucratic domination of Chinese society served to absorb technological changes which had revolutionary consequences in European society. 'Science and China's Influence in the World,' in *The Legacy of China*, ed. Raymond Dawson (Oxford: Oxford Univ. Press, 1964), pp. 234–308.
61. D.C. Twitchett, 'The Composition of the T'ang Ruling Class: New Evidence from Tunhuang,' in *Perspectives on the T'ang*, eds. Arthur Wright and Denis Twitchett (New Haven: Yale University Press, 1973), p. 79.
62. David Johnson, 'The Last Years of a Great Clan,' pp. 59–68.
63. Sung Shee, 'Sung-tai shih-ta-fu tui shang-jen ti t'ai-tu,' in *Sung-shih yen-chih lun-ts'ung* (Taipei: Shang-te yin-shu-kuan, 1962), p. 2.
64. For a persuasive discussion of why this was the case, see Ch'en Chung-mien, 'Chin-shih k'o t'ai-t'ou chih yüan-yin chi ch'i liu-pi,' in *Sui T'ang shih* (Peking: K'ao-teng chiao-yü ch'u-pan-she, 1957), pp. 181–90.
65. For a number of years prior to 710, figures for graduates who had been recommended by local officials are available. For those years, their proportion (of all graduates) varied for 1/11 to 1/55. This was the case despite the fact that provincial candidates outnumbered those from the capital. Thereafter, provincial candidates probably fared somewhat better, but not enough to reverse the imbalance. D.C. Twitchett, 'T'ang Governmental Institutions: the Bureaucracy,' *Cambridge History of China*, vol. IV, forthcoming.
66. Twitchett op. cit., estimates that the examinations accounted for roughly 15–16% of the T'ang bureaucracy in the ninth century. Another historian, Sun Kuo-tung, has a considerable lower estimate of 6%. 'T'ang Sung chih chi she-hui men-ti chih hsiao-jung,' *Hsin-ya hsüeh-pao* 4 (1959):246.
67. David G. Johnson, *The Medieval Chinese Oligarchy* (Boulder, Co.: Westview Press, 1977), p. 149.
68. Ibid.; Twitchett, 'T'ang Governmental Institutions.'

69. WHTK ch. 29–30. There is some doubt as to the completeness of the T'ang examination figures in the WHTK, but the actual figure, if somewhat higher, still could not have begun to approach the Sung average. During the Five Dynasties and the Sung before 977, for which the figures are quite reliable, the degree averages were 33 and 19 respectively.

70. See Chapter 3 for an elaboration of these concerns.

71. Sadao Aoyama, 'The Newly-risen Bureaucrats in Fukien at the Five Dynasty–Sung Period with Special Reference to their Genealogies,' *Memoirs of the Research Department of the Tōyō Bunko* 21 (1962):1–48.

Notes to Chapter 2

1. Max Weber, 'Bureaucracy,' *From Max Weber: Essays in Sociology*, trans. and ed. H.H. Girth and C. Wright Mills (New York: Oxford University Press, 1958), pp. 196–244. See also C.K. Yang, 'Some Characteristics of Chinese Bureaucratic Behavior,' in *Confucianism in Action*, eds., David S. Nivison and Arthur F. Wright (Stanford: Stanford University Press, 1959), pp. 134–64.

2. See Edward A. Kracke, Jr., *Civil Service in Sung China: 960–1067* (Cambridge, Mass.: Harvard University Press, 1953), Ch. 3.

3. Ibid., Ch. 5–10.

4. Ping-ti Ho, 'An Estimate of the Total Population of Sung–Chin China,' in *Études Song/Démographie* (Paris: Mouton & Co., 1970), pp. 33–53. Robert Hartwell has estimated Sung land area to have been 2,108,000 sq. mi., 'Transformations of China,' p. 369.

5. Brian E. McKnight, *Village and Bureaucracy in Southern Sung China* (Chicago: University of Chicago Press, 1971), esp. Ch. 2–3.

6. Arthur F. Wright, 'Symbolism and Function, Reflections on Changan and other Great Cities,' *Journal of Asian Studies* 24 (1965):667–79.

7. Kracke, *Civil Service*, p. 56.

8. Kracke describes the importance and uses of titular (or stipendiary) offices (*pen-kuan, chi-lu-kuan*) in their pre-1082 form in Ibid., pp. 78–80. For a more comprehensive treatment which analyzes the nine-grade system as well, see Umehara Kaoru, 'Sōsho no kirokukan to sono shuhen: Sōdai kansei no rikai no tame ni,' *Tohō gakuho* 48 (1975):135–182.

9. Kracke, *Civil Service*, p. 8.

10. Ibid., p. 89; Umehara, 'Sōsho no kirokukan,' p. 142.

11. For a revealing description of the clerical recruitment and organization in one agency, the Imperial Library, see John H. Winkleman, 'The Imperial Library in Southern Sung China, 1127–1279: A Study of the Organization and Operation of the Scholarly Agencies of the Central Government,' *Transactions of the American Philosophical Society*, n.s. 64, pt. 8 (1974):24–6.

12. McKnight, *Village Bureaucracy*, pp. 20–2.

13. Chao I, *Nien-er-shih tsa-chi*, 2 vols. (Taipei: Shih-chieh shu-chü, 1972), 2:334.

14. Control of clerks was a persistent and serious problem, for they were in an excellent position to accumulate power and wealth. See James T.C. Liu (Liu Tzu-chien), 'The Sung Views on the Control of Government Clerks,' *Journal of the Economic and Social History of the Orient* 10 (1967):317–34.

15. See below Chapter 3, pp. 55–6 for a discussion of clerks and the examinations.

16. Kracke, *Civil Service*, p. 56.

17. On the growing numbers of imperial clansmen in the civil service, see p. 24 below.

18. The group of officials promoted from the ranks is particularly striking, for it accounted for 33.2% of the administrative officials but just 10.4% of the executory group. It may be that because of the war with the Chin, irregular armed units were incorporated into the army and their leaders given officer status.

19. See Appendix 1 for a complete list.

20. The grade required for an official to have this privilege varied. In 1195 it was the lower sixth grade, using the Yüan-feng (1082) system of grades. CYTC 2.14:528. There are no general treatments of this extremely important and complicated institution. For useful discussions of it, see Karl Wittfogel, 'Public Office in the Liao and the Chinese Examination System,' pp. 13–40; Kracke, *Civil Service*, pp. 73–5; and Sung Shee, *Sung shih*, 2 vols. (Taipei: Hua-kang shu-chu, 1968), 1:81–2.

21. WHTK 34:326–7.

22. In addition, the promotion requirements for protected officials (and other non-degree holders) were more stringent than were those for degree holders. Kracke, *Civil Service*, pp. 91–3; Umehara, 'Sōsho no Kirokukan,' pp. 146–55, 167–74.

23. For example, regulations in 1195–1200 permitted titular counselors (*shih-hsiang*), who were officials of the lower first grade, to name eighteen. CYTC 2.14:528.

24. According to tenth century Wang Ting-pao's entertaining and informative book on T'ang examinations, *T'ang chih-yen*, 15 ch. (Shanghai: Ku-tien wen-hsüeh ch'u-pan she, 1957) 2:17–19, prefects sometimes held tests for selecting candidates, but these were informal affairs open to all aspiring literati, not merely those from the prefecture. This work will hereafter be cited as TCY.

25. See Chapter 5 for an analysis of these very important examinations.

26. In the *chin-shih* examination, graduates were usually ranked into five classes. Those in the first two classes were designated as having 'passed with distinction' (*chi-ti*); those in the third class 'formally qualified' (*ch'u-shen*); while those in the fourth and fifth classes simply 'passed' (*t'ung ch'u-shen*). Kracke, *Civil Service*, pp. 66–7. A high place in the examinations was of great benefit to one's career. See, for example, Winkleman, 'The Imperial Library,' pp. 23, 43.

27. See Kracke, *Civil Service*, pp. 71–2, 95–9, and Wang Te-i, *Sung-tai hsien-liang fang-cheng-k'o chi tz'u-k'o k'ao* (Taipei: Ch'ung-wen shu-tien, 1971).

28. For example, Fu-chou (Fu-chien), which produced more *chin-shih* than any other prefecture save K'ai-feng during the Sung, had only one imperial clansman receive a *chin-shih* degree prior to 1190. But from 1190 to the end of the dynasty they were represented in virtually every examination and numbered 391 out of a total of 1,544. Liang K'o-chia, *San-shan chih*, 42 ch., addendum by Chu Chin, ch. 31–2 (Ming woodblock ed.) 28–32; Huang Chung-chao, *Pa Min t'ung-chih*, 87 ch. (1490 ed.) ch. 46.

29. The only study of purchase of office during the Sung is that by Wei Mei-yüeh, 'Sōdai shinna seido ni tsuite no ichi kōsatsu: toku ni sono chokuri no enkakuhyō o chūshin ni,' *Makasan ronsō* 7 (1974):23–41. But while useful for its description of the purchase system, the status of officials by purchase, and the variations in the prices of various offices, it does not deal with the question of the numerical importance of purchase.

30. CWCKC 11/6a. This is from a policy-discussion answer (*ts'e*) which Chou, an 1151 *chin-shih*, gave while taking the prestigious institutes examination (*kuan-chih-shih*). According to Chou's biography in SS 391/1a, this answer, which dealt with military, personnel and fiscal problems, so impressed the emperor that he exclaimed, 'These are hands (fit) to direct government.'

31. Ibid. 11/6b. Thirteen years earlier, another official, Chao Ssu-ch'eng, claimed that the wait for a post averaged some ten years. WHTK 34:326.

32. In the twelve examinations (thirty-six years) prior to 1213, 5,256 *chin-shih* degrees were given.

33. The major variable here would be the average age at which people received their degrees. This changed not at all between 1148 and 1256, for the mean ages in those two examinations were 35.6 and 36.1 years respectively. SYKCSL passim. Thomas H.C. Lee, using Weng T'ung-wen's *Répertoire des dates des hommes célèbres des Song* (Paris: Mouton & Co., 1962), has calculated average ages for

those receiving *chin-shih* degrees as 28.52 years in the Northern Sung and 31.54 years in the Southern Sung. As he admits, his sample is a selective one, but even accepting his three-year difference, it would affect the findings in Table 5 only marginally, and then its effect would be to heighten the trend. 'Schools of Sung China,' p. 52.

34. SHY:HC 7–8. See also Appendix 2.
35. Ibid.
36. Kracke, *Civil Service*, pp. 79, 235.
37. SHY:CK 55; Wei Mei-yüeh, 'Sōdai shinna seido,' p. 30.
38. SHY:HC 4/17a; CYTC 1.13:182.
39. WHTK 32:301; CYTC 2.15:540–41; SHY:HC 2/23b, 26b–27a. Some, however, defended their large numbers. In the last citation above, the Emperor Hsiao-tsung argued that facilitated degree recipients were elderly scholars worthy of respect rather than derision as 'playthings'.
40. See, for example, Hung Mai, *Jung-chai ssu-pi* 4.4/1b–2a.
41. In 1165 and 1182. CYTC 2.14:534; WHTK 32:301.
42. CYTC 1.6:86; 2.14:533–4.
43. CWCKC 11/7b.
44. *Sōdai kanryōsei to daitochi shoyū* (Tokyo: Nippon Hyōronsha, 1950) pp. 20–5.
45. Ibid., p. 66. The prefectures are T'ai-chou and Ming-chou in Liang-che-tung, Ch'ang-chou and Lin-an fu in Liang-che-hsi, and Chien-k'ang fu and Hui-chou in Chiang-nan-tung. During the Northern Sung, 5.8% of their graduates reached the lower fourth grade or above; this fell to 3.2% in the Southern Sung. In Ch'ang-chou and Hui-chou there is comparable information for those who reached the upper sixth grade or above (but not counting those of the fourth grade or above) and there the drop was from 16.4% to 12.2%.
46. 'Chu Hsi and the World He Lived In,' paper presented to the International Conference on Chu Hsi (1130–1200), Honolulu, Hawaii, July 1982, pp. 15–17.
47. In 1195, even after the 1182 cutbacks in protection, a titular councilor could name 10 kinsmen to office (subject, of course, to the placement examination) and another 8 upon his retirement and death. An assistant councilor could name 8 and 6 respectively. CYTC 2.14:533–4.
48. 'Transformations of China,' pp. 420–5.
49. See Chapter 5 for descriptions of the University entrance examination, the privileged entry given to some, its preliminary examination, and exemptions from the preliminary examination.
50. See Wang Chien-ch'iu, *Sung-tai T'ai-hsüeh*, pp. 232–42; and Thomas H.C. Lee, 'The Schools of Sung China,' pp. 52–7.
51. Ibid., p. 56.
52. See Huang Hsien-fan, *Sung-tai T'ai-hsüeh-sheng chiu-kuo yün-tung*, and Wang Chien-ch'iu, *Sung-tai T'ai-hsüeh*, pp. 256–349.
53. In 1107, University students who had been admitted because of their virtuous conduct were granted official family (*kuan-hu*) status, and service exemption (or the right to cash payment for their service obligations), depending on their status at the University. Ibid., p. 205. In 1117, even county school students received exemptions from service obligations. Thus University students would certainly have been exempted. WHTK 46:433.
54. Li Hsin-ch'uan, *Chien-yen i-lai hsi-nien yao-lu*, 200 ch. (Taipei: When-hai ch'u-pan-she, 1968) 60/3b–4b. This source will be cited hereafter as HNYL.
55. In 1133 lenient regulations were promulgated exempting current *chü-jen* and past *chü-jen* with preliminary examination exemptions, but this was restricted in 1149 to only those who had attempted the departmental examination and who were the only adult males in their households. See McKnight, *Village and Bureaucracy*, pp. 106–7, and 'Fiscal Privileges and the Social Order,' in *Crisis and*

Properity in Sung China, ed. John W. Haeger (Tucson: University of Arizona Press, 1975), pp. 91–2.

56. See John W. Chaffee, 'Education and Examinations in Sung Society' (Ph.D. Dissertation, University of Chicago, 1979), pp. 197–203.

57. In 1021, *chü-jen* who had qualified twice in the *chin-shih* examinations or three times in the *chu-k'o* examinations were allowed to serve as irregular officials. *Sung hui-yao chi-kao*: *Chih-kuan* section 62/40b–41a. This section of the SHY will hereafter be cited as SHY:CK. For a criticism of these provisions for Kuang-nan *chü-jen*, see Ou-yang Hsiu, *Ou-yang wen-chung kung wen-chi*, 158 ch. (SPTK ed.) 113/10b–11a.

58. McKnight, 'Fiscal Privileges,' p. 92.

59. See p. 7 above.

60. Yang Wan-li, *Ch'eng-chai chi* 72/2a–3b.

61. Cited by Sadao Aoyama in 'The Newly-Risen Bureaucrats in Fukien at the Five Dynasty-Sung Period with Special Reference to Their Genealogies,' *Memoirs of the Research Department of the Toyō Bunko* 21 (1962):35.

62. Dun J. Li, *The Essence of Chinese Cultivation* (New York: D. Van Nostrand Company, 1967), p. 172. The quotation was taken from an essay by the famous early Ch'ing writer, Ku Yen-wu.

63. See Chapter 7, pp. 172–4 for an elaboration on this theme.

64. SHY:HC 15/29b.

65. This figure is the sum of a list of prefectural examination quotas which appears on an anonymous and undated Southern Sung map described in note 5, page 211 above.

66. The figure for 1124 is an exception but so was that examination. For the first time in over twenty years the examinations were not tied to the school system and there was some confusion over quotas. Far more *chü-jen* appeared in the capital than had been expected and the number of degrees to be given was raised by one hundred. SS 155/22a; SHY:HC 4/14a; WHTK 31:297.

67. The most common reason was the difficulty and expense of making the trip to the capital but there were others. For example, in 1121 Liu Yen-chung of Chi-chou was selected from his prefectural school class to go to the University (this was then the equivalent of being selected as a *chü-jen*), but did not go because his father's fiftieth birthday was approaching and he did not want to miss it. Liu Ts'ai-shao, *Shan-ch'i chü-shih chi* 12/25a–b.

68. Ping-ti Ho, reply to 'The Comparative Study of Social Mobility' by Vernon Dibble, pp. 321–2. Chung-li Chang's figures for the Ch'ing in *The Chinese Gentry* (pp. 97–113) are somewhat higher. Using Ho's method of calculating the adult male population (20% of the total population), Chang's data yield percentages of 2.7 for the early nineteenth century and 3.8 for the late nineteenth century.

69. The four references that I have found to non-University student service exemptions are all from the period of the Three Hall System and it is likely that they did not survive the system's demise in 1121. SHY:CJ 2/24a–b, 29a; WHTK 46: 433; *Sung ta-chao ling-chi*, 240 ch. (Peking: Chung-hua shu-chü, 1962) 157:593.

70. Tseng Feng, *Yüan-tu chi*, 20 ch. (SKCS ed.) 17/6a. The translation follows, in part, that of Mark Elvin in Shiba, *Commerce and Society*, p. 186.

71. The figure of seventy-nine thousand is from SHY:HC 15/29a–b. The others are estimates based upon information concerning legislated quota-ratios and *chü-jen* numbers, which are detailed in Chaffee, 'Education and Examinations,' p. 59.

72. Ho Ch'iao-yüan, *Min shu*, 154 ch. (1629 ed.) 32/9a–b; Liu Tsai, *Man-t'ang wen-chi*, 36 ch. (1604 ed.) 13/10a; SHY:HC 15/29b. The earlier *chü-jen* figure, which was taken from the *Sung hui-yao*, was actually from 1104. The 18,000 figure for 1207 is not the highest figure that we have for Fu-chou. *Min shu* 32/9b reports that there were 20,000 candidates in 1174. The *Min shu* will be cited hereafter as MS.

73. Liu Wen-fu, *Yen-chou t'u-ching*, 3 ch. (TSCC ed.) 1:13; Fang Jen-jung, *Ching-ting Yen-chou hsü-chih*, 10 ch. (TSCC ed.) 3:33.

74. SS 156/16b.

75. For the 1102 prefectural population statistics, I used the compilation of the *Sung shih* data made by Chao Hui-jen in 'Sung-shih ti-li-chih liu-k'ou piao,' *Yü kung* 2 (1934):59–67. For the 1162 and 1223 circuit figures, I used the *Sung hui-yao: Shih-huo* section 69/71a and WHTK 11:116–7, respectively, and also Kracke, 'Region,' p. 257.

76. Yüan Chüeh, *Yen-yu Ssu-ming chih*, 20 ch. (Sung Yüan Ssu-ming liu chih ed.) 14/8b–9a. The writer was Hu Kang-chung of Ming-chou, who received a *chin-shih* degree in 1208. This work will hereafter be cited as YYSMC.

77. This classification, which did not include rulers and officials or servants and slaves, dates back at least to the late Chou, for we have several works from that period which use it. See, for example, *Kuan-tzu*, 24 ch. (SPPY ed.) 8/6b–8a; *Kuo-yü*, 21 ch. (SPPY ed.) 6/2b–4a; Chung Wen-cheng, *Ku-liang pu-chu*, 24 ch. (SPPY ed.) 17/1b. While the categories remained constant and were frequently used to describe the social order thereafter, some of their meanings changed. This was especially true of the term *shih*, which originally denoted a semi-aristocratic group of men but by the Han had come to mean 'men of learning' or 'scholars'. See Cho-yun Hsu, *Ancient China in Transition: An Analysis of Social Mobility, 722–222 B.C.* (Stanford, Calif.,: Stanford University Press, 1965), pp. 7–8, 34–7, and T'ung-tsu Ch'ü, *Han Social Structure*, ed. Jack L. Dull (Seattle: University of Washington Press, 1972), pp. 101–7.

78. See the section on occupational prohibitions in Chapter 3 below.

79. WHTK 35:332.

80. Cited in Ch'eng Yün, 'Sung-tai chiao-yü tsung-chih ch'an-shih,' *Chung-cheng hsüeh-pan* 2 (1967):93.

81. Su Ch'e, *Luan-ch'eng chi*, 50 ch. (Taipei: Commercial Press, 1968), 21:292.

82. Yüan Ts'ai, *Yüan-shih shih-fan* (Chih pu tsu chai ts'ung-shu ed.) 2/23b–24a. The translation follows Mark Elvin's in Shiba, *Commerce and Society*, p. 213.

83. 'Doctors in Sung and Yüan: A Local Case Study,' paper presented to Columbia University's Traditional China Seminar, 1981.

84. 'Prominence and Power,' pp. 56–8.

85. This point, particularly as it relates to the question of guarantees, is argued at length in Chapter 3 below.

86. SYKCSL passim. More precisely, in 1148 the average was 3.2 brothers and in 1256, 1.8, though the latter figure is based upon only 329 (out of a total of 600) *chin-shih* for whom information on brothers is given. Why families should have averaged as many as 8–10 members (2–3 brothers, 2–3 sisters and parents) is an intriguing question which I am currently investigating.

87. CWCKC 58/8b–9a.

88. This is a reference to the Neo-Confucian master Chu Hsi (1130–1200).

89. YYSMC 13/7a–b.

90. Wang T'ing-kuei, *Lu-ch'i wen-chi* 46/6a.

91. Tseng Kuo-ch'üan, *Hu-nan t'ung-chih*, 288 ch. (1885 ed.) 66/23a–b.

92. See pp. 1–2 above.

93. SHY:HC 16/34b–35a. The disturbances were blamed upon outsiders who had falsely claimed residence in those prefectures.

94. Wang Yen-wu, *Wu-wen kao*, 10 ch. (SPTK ed.) 9/17a–b.

Notes to Chapter 3

1. *Confucian China and Its Modern Fate: A Trilogy* (Berkeley: University of California Press, 1968).

2. See Donald Munro, *The Concept of Man in Early China* (Stanford: Stanford University Press, 1969), on Confucian notions of equality and inequality.
3. James Legge, trans., *The Works of Mencius*, in *The Four Books* (Shanghai: Chinese Book Company; reprint ed., Taipei: I-shih Book Company, 1971), pp. 242–3 (Sec. 2.A.5).
4. Chu Hsi, *Reflections on Things At Hand*, trans. Wing-tsit Chan (New York: Columbia University Press, 1967), 199–200.
5. Ibid.
6. In 964 the Latter Chou examination regulations of 955 were formally adopted. SHY:HC 14/13a–14a.
7. Robert M. Hartwell, 'Financial Expertise, Examinations, and the Formulation of Economic Policy in Northern Sun China,' in *Enduring Scholarship Selected from the Far Eastern Quarterly – The Journal of Asian Studies, 1941–1971. Volume I: China*, ed. John A. Harrison (Tucson: University of Arizona Press, 1972):52.
8. HCP, addendum from the *Yung-lo ta-tien* 14,308/3b.
9. SHY:HC 3/1b–2a.
10. Ch'en Chün, *Huang-ch'ao pien-nien kang-mu pei-yao*, 30 ch. (Ching-chia-t'ang ts'ung-shu ed.; Taipei: Ch'eng-wen ch'u-pan she, 1966) 1:125. According to Araki Toshikazu, this is the first known reference to *tu-shu-jen*, a common term even today for a literatus.
11. SHY:HC 7/1a–2a. See also SKSK, pp. 284–9 and also Ichisada Miyazaki, *China's Examination Hell*, trans. Conrad Schirokauer (New York: John Weatherhill, Inc., 1976), pp. 74–5.
12. WHTK 30:284; HCP 18/1b–2b.
13. WHTK 32:305; HCP 18/1b–2b. The facilitated degree figure is not given in WHTK 32, but WHTK 30:284, has it as 180 +, but in view of the agreement of the other two sources, this is probably a copying error.
14. Under T'ai-tsu, 188 *chin-shih* and 120 *chu-k'o* degrees were given. Ibid. 32:305.
15. HCP 18/2b.
16. Ibid. 30:282. These were the degrees given in the northern dynasties. There are no dates for the southern kingdoms.
17. Ibid. 32:305.
18. Ibid. 32:305–7.
19. WHTK 30:284. HCP 18/2a has 5,300.
20. Ibid. 24/1a.
21. Ibid. 33/1a. SHY:HC 1/4a has 17,000. Tseng Kung (1019–83) in the mid-eleventh century cited both this figure and the 10,760 and argued that that increase was caused by the increase in degree numbers in 977. *Tseng Wen-ting kung ch'üan-chi* (1693 ed.) 17/2a–b.
22. See Appendix 2 which lists the degree totals by year.
23. WHTK 32:305.
24. HCP 18/2b.
25. Wang Yung, *Yen-i i-mou lu*, 5 ch. (TSCC ed.) 1. Cited in SKSK, p. 102. This same reason was given by Chou Pi-ta in an examination essay. CWCKC 11/6a.
26. 'Sung-tai ti k'o-chü yü chiao-yü,' *Hsüeh-feng* 2, no. 9 (1932):6.
27. Ichisada Miyazaki, *China's Examination Hell*, p. 116.
28. This point is well argued by Thomas Lee in 'Education in Sung China.'
29. HCP 33/2a; SHY:HC 7/5b. The most thorough treatment of this topic is Araki Toshikazu's. SKSK, pp. 22–3, 208–14, and 243–66.
30. HCP 67/15b–16a; SHY:HC 3/8b.
31. Ibid. 15/9a.
32. YH 116/21a–b; SS 155/9a.
33. SHY:HC 15/10a; YH 116/31a.

34. See Arthur Waley, *The Life and Times of Po Chu-i (772–846 A.D.)*(London: George Allen & Unwin Ltd., 1949), pp. 18–19, 23.
35. HCP 133/3a. See also Ibid. 61/18a–19a.
36. HCP 67/15b–16a.
37. Ibid. 68/4b–5a; SHY:HC 3/9a.
38. Ibid. 3/38a–b, 15/17b.
39. John Steele, trans., *The I-li or Book of Etiquette and Ceremonial*, 2 vols. (London: Probsthain & Co., 1917), v. 1, p. 272. Regarding the ceremony, see Chapter 6 below.
40. Wei Liao-weng, *I-li yao-i*, 50 ch. (SKCS ed.) 8/3b. See also TCY 1:1.
41. SHY:HC 3/38a–b.
42. SHY:HC 14/13a–14a.
43. TCY 1:1.
44. Ibid. 14/16a–17b.
45. See, for example, complaints from 1005, 1011, and 1025. Ibid. 3/7a, 14/19a–b, 21a–b, 22b–23a; HCP 103/6b.
46. Ibid. 61/19a; SHY:HC 14/20b.
47. Specifically, the quota was to be 5/10 of the highest number of prefectural candidates in the past five examinations. The Board of Rites had suggested a quota-ratio of 3/10 but the emperor decided on the higher figure 'in order to extend the selection of talent.' Ibid.
48. For examples, see SHY:HC 14/20a, 20b–21a, 24a.
49. See HCP 47/6a, 8a, 49/5a; SHY:HC 14/18b.
50. HCP 120/1a. SS 10/9a states that the edict ordered the equalization of all prefectural quotas. See also a complaint of quota inequality in 1067. SHY:HC 15/17a–b.
51. HCP 14/14a–b.
52. Ibid. 14/15b–16a.
53. Ibid. 14/26b.
54. See TCY 2:17–19 on T'ang literati trying for selection in prefectures not their own.
55. Ibid. 16/89b–9a; HNYL 160/10a–b. The two versions vary considerably. Each has information missing from the other, though they do not contradict each other. Both are used for the description below.
56. At that time, either participation in two such ceremonies or a half-year's attendance in a government school was required of all candidates. Ibid. 16/6a.
57. SHY:HC 3/24b–25b.
58. Ibid. The former could take the examinations if they had guarantees either from one official or three *chü-jen* who had taken the departmental examination. The latter could attend the school where the official was serving and use that attendance time to qualify for the examinations in their home prefectures.
59. These were violations of regulations (*fan t'iao-hsien*) whose penalties could be commuted into fines (*shu-fa*). By contrast, the violations referred to in the second condition were more serious with penalties such as flogging and banishment.
60. These were particularly heinous crimes which merited the death penalty. The first four all involved some form of rebellion. For their provisions in the T'ang Code, which was adopted with few changes by the Sung, see Wallace Johnson, 'The T'ang Code: An Analysis and Translation of the Oldest Extant Code (A.D. 653), Ch. 1–3' (Ph.D. Dissertation, University of Pennsylvania, 1968), pp. 63–96.
61. Following SKSK, p. 78, I have taken the rather ambiguous term '*tsa-lei*' ('miscellaneous types') to mean clerks.
62. SHY:HC 3/25a.

63. See Chapter 4.
64. HCP 24/21b; SHY:HC 3/4b.
65. Ibid.
66. WHTK 30:285; 31:297; 35:332; HCP 30/12a.
67. SHY:HC 14/15b–16a.
68. Ibid.
69. 'Sung-tai shih-ta-fu,' pp. 3–4.
70. James T.C. Liu, 'Control of Government Clerks,' pp. 327–8. See TCY 8:88–9, for an example of a T'ang clerk passing the examinations.
71. WHTK 35:330.
72. HCP 202/1b–2a. This is a memorial which mentions an earlier provision allowing very talented artisans, merchants and clerks to take the examinations.
73. WHTK 31:297.
74. *The Medieval Chinese Oligarchy*, p. 203. Also see p. 30. Robert Hartwell has reported that many members of the Northern Sung professional elite used choronyms and claimed descent from august T'ang families. 'Transformations of China,' p. 411–12. Whatever the truth of these claims, their use would seem to have been primarily social, for I have encountered no references to or uses of choronyms in documents relating to the examinations.
75. Ibid., p. 203.
76. SHY:HC 3/21b–22a.
77. For example, in 997, 'temporarily buying productive fields and establishing a household' outside one's native place was prohibited. Ibid. 14/19a; HCP 60/17a–b; WHTK 30:287.
78. For example, see HCP 60/17a–18b.
79. See SHY:HC 14/25a–b, 15/7b–8b, 11a; HCP 83/10a, 108/14a, 132/15a.
80. SHY:HC 6/11b–12a.
81. Ibid. 16/17b.
82. Ibid. 3/36a; HCP 187/6a. Also see SHY:HC 15/7b–8b.
83. Ibid. 16/20b. The SHY gives his surname as Kung, but according to Ch'ang Pi-te et al., *Sung-jen ch'uan-chi tzu-liao suo-in*, 6 vols. (Taipei: Ting-wen shu-chü, 1974–6) 5:4,497, it was Hsi, a very similar character.
84. Ibid. 16/20b. The official was Tan K'uei.
85. HCP 47/4a.
86. SHY:HC 15/5a–b.
87. HCP 186/13b. Official investigation into the conduct of candidates together with prohibitions against the 'unfilial', merchants, Buddhists and Taoists can also be found in a general description of the examinations in both SS 155/2a–3b and WHTK 30:283. But while this description is undated, internal evidence places it before 1057.
88. SHY:HC 15/7b. See also Ibid. 15/3b–4a for a complaint about those coming to K'ai-feng to avoid the rule of not taking the examinations while in mourning for one's parents.
89. Ibid. 14/25a–b; HCP 83/9b–10a. The official who made the second protest was also demoted on the grounds that his complaint, which simply pointed out that Liu's accusation was correct, indicated partial responsibility.
90. We will see in Chapter 4 how an attempt to seek out the exceptionally virtuous was made under the emperor Hui-tsung (r. 1101–26), but that was not a character qualification.
91. Ibid. 14/22a–b; SHY:HC 14/21b–22a.
92. Ibid. 5/8a.
93. SKSK, pp. 12–18.

94. This is the information provided on the official lists of *chin-shih* in 1148 and 1256, and one would assume that each candidate compiled such a biographical profile. SYKCSL. See also the 1005 proposal by the Board of Rites that candidates be required to copy their 'family certificates' (*chia-chuang*) onto their examination papers. HCP 61/18a–19a.
95. SHY:HC 16/24a–b. See also Ibid. 5/4b–5a.
96. 'Prominence and Power,' pp. 55–8. See also Hartwell, 'Transformations,' p. 419.
97. Hymes's argument rests upon three Fu-chou references to 'recommendation' (*chien*) or 'recommendation [for] selection' (*chien-chü*) (terms which I have not encountered in the sense of recommendation for the prefectural examinations), and a description of a Chi-chou scholar who, to encourage those who had yet to acquire great reputations, guaranteed several candidates per examination. This evidence is open to other interpretations, however. First, since *chien* was also used to describe the selection of *chü-jen* (cf., ICC 3.2:11–2, 3.11:83–4; CCCW 1:5), Hymes's second example citing the difficulty of *chien-chü* can be read as applying to prefectural examination selection, especially in light of the great competitiveness of that process. Second, in the initial case of a lineage with seven or eight who were *chien-chü* but with only two prefectural *chü-jen*, it is possible that the others passed one of the special preliminary examinations described below in Chapter 5 and thus *chien-chü* refer to *chü-jen* selection. Similarly, the third reference to people discussing who would be recommended *to* the examinations can be read as who would be selected *in* them. Who would succeed in the prefectural examinations was a matter of great public interest and the fact that 'only those whose talents are well known' succeeded in them could simply reflect the fact that those with the best education and literary renown tended to dominate the examinations. Finally, the fact that a single scholar, however eminent, could recommend as many as several hundred literati per examination testifies, it would seem, to the looseness rather than the exclusiveness of the guarantee requirement.
98. See ICC 3.11:83–4; 1.11:87; 2.14:102.
99. K'ai-feng, the eastern capital, was in theory just one of four capitals, the others being Ta-ming fu, the northern capital, Ying-t'ien fu, the southern capital, and Ho-nan fu, the western capital. But as Kracke has noted, the others 'had no capital functions apart from the titles of their officials and a few other ceremonial attributes.' 'Sung K'ai-feng: Pragmatic Metropolis and Formalistic Capital,' in *Crisis and Prosperity in Sung China*, ed. John Winthrop Haeger (Tucson: University of Arizona Press, 1975), p. 49.
100. SHY:HC 1/6b. Hung Mai (1123–1202) is cited as the source for this item.
101. Ssu-ma Kuang, *Wen-kuo wen-cheng Ssu-ma kung wen-chi*, 80 ch. (SPTK ed.) 30/2a–3b. See Chapter 6 for a discussion of the debate between Ssu-ma Kuang and Ou-yang Hsiu from which these figures are drawn.
102. 'Sung K'ai-feng', p. 53.
103. See especially Robert M. Hartwell, 'Transformations of China,' and 'Kinship, Status and Region.'
104. TMH 1:11.
105. Ibid. 3:25.
106. SHY:HC 3/45b; 14/16a, 16b, 19a, 25a–b; 15/3b–4a, 6a, 6b–7a, 7b–8b, 17b–19a; HCP 60/17a–b; 83/9b–10a; 95/7a; 102/1a; 108/14a.
107. *Su wei-kung wen-chi*, 72 ch. (SKCS) 15/18b.
108. SHY:HC 15/22b.
109. In 1020, when the general quota-ratio was 5/10, K'ai-feng's was 3/10 for *chin-shih* and 5/10 for *chü-k'o*. Again in 1052, K'ai-feng and the Directorate were both assigned quota ratios of 15/100 compared to 2/10 for the empire. SHY:HC 14/20b; 15/3b–4a, 13a–b, 14b.

110. SHY:HC 14/20a, 20b–21a, 24a. On the latter two occasions the Directorate of Education was included as well.
111. Ibid. 15/1b–2a, 6b, 11a–b, 16a–b, 21a, 22a, 23a, 23b, 24b–25a, 25a–b, 26a–b, 27a, 27b, 28a, 28b–29a, 30a, 30a–b.
112. See Chaffee, 'Education and Examination,' pp. 197–203.
113. WHTK 31:291–2. See too SKSK, p. 52, and Chin Chung-shu, 'Pei-Sung k'o-chü chih-tu yen-chiu,' *Hsin-ya hsüeh-pao* 6, no. 1 (1964):242–3.
114. Ssu-ma Kuang, *Ssu-ma kung wen-chi* 30/2a–3b. See also Table 19 in Chapter 6.
115. SS 157/1a.
116. WHTK 42:395.
117. Ibid.; SHY:HC 15/11b–12a; SHY:CJ 1/29a–30a. 500 days of school attendance were required of those who wished to take the Directorate examination.
118. WHTK 42:395.
119. See Li Hung-chi, 'Sung-ch'ao chiao-yü chi k'o-chü san-lun chien p'ing san pen yu-kuan Sung-tai chiao-yü chi k'o-chü shu,' *Ssu yü yen* 13 (1975):17–19, on the confused relationship between the University, the Directorate, and the Directorate school.
120. 'Transformation of China,' pp. 405–25. The first of five characteristic features which Hartwell ascribes to this group on p. 406 is that they 'established their main residence in the primary or subordinate Sung capitals.'
121. For examples, which span the years 1005–76, see HCP 60/17a–18b; 83/10a; 95/7a; 102/1a; 108/14a; 132/15a; SHY:HC 3/21b–22a, 45b; 14/25a–b; 15/3b–4a, 6a, 7b–8b, 11a, 17b–19a.
122. Ibid. 15/22b. During the intervening years, the two quotas had been briefly merged, and in the following twenty-five years, they merged and separated two more times. Meanwhile, K'ai-feng's quota dropped to 100. Ibid. 15/23a–b, 27a.

Notes to chapter 4

1. Quoted from James T.C. Liu, *Ou-yang Hsiu: An Eleventh Century Confucianist* (Stanford: Stanford University Press, 1967), p. 41, which also contains most of the above information.
2. See James T.C. Liu, 'An Early Sung Reformer: Fan Chung-yen,' in *Chinese Thought and Institutions* (Chicago: University of Chicago Press, 1957), pp. 105–31.
3. See HCP 141/9a–11a for Ou-yang's suggestion and Ibid. 143/1b–14a for the memorial.
4. Ibid. 143/4a–5b; Ch'en Chün, *Huang-ch'ao pien-nien kang-mu pei-yao* 12:552–3; Liu, 'Fan Chung-yen,' pp. 112–3.
5. HCP 143/5b–7b; Liu, 'Fan Chung-yen,' pp. 114–5; Chin Chung-shu, 'Pei-Sung k'o-chü chih-tu yen-chiu,' *Hsin-Ya hsüeh-pao* 6, no. 1 (1964):248–53.
6. SHY:HC 3/23b–30a.
7. Ibid. 3/25b–28b.
8. Ibid. 3/25a–b. See Chapter 3 for a translation and discussion of these.
9. Where such officials were not available, *chü-jen* or even local scholars could be used provided they received the appropriate authorization and guarantees. Ibid. 3/24b.
10. Ibid. 3/24b–25a and SHY:CJ 2/4a–b.
11. SHY:HC 3/23b.
12. WHTK 42:395; HCP 148/14a. See Chapter 3 on the social significance of this development.
13. SHY:HC 3/30a; HCP 147/10a–11a. In mid-1044, well before their recision, the school residency requirements had been considerably weakened. SHY:CJ 2/3b–4a; SHY:HC 15/121a–b.

14. WHTK 42:395.
15. In his biography in SS 432/10b, it states that his students accounted for four or five out of every ten who were successful on the examinations during those years when he was at the University.
16. Ibid.
17. HCP 185/2a; WHTK 31:290. For good accounts of this incident, see James Liu, 'Ou-yang Hsiu,' pp. 70, 151–2, and especially Chin Chung-shu, 'Sung-tai ku-wen yün-tung chih fa-chan yen-chiu,' *Hsin-Ya hsüeh-pao* 5, no. 2 (1963):105–9.
18. HCP 186/12b–14a.
19. Chin Chung-shu, 'Pei-Sung k'o-chü,' pt. 1, pp. 219–20. The major classics were the *Classic of Rites* (*Li-chi*) and the Tso commentary to the *Spring and Autumn Annals* (*Tso chuan*); the middle classics, Mao's edition of the *Classic of Poetry* (*Mao-shih Shih-ching*), the *Rites of Chou* (*Chou-li*) and the *I-li*; and the minor classics, the *Classics of History* (*Shu-ching*) and the Ku-liang and Kung-yang commentaries to the *Spring and Autumn Annals* (*Ku-liang chuan, Kung-yang chuan*).
20. See James T.C. Liu, *Reform in Sung China: Wang An-shih* (1021-1086) and *His New Policies* (Cambridge, Mass.: Harvard University Press, 1959), pp. 88-90.
21. HCP 220/1a–2a; SHY:HC 3/43b–44b.
22. Ibid. 14/1a.
23. Ibid. 14/1b.
24. See, for example, HCP 68/4b–5a; WHTK 31:295; Ou-yang Hsiu, *Ou-yang wen-chung kung wen-chi* 113/9b.
25. HCP 220/1b. This item is missing from the less complete version of this edict in SHY:HC 3/43b–44a.
26. Ibid. 3/48b; 14/2a.
27. Ibid. 3/50b–51a.
28. Ibid. 3/55a.
29. Ibid. 4/17a–b.
30. See Ibid. 4/25b, 31b–32a; 5/13b–14b. The first reference is noteworthy for its defense of the classics degree.
31. Biography of Su Shih in *Sung Biographies*, ed. Herbert Franke (Wiesbaden: Franz Steiner Verlag GMBH, 1976), pp. 921–2.
32. Ibid.; James Liu, *Ou-yang Hsiu*, p. 74; Chin Chung-shu, 'Pei-Sung k'o-chü,' 1:261.
33. SHY:HC 8/36b–37a. These are the numbers as given. There is obviously an error in arithmetic, for the poetry and classics numbers add up to 2,176, not 2,175.
34. Ibid. 14/4b. This is according to an 1146 memorial which describes the 1102 action.
35. WHTK 31:295.
36. Lü Tsu-ch'ien, *Li-tai chih-tu hsiang-shuo*, 12 ch. (SKCS ed.) 1/13a.
37. Ibid.
38. Yüeh K'o, *T'ing-shih*, 15 ch. (TSCC ed.) 10:81–2. This will be cited hereafter as TS.
39. Wang T'ing-kuei, *Lu-ch'i wen-chi* 46/3b–5a.
40. Ibid. 46/10a–12a.
41. Ibid. 46/12a–14a.
42. For descriptions of schools in antiquity, see James Legge, trans., *The Works of Mencius*, pp. 242–3 and James Legge, trans., *The Li Chi*, eds. Ch'u Chai and Winberg Chai, 2 vols. (New York: University Books, Inc., 1967), 2:83. YH 102/8a and WHTK 46:429–31 detail earlier dynastic orders to establish schools, most notably in the first year of the Sui and the seventh year of the T'ang.
43. Legge, *The Works of Mencius*, pp. 242–3.

44. SHY:CJ 2/1a–b. The purpose of this seems not to have been to increase knowledge of the classics but rather to insure textual accuracy through the distribution of officially edited texts.
45. Ibid. 2/3a; HCP 99/12a; WHTK 46/431.
46. *Yen-shih hsü cha* (Shanghai: Shanghai jen-min ch'u-pan-she, 1958), pp. 144–52. See also Hou Shao-wen, who in his periodization of the history of the Sung examinations, characterizes 1043–1126 as the period in which the schools and examinations 'mutually waxed and waned.' *T'ang Sung k'ao-shih chih-tu shih*, p. 82.
47. Terada Gō lists some 42 imperially-sanctioned school foundings from the 1020s and 1030s mentioned in the HCP. SKG, pp. 27–31. See also Tables 11 and 12 below.
48. SHY:CJ 2/4a.
49. Although Wang instituted this system, it had previously been suggested by Ch'eng Hao (992–1058) and Ou-yang Hsiu. SKG, pp. 98–9. For a description of the University at this time, see pp. 30–1 above.
50. SHY:CJ 2/5a; HCP 221/5a; WHTK 46:432.
51. SHY:CJ 2/5a; HCP 220/1a–2b; WHTK 46:432.
52. SHY:CJ 2/5a–b; WHTK 46:432.
53. See, for example, H.R. Williamson, *Wang An-shih: A Chinese Statesman and Educationalist of the Sung Dynasty*, 2 vols. (London: Arthur Probsthain, 1935), 1:337.
54. Ibid. This does not mean that there were only 53 active prefectural schools. We have records of many prefectural schools that were active in 1078 which had no preceptor or teaching official.
55. SKG, p. 132.
56. This was particularly true during the Yüan-yu period (1086–93), when the anti-reform faction was in power and almost no actions concerning local education were taken by the central government. In the late 1090s the movement towards local school reform and development began again. Most notably, the University's three hall system of organization was extended to the prefectural schools in 1099, though the consolidation of all schools into a hierarchical system replacing the examination system did not occur until the reign of Hui-tsung. SHY/CJ 2/7a; WHTK 46:432.
57. Ch'en Chün, *Huang-ch'ao pien-nien kang-mu pei-yao* 26:1217.
58. In addition approximately 30 *chin-shih* degrees were given in each of the off years to students who passed the University examinations given to upper hall students. SHY:HC 1/13a–15a.
59. SHY:CJ 2/7b–8a; 8b–9a. Students promoted from prefectural schools to the University had to be guaranteed by the preceptor, prefect, vice-prefect, and circuit educational intendent.
60. See Ibid. 2/7b–9a for Ts'ai Ching's memorial proposing the system and describing its salient features. See, too, Kracke, 'The Expansion of Educational Opportunity in the Reign of Hui-tsung of the Sung and Its Implications.' *Sung Studies Newsletter* 13 (1978), pp. 6–30.
61. See Tilemann Grimm, 'The Inauguration of *T'i-chu hsüeh-shih ssu* (Education Intendents) During the Northern Sung Dynasty,' in *Études Song/Institutions* (Paris: Mouton & Co., 1976) pp. 259–74.
62. SHY:CJ 2/7b.
63. For the land holdings of the government schools as well as other statistics on the number of buildings owned, income and expenses, see Ko Sheng-chung, *Tan-yang chi*, 24 ch. (Ch'ang-chou hsien-che i-shu ed.) 1/2a. The same source gives the number of non-capital students in 1109 as 167,622. Two other sources give com-

parable student figures: 210,000 for 1104 and 'over 200,000' for 1116. Ch'in Hsiang-yeh, *Hsü Tzu-chih t'ung-chien ch'ang-pien shih-pu*, 60 ch. (Taipei: Shih-chieh shu-chu) 24/15b–16a; *Sung ta-chao ling-chi* 157:593.

64. This was computed using the population figure of 20,282,438 households (over 100 million individuals, figuring five people per household) given in *Sung hui-yao: Shih-huo* section 11/27b–28a for the year 1109. See, too, Ping-ti Ho, 'An Estimate of the Total Population of Sung-Chin China,' pp. 33–53.

65. These were filiality (*hsiao*), brotherly love (*ti*), friendliness towards agnatic kin (*mu*), good relations with affinal kin (*yin*), trustworthiness with friends (*jen*), sympathy towards neighbours (*hsü*), loyalty towards the ruler (*chung*), and a sense of harmony in distinguishing the right from the profitable (*ho*). The initial edict can be found in WHTK 46:433. These definitions are based upon a measure from 1107 defining them in Ch'in Hsiang-yeh, *Hsü ch'ang-pien shih-pu* 27/4a–5a.

66. WHTK 42:433.

67. Ch'in Hsiang-yeh, *Hsü ch'ang-pien shih-pu* 27/9a, 10b.

68. Although curtailed and apparently abolished in 1118 (SHY:CJ 2/29b–30a), it apparently continued for in 1120 an edict was issued that forbids providing 'eight conduct' students with school documents. Ibid. 2/30a–b.

69. For the Nine Rank Arbiter system, see Patricia Buckley Ebrey, *The Aristocratic Families of Early Imperial China* (Cambridge: Cambridge University Press, 1978), pp. 17–19. For complaints about the 'eight conduct' system, see SHY:CJ 2/19b; Ch'in Hsiang-yeh, *Hsü ch'ang-pien shih-pu* 32/9a; *Sung ta-chao-ling chi* 157:593.

70. Teaching positions were forbidden for any with 'heterodox views or strange writings.' SHY:CJ 2/9a, 23a.

71. WHTK 31:293.

72. This was a legacy of Wang An-shih's utopian, anti-historical approach to the classics, for he too had banned history – specifically the *Spring and Autumn Annals* – from the examinations. See Hoyt Tillman, *Utilitarian Confucianism: Ch'en Liang's Challenge to Chu Hsi* (Cambridge, Mass.: Harvard University Press, 1982), pp. 40–53. For a complaint about the lack of historical instruction under Hui-tsung, see TMH 3:30.

73. Li Hsin-ch'uan, *Tao-ming lu*, 10 ch. (TSCC ed.) ch. 2.

74. For a detailed and strongly argued condemnation of Ts'ai's activities, see Robert M. Hartwell, 'Historical Analogism, Public Policy, and Social Science in Eleventh and Twelfth Century China,' *American Historical Review* 76 (1971):715 ff.

75. ICC 1.17:134.

76. WHTK 46:433.

77. TMH 3:26. The speaker is one Fan Pien-shu. For other complaints, see SHY:CJ 2/15a, 19a, 19a–b; *Sung ta-chao ling-chi* 157:593; WHTK 46:433.

78. *Min-chung chin-shih chih*, 14 ch. (Chia-yeh t'ang chin-shih ts'ung-shu ed.) 8/26b.

79. SHY:CJ 2/18a.

80. 'Education in Sung China,' pp. 143, 148, 167–8.

81. Cited in Wang Yün-wu, *Sung Yüan chiao-hsüeh ssu-hsiang* (Taipei: Commercial Press, 1971), p. 92.

82. See for example, Liang K'o-chia, *San-shan chih* 12/3a; MS 32/10b.

83. To cite two examples, Hu Yüan reportedly attracted over a thousand students to the Su-chou prefectural school in the late 1030s, and twenty years later the classicist Chou Hsi-meng had some seven hundred students in Fu-chou (in Fu-chien). Fan Ch'eng ta, *Wu-chun chih*, 50 ch. (TSCC ed.) 4:21; Huang Tsung-hsi, *Sung Yüan hsüeh-an*, 100 ch. (SPPY ed.) 5/10a.

84. For the evidence on these changes, most of which occurred during the Three Hall System, see Chaffee, 'Education and Examinations,' pp. 148–54 and also 92–100.

85. SHY:HC 3/31a–b; HCP 5/13a.
86. SHY:HC 5/13a.
87. Ch'eng Tuan-li, *Ch'eng-shih chia-shu tu-shu fen-nien jih-ch'eng*, 3 ch. (PPTK ed.) 3/40b–50a.
88. See Miyazaki, *China's Examination Hell*, pp. 18–32.
89. Ho, *The Ladder of Success*, p. 171.
90. Huang P'eng-nien, *Chi-fu t'ung-chih*, 300 ch. (1885 ed.) 117/72a–b.
91. SHY:CJ 2/24a.
92. Chang Chia-chü, *Liang-Sung ching-chi chung-hsin ti nan-i* (Wuhan: Hu-pei jen-min ch'u-pan-she, 1957), pp. 44–9.
93. Preceptorships established under Hui-tsung were ordered abolished in 1121 and in 1129, 43 specific preceptorships were discontinued. SHY:CJ 2/31a–b, 32b–33a.
94. CKC 28/4b–5a.
95. ICC 1.12:92–3.
96. *Min-chung chin-shih chih* 8/11b–12a; MS 32/46b; Tseng Kuo-ch'üan, *Hu-nan t'ung-chih* 62/31a–b.
97. YYSMC 13/3a–5b; Chang Chin, *Ch'ien-tao Ssu-ming t'u-ching* 9/5a–8a.
98. Ibid.
99. See SHY:CJ 2/34a–38b.
100. Ibid. 1/36a.
101. SHY:HC 16/6a. For more on the community ceremony, see Chapter 7.
102. For example, Chu Hsi tells of the prefectural school of Nan-chien chou (Fu-chien) falling under the influence of Yin–Yang doctrines. *Min-chung chin-shih chih* 9/8b–9a. For a discussion of the problems involved in maintaining land holdings, see Chaffee, 'Education and Examinations,' pp. 120–1, 128.
103. According to Chao Sheng's thirteenth-century glossary of terms relating to Sung public life, registering for the prefectural examinations was far easier if one was already registered as a government school student. *Ch'ao-yeh lei-yao* 2:34. Also see ICC 3.7:53, a story about a test at the Hu-chou prefectural school, which is described in Chapter 7.
104. Chu Hsi, *Chu Wen-kung wen-chi* 80/20b; MS 32/12a. He also used this image of 'men on the highway' to describe conditions at the University in his critique of schools and the examinations, 'Hsüeh-hsiao kung-chü ssu-i,' in WHTK 42:433.
105. Quoted in Dun J. Li, *The Essence of Chinese Civilization*, p. 167.
106. SS 157/15a.
107. WHTK 42:399.
108. Lu Hsien, comp., *Chia-ting Chen-chiang chih*, 22 ch. (Ching-chia t'ang wen-k'u ed.) 11/25b.
109. See, for example, CKC 30/14b, 20a–21b, and Sun Shih-ch'ang, *Kuang-hsin fu chih*, 20 ch. (1683 ed.) 12/3b–5a.
110. The differences between *ching-she* ('house of refinement') and *shu-yüan* ('hall of study') were not great, but their origins were quite different. Whereas shu-yüan had originally been the studies or libraries of scholars during the T'ang and Five Dynasties, *ching-she* dated back to the Han, when it denoted the chambers where a teacher received his students, and was subsequently appropriated by the Taoists to mean a hall for meditation, and the Buddhists, who used it for libraries, temples and country retreats. In the Southern Sung it was taken up by the Neo-Confucians and in practice seems to have been similar to *shu-yüan*, although according to James T.C. Liu it retained the connotation of the religiosity. Wu Tseng, *Neng-kai' chai man-lü*, 18 ch. (Pi-chi hsiao-shuo Ta-kuan hsu pien ed.) 3/14a; and James T.C. Liu, 'How Did a Neo-Confucian School Become the State Orthodoxy?,' *Philosophy East and West* 23 (1973):494.
111. Su Chia-ssu, *Ch'ang-sha fu chih*, 20 ch. (1665 ed.) 4/71a–b. The essay, which

includes a history of the academy to 1165, appears in Chang Shih, *Nan-hsien hsien-sheng wen-chi*, 7 ch. (TSCC ed.) 4/15a–16b.

112. *Ta-Ming i-t'ung chih*, 90 ch. (1461 ed.) 64/8a.

113. The most comprehensive source for this much studied academy is the Ming *Pai-lu shu-yüan chih*, 17 ch. (Ch'ing ed.; first foreword dated 1622). See also Ch'en Tung-yüan, 'Lu-shan Pai-lu-tung shu-yüan yen-ko k'ao,' *Min-tuo tsa-chih* 7 (1937), no. 1, pp. 1–32; no. 2, pp. 1–25; and John Chaffee, 'Chu Hsi and the Revival of the White Deer Grotto Academy,' paper prepared for the International Conference on Chu Hsi, University of Hawaii, July 1982.

114. For the wide geographical distribution of the prominent followers of these and other leading thinkers, see Ho Yu-sen, 'Liang-Sung hsüeh-feng ti ti-li fen-pu,' *Hsin-Ya hsüeh-pao* 1 (1955):331–79.

115. Tseng Kuo-ch'üan, *Hu-nan t'ung-chih* 66/23a–b.

116. See James Liu, 'State Orthodoxy,' p. 497, on the Buddhist and Taoist aspects of Neo-Confucian withdrawal.

117. Ch'eng Tuan-meng and Tung Chu, *Ch'eng Tung er hsien-sheng hsüeh-tzu* (Pai-pu ts'ung-shu chi-ch'eng ed.).

118. Lu Chiu-yüan, *Hsiang-shan ch'üan-chi*, 36 ch. (Kuo-chi chi-pen ts'ung-shu chi-ch'eng ed.) ch. 36.

119. Conrad Schirokauer, 'Neo-Confucians Under Attack: The Condemnation of *Wei-hsüeh*,' in *Crisis and Prosperity in Sung China*, pp. 177–83. For an account of one examiner who refused to make a similar pledge, see YHCW 9/9b–10a.

120. 'Protests Against Convention and Conventions of Protest,' in *The Confucian Persuasion*, ed. Arthur F. Wright (Stanford, Calif.,: Stanford University Press, 1960), pp. 177–201.

121. Huang Tsung-hsi, *Sung Yüan hsüeh-an* 58/136.

122. See James Liu, 'State Orthodoxy,' pp. 496–7, on this pattern of alteration.

123. CKC 28/5b–6a. It was quasi-official in that local officials had founded it in 1174 and subsequently appointed its headmasters and was also located within the city walls. However, it was not a part of the well developed system of government schools in Chien-k'ang fu.

124. For accounts of these occasions, see Carson Chang, *The Development of Neo-Confucian Thought* (New Haven, Conn.,: College and University Press, 1963), pp. 297–301.

125. Terada Gō lists over twenty academies founded at the command of the emperor. SKG, pp. 311–7.

126. For examples, see *Lin T'ing chih*, 7 ch., in *Yung-lo ta-tien*, ed. Yao Kuang-hsiao (Peking: Chung-hua shu-chu, 1960) 7892/24b–25a, 24a–b; CKC 30/10a–13b; Lo Chün, *Pao-ch'ing Ssu-ming chih* 16/9a–b. This last work will be cited hereafter as PCSMC.

127. 'The Price of Autonomy: Intellectuals in Ming and Ch'ing Politics,' *Daedalus* 101, no. 2 (1972):35.

Notes to chapter 5

1. For an analysis of how the Sung survived the critical first four years of this period, see James T.C. Liu, 'China's Imperial Power in Mid-Dynastic Crises: The Case in 1127–1130,' paper presented to the Conference on the Exercise of Imperial Power, 10th–14th Centuries, Germany, September 1982. See too, Chang Chia-chü, *Liang-Sung ching-chi*, pp. 41–51, for a detailed treatment of migrations in the early Southern Sung.

2. Hartwell, 'Transformations of China,' pp. 397–8. The systems were (1) Hu-kuang, comprising Ching-hu-nan and -pei, (2) Ssu-ch'uan with the circuits of Ch'eng-tu, Tzu-chou, Li-chou and K'uei-chou, (3) Huai-hsi with Huai-nan-hsi and

Chiang-nan-tung and -hsi, and (4) Huai-tung with Huai-nan-tung, Liang-che-tung and -hsi, and Fu-chien.
3. Ibid., pp. 401–5.
4. Liu, 'China's Imperial Power,' pp. 33–4; Hellmut Wilhelm, 'From Myth to Myth: The Case of Yüeh Fei's Biography,' in *Confucianism and Chinese Civilization*, ed. Arthur F. Wright (Stanford, Calif.: Stanford University Press, 1975), p. 225. For a discussion of how the principle of 'civilism' was manifested in the events of 1126–7, see John W. Haeger, '1126–27: Political Crisis and the Integrity of Culture,' in *Crisis and Prosperity in Sung China*, pp. 155–160.
5. Ch ien Yüeh-yu, *Hsien-ch'un Lin-an chih*, 100 ch. (1268 ed.) 11/32a–b. This will hereafter be cited as HCLAC.
6. *Chin-shih* were named in 1124, 1128, 1132, 1135, 1138 and 1142.
7. See SHY:HC 16/2a–4b on the problem of lost records.
8. Ibid.
9. Ibid. 16/2b–3a. This request was sent out in 1130, shortly after the most serious Jurchen invasion had been turned back.
10. Ibid. 16/2a. This was in 1130.
11. Ibid. 16/5a.
12. CKC 32/1b–2a is clearest about this, saying that this ratio had been ordered by the government, but Hsü Shih, *Chih-yüan Chia-ho chih*, 32 ch. (1288 ms.) 7/6a–b, mentions that in the early Southern Sung, Hsiu-chou had a quota of one for her seventy-five refugee literati.
13. The quotas of one were from Chien-k'ang fu, T'ai-p'ing-chou and Kuang-te chün in Chiang-nan-tung, and Hsiu-chou, Hu-chou and Su-chou in Liang-che-hsi. Those of two were from Ch'ang-chou and Yen-chou in Liang-che-hsi and Ming-chou in Liang-che-tung. T'ai-chou in Liang-che-tung and Lin-an fu had quotas of three. SHY:HC 16/3b; Hsü Shih, *Chia-ho chih* 7/6a–b; T'an Yao, *Wu-hsing chih*, 20 ch. (1201 ed.) 11/2b; Kung Ming-chih, *Chung-wu chi-wen*, 1 ch. (TSCC ed.) pp. 6–7; Chu Yü, *Hsien-ch'un P'i-ling chih*, 30 ch. (1268 ed.) 11/4a–5a; Liu Wen-fu, *Yen-chou t'u-ching*, 3 ch. (TSCC ed.) 1:101–2; PCSMC 2/19b; Ch'en Ch'i-ch'ing, *Chih-ch'eng chih*, 40 ch. (Ming Wan-li ed.) 4/10b; HCLAC 56/16b.
14. SHY:HC 4/17b–18a.
15. Ibid. 4/23a–b.
16. See Chapter 6 for discussion of the Ssu-ch'uan examination.
17. See Appendix 3.
18. As Hartwell has shown, however, there was a striking regional component to office-holding at the capital, with some 41% of high policy officials coming from what he calls the lower Yangtze macroregion during the period 1127–62. 'Transformations of China,' pp. 404, 415.
19. SHY:HC 16/7a–b.
20. SHY:HC 15/22b; HCLAC 56/16b.
21. HCP 42/5a–b.
22. Ibid. 42/5a–b.
23. The first case of officials being awarded degrees occurred in 980 and involved four men, but the first mention of the *suo-t'ing-shih* was in 985. Ibid. 14/8b.
24. SHY:HC 14/9a.
25. Holding the two together in K'ai-feng and in the circuit capitals was ordered in 1039 and again in 1070. Ibid. 14/11a–b; HCP 125/10a–b; SS 155/18a.
26. Loss of office was specified in 985. SHY:HC 14/8b. The personal offense, which was considered to be more serious than a public offense (*kung-tsui*), was first ordered in 1018 and then abolished in 1034. Ibid. 14/10b; HCP 114/12a–b. The fine, ten *chin* of copper, was established in 1024. SHY:HC 14/10a.
27. SHY:HC 2/18b; Yü Chih-chen, *Chi-an fu chih* 22/17a.
28. Hou Shao-wen claims that the *sou-t'ing-shih* was far more competitive than the

prefectural examinations. *T'ang Sung k'ao-shih*, p. 85. But the only quota-ratio which I have found for it was 3/10 for 1039, which was more liberal than the 2/10 quota-ratio then being used for the prefectural examinations, and 1/10 for 1061, which was more restrictive in theory but probably not in fact, since prefectures operated under set quotas and their actual competition was probably greater than 1/10. SHY:HC 14/11a–12a; HCP 125/10a–b.

29. Ibid. 43/9b.
30. *Pieh-shih* and *pieh-t'ou-shih* ('separate heads examination') were its standard names during the Northern Sung; in the Southern Sung *tieh-shih* ('official-list examination') was its proper name but *chüan-yün-ssu shih* ('fiscal intendency examination' – that is where it was held) and *ts'ao-shih* ('office examination') were also common.
31. SHY:HC 15/9b–10a; HCP 112/2b. 'Relatives' were defined as those within the five degrees of mourning (*wu-fu*), in practice, those with a great-great-grandfather in common.
32. SHY:HC 15/20b.
33. Ibid. 16/29b–30a.
34. CYTC 1.13:172–3.
35. SS 156/19b–20a.
36. See Ibid. 4/36b; 16/12b–14a.
37. Ibid. 16/13a–b.
38. Such relatives were permitted to take the *tieh-shih* in 1168, barred in 1180, permitted again in 1182 and barred again in 1189. Ibid. 16/14b–15a, 22b–23a, 24b–25a.
39. SHY:HC 16/14b–15b. This codification was known as the Detailed Regulations for the Avoidance Examination (*tieh-shih t'iao-fa*) or the New Regulations of the Ch'ien-tao Period (*Ch'ien-tao hsin-fa*), and for at least the following thirty years it served as the definitive authority.
40. From 1171 on, Fu-chien was included as well. Ibid. 16/17a, 22b–23a, 24a.
41. The circuit officials so affected were specified in the text of the regulations.
42. See Ibid. 16/13a, dated 1165, for an earlier reference to this provision.
43. This degree of mourning would have included an individual's paternal grandfathers, paternal uncles, paternal cousins, all grandsons and of course parents, siblings and children.
44. See SHY:HC 6/47a–48a; 16/13a–b, 23b–24a; and ICC 1.19:152–3. This last reference will be discussed in Chapter 8.
45. SHY:HC 4/36b. See also Ibid. 16/13a–b.
46. SS 156/16a–b. Liu Tsai had proposed a similar reform in 1207. *Man-t'ang wen-chi* 13/10a–b.
47. Ibid.
48. Ibid. 156/19b.
49. This was well understood by Lin Ta-chung (1131–1208) who in 1192 proposed equalizing the avoidance and prefectural examination quota-ratios: 'If [the avoidance examination] does not differ from prefectural selection, then all but those who truly cannot manage it will return [home] and go to the prefectural examination.' SHY:HC 16/26b.
50. CKC 32/6b.
51. After the creation of the University, the two terms were used interchangeably.
52. WHTK 32:306.
53. The prestige of this *shih-ho* degree was comparable to that of a first-class *chin-shih* degree. See Chao Sheng, *Ch'ao-yeh lei-yao*, 5 ch. (TSCC ed.) 2:23.
54. For example, in 1042 when the Directorate examination's quota-ratio was 3/10, a prefectural quota-ratio of 2/10 was then in use. SHY:CJ 1/29a–30a; HCP 111/9a; SHY:HC 15/13a–b.

55. Ibid. 6/6b–7a.
56. Ibid. 4/23a. This was from 1131 and was obviously intended for the small group of University students who had followed Kao-tsung south. But because it represented only an increase in established exemption privileges and not new privileges, it is reasonable to assume that the regulations remained in effect after the re-establishment of the University in Lin-an.
57. Ch'en Yüan-ching, *Shih-lin kuang-chi* (Japanese ed., 1699), 'Sung-tai T'ai-hsüeh chiu-kuei.' Ch'en lived from ca. 1200 to 1266; the book is undated.
58. Ch'eng Tuan-li, *Ch'eng-shih chia-shih tu-shu* 3/42a.
59. The most informative source for the Southern Sung entrance examination is SHY:CJ 1, which deals exclusively with the Sung University. The best modern treatment of the examination is Li Hung-chi, 'Sung-ch'ao chiao-yü,' pp. 22–5.
60. SHY:CJ 1/42b. See YHCW 2/5b on the complaints of literati who were excluded from the examination as a result and who ridiculed the official contention that the new method was 'fairer'.
61. SHY:CJ 1/39a. In 1163 a third method, direct prefectural nomination of students to the University, but it was discontinued in 1166. Ibid. 1/38a–b.
62. Ibid. 1/35b.
63. Ibid. 1/41a.
64. SHY:HC 5/26a–b.
65. SHY:CJ 1/39a; CYTC 1.13:179–80. SHY:HC 5/26a–b gives the number as 39,000 +.
66. Yü Chih-chen, *Chi-an fu chih* 22/42a.
67. The number selected varied according to the number of vacancies that existed, but the specific figures that I have found are all in this range: 300 in 1143, 133 in 1169, 268 in 1184, and 247 in 1214. SHY:CJ 1/35b, 39b, 44a–b; SHY:HC 6/22a.
68. See p. 104.
69. See HNYL 33/11a and SHY:HC 16/2a for 1130; Ibid. 15/5a–b and SS 156/4b for 1137; and SHY:HC 16/26b–27a for 1192.
70. *Chih-shih-kuan* and *li-wu-kuan* are both rarely encountered terms whose meaning and significance are far from clear. Both appear to have been broad categories for high grade active officials, with the *chih-shih-kuan* the more important of the two. Araki Toshikazu, for example, take the two terms to refer to the officials in the capital generally. SKSK, pp. 177–8. Some idea of the significance of *chih-shih-kuan* may be gotten from the already mentioned 1165–8 regulations allowing tutors of '*chih-shih-kuan* [with the titular office of] investigating censor and above' to take the avoidance examination. SHY:HC 16/13a, 15a.
71. The provisions concerning the eligibility of relatives were complicated. For *chih-shih-kuan*, relatives within the five degrees of mourning who were fellow clansmen and who lived with them and those within the third degree of mourning living apart were eligible. For the *li-wu-kuan* only fellow clansmen within the fourth degree of mourning living with the official could take the University examination. Ibid. 16/26b–27a.
72. Ch'en Yüan-ching. *Shih-lin kuang-chi* 'Sung-tai t'ai-hsüeh chiu-kuei.' HCLAC 11/33b gives a lower quota of 80 for the Hsien-ch'un period (1265–75).
73. Wu Tzu-mu, *Meng-liang lu* 4/5a.
74. SS 156/21b. Between these extremes, officials were listed who had quotas of 27, 20, 15 and 10.
75. I.e., the relatives of circuit officials, prefects, vice-prefects and examination officials (degree holders who were frequently prefects or vice-prefects).
76. SS 155/13a.
77. SHY:HC 3/8b; HCP 67/16b–17a. The phrase occurred during an exchange between Chen-tsung and one of his ministers just after Chen-tsung had asked how many men were normally recommended. They were concerned with the

large number of candidates at the departmental examination (there had been over 13,000) and not with the ratio as such.

78. SHY:HC 3/17a.
79. Ibid. 3/8b; HCP 181/10a–11a.
80. In general, quotas were used for the rest of the Northern Sung and quota-ratios during the Southern Sung.
81. For example, in 1124, the first year in a quarter of a century that had an open preliminary examination instead of selection of *chü-jen* by the schools, the degree quota was raised by a hundred because of the large number of *chü-jen* who had come for the departmental examination. SHY:HC 4/14a; SS 155/22a.
82. Hung Mai, *Jung-chai sui-pi* 4:8/3a; SHY:HC 4/6b.
83. Ibid. 4/17b–18a, 36; 5/3a.
84. Ibid. 5/3b, 5a–b.
85. Li Yu, *Sung-ch'ao shih-shih*, 20 ch. (Taipei: Commercial Press, 1975) 8:128.
86. Ibid. 8:127–8.
87. For the Northern Sung, there are records of imperial clansmen being examined for the *chin-shih* degree in 1049, 1053 and on four occasions between 1079 and 1085, but the numbers involved were extremely small. YH 116/27b–28a.
88. Li Yu, *Sung-ch'ao shih-shih* 8:128–9. The *liang-shih* had been abolished during the anti-reform Yüan-yu period and the primary reason given for reviving it under Hui-tsung was that the lack of opportunities for advancement was making growing numbers of clansmen destitute.
89. SHY:HC 16/7b–8a.
90. CYTC 1.13:179–80.
91. SHY:HC 18/21a–25a.
92. Ibid. There were 50 degrees awarded in 1163, 39 in 1166, 38 in 1169 and 41 in 1172. In addition, candidates who had failed in the past were reexamined on two occasions and given titular offices lower than those given to the regular *liang-shih* graduates. There were 221 such candidates in 1166 and 8 in 1169.
93. See p. 216, n. 28, concerning the increase. In 1256, there were an additional 19 *chin-shih* with the surname Chao who were not identified as imperial clansmen. SYKCSL passim.
94. HCP 68/18b–19a.
95. SS 156/15b.
96. Ibid.
97. The term used here is '*chou-tzu-shih*' or 'eldest son's examination'. See pp. 104–5 above for a discussion of the similar *chou-tzu tieh-shih.*
98. Ibid. 156/19b.
99. MS 103/15 et seq.
100. *Chiang-su chin-shih chih*, 24 ch. (1927 ed.) 10/6a–13a.
101. T'ao Ch'eng, comp., *Chiang-hsi t'ung-chih*, 162 ch. (1732 ed.) 49–51 and Liu I, *Chi-an fu chih*, 53 ch. (1876 ed.) 22. The former source is the one that I have used in the tables below.
102. The numbers of names per examination are extremely close to the prefectural quotas. The correspondence is almost exact for Su-chou, while for Chi-chou the list figures are generally a little lower than the quotas but still close. See Chaffee, 'Education and Examinations,' p. 255, notes 1 and 2.
103. Sudō Yoshiyuki, *Sōdai kanryosei*, pp. 10–25.
104. Kung Ming-chih, *Chung Wu chi-wen*, pp. 6–7.
105. 'Transformations of China,' p. 417.
106. The *Yü-ti-t'u* gives 68. Aoyama, *Kōtsū to chishi*, appended.
107. For example, Wang T'ing-kuei stated that 5,000 took the prefectural examination in 1144. *Lu-ch'i wen-chi* 45/2a.
108. Sudō Yoshiyuki, *Sōdai kanryosei*, pp. 10–25.

109. See especially Figure 13.
110. For reasons I have not discovered, in the examinations of 1163, 1166, 1172, 1190 and 1193, departmental graduates virtually equalled *chin-shih*. If one discounts those years, the figures for the remaining periods are close:

Period	Departmental graduates	Chin-shih	Triannual difference	Dept. grads. per chin-shih
1135–1162	2,069	3,319	−138	1.60
1175–1189	1,295	2,052	−151	1.58
1190–1207	1,226	2,793	−140	1.46
1208–1225	1,698	2,941	−207	1.73

111. These estimates are probably high, for in those years when departmental graduates equalled *chin-shih*, the Ssu-ch'uan graduates must either have been included with the former or not counted with the latter. The Ssu-ch'uan percentages come from Table 18 in Chapter 6.
112. SHY:CJ 1/39b. The 592 figure is from WHTK 42. SHY:HC 8/13a gives the number as 391, or just two more than the departmental figure. In that case, the 133 would represent 34% of all *chin-shih*, a very high figure indeed.
113. SYKCSL passim. These were only those Chaos who were specifically identified as belonging to the imperial clan.
114. See, for example, SHY:HC 16/32b–33a, which describes a scandal in Ssu-ch'uan involving bribery, substituted names, special identifying marks on the examination paper, and an official writing on one candidate's paper that he was related to an official.
115. Ibid. 6/48a–49b lists twelve forms of examination abuse. For a short but useful analysis of the kinds of cheating and corruption, see James T.C. Liu, 'Sung-tai k'ao-ch'ang pi-tuan – chien lun shih-feng wen-t'i' ('Misconducts at the Sung State Examinations – A Further Discussion on Literati Moral Standards'), in *Ch'ing-chu Li Chi Hsien-sheng Ch'i-shih sui lun-wen chi* (Taipei, 1965), Pt. 1, pp. 189–202.
116. SHY:HC 4/7b–8a. The earliest reference to cribs that I have found is from 1005, when seventeen candidates were caught with them and were barred from the next two examinations. Ibid. 3/7a.
117. Ibid. 6/49b–50a.
118. ICC 1.19:152–3.
119. See Chapter 7 for a discussion of such dreams and spirits and the stories that tell about them.
120. Ibid. 4/28b. For other references to this scandal, see Ibid. 4/29a–b, 16/8a.
121. Ibid. 4/30b–31a.
122. 'Sung-tai k'ao-ch'ang pi-tuan,' p. 201.
123. SS 156/15a; WHTK 32:300.
124. For a reference to the use of candles in the examination cells which was theoretically forbidden to keep the examinees from running into the night but often allowed, see SS 156/15a–b.
125. Liu Cheng, *Huang-Sung chung-hsing liang-ch'ao 'sheng-cheng* (Yüan-wei pieh-ts'ang ed.) 55/14; cited by Liu, 'Sung-tai k'ao-ch'ang pi-tuan,' p. 200. For a slightly different version, see SHY:HC 16/21a–b.
126. Ibid. 4/31a.
127. Ibid. 4/31a. See p. 82 above for the full quotation.

Notes to chapter 6

1. The literature on this process is large and conclusive. See Yü Ying, 'Sung-tai ju-che ti-li fen-pu ti t'ung-chi,' *Yü kung* 1 (1933):170–6; Ho Yu-sen, 'Liang-Sung

ti hsüeh-feng ti-li fen-pu,' *Hsin-ya hsüeh-pao* 1 (1955):331–79; Kracke, 'Region, Family and Individual,' pp. 251–68; Chang Chia-chü, *Liang-Sung ching-chi chung-hsin ti nan i.* Other noteworthy studies include Sudō Yoshiyuki, *Sōdai kanryosei,* pp. 9–29, and Sun Yen-min, *Sung-tai shu-yüan chih-tu chih yen-chiu* (Taipei: Kuo-li Cheng-chih ta-hsüeh, 1963).

2. On the long-term north to south shift, see Aoyama Sadao, 'Zui, Tō, Sö sandai ni okeru kosū no chiiki teki kōsatsu, *'Rekishigaku kenkyū* 6 (1936):411–46. Shiba gives a useful summary of much of Aoyama's data in 'Urbanization and the Development of Markets in the Lower Yangtze Valley, in *Crisis and Prosperity in Sung China,* pp. 13–20. For a comprehensive study of these changes during the Sung, see Chang Chia-chü, *Liang-Sung ching-chi,* especially pp. 41–66.

3. See figure 7 below and Hartwell, 'Transformations of China,' Table 10, pp. 414–15.

4. See Sudō Yoshiyuki, *Sōdai kanryosei,* passim.; Chin Chung-shu, 'Pei-Sung k'o-chü,' pt. 1, pp. 237–47; and Aoyama Sadao, 'Newly-Risen Bureaucrats.' James T.C. Liu has a succinct discussion of the role of region in Northern Sung politics in *Reform in Sung China,* pp. 27–29.

5. Cited in Chin Chung-shu, 'Pei-Sung k'o-chü,' pt. 1, p. 244.

6. SHY:HC 3/35b–39a; 15/15b, 17b.

7. Ibid. 3/38a–39a; 15/17b; HCP 208/15a–b.

8. The original proposal came from the prefect of Fen-chou (Kuang-nan-tung), Liu Ts'ai, about whom we know nothing. Ssu-ma Kuang, *Ssu-ma kung wen-chi* 30/1b.

9. SHY:HC 1/11a, 11b.

10. Ssu-ma Kuang, *Ssu-ma kung wen-chi* 30/1b–5a.

11. *Ou-yang kung wen-chi* 113/8b–13a.

12. Ibid. 113/11a.

13. Ibid. 113/11b.

14. For a twelfth century example of a frustrated scholar turned rebel who later returned to the fold and passed an examination for amnestied literati, see TS 1:6–7.

15. Kracke, 'Region, Family and Individual,' pp. 262–5.

16. See Ping-ti Ho's discussion of the biases inherent in biographical collections. *The Ladder of Success,* pp. 92–6.

17. Kracke, 'Region, Family and Individual,' pp. 253–6.

18. That was in 1045. SHY:HC 15/13a–b.

19. Ibid.

20. The increases are given in both HNYL 172:2833 and SHY:HC 16/10a, but the special strictures on the 'three prefectures' *(san chün)* are mentioned only in the former source. There are two reasons for taking the three to be Wen-chou, T'ai-chou and Wu-chou. First, they were the only prefectures to be given increases larger than two. Second, we know from other sources that both Wen-chou and T'ai-chou were among the most competitive prefectures in the empire in the early thirteenth century. Wen-chou had 8,000 competing for 17 positions and T'ai-chou had a like number competing for 11 positions. Liu Tsai, *Man-t'ang wen-chi* 13/10a–b; Ch'en Ch'i-ch'ing, *Chia-ting Chih-ch'eng chih,* 4/10a.

21. See, for example, SHY:HC 15/15b.

22. Ibid. 15/4a; HCP 95/7b.

23. Ibid. 102/2a–b.

24. Ibid. 104/10b and SHY:HC 15/5b–6a for 1026; Ibid. 15/4a and HCP 108/2b for 1029.

25. SHY:HC 16/11a.

26. A complaint from 1178 makes this point very well. Ibid. 16/21b–22a. See also Ibid. 6/11b–12a and 16/17b.

27. SS 156/20a–b. This is a request dated 1252 asking that Kuang-nan-hsi be allowed to follow the example of Huai-nan, Ching-hsi and Ching-hu-pei in being examined separately and it was granted. That the origin of separate examinations for Ching-hsi and Ching-hu-pei was related to wartime disruptions is made clear in Ibid. 156/18a.

28. See SKSK, pp. 238–42, on the origins of the Ssu-ch'uan departmental examination. As to how long it continued, the latest reference that I have found is to a Ssu-ch'uan *sheng-yüan* (that is, the top graduate in the Ssu-ch'uan departmental examination) in the examination of 1256. He placed ninety-sixth in the fourth class. SYKCSL.

29. SHY:HC 5/5a–b; 4/17b–18a, 23a–b.

30. Lin T'ien-wei, 'Nan-Sung shih Ssu-ch'uan t'e-shu hua chih fen-hsi,' *Tung-fang wen-hua* 18 (1980):225–46, especially 225–42.

31. HNYL 177/2b–3a; CYTC 1.13:169.

32. For evidence of resentment by others of Ssu-ch'uan's special status, see the complaint from 1189 in SHY:HC 1/20b which claimed that Ssu-ch'uan's lax examination procedures had made its examinations easy to pass.

33. That is, all *chin-shih* degrees that we know to have been given. If we take instead all *chin-shih* of which we have record, the percentages would be 1.4% and 4.0% for the two periods.

34. I have used the circuit totals given by Kracke in 'Region, Family and Individual,' p. 257.

35. SS 156/20a–b.

36. Most important are those for the Southern Sung population. There are circuit population figures for 1162 and 1223, but no empire-wide prefectural figures between the years 1100 and 1290. *Sung hui-yao: Shih-huo* section 69/71a–b; WHTK 11:116–17.

37. Kracke, *Civil Service*, pp. 50–1.

38. 'Introduction: Urban Development in Imperial China,' in *The City in Late Imperial China*, ed. G. William Skinner (Stanford, Calif.: Stanford University Press, 1977), pp. 3–31; 'Regional Urbanization in Nineteenth Century China,' in Ibid., pp. 211–49; and 'Cities and the Hierarchy of Local Systems,' in Ibid., pp. 275–351. Robert Hartwell has also used Skinner's model with modifications in his recent article, 'Transformations of China.'

39. Skinner, 'Introduction: Urban Development,' p. 12. These were Northwest China, North China, Upper Yangtze, Middle Yangtze, Lower Yangtze, Southeast Coast, Ling-nan, Yun-kwei, and Manchuria. The last two lie outside areas controlled by the Sung.

40. Skinner, 'Mobility Strategies in Late Imperial China: A Regional Systems Analysis,' in *Regional Analysis*, 2 vols., ed. Carol A. Smith (New York: Academic Press, Inc., 1976), 1:330.

41. Ibid.

42. Skinner, 'Introduction: Urban Development,' p. 16.

43. 'Mobility Strategies,' pp. 342–3.

44. 'Introduction: Urban Development,' pp. 13–17. Here I follow Skinner rather than Hartwell, who outlines developmental cycles for seven macroregions from the eighth through the sixteenth centuries. 'Transformations of China,' pp. 367–83.

45. In 1059, 1061 and 1063, K'ai-feng alone accounted for 26.7%, 37.7% and 34.2% of all *chin-shih* (see Table 8). Using the lowest percentage of 26% to extrapolate, K'ai-feng would have accounted for 4,891 of the 18,812 Northern Sung *chin-shih*.

46. Lu Yu, *Wei-nan wen-chi*, 41 ch. (SPTK ed.) 3:46.

47. 'Transformations of China,' p. 414. Sudō Yoshiyuki also found that Shen-tsung's reign was the first in which southern chief councilors predominated. *Sōdai kan-ryosei*, p. 16.

48. Again, if we count only those *chin-shih* listed in the local histories, the figure would be 93%.
49. I have found references to only three academies in Sung local histories (all from the late Southern Sung), from Yen-chou (Liang-che-hsi), Shou-ch'ang chün (Ching-hu-pei) and Chien-k'ang fu. Fang Jen-jung, *Yen-chou hsü-chih* 3:27 -8; *Shou-ch'ang ch'eng* 14a–15a; CKC 28/5b–6a.
50. *Shou-ch'ang ch'eng* 4b–15a.
51. Ibid. 4b–7a, 13b–14a.
52. Ibid. 14a–15a.
53. Ibid. 7b.
54. Ibid. 7b, 11a–12b.
55. We might note that of the 178 *chin-shih* from prefectures not on the Yangtze or Grand Canal, 110 were from T'ai-chou in southern Huai-nan-tung, which was near to but not actually on both.
56. Yet even in these cases, we cannot assume an absence of educational activity. Wan-chou in K'uei-chou lu, which was mentioned above, had no *chin-shih* or schools (so far as we know), yet it had five hundred examination candidates in 1163. SHY:HC 4/37a–b.
57. Ibid. 15/14a–b.
58. Tseng Feng, *Yüan-tu chi* 17/5b.
59. Ibid. 16/33b.
60. See Chapter 2, p. 32 above.
61. 'Readers and Audiences: An Exploration of the Spread of Traditional Chinese Culture,' in *Text and Context: the Social Anthropology of Tradition*, ed. Ravindra K. Jain (Philadelphia: Institute for the Study of Human Issues, Inc., 1977), pp. 184–5.
62. SHY:CJ 2/10b–11a. For two similar cases from the south, see Ibid. 2/12a, 14a.
63. SHY:HC 16/17b–18a.
64. Ch'ao-ting Chi, *Key Economic Areas in Chinese History, as Revealed in the Development of Public Works for Water Control* (London: Allen & Unwin, 1936), p. 132.
65. Shiba, *Commerce and Society,* pp. 103–11; Chang Chia-chü, *Liang-Sung ching-chi,* pp. 6–28.
66. Ibid., pp. 23–26; Shiba, *Commerce and Society*, pp. 103–11; Chang Hsiu-min, 'Nan-Sung k'o-shu ti-yü k'ao,' pp. 52–6.
67. Shiba, 'Urbanization and the Development of Markets,' pp. 24–33; Kracke, 'Sung Society: Change Within Tradition,' in *Enduring Scholarship*, pp. 65–9.
68. Carter, *The Invention of Printing in China*, pp. 56–62.
69. Shiba, 'Urbanization and the Development of Markets,' p. 15.
70. Linda Walton-Vargo, 'Education, Social Change, and Neo-Confucianism,' p. 31.
71. For a description of Ming-chou's commercial importance during the Sung, see Shiba, 'Ningpo and its Hinterland,' in *The City in Late Imperial China*, pp. 396–7.
72. Skinner, 'Introduction: Urban Development,' p. 13.
73. Chi-chou, for example, was an extremely prosperous prefecture which had one of the highest tax quotas in the empire because of its rice production. Shiba, *Commerce and Society*, p. 65. For the similar characteristics of neighbouring Fu-chou, see Hymes, 'Prominence and Power,' Introduction.
74. Ping-ti Ho, *The Ladder of Success*, p. 227. The role of Chi-chou (Ming Chi-an fu) was central in both periods, for in the years 1225–75 its 499 *chin-shih* were second only to Fu-chou's (Fu-chien) 865, while the 1,020 *chin-shih* it produced in the Ming were unequalled by any other prefecture. Ibid., pp. 246–8.
75. Shiba, *Commerce and Society*, pp. 63–4.
76. These ten accounted for 44% of the 3,078 south China *chin-shih* for those years.

77. For example, Ch'üan-chou produced only thirteen *chin-shih* and nine *ming-ching* degrees during the T'ang. Hugh R. Clark, 'Quanzhou (Fujian) During the Tang–Song Interregnum, 879–978,' *T'oung Pao* 68 (1982):144.
78. Ibid., pp. 145–7; Shiba, 'Urbanization and the Development of Markets,' pp. 16–19.
For migration into Fu-chien, see Aoyama, 'Newly-Risen Bureaucrats,' and Hans Bielenstein, 'The Chinese Colonization of Fukien until the End of the T'ang,' in *Studia Serica Bernard Karlgren Dedicata: Sinological Studies Dedicated to Bernard Karlgren on his Seventieth Birthday, October Fifth, 1959*, ed. Soren Egerod and Else Glahn (Copenhagen: Ejnar Munksgaard, 1959), pp. 98–122.
79. 'Quanzhou,' pp. 145–9.
80. This commitment, like the later educational culture of the Southeast Coast described below, can be viewed as a 'mobility strategy,' which, according to Skinner, involved local systems specializing occupationally and exporting their skills. 'Mobility Strategies,' p. 327. The ubiquity of the literati in later times should not obscure the occupational options, especially of merchant and soldier, open to elite men in the tenth century.
81. Cited by Shiba Yoshinobu, *Sōdai shōgyō-shi kenkyū* (Tokyo: Kazama-Shopbo, 1968), p. 424.
82. This statement is based upon Hartwell's comments on a paper of mine at the University of Pittsburgh's Tristate Seminar on Modern China, September 1978, in which he said that these lineages were centered in the four capitals in the north, Ch'eng-tu fu and Mei-chou in Ssu-ch'uan, the Kan Basin, and Ch'ang-chou and Su-chou in the Yangtze Delta.
83. This was especially the case after the establishment of a Superintendency of Foreign Trade (*shih-po-ssu*) in 1086. Laurence J.C. Ma, *Commercial Development and Urban Change in Sung China (960–1279)* (Ann Arbor: Department of Geography, University of Michigan, 1971), pp. 33–7.
84. Jung-pang Lo, 'The Emergence of China as a Seapower During the Late Sung and Early Yüan Periods,' in *Enduring Scholarship*, pp. 92–3.
85. Chang Ch'i-yün, 'Sung-tai Ssu-ming chih hsüeh-feng,' in *Sung-shih yen-chiu*, vol. 3 (Taipei: Chung-hua ts'ung-shu pien-shen wei-yuan-hui, 1966), p. 63. Note, too, the statement by Su Shih that 'the entire province of Fukien made its living by the practice of sea-borne commerce.' Shiba, *Commerce and Society*, p. 187.
86. PCSMC 12/7b–8b.
87. Ping-ti Ho, *The Ladder of Success*, pp. 227–8. For a more exact comparison, the Sung prefectures that lay within the Ming and Ch'ing boundaries of Chekiang and Fukien accounted for 47% of all Southern Sung *chin-shih*.
88. YYSMC 13/7b.
89. The teachers were Tu Ch'un, Yang Chih, Wang Shih, Wang Shuo, and, most renowned, Lou Yu, who was to teach at the prefectural school for over thirty years. Linda Walton-Vargo, 'Education, Social Change, and Neo-Confucianism,' p. 58; Chang Ch'i-yün, 'Sung-tai Ssu-ming chih hsüeh-feng,' p. 48.
90. These were Wang An-shih when he served as Tz'u-chi county magistrate in 1048 and Tu Hsing who as magistrate in Hsiang-shan country ten to twenty years later did much to foster local education. Chang Chin, *Ch'ien-tao Ssu-ming t'u-ching* 9/13a–16b; Wang P'i-chih, *Sheng-shui yen-t'an lu*, 10 ch. (TSCC ed.) 3:22. This will hereafter be cited as SSYTL.
91. Chang Chin, *Ch'ien-tao Ssu-ming t'u-ching* 9/16b–18a. The writer, Li Kang, was generalizing about Sung education, but we can assume that conditions in Ming-chou accorded with his description, since he subsequently discussed the prefecture in very favorable terms.
92. Chang Ch'i-yün, 'Sung-tai Ssu-ming,' pp. 52–7.
93. Schirokauer, 'Neo-Confucians Under Attack,' pp. 184–8.
94. *Liang-Sung ching-chi*, pp. 138–9.

95. MS 32/9b; SHY:HC 22/6b; Liu Tsai, *Man-t'ang wen-chi* 13/10a–b.
96. Ibid.; Ch'en Ch'i-ch'ing, *Chih-ch'eng chih* 4/10a.
97. CCC 11/35b–36a; Kung Ming-chih, *Chung Wu chi-wen* 1:6–7; Lo Yüan, *Hsin-an chih*, 10 ch. (1888 ed.) 8/2a–b.
98. Shih O, comp., *Ch'un-yu Lin-an chih*, ch. 5–10 extant (Wu-lin chang ts'ung-pien ed.) 6/4b–5a; HCLAC 56/3b.
99. Population pressure is also the reason given by James Cole to explain the strong scholarly/clerical emigrant tradition of Shao-hsing during the Ch'ing. 'Shaohsing: Studies in Ch'ing Social History' (Ph.D. Dissertation, Stanford University, 1975), p. 8.
100. Tseng Feng, *Yüan-tu chi* 17/11a. The translation follows, in part, that of Mark Elvin in Shiba, *Commerce and Society*, p. 186. Shiba also quotes Fang Ta-tsung (1183–1247), who with a touch of poetic license described his county of Yung-fu in Fu-chou: 'Every family is adept at music and the chanting of texts. People know the laws; and this is true not only of scholars; every peasant, artisan and merchant teaches his sons how to read books. Even herdsmen and wives who bring food to their husbands at work in the fields can recite the poems of the men of ancient times.'
101. See Table 15. I have been unable to examine *chü-jen* lists for three counties in Fu-chou (Chiang-nan-hsi), but according to Robert Hymes, 20% of them became *chin-shih*. 'Prominence and Power,' p. 58.
102. Ch'eng Tuan-li, *Ch'eng-shih chia-shu* 3/42a–b.

Notes to chapter 7
1. Wei Liao-weng, *I-li yao-i*, 50 ch. (SKCS ed.) 8/3b.
2. ICC 4.12:89. This is actually from a dream that Kung had which later supposedly came to pass, but Hung Mai, who received his *chin-shih* in 1145, knew whereof he was writing.
3. See, for example, TCY 3:24–7.
4. The principal source for it was the Western Han classic, *I-li*. See John Steele, *The I-li* 1:51–73.
5. See Wei Liao-weng, *I-li yao-i* 8/2a–b, and Chu Hsi, *I-li ching-chuan t'ung-chieh*, 37 ch. (Hsi-ching ch'ing-lu ts'ung-shu ed.) Mu-lu 9a.
6. TCY 1:1.
7. SHY:HC 16/6a.
8. Ibid. 16/10a. See also 6b and 8b–9a.
9. PCSMC 2/16a. See also the 'community pact' (*hsiang-yüeh*) of Lü Ta-chün (1030–81) to which Chu Hsi added his own emendations, for its prescribed ceremonies were very like the *I-li's* district drinking ceremony. *Chu Wen-kung wen-chi* 74/25a–32a. This has been translated by Monica Übelhör: 'Mr. Lu's Community Pact, With Additions and Deletions by Chu Hsi,' paper presented to the International Conference on Chu Hsi, University of Hawaii, July 1982.
10. PCSMC 2/16a. The last occurred as the result of a report to the court by an official from Ming-chou, Lin Pao (1079–1149).
11. Ibid. 2/17a–18b. Also included is a listing of the financial assets supporting the ceremony as of 1246.
12. See Walton-Vargo, 'Education, Social Change, and Neo-Confucianism.'
13. PCSMC 2/17b. The quotation is from 1246.
14. Mei Ying-fa, *K'ai-ch'ing Ssu-ming chih*, 12 ch. (Sung Yüan Ssu-ming liu chih ed.) 1/16a–17b.
15. Ibid. 1/17a. The Chinese dimensions were one *ch'ih* five *ts'un* in length, six *ts'un* in width.
16. Chou Pi-ta, *I-kung t'i-pa* (TSCC ed.) 3:34.

17. The congratulatory banquet following the palace examination at the capital was called the Feast of Hopeful Expectation (*Ch'i-chi yen*). See SKSK, pp. 343–5.
18. See CKC 32/11a–12b. For an intriguing comparative example of the uses of ritual feasting, see Richard C. Trexler, *Public Life in Renaissance Florence* (New York: Academic Press, 1980), pp. 539–40.
19. ICC 1.17:135. See too YHCW 6/6b–7a.
20. ICC 2.9:66–67.
21. Ibid. 4.5:37.
22. SHY:HC 8/23b–24b; Wu Tzu-mu, *Meng-liang lu* 2/2b–2a, 4/4b. These were the standard dates in the Southern Sung.
23. Denis Twitchett, 'The Fan Clan's Charitable Estate,' pp. 105–7; and 'Documents on Clan Administration: I. The Rules of Administration of the Charitable Estate of the Fan Clan,' *Asia Major* n.s. 8 (1960):1–35.
24. Yang Lien-sheng, 'K'o-chü shih-tai ti fu k'ao lü-fei wen-t'i,' *Ch'ing-hua hsüeh-pao* n.s. 2 (1961):122.
25. Twitchett, 'Fan Clan's Charitable Estate,' pp. 109–10.
26. Ho Ping-ti notes that the Neo-Confucians Ch'eng I (1033–1107) and Chu Hsi (1133–1200) argued for such a revival 'in the hope that the integrity of ancestral property might thus be permanently maintained and that the clan as a whole might not decline.' *The Ladder of Success in Imperial China*, pp. 162–3.
27. Lu Yu, *Wei-nan wen-chi* 21:124. Lu was writing in 1207.
28. See Yang Lien-sheng, 'K'o-chü shih-tai,' pp. 116–30, and Sudō Yoshiyuki, *Chūgoku tochi seido shi kenkyū* (Tokyo: Tokyo University Press, 1954), pp. 204–7.
29. SS 247/20b. See also Yang, 'K'o-chü shih-tai,' p. 118, which quotes variants of this passage from other sources.
30. Yü Hsi-lu, *Chih-shun Chen-chiang chih*, 21 ch. (Taipei: Wen-hua shu-chü, 1958) 11/19b. This will hereafter be cited as CCC.
31. In addition to the six estates mentioned by Sudō and Yang, I have found references to another sixteen, dating from between 1197 and 1274.
32. See CCC 11/19a–20a; Hsü Shih, *Chih-yüan Chia-ho chih*, 32 ch. (1288 ms.) 7/6a–b; YYSMC 14/48b–49a.
33. Wen T'ien-hsiang, *Wen Shen hsien-sheng ch'üan-chi* 9:291.
34. CCC 11/19b.
35. CKC 32/9a–10b.
36. Chu Hsi, *Chu wen-kung wen-chi*, 100 ch. (SPTK ed.) 100/14b.
37. PCSMC 1/16a–17b.
38. See *chüan* 113 (pp. 1019–27) on the dress of Sung officials in WHTK.
39. In separate measures from 982, *chü-jen* were on the one hand grouped with clerks, artisans, merchants and other commoners in the wearing of the lowly 'iron-plated belts' (*t'ieh-chiao-tai*), but on the other hand were specifically permitted to wear black robes at their residences. Ibid. 113:1020.
40. For the importance of such dress at local ceremonies, see Chu Hsi, *Chu Wen-kung wen-chi* 74/27a–b, 28b; Übelhör, 'Mr. Lu's Community Pact,' pp. 7–8, 16.
41. ICC 2.20:158.
42. See ICC 1.11:87; 1.16:128.
43. See SKSK, pp. 147–8.
44. For example, Lin-an's was built in 1135, Ming-chou's in 1169, and Jun-chou's in 1177. HCLAC 12/1a–18a; PCSMC 1/29a–b; CCC 11/35b–36a.
45. SHY:HC 4/37a–b, 16/26a.
46. CKC 32/2a, 5a, 13a.
47. Ibid. 29/14.
48. See, for example, CKC 32/5a, 6b; PCSMC 1/29a–b; CCC 11/35b–36a.

49. There was sometimes a permanent staff of functionaries who maintained the buildings and kept records, but the examining area remained empty.

50. See especially Chang Chung-li, _The Chinese Gentry: Studies on Their Role in Nineteenth Century Chinese Society_ (Seattle: University of Washington Press, 1955).

51. One is reminded of Clifford Geertz's Balinese 'theater state', where a central aim of its elaborate ritual was to communicate the status of its participants to the people at large. _Nagara: The Theater State in Nineteenth Century Bali_ (Princeton, N.J.: Princeton University Press, 1980).

52. _I-kung t'i-pa_ 3:34.

53. CKC 32/3a.

54. But this result did not always follow. See Yüeh K'o's account of an examination riot in 1180 at the just renovated examination hall in Ch'eng-tu. TS 10:80–2.

55. See Peter Kees Bol's excellent dissertation, 'Culture and the Way in Eleventh Century China' (Ph.D. Dissertation, Princeton University, 1982), especially Chapters 1 and 2.

56. Pao Lien, _Ch'in-ch'uan chih_, 15 ch. (Ch'ing copy of a Yüan edition) 12/8a.

57. CKC 28/14a–b. The authors of the essay were Huang Fu and Chang Ju-chieh.

58. In addition to the 'thorny gates' mentioned earlier, there were the 'gates of rites' (_li-wei_) and 'departmental gates' (_sheng-wei_) used for the departmental examinations, the 'tribute gates' (_kung-wei_) for the prefectural examinations, and the 'office gates' (_ts'ao-wei_) for the avoidance examinations.

59. TCY, first cited on p. 216 n.24. For a partial translation, see Patricia Buckley Ebrey, _Chinese Civilization and Society: A Sourcebook_ (New York: Macmillan Publishing Co., 1981), pp. 58–61.

60. See especially _chüan_ 7 which is devoted to accounts of the successes of men of humble birth.

61. TMH, first cited on p. 212 n.18.

62. _Sheng-shui yen-t'an lu_ ('Compilation of banquet conversations on the Sheng River bank'), 10 ch. (TSCC ed.). This will be cited hereafter as SSYTL.

63. _Ch'un-chu chi-wen_ ('Record of hearsay at a spring waterside') or CCCW, first cited on p. 212 n. 28.

64. _T'ing-shih_ ('Stores noted at home on a small table') or TS, first cited on p. 225 n. 28.

65. _Yu-huan chi-wen_ ('Experiences of a provincial official') or YHCW, first cited on p. 213 n. 49.

66. ICC, first cited on p. 212 n. 29. This served as the primary sourcebook for Hung Pien's famous Ming collection, _Liu-shih-chia hsiao-shuo_ ('Sixty Stories'). See Patrick Hanan, _The Chinese Vernacular Short Story_ (Cambridge, Mass.: Harvard University Press, 1981), p. 56.

67. Modern anthropologists have been particularly insightful on the vital role played by gods, ghosts and ancestors in everyday Chinese life. See Arthur P. Wolf, 'Gods, Ghosts, and Ancestors' in Arthur P. Wolf, ed. _Religion and Ritual in Chinese Society_ (Stanford, Calif.: Stanford University Press, 1974), pp. 131–82; and Emily Ahern, _Chinese Ritual and Politics_ (Cambridge: Cambridge University Press, 1982).

68. D.R. Jonker, biography of Lü Pen-chung in _Sung Biographies_, ed. Herbert Franke, pp. 735–41. On Lü's social and intellectual milieu, see TMH 1:7.

69. Yves Hervouet, ed., _A Sung Bibliography (Bibliographie des Sung)_ (Hong Kong: The Chinese University Press, 1978), pp. 102, 339, 338.

70. Ibid., p. 336.

71. Chang Fu-jui, biography of Hung Mai in _Sung Biographies_, ed. Herbert Franke, pp. 469–78.

72. I am indebted to Professor Peter Bol for this idea.

73. _Daedalus_, v. 105 (Spring 1976):109–23.

74. *Analects* 2.4. I have followed Tu's translation. 'Confucian Perceptions,' p. 117.
75. Ibid., p. 109; *Li-chi* (1815 ed.) 28/20a–21b.
76. See Lee, 'The Schools of Sung China,' pp. 45–60.
77. That, at least, was the average in the examinations of 1148 and 1256, the only examinations for which we have comprehensive biographical data. It may have been somewhat lower during the Northern Sung. SYKCSL.
78. Kracke, *Civil Service*, p. 82.
79. See Chapter 1 for a discussion of their alternatives.
80. CCCW 6:73–4.
81. ICC 3.7:53–4.
82. Mei Yao-ch'en, *Wan-ling hsien-sheng chi*, 60 ch. (SPTK ed.) 34/15a. With a few changes the translation is that of Jonathan Chaves in *Sunflower Splendor* ed. (Bloomington: Indiana University Press, 1976), p. 318.
83. See ICC 3.6:44–5 for a portrait of the wandering literatus as bully.
84. Liu Tsai, *Man-t'ang wen-chi* 3/8a–11b.
85. Ibid. 3/8b–9a.
86. Presumably to guard against such connivance and against literati using official connections to their own ends, Li Yüan-pi in his 1117 *Guide for Magistrates* (*Tso-i tzu-chen*) suggested that a new magistrate post placards stating that his retinue contained neither degree candidates (*hsiu-ts'ai*) nor relatives, retainers, doctors, monks, attendants or the like. Peter Kees Bol, 'The *Tso-i tzu-chen*; A Twelfth Century Guide for Subprefects.' Unpublished manuscript, pp. 9–10, 37–8.
87. ICC 1.8:62. See also 4.15:115.
88. Ibid. 3.11:84.
89. Ibid. 1.13:99.
90. Ibid. 4.11:85.
91. This was for the preliminary examination for refugee literati, for Liu was from K'ai-feng.
92. Ibid. 4.17:134. They also learn that he would have passed in first place had it not been for the seduction.
93. Ibid. 1.2:15–16.
94. Ibid. 3.3:19.
95. *Analects* 16.7.
96. This was a degree given to elderly *chü-jen* who had taken the departmental examination in the past which I dealt with at length in Chapter 2. Ts'ai T'ao, in his discussion of facilitated degrees, states that the recipients had to have failed before and be elderly and pitiable. *T'ieh-wei-shan ts'ung-shu*, 6 ch. (Chih-pu-tsu-chai ts'ung-shu ed.) 2/9a.
97. ICC 2.3:21–2. For other cases of older literati being scoffed at, see Ibid. 1.4:29 and CCCW 2:14.
98. ICC 3.12:95–6. But then he died after inadvertently fulfilling the conditions of a death prophecy that he had had in a third dream.
99. Ibid. 4.11:87.
100. Ibid. 1.5:34–5. His efforts were eventually successful but only after much trying. For a similar accumulation of *yin* virtue by a literatus, see Ibid. 1.12:89.
101. SSYTL 10:87.
102. ICC 4.5:37.
103. TMH 1:9. The other two were 'becoming an official by virtue of the power of one's father or brothers' and 'having a lofty talent for writing essays.'
104. SSYTL 6:53.
105. See WHTK 35:329–30.
106. SS 46/6a.
107. Chu Hsi, *Reflections on Things at Hand*, p. 149.

108. CCCY 5:59 provides two such examples.
109. ICC 1.9:72.
110. Both are described in YHCW 4/5a–6a.
111. ICC 2.4:29.
112. See ICC 4.11:84–85 and *Ta Ming i-t'ung chih*, 90 ch. (1461 ed.) 54/8a.
113. For examples, see Tseng Kuo-ch'üan, *Hu-nan t'ung-chih* 64/35a–b, 65/13b, and most especially 63/18a–b.
114. See Robert Hymes's description of the collapse and rebuilding of the Writing Brush Pagoda in Fu-chou. 'Prominence and Power,' pp. 285–95.
115. ICC 3.19:143.
116. Ibid. 1.9:67–8; TS 1:6–7; SSYTL 6:52.
117. ICC 1.10:74, 1.19:151–2.
118. Ibid. 8:65; ICC 1.15:120.
119. SSYTL 6:54.
120. ICC 2.14:104, 4.6:45–6.
121. Ibid. 1.9:67–8, 1.10:74.
122. Ibid. 1.18:139, 3.5:34.
123. Ibid. 1.5:34, 4.10:76; CCCW 2:14; SSYTL 3:19.
124. ICC 3.3:23–4.
125. YHCW 4/1a–3b. Chang cites his source as 'village elders' (*hsiang-li chang-lao*).
126. ICC 1.16:124; 2.15:115.
127. Ibid. 1.1:1.
128. Ibid. 1.19:152–3. The others are in Ibid. 1.18:144 and 3.1:5–6.
129. Ibid. 1.6:47–8; 1.18:138; 2.1:3–4.
130. Ibid. 1.9:67, 3.5:37–38. See also Ibid. 1.3:21 where a woman dreams of a boy dressed in blue atop a mountain. He is her future son who passes the examination only to be killed by bandits when serving as a county registrar.
131. SSYTL 6:53. See also Ibid. 6:55 where the literatus dreams of a meeting he is to have with the Sung emperor Ying-tsung some thirty years hence.
132. ICC 3.7:53.
133. Ts'ai T'ao, *Tieh-wei-shan ts'ung-shu*, 6 ch. (Chih-pu-tsu-chai ts'ung-shu ed.) 4/4b–5a.
134. ICC 2.8:56.
135. See Henri Maspero, 'The Mythology of Modern China,' in *Asiatic Mythology*, Intro. by Paul-Louis Chochoud (London: 1932; reprint ed. New York: Crescent Books), pp. 310–12.
136. Ibid., p. 311. Maspero is talking specifically about Chang Ya(-tzu) as an incarnation of the god Wen-ch'ang, but Morahashi identifies Chang Ya-tzu with Tzu-t'ung. *Hanwa daijiten*, v. 6, p. 368.
137. Maspero, 'Mythology,' p. 312; R.H. van Gulik, 'On the Seal Representing the God of Literature on the Title Page of Old Chinese and Japanese Popular Editions,' *Monumenta Nipponica* 4 (Jan. 1941), esp. 34–7; and Henri Doré, S.J., *Researches into Chinese Superstitions*, trans. M. Donnelly, S.J. (Shanghai: T'usewei Press, 1921), v. 6, pp. viii–xi, 4–57.
138. See Ibid. 4.12:89 and CCCW 1:5.
139. See ICC 1.18:138; 2.19:151; 2.20:157–8; 3.7:54; and 3.11:83–4. One man was actually delighted with his new status, for in life he had never passed the examinations but upon dying he was made vice-administrator in the City God's government. Ibid. 2.20:158.
140. Ibid. 2.20:157–8.
141. On classics, see ICC 4.16:122; on poems, Ibid. 1.13:98; CCCW 2:13; SSYTL 6:52; and on biographies, Ibid. 6:53.
142. See ICC 4.6:42 and especially 4.2:11–12.
143. SSYTL 6:55.

144. ICC 1/17:133–4 and also CCCW 2:17. The prophecy was: 'Twenty-seven A; connected with the seventh class' (*er-shih-ch'i chia; hsi ti ch'i k'o*). Since *chia* and *k'o* were terms commonly used in the examinations, Hsu assumed that that was what it referred to, though he didn't fully understand it. What it meant was the seventh space in the twenty-seventh row. Perhaps coincidentally, Chin-chia (Golden Armor) was the name of another god associated with the God of Literature cult in Ch'ing times. See Doré, *Chinese Superstitions*, V. 6, p. 59.
145. See, for example, ICC 1.2:11–12; 1.15:120; 2.9:66–7.
146. ICC 1.4:29–30; 1.7:51; 1.9:65; 1.11:84; 3.15:113; 4.15:113. In a slight variation, one man had once seen a snake in a temple before passing the prefectural examinations, so when preparing again for the examinations, he prayed to see another snake. He saw a large one and was placed first.

Notes to chapter 8

1. Hsü Shih, *Chia-ho chih* 16/16a.
2. See Miyakawa Hisayuki, 'An Outline of the Naito Hypothesis and Its Effects on Japanese Studies of China,' *Far Eastern Quarterly* 14 (1954–5):533–2, and Miyazaki, *China's Examination Hell*, pp. 115–16, where this is argued. The objection is not to the effects of the Sung examination reforms, which certainly enhanced imperial power, but to the characterization of Sung rule as autocratic.
3. See pp. 95–6 above.
4. Lawrence Stone, 'The Educational Revolution in England, 1560–1640,' *Past and Present* 28 (July 1964).
5. See pp. 120–3 above.
6. Ho, *The Ladder of Success*, pp. 149–53.
7. This, at least, was the case in the Ch'ing. See Chang, *The Chinese Gentry*, p. 170, especially note 23.
8. See Chaffee, 'Education and Examinations,' pp. 90–92. The primary sources on these schools are SHY:CJ 3 and SS 157/17a–20a, 24a–34b.
9. This point originated with Max Weber who characterized Chinese education as a 'pedagogy of cultivation' while acknowledging the late Northern Sung as the primary exception to his generalization. *The Religion of China: Confucianism and Taoism*, trans. Hans H. Gerth (New York: Macmillan Co., 1964), pp. 119–21.
10. *Centuries of Childhood: A Social History of Family Life*, trans. Robert Baldick (New York: Vintage Books, 1962), Part II, especially Chapter 2.
11. See Bol, 'Culture and the Way,' and, for an analysis of Su's approach as seen in literary theories of painting, Susan Bush, *The Chinese Literati on Painting: Su Shih (1037–1101 to Tung Ch'i-ch'ang (1555–1636))*(Cambridge, Mass.: Harvard University Press, 1971).
12. Quoted in Tillman, *Utilitarian Confucianism*, p. 53.
13. See p. 91 above for a discussion of the religious character of the Neo-Confucian academies.
14. For the yeshiva, see Jacob Katz, *Tradition and Crisis: Jewish Society at the End of the Middle Ages* (New York: Schocken Books, 1961), pp. 192–8.
15. ICC 1.16:125.
16. See especially, 'Transformation of China.'
17. See CCCW 2:11–12 and SSYTL 4:28 for two famous examples.
18. For only 10 of the 72 families that Hymes identified as the Fu-chou local elite is there no record of office-holding. 'Prominence and Power,' pp. 108–9.
19. ICC 1.7.51. The student followed the spirit's advice and set off for home but died en route. For story of a University student who is sent home to bury his father and lives, see Ibid. 1.7:52.

Notes to appendix 4

1. In the first prefecture surveyed (Fu-chou in Fu-chien) I kept track of the *chin-shih* by county and found considerable disagreement concerning the counties from which they came, especially for the thirteenth century.
2. The sources were *Che-chiang t'ung-chih* by Fu Wang-pa, *Ch'ü-chou fu chih* by Lin Ying-hsiang, and *Ch'ü-chou fu chih* by Yang T'ing-wang. For a given year, if one source differed from the other two, the figure given by the two was used. If all three differed, the middle figure was used.
3. PCSMC 10/1a.
4. See Appendix 2 and its description of the sources used for the empire-wide examination figures.
5. For example, the list for Hu-chou in T'an Yao's *Wu-hsing chih* begins only with 1042, but the *Che-chiang t'ung-chih* by Fu Wang-pa lists *chin-shih* from the prefecture beginning with the early Sung.
6. Ssu-ma Kuang, *Ssu-ma kung wen-chi* 30/1a—5b. See also Table 9 above.
7. See the discussion on K'ai-feng in Chapter 3.
8. SHY:HC 1/6b.
9. For a discussion of these lists and of their bibliographical histories, see Kracke, 'Family vs. Merit,' pp. 108—9.

LIST OF CHARACTERS

an-ch'a-shih 按察使
An-hua hsien (T'an-chou) 安化縣
Ch'an 禪
Chang-chou (Fu-chien) 漳州
Chang Chün 張浚
Chang Hsien-t'u 張獻圖
Chang K'o-ching 張克敬
Chang Shih 張栻
Chang Shih-nan 張世南
Chang Shih-sun 張士遜
Chang Tsai 張載
Chang Tz'u-hsien 張次賢
Chang Ya-tzu 張亞子
Ch'ang-an 長安
Ch'ang-chou (Liang-che-hsi) 常州
ch'ang-p'ing-ts'ang 常平倉
ch'ang-shih 長史
Chao 趙
Chao-chün Li 趙郡李
Chao Ju-yü 趙汝愚
Chao K'uang-yin 趙匡胤
ch'ao-kuan 朝官
Che-tsung 哲宗
Chen-chiang fu (Liang-che-hsi)
    鎮江府
Chen-chou (Huai-nan-tung) 眞州
Chen Te-hsiu 眞德秀
Chen-tsung 眞宗
chen-wang en-tse 陣亡恩澤
chen-wang nü-fu 陣亡女夫
Chen Ying 眞穎
Ch'en Fu-liang 陳傅良
Ch'en Hsiang 陳襄
Ch'en Hsiu-kung 陳秀公
Ch'en Kung-fu 陳公輔
Ch'en Liang 陳亮

Ch'en Mao-lin 陳茂林
Ch'en Shu 陳恕
Ch'en Te-kao 陳德高
Ch'en Te-kuang 陳德廣
Ch'en Yen 陳炎
Cheng-chou (Ching-hsi-pei) 鄭州
Cheng-t'ing 正廳
ch'eng 成
Ch'eng Hao 程灝
Ch'eng-huang 城皇
Ch'eng I 程頤
ch'eng-jen 成人
Ch'eng-tu fu 成都府
Ch'eng-tu fu lu 成都府路
Chi 濟
Chi-chou (Chiang-nan-hsi) 吉州
chi-lu-kuan 寄祿官
chi-ti 及第
chi-wei 棘闈
Ch'i-chi Yen 期集宴
chia 甲
chia-chuang 家狀
chia-pao-chuang 家保狀
Chiang-nan-hsi lu 江南西路
Chiang-nan-tung lu 江南東路
Chiang-ning fu (Chiang-nan-tung)
    江寧府
Chiang-tso 江左
chiao-hua 教化
chiao-kuan 教官
chiao-shou 教授
chieh-shih 解試
chien (industrial prefecture) 監
chien (recommend) 薦
chien (room) 簡
chien-ch'a yü-shih 監察御史

Chien-chou (Fu-chien) 建州
chien-chü 薦舉
Chien-k'ang fu (Chiang-nan-tung) 建康府
Chien-yang hsien (Chien-chou) 建陽縣
Ch'ien-chou (Chiang-nan-hsi) 虔州
Ch'ien Han Shu 前漢書
Ch'ien-t'ang River 錢塘江
Ch'ien-tao 乾道
Ch'ien-tao hsin-fa 乾道新法
Ch'ien-tzu wen 千字文
chih-cheng 制政
chih-k'o 制科
chih-kung 至公
chih-shih-kuan 職事官
chih-shih pu-kuan 致仕補官
ch'ih 尺
chin 斤
Chin-chia 金甲
chin-hua p'ang-tzu 金花榜子
chin-na pu-kuan 進納補官
chin-shih 進士
Ch'in-feng lu 秦鳳路
Ch'in Kuei 秦檜
Ch'in-tsung 欽宗
Ching-chi lu 京畿路
Ching-hsi 京西
Ching-hsi-nan lu 京西南路
Ching-hsi-pei lu 京西北路
Ching-hu-nan lu 荊湖南路
Ching-hu-pei lu 荊湖北路
ching-i chih-shih 經義進士
ching-kuan 京官
ching-she 精舍
Ching-tung 京東
Ching-tung-hsi lu 京東西路
Ching-tung-tung lu 京東東路
ch'ing (land unit) 頃
Ch'ing-ho Chang 清河張
Ch'ing-li 慶歷
Chiu-ching 九經
Chiu-lung 九龍
chiu-p'in chung-cheng 九品中正
Ch'iung-chou (Kuang-nan-hsi) 瓊州
chou 州
Chou Hsi-meng 周希孟
chou-hsüeh 州學
Chou-li 周禮

Chou Pi-ta 周必大
chou-tzu 冑子
chou-tzu-shih 冑子試
chou-tzu tieh-shih 冑子牒試
chu-chiao 助教
Chu Hsi 朱熹
chu-k'o 諸科
chu-kuan chin-feng 主官進奉
Ch'u-chou (Liang-che-tung) 處州
ch'u-shen 出身
chü-jen 舉人
Ch'ü-chou (Liang-che-tung) 衢州
Ch'üan-chou (Fu-chien) 泉州
chüan-yün-shih 轉運使
chüan-yün-ssu shih 轉運司試
ch'üan-shih 銓試
chuang 壯
chuang-yüan (estate) 莊院
chuang-yüan (top examination graduate) 狀元
chün 軍
chün-kung 軍功
chün-pan 軍班
chün-wang 郡望
Ch'un-ch'iu 春秋
Ch'un-hsi 淳熙
Ch'un-yu 淳祐
chung 忠
Chung-men 中門
E-chou (Ching-hu-pei) 鄂州
en-yin 恩蔭
er-shih-ch'i chia; hsi ti ch'i K'o 二十七甲, 係第七科
Er-ya 爾雅
Fan Chih 范時
Fan Chung-yen 范仲淹
Fan-hsüeh 蓄學
Fan Pien-shu 范辯叔
Fan Yen-hui 范彥煇
fan t'iao-hsien 犯條憲
Fang Ta-tsung 方大宗
fei kung-hsin 非公心
Feng-chou (Kuang-nan-tung) 封州
feng-mi 封彌
feng-piao pu-kuan 奉表補官
feng-shui 風水
feng-wen 風聞
fu (poetic description) 賦

fu (prefecture) 府
Fu-chien lu 福建路
Fu-chou (Chiang-nan-hsi) 撫州
Fu-chou (Fu-chien) 福州
Fu Pi 富弼
Fu River 撫江
fu-shih 附試
Han 漢
Han Ch'i 韓琦
Han-lin 翰林
Han River 韓江
Han Shih-chung 韓世忠
Hang-chou (Liang-che-hsi) 杭州
Heng-chou (Ching-hu-nan) 衡州
ho 和
Ho-nan fu 河南府
Ho-pei 河北
Ho-pei-hsi lu 河北西路
Ho-pei-tung lu 河北東路
Ho-tung lu 河東路
Ho Wei 何蘧
hou-chi ch'in-shu 后妃親屬
Hou Han Shu 後漢書
Hsi-ch'ing Hall 錫慶院
hsi-feng pu-kuan 襲封補官
Hsi Kai-ch'ing 襲蓋卿
hsiang 鄉
hsiang-li chang-lao 鄉里長老
hsiang-jen 鄉人
hsiang-kung 鄉貢
Hsiang River 湘江
Hsiang-shan hsien (Ming-chou) 象山縣
hsiang yin-chiu li 鄉飲酒禮
Hsiang Yü 項羽
hsiang-yüeh 鄉約
hsiao 孝
hsiao-chü 校舉
Hsiao Hsien 蕭銑
Hsiao-hsüeh 小學
hsiao-shih-ch'en 小使臣
Hsiao-tsung 孝宗
hsien 縣
Hsien-hsien Tz'u 先賢祠
hsien-hsüeh 縣學
hsien-sheng hsien-shih 先生先師
Hsin-chou (Chiang-nan-hsi) 信州
hsin-k'o ming-fa 新科明法

Hsing-chou (Li-chou lu) 興州
hsing-hsien-chuang 興賢莊
Hsing-hua chün (Fu-chien) 興化軍
Hsiu-chou (Liang-che-hsi) 秀州
hsiu-ts'ai 秀才
hsü 恤
Hsü Chi-chih 許及之
Hsü Kuo-hua 徐國華
Hsü Shu-wei 許叔微
Hsüan-ho 宣和
hsüan-jen 選人
hsüeh ch'i 血氣
Hsüeh-chiu Mao Shih 學究毛詩
hsüeh-t'ien 學田
hu-chi 戶籍
Hu-chou (Liang-che-hsi) 湖州
Hu Chü 胡榘
hu-chüeh-t'ien 戶絕田
Hu Hung 胡宏
Hu Kang-chung 胡剛中
hu-ming 糊名
Hu Yüan 胡瑗
Hua-chou (Kuang-nan-hsi) 化州
Huai-nan-hsi lu 淮南西路
Huai-nan-tung lu 淮南東路
Huang Ch'ao 黃巢
Hui-chou (Chiang-nan-tung) 徽州
Hui-tsung 徽宗
hun-pu 混補
Hung Mai 洪邁
Hung P'ien 洪梗
I-ching 易經
i-chuang 義莊
i-hsüeh 義學
I-li 儀禮
i-piao pu-kuan 遺表補官
jen 任
Jen-tsung 仁宗
Ju 儒
Ju-fu 儒服
Ju-lin 儒林
ju-tsao su pu-li 汝曹素不立
Jun-chou (Liang-che-hsi) 潤州
jung-kuan 冗官
K'ai-feng fu 開封府
K'ai-yuan li 開元禮
Kan River 贛江
Kao-tsung 高宗

k'ao-shih 考試
k'o 科
k'o-chu 科舉
Ku-liang Chüan 穀梁傳
Ku-t'ien hsien (Fu-chou) 古田縣
kuan 官
kuan-chih-shih 館職試
kuan-hu 官戶
kuan-li 冠禮
Kuang-chou (Huai-nan-hsi) 光州
Kuang-chou (Kuang-nan-tung) 廣州
Kuang-nan 廣南
Kuang-nan-hsi lu 廣南西路
Kuang-nan-tung lu 廣南東路
kuei-chi 桂籍
kuei-ming kuei-cheng 歸明歸正
K'uei-chou lu 夔州路
k'uei-shou 魁首
kung 公
Kung 龔
kung-chü 貢舉
kung-chüan 公卷
kung-tao 公道
Kung P'i-hsien 龔丕顯
kung-shih 公試
kung-shih-chuang 貢士莊
kung-tsui 公罪
kung-wei 貢闈
Kung-yang chuan 公羊傳
kung-yüan 貢院
K'ung-tzu miao 孔子廟
kuo-tzu 國子
Kuo-tzu-chien 國子監
Kuo-tzu-chien chieh-shih 國子監解試
Kuo-tzu-hsüeh 國子學
Kuo-tzu-sheng 國子生
lan-shan 襴衫
lei-shih 類試
li (ritual) 禮
li (unit of distance) 里
Li-chi 禮記
Li Ch'ien 李潛
li-chih 吏職
Li-chou lu 利州路
Li Chün-hsing 李君行
Li-hsüeh 理學
Li K'ang 李閌
Li Kou 李覯

Li Mo 李謨
Li-pu 禮部
Li-tsung 理宗
li-wei 禮闈
li-wu-kuan 釐務官
Li Yu 李攸
Li Yüan-pi 李元弼
Liang-che 兩浙
Liang-che chüan-yün-ssu fu-shih
　　兩浙轉運司附試
Liang-che-hsi lu 兩浙西路
Liang-che-tung lu 兩浙東路
liang-shih 量試
Lien-chiang hsien (Fu-chou) 連江縣
Lin-an fu (Liang-che-hsi) 臨安府
Lin Pao 林保
Lin Ta-chung 林大中
Liu Ch'eng-pi 劉承弼
Liu Chi-ming 劉紀明
Liu-ho hsien (Chen-chou) 六合縣
Liu Kai 劉漑
Liu Kung 劉珙
Liu Nan-fu 劉南甫
liu-nei 流內
Liu Pang 劉邦
Liu Shih 劉實
Liu T'ing-chih 劉廷直
Liu Tsai 劉宰
Liu Ts'ai 柳材
Liu Tsao 劉璪
liu-wai 流外
liu-wai pu-kuan 流外補官
Liu Yao-chü 劉堯舉
Liu Yü-hsi 劉禹錫
liu-yü-shih 流寓試
Lou Yu 樓郁
lu 路
Lu Chiu-ling 陸九齡
Lu Chiu-yüan 陸九淵
Lu-ling hsien (Chi-chou) 廬陵縣
Lu-ming yen 鹿鳴宴
lu-shih ts'an-chün 錄事參軍
Lu T'ang 陸棠
Lu Yu 陸游
Lü I-chien 呂夷簡
Lü Pen-chung 呂本中
lü-shih 律詩
Lü Ta-chün 呂大鈞

Lü Tsu-ch'ien 呂祖謙
Luan 鸞
lun 論
Lun-yü 論語
Lung-chou (Li-chou lu) 龍州
lung-shou 龍首
Ma Jen-yü 馬仁瑀
Ma Tuan-lin 馬端臨
Man 蠻
Mao-shih Shih-ching 毛氏詩經
Mei-chou (Ch'eng-tu fu lu) 眉州
Mei Yao-ch'en 梅堯臣
men-k'o 門客
meng-jen 夢人
Min 閩
ming 命
ming-ching 明經
Ming-chou (Liang-che-tung) 明州
ming-fa 明法
ming-shu 明書
ming-suan 明算
Ming-tao Shu-yüan 明道書院
mo-i 墨義
mou 畝
mu 睦
Nan-chien chou (Fu-chien) 南劍州
Nan-k'ang chün (Chiang-nan-tung)
　　南康軍
Ou-yang Hsiu 歐陽修
Ou-yang Shou-tao 歐陽守道
pa-hsing (eight forms of virtuous
　　conduct) 八行
pa-hsing (eight punishments) 八刑
Pai-chia hsing 百家姓
Pai-lu-tung Shu-yüan 白鹿洞書院
p'an-kuan 判官
p'ang 榜
pen-kuan 本貫
pen-wang 本望
P'eng 鵬
Pi-yung 辟雍
pieh-chia 別駕
pieh-shih 別試
pieh-t'ou-shih 別頭試
pieh-yüan-shih 別院試
p'o-lo 破落
P'o-yang Lake 鄱陽湖
pu ch'eng-ming 不成名

pu-chün 不均
pu-i chih shih 布衣之時
pu-shih 補試
San-chuan 三傳
san chün 三郡
san Han 三韓
San-li 三禮
san-she 三舍
San-she-fa 三舍法
san-sheng pu-kuan 三省補官
San-shih 三史
San-tzu ching 三字經
San-tzu hsün 三字訓
Shan-hsi 陝西
shan-jen 山人
shang-she 上舍
shao 少
Shao-hsing 紹興
she-kuan 攝官
she-kuan pu-kuan 攝官補官
shen 神
shen-fu 沈服
Shen Huan 沈煥
Shen Shu 沈樞
Shen-tsung 神宗
Shen Wei-fu 沈緯甫
sheng-shih 省試
sheng-yuan 省元
sheng-wei 省闈
shih (literatus) 士
shih (poetry) 詩
Shih-chi 史記
Shih Chieh 石介
Shih-ching 詩經
shih-fu chin-shih 詩賦進士
Shih Hao 史浩
shih-ho 釋褐
shih-hsiang 使相
Shih-ku Shu-yüan 石鼓書院
shih-o 十惡
shih-po-ssu 市舶司
shih-ta-fu 士大夫
Shou-ch'ang chün (Ching-hu-pei)
　　壽昌軍
shou-kuan 授官
Shu-ching 書經
shu-fa 贖罰
Shu Lin 舒璘

shu-shih 術士
shu-yüan 書院
Shun-ch'ang hsien (Nan-chien chou)
    順昌縣
Ssu-ch'uan 四川
Ssu-ch'uan lei-sheng-shih 四川類省試
ssu-hsüan 四選
ssu-ma 司馬
Ssu-ma Kuang 司馬光
Ssu-men-hsüeh 四門學
ssu-min 四民
ssu-tsui 私罪
Su Ch'e 蘇轍
Su-chou (Liang-che-hsi) 蘇州
Su Shih 蘇軾
Su Sung 蘇頌
Sui Wen-ti 隨文帝
Sun Fu 孫復
Sung Ch'i 宋祁
Sung Chiang 宋江
suo-t'ing-shih 鎖廳試
ta Fan 大藩
ta-i 大義
Ta-kuan 大觀
ta-k'uei 大魁
ta-kung 大功
Ta-li chien-tsou pu-kuan 大禮薦奏
    補官
Ta-ming fu (Ho-pei-tung) 大名府
ta-pi 大比
ta-shih-ch'en 大使臣
Tai 戴
tai-pu 待補
T'ai-chou (Huai-nan-tung) 泰州
T'ai-chou (Liang-che-tung) 台州
T'ai-hsüeh 太學
T'ai-hsüeh chieh-shih 太學解試
T'ai-p'ing 太平
T'ai-tsu 太祖
T'ai-tsung 太宗
T'an-chou (Ching-hu-nan) 潭州
tao 道
Tao-hsüeh 道學
t'e shou wen-hsüeh pu-kuan 特受文學
    補官
t'e-tsou-ming chin-shih 特奏名進士
t'e-tsou-ming chu-k'o 特奏名諸科
t'eng-lu 謄錄

ti 弟
t'i-chü hsüeh-shih 提舉學士
tieh-shih 牒試
tieh-shih t'iao-fa 牒試條法
t'ieh-chiao-tai 鐵角帶
tien-shih 殿試
tsa-lei 雜類
tsa-liu fei-fan li-chih 雜流非泛吏職
tsai 宰
tsai-hsiang 宰相
Ts'ai Ching 蔡京
ts'ao-shih 漕試
ts'ao-wei 漕闈
tseng fan hsing-tse 增犯刑責
Tseng Feng 曾丰
Tseng Kung 曾鞏
tseng-tsu 曾祖
Tso-i tzu-chen 作邑自箴
tsou-chien 奏薦
ts'un 才
ts'e (policy questions) 策
ts'e (volumes) 冊
Tso-chuan 左傳
tsou-pu 奏補
tsung-nu-fu 宗女夫
tsung-shih kai en 宗室該恩
tsung-shih kuo li pu-kuan 宗室過禮
    補官
tsung-tzu 宗子
Tu Ch'un 杜醇
Tu Hsing 篤行
tu-shu-jen 讀書人
Tuan-p'ing 端平
Tung Chung-shu 董仲舒
Tung Te-yüan 董德元
Tung-t'ing Lake 洞庭湖
Tung-yang hsien (Wu-chou) 東陽縣
t'ung ch'u-shen 同出身
t'ung-tzu-k'o 童子科
T'ung-wen-kuan shih 同文館試
Tzu-hsia 子夏
tzu-sung-chai 自訟齋
Tzu-t'ung-shen 梓潼神
tz'u 祠
Tz'u-ch'i hsien (Ming-chou) 慈溪縣
Wan-chou (K'uei-chou lu) 萬州
wan-kuei-chuang 萬桂莊
Wang An-shih 王安石

Wang Chi 王濟
Wang Chih 王致
Wang Hsien-chih 王仙芝
Wang Hung-chih 王鴻志
Wang Lo-hsien 王樂仙
Wang Lun 王倫
Wang P'i-chih 王闢之
Wang Shuo 王說
Wang Tan 王旦
Wang Ting-pao 王定保
Wang T'ing-chang 王庭璋
Wang T'ing-chen 王庭珍
Wang T'ing-kuei 王庭珪
Wang Yen-wu 王炎午
Wang Ying-lin 王應麟
wei 闈
Wei-hsüeh 偽學
Wei Wen-ti 魏文帝
wen 文
Wen-ch'ang ti-chün 文昌帝君
Wen-chou (Li-chou lu) 文州
Wen-chou (Liang-che-tung) 溫州
Wen-hsüan wang miao 文宣王廟
wen-hsüeh 文學
wu 武
Wu-ch'ang hsien (E-chou) 武昌縣
Wu-ching 五經
Wu-chou (Liang-che-tung) 婺州
wu-chü 武舉
wu-fu 五服
Wu-hsi hsien (Ch'ang-chou) 無錫縣
wu-hsüeh 武學
wu-nei fen-lieh 五內分裂
Wu Shih-jen 吳師仁
Wu Wei-tao 吳味道
yamen 衙門
yang 陽

Yang Chien 楊簡
Yang Ch'un 楊椿
Yang Hung-chung 楊宏中
Yang Shih 楊適
Yang Wan-li 楊萬里
yeh 業
Yeh Meng-te 葉夢得
Yeh Shih 葉適
Yen-chou (Ching-tung-hsi) 兗州
Yen-chou (Liang-che-hsi) 嚴州
Yen-ch'un (style for Liu Ch'eng-pi) 彥純
yin (good relations with affinal kin) 姻
yin (female principle) 陰
yin (protection) 蔭
yin-kung 陰功
yin-pu 蔭補
yin-te 陰德
yin yu ni fu 隱憂匿服
Ying-t'ien fu (Ching-tung-hsi) 應天府
Ying-t'ien-shan Ching-she 應天山精舍
yu-shih 游士
yü-chi 寓寄
yü-shih 御試
Yü-ti-t'u 輿地圖
Yüan-feng 元豐
Yüan Hsieh 袁燮
Yüan River 袁江
Yüan Ts'ai 袁采
Yüan-yu 元祐
Yüeh Fei 岳飛
Yüeh K'o 岳珂
Yüeh-lu Shu-yüan 嶽麓書院
Yung-chia hsien (Wen-chou) 永嘉縣
Yung-fu hsien (Fu-chou) 永福縣
Yung-hsing lu 永興路

BIBLIOGRAPHY

Local Histories

Chang Chin 張津. *Ch'ien-tao Ssu-ming t'u-ching* 乾道四明圖經, 12 ch. 1169. Sung Yüan Ssu-Ming liu chih ed.

Chang Hsüan 張鉉. *Chin-ling hsin-chih* 金陵新志, 15 ch. 1344.

Chang I-ying 張一英. *T'ung-chou fu chih* 同州府志, 18 ch. 1625.

Chang Liang-chih 張艮知. *Han-chung fu chih* 漢中府志, 10 ch. 1588.

Chang Mu 張沐. *K'ai-feng fu chih* 開封府志, 40 ch. 1695.

Chao Pen 趙本. *Ta-ming fu chih* 大名府志, 10 ch. 1445.

Ch'en Ch'i-ch'ing 陳耆卿. *Chih-ch'eng chih* 赤城志, 40 ch. 1223. Ming Wan-li ed.

Ch'en Ken-shan 陳艮山. *Huai-an fu chih* 淮安府志, 16 ch. 1518.

Chiang Hsiang-nan 蔣湘南. *T'ung-chou fu chih* 同州府志, 34 ch. 1852.

Ch'iao Shih-ning 喬世寧. *Yao-chou fu chih* 耀州府志, 11 ch. 1557.

Ch'ien Chen-lun 錢振倫. *Yang-chou fu chih* 揚州府志, 24 ch. 1810.

Ch'ien Yüeh-yu 潛說友. *Hsien-ch'ün Lin-an chih* 咸淳臨安志, 100 ch. 1268 ed.

Chou Fang-ching 周方炯. *Feng-hsiang fu chih* 鳳翔府志, 12 ch. 1766.

Chou Hsüeh-chün 周學濬. *Hu-chou fu chih* 湖州府志, 96 ch. 1874.

Chou Jung-ch'un 周榮播. *Ch'u-chou fu chih* 處州府志, 30 ch. 1877.

Chou Ying-ho 周應合. *Ching-ting Chien-k'ang chih* 景定建康志, 50 ch. 1261. 1801 ed.

Chu Yü 朱昱. *Hsien-ch'un P'i-ling chih* 咸淳毗陵志, 30 ch. 1268.

Chu Yüan 朱沅. *Ho-chou chih* 和州志, 7 ch. 1441.

Chung Wang 鍾汪. *T'ung-chou chih* 通州志, 34 ch. 1530.

Fan Ch'eng-ta 范成大. *Wu-chün chih* 吳郡志, 50 ch. 1229. Ts'ung-shu chi-cheng ed.

Fang Jen-jung 方仁榮. *Ching-ting Yen-chou hsü chih* 景定嚴州續志, 10 ch. 1262. Ts'ung shu chi-ch'eng ed.

Fang Yü 方瑜. *Nan-ning fu chih* 南寧府志, 1564.

Fu Shu-hsün 傅叔訓. *P'ing-yang fu chih* 平陽府志. 1615.

——. *Tse-chou chih* 澤州志, 18 ch. 1615.

Fu Wang-pa 傅王露. *Che-chiang t'ung-chih* 浙江通志, 280 ch. 1736.

Ho Ch'iao-yüan 何喬遠. *Min shu* 閩書, 154 ch. 1629.

Ho Shao-chi 何紹基. *An-hui t'ung-chih* 安徽通志, 350 ch. 1877.

Hsü Hao 徐顥. *Lin-chiang fu chih* 臨江府志, 9 ch. 1538.

Hsü Jung 許容. *Kan-su t'ung-chih* 甘肅通志, 50 ch. 1736.

Hsü Shih 徐碩. *Chih-yüan Chia-ho chih* 至元嘉禾志, 32 ch. 1288. Ms. ed.

Huang Ch'i-chin 黃其勤. *Chih-li Nan-hsiung chou chih* 直隸南雄州志, 34 ch. 1818.

Huang Chung-chao 黃仲昭. *Pa-Min t'ung chih* 八閩通志, 87 ch. 1490 ed.

Huang P'eng-nien 黃彭年. *Chi-fu t'ung-chih* 畿輔通志, 300 ch. 1872. 1885 ed.

Jen Te 任德. *Sui chih* 隨志. 1539. 1539 ed.

K'ang K'ung-kao 康孔高. *Nan-yang fu chih* 南陽府志, 8 ch. extant. 1437.

Kao Ssu-sun 高似孫. *Shan lu* 剡錄, 10 ch. 1214. 1870 ed.

Ku Ch'ing 顧清. *Sung-chiang fu chih* 松江府志, 32 ch. 1512.

Kuo Chung 郭忠. *Ch'u-chou fu chih* 處州府志, 30 ch. 1486.

Li Meng-hsiung 李夢熊. *Ts'ang-chou chih* 滄州志, 6 ch. extant. 1603.

Li Ssu-kung 李思恭. *Ch'ih-chou chih* 池州志, 10 ch. 1612.

Li Sung 李嵩. *Kuei-te fu chih* 歸德府志, 6 ch. extant. 1568.

Li Yüan-fang 李元芳. *Yüeh-chou fu chih* 岳州府志, 7 ch. extant. 1567.

Liang K'o-chia 梁克家. *San-shan chih* 三山志, 42 ch. plus addendum (ch. 31-2) by Chu Chin 朱謹. 1174-1189. Ming woodblock ed.

Lin-T'ing chih 臨汀志, 7 ch. Ca. 1265. In *Yung-lo ta-tien* 永樂大典. Edited by Yao Kuang-hsiao 姚廣孝. Peking: Chung-hua shu-chü, 1960.

Lin Ying-hsiang 林應翔. *Ch'ü-chou fu chih* 衢州府志, 16 ch. 1622.

Ling Wan-ch'ing 凌萬頃. *Yü-feng-chih* 玉峯志, 3 ch. 1251. 1251 ms.

Liu Fang-sheng 劉芳聲. *Ho-chou chih* 合州志, 8 ch. 1579.

Liu I 劉繹. *Chi-an fu chih* 吉安府志, 53 ch. 1876.

Liu Kuo-kuang 劉國光. *Te-an fu chih* 德安府志, 20 ch. 1888.

Liu Wan-ch'un 劉萬春. *T'ai-chou chih* 台州志, 10 ch. 1633.

Liu Wen-fu 劉文富. *Yen-chou t'u-ching* 嚴州圖經, 3 ch. 1186. Ts'ung-shu chi-ch'eng ed.

Lo Ch'ing-hsiao 羅青霄. *Chang-chou fu chih* 漳州府志, 33 ch. 1573.

Lo Chün 羅濬. *Pao-ch'ing Ssu-ming chih* 寶慶四明志, 21 ch. 1227. Sung Yüan Ssu-ming liu chih ed.

Lo Hsü 羅許. *Ching-chou chih* 景州志, 3 ch. extant. 1572.

Lo Yüan 羅願. *Hsin-an chih* 新安志, 10 ch. 1175. 1888 ed.

Lu Feng-i 陸鳳儀. *Chin-hua fu chih* 金華府志, 30 ch. 1598.

Lu Hsien 盧憲. *Chia-ting Chen-chiang chih* 嘉定鎮江志, 22 ch. 1213. Ching-chia-t'ang wen-k'u ed.

Lu Hsiung 盧熊. *Su-chou fu chih* 蘇州府志, 50 ch. 1379. 1379 ed.

Lu I 陸鈇. *Chia-ching Shan-tung t'ung-chih* 嘉靖山東通志, 40 ch. 1533.

Lung Wen-ming 龍文明. *Lai-chou fu chih* 萊州府志, 8 ch. 1604.

Mei Ying-fa 梅應發. *K'ai-ch'ing Ssu-ming hsü-chih* 開慶四明續志, 12 ch. 1259. Sung Yüan Ssu-ming liu chih ed.

Pao Lien 鮑廉. *Ch'in-ch'uan chih* 琴川志, 15 ch. 1141. Ch'ing copy of a Yüan ed.

P'eng Tse 彭澤. *Hui-chou fu chih* 徽州府志, 12 ch. 1502.

Pien Hsiang 邊像. *P'u-chou chih* 蒲州志, 3 ch. 1559.

Shih O 史諤. *Ch'un-yu Lin-an chih* 淳祐臨安志, ch. 5-10 extant. 1241-53. Wu-lin chang ts'ung-pien ed.

Shih Su 施宿. *K'uai-chi chih* 會稽志, 20 ch. 1225. Ming Cheng-te ed.

Shou-ch'ang ch'eng 壽昌乘, 1 ch. Late Southern Sung. Southern Sung ed.

Su Chia-ssu 蘇佳嗣. *Ch'ang-sha fu chih* 長沙府志, 20 ch. 1665. 1665 ed.

Sun Hao 孫灝. *Ho-nan t'ung-chih* 河南通志, 80 ch. 1735.

Sun Shih-ch'ang 孫世昌. *Kuang-hsin fu chih* 廣信府志, 20 ch. 1683. 1683 ed.

Sun Ts'un 孫存. *Ching-chou fu chih* 荆州府志, 8 ch. extant. 1532.

Tai Ching 戴璟. *Kuang-tung t'ung-chih*廣東通志, 40 ch. 1535.

T'an Yao 談瑢. *Wu-hsing chih* 吳興志, 20 ch. 1201.

T'ang Ch'en 唐臣. *Chen-ting fu chih* 眞定府志, 33 ch. 1547.

T'ang Jih-chao 唐日照. *Wen-chou fu chih* 溫州府志, 16 ch. extant. 1605.

T'ang Ning 唐寧. *Hsing-kuo chou chih* 興國州志, 6 ch. extant. 1554.

T'ao Ch'eng 陶成. *Chiang-hsi t'ung-chih* 江西通志, 162 ch. 1732. 1732 ed.

T'ao Lü-chung 陶履中. *Jui-chou fu chih* 瑞州府志, 24 ch. 1628. 1628 ed.

Teng Ch'en 鄧璨. *Huang-chou fu chih* 黃州府志, 40 ch. 1884.

Teng Lun-pin 鄧掄斌. *Hui-chou fu chih* 惠州府志, 45 ch. 1881.

Tseng Kuo-ch'üan 魯國荃. *Hu-nan t'ung-chih* 湖南通志, 288 ch. 1885. 1885 ed.

Tu Ssu 杜思. *Ch'ing-chou fu chih* 青州府志, 14 ch. 1565.

Tu Ying-fang 杜應芳. *Ssu-ch'uan tsung-chih* 四川總志, 27 ch. 1619.

Wang Hsin-ming 王新命. *Chiang-nan t'ung-chih* 江南通志, 76 ch. 1684.

Wang Hsüan 王軒. *Shan-hsi t'ung-chih* 山西通志, 184 ch. 1892.

Wang I-hua 王一化. *Ying-t'ien fu chih* 應天府志, 33 ch. 1577.

Wang Kuo-chen 王國楨. *Pao-ting fu chih* 保定府志, 37 ch. 1607.

Wang Ming-chüeh 王命爵. *Tung-ch'ang fu chih* 東昌府志, 6 ch. extant. 1600.

Wang Tao-i 王道一. *Fen-chou fu chih* 汾州府志, 16 ch. 1609.

Wang Yüan-kung 王元恭. *Chih-cheng Ssu-ming hsü-chih* 至正四明續志, 12 ch. 1342. Sung Yüan Ssu-ming liu chih ed.

Wei-hui fu chih 衛輝府志, 16 ch. 1603.

Wu Chen 吳臻. *Wu-wei chou chih* 無爲州志, 9 ch. 1506–21.

Wu Tao-ming 吳道明. *Lu-chou fu chih* 廬州府志, 13 ch. 1575.

Yang Ch'eng-hsi 楊承禧. *Hu-pei t'ung-chih* 湖北通志, 172 ch. 1911.

Yang En 楊恩. *Kung-ch'ang fu chih* 鞏昌府志, 8 ch. 1621.

Yang Fang 楊芳. *Kuang-hsi t'ung-chih* 廣西通志, 40 ch. 1599.

Yang Fang-ts'an 楊芳燦. *Ssu-ch'uan t'ung-chih* 四川通志, 204 ch. 1816.

Yang Hui 楊譓. *K'un-shan chün-chih* 崑山郡志, 6 ch. Ch'ing ms.

Yang Ssu-chen 楊思震. *Pao-ning fu chih* 保寧府志, 14 ch. 1543.

Yang T'ing-wang 楊廷望. *Ch'ü-chou fu chih* 衢州府志, 40 ch. 1711.

Yao Chih-lang 姚之琅. *Teng-chou chih* 鄧州志, 24 ch. 1711.

Yao Wen-t'ien 姚文田. *Yang-chou fu chih* 揚州府志, 72 ch. 1664.

Yao Ying-lung 姚應龍. *Hsü-chou chih* 徐州志, 6 ch. 1574.

Yen Ch'ang-ming 嚴長明. *Hsi-an fu chih* 西安府志, 80 ch. 1779.

Yü Chih-chen 余之楨. *Chi-an fu chih* 吉安府志, 36 ch. 1585. 1585 ed.

Yü Hsi-lu 俞希魯. *Chih-shun Chen-chiang chih* 至順鎮江志, 21 ch. 1332. Taipei: Wen-hua shu-chü, 1958.

Yü Tzu-ming 虞自明. *Yung-chou fu chih* 永州府志, 12 ch. 1383.

Yüan Chüeh 袁桷. *Yen-yu Ssu-ming chih* 延祐四明志, 20 ch. 1320. Sung Yüan Ssu-ming liu chih ed.

Other works in Chinese and Japanese

Aoyama Sadao 青山定雄. *Tō Sō jidai no kōtsū to chishi chizu no kenkyū* 唐宋時代の交通と地誌地圖の研究. Tokyo: Yoshikawa Kobunkan, 1963.

——. 'Zui, Tō, Sō sandai ni okeru, Kosū no chiiki teki kōsatsu 隨唐宋三代に於ける戸類の地域的考察. *Rekishigaku kenkyū* 歷史學研究 6 (1936):411–46.

——. ed. *Sōdaishi nempyō* 宋代史年表, 2 vols. Tokyo: Toyo Bunko, 1964–74.

Araki Toshikazu 荒木敏一. *Sōdai kakyo seido kenkyū* 宋代科舉制度研究. Kyoto: Dobosha Press Co., 1969.

Chang Ch'i-yün 張其昀. 'Sung-tai Ssu-ming chih hsüeh-feng 宋代四明之學風'. In *Sung-shih yen-chiu chi* 宋史研究集, 7 vols. Taipei: Chung-hua ts'ung-shu wei-yüan-hui, 1954–74. 3:33–71.

Chang Chia-chü 張家駒. *Liang-Sung ching-chi chung-hsin ti nan i* 兩宋經濟中心的南移. Wuhan: Hu-pei jen-min ch'u-pan-she, 1957.

Chang Hsiu-min 張秀民. 'Nan-Sung k'o-shu ti-yü k'ao 南宋刻書地域考.' *T'u-shu kuan* 圖書館 3 (1961):52–6.

Chang Shih 張栻. *Nan-hsien hsien-sheng wen-chi* 南軒先生文集, 7 ch. Ts'ung-shu chi-ch'eng ed.

Chang Shih-nan 張世南. *Yu-huan chi-wen* 游宦紀聞, 10 ch. Ts'ung-shu chi-ch'eng ed.

Ch'ang Pi-te 昌彼得; Wang Te-i 王德毅; Ch'eng Yüan-min 程元敏; and Hou Chün-te 侯俊德. *Sung-jen ch'uan-chi tzu-liao suo-yin* 宋人傳記資料索引, 6 vols. Taipei: Ting-wen shu-chü, 1974–6.

Chao Hui-jen 趙惠人. 'Sung-shih ti-li-chih hu-k'ou piaŏ 宋史地理志戶口表.' *Yü kung* 禹貢 2 (1934):59–67.

Chao I 趙翼. *Nien-er-shih tsa-chi* 廿二十箚記, 2 vols. Taipei: Shih-chieh shu-chü, 1972.

Chao Sheng 趙升. *Ch'ao-yeh lei-yao* 朝野類要, 5 ch. Ts'ung-shu chi-ch'eng ed.

Chao T'ieh-han 趙鐵寒. 'Sung-tai ti chou-hsüeh 宋代的州學.' *Ta-lu tsa-chih* 大陸雜誌 7, no. 10 (1953):15–20, and no. 11, pp. 15–18.

Ch'en Chün 陳均. *Huang-ch'ao pien-nien kang-mu pei-yao* 皇朝編年綱目備要, 30 ch. Ching-chia-t'ang ts'ung-shu ed.; Taipei: Ch'eng-wen ch'u-pan she, 1966.

Ch'en Chi-hsin 陳繼新. 'Ts'ung chiao-yü kuan-tien hsi-lun Sung-tai shu-yüan chih-tu 從教育觀點析論宋代書院制度.' *Hsüeh-chi* 學記 3 (1971):75–124.

Ch'en Chung-mien 岑仲勉. 'Chin-shih-k'o t'ai-t'ou chih yüan-yin chi ch'i liu-pi 進士科擡頭之原因及其流弊.' In *Sui T'ang shih* 隨唐史. Peking: Kao-teng chiao-yü ch'u-pan-she, 1957. Pp. 181–90.

Ch'en Tung-yüan 陳東原. *Chung-kuo chiao-yü shih* 中國教育史. Shanghai: Commercial Press, 1936.

——. *Chung-kuo k'o-chü shih-tai chih chiao-yü* 中國科舉時代之教育. Shanghai: Commercial Press, 1933.

——. 'Lu-shan Pai-lu-tung shu-yüan yen-ko k'ao 廬山白鹿洞書院沿革考.' *Min-tuo tsa-chih* 7 民鐸雜誌 (1937), no. 1, pp. 1–32; no. 2, pp. 1–25.

——. 'Sui T'ang ti k'o-chü 隨唐的科舉.' *Hsüeh-feng* 學風 2, no. 8 (1932):8–25.

——. 'Sung-tai ti k'o-chü yü chiao-yü 宋代的科舉與教育.' *Hsüeh-feng* 學風 2, no. 9 (1932):5–39.

Ch'en Yüan-ching 陳元靚. *Shih-lin kuang-chi* 事林廣記. Japanese edition, 1699.

Ch'eng Tuan-li 程端禮. *Ch'eng-shih chia-shu tu-shu fen-nien jih-ch'eng* 程氏家塾讀書分年日程, 3 ch. Pai-pu ts'ung-k'an ed.

Ch'eng Tuan-meng 程端蒙 and Tung Chu 董銖. *Ch'eng Tung er hsien-sheng hsüeh-tse* 程董二先生學則. Pai-pu ts'ung-shu chi-ch'eng ed.

Ch'eng Yün 程運. 'Sung-tai chiao-yü tsung-chih ch'an-shih 宋代教育宗旨闡釋.' *Chung-cheng hsüeh-pao* 中正學報 2 (1967):90–3.

Chiang-su chin-shih chih 江蘇金石志, 24 ch. 1927 ed.

Chin Chung-shu 金中樞. 'Pei-Sung k'o-chü chih-tu yen-chiu 北宋科舉制度研究.' *Hsin-ya hsüeh-pao* 新亞學報 6, no. 1 (1964):205–81, and 6, no. 4, pp. 163–242.

——. 'Sung-tai ku-wen yün-tung chih fa-chan yen-chiu 宋代古文運動之發展研究.' *Hsin-ya hsüeh-pan* 新亞學報 5, no. 2 (1963):105–9.

Chin Yü-fu 金毓黻. 'Sung-tai kuan-chih yü hsing-cheng chih-tu 宋代官制與行政制度.' *Wen-shih tsa-chih* 文史雜誌 2, no. 4 (1942):3–26.

Ch'in Hsiang-yeh 秦湘業. *Hsü Tzu-chih t'ung-chien ch'ang-pien shih-pu* 續資治通鑑長編拾補, 60 ch. Taipei: Shih-chieh shu-chü, 1964.

Chou Pi-ta 周必大. *Chou wen-kung chung chi* 周文公忠集, 200 ch. Ssu-k'u ch'üan-shu ed.

——. *I-kung t'i-pa* 益公題跋. Ts'ung-shu chi-ch'eng ed.

Chu Hsi 朱熹. *Chu wen-kung wen-chi* 朱文公文集, 100 ch. Ssu-pu ts'ung-k'an ed.

——. *Hsiao-hsüeh chi-chu* 小學集注, 6 ch. Ssu-pu pei-yao ed.

——. *I-li ching-chuan t'ung chieh* 儀禮經傳通解, 37 ch. Hsi-ching ch'ing-lu ts'ung-shu ed.

Chu Yü 朱彧. *Ping-chou k'o-t'an* 萍洲可談, 3 ch. Ts'ung-shu chi-ch'eng ed.

Ch'üan Han-sheng 全漢昇. 'Pei-Sung wu-chia ti pien-tung 北宋物價的變動.' *Li-shih yü-yen yen-chiu-suo chi-k'an* 歷史語言研究所集刊 11 (1944):337–94.

——. 'Sung-mo ti t'ung-huo p'eng-chang chi ch'i tui-yu wu-chia ti ying-hsiang 宋末的通貨膨脹及其對於物價的影響.' *Li-shih yü-yen yen-chiu-suo chi-k'an* 歷史語言研究所集刊 10 (1943):193–222.

Chung Wen-cheng 鍾文烝. *Ku-liang pu-chu* 穀梁補注, 24 ch. Ssu-pu pei-yao ed.

Fan Chung-yen 范仲淹. *Fan wen-cheng kung chi* 范文正公集, 20 ch. plus appendices. Taipei: Commercial Press, 1965.

Ho Wei 何薳. *Ch'in-chu chi-wen* 春渚紀聞, 10 ch. Sung-jen pai-chia hsiao-shuo ed.

Ho Yu-sen 何佑森. 'Liang-Sung hsüeh-feng ti ti-li fen-pu 兩宋學風的地理分佈', *Hsin-ya hsüeh-pao* 新亞學報 1 (1955):331–379.

Hou Shao-wen 侯紹文. *T'ang Sung k'ao-shih chih-tu shih* 唐宋考試制度史. Taipei: Commercial Press, 1973.

Hsü Nai-ch'ang 徐乃昌, ed. *Sung Yüan k'o-chü san lu* 宋元科舉三錄. 1923 ed.

Huang Hsien-fan 黃現璠. *Sung-tai T'ai-hsüeh-sheng chiu-kuo yün-tung* 宋代太學生救國運動. Shanghai: Commercial Press, 1936.

Huang Tsung-hsi 黃宗羲. *Sung Yüan hsüeh-an* 宋元學案, 100 ch. Ssu-pu pei-yao ed.

Hung Mai 洪邁. *I-chien chih* 夷堅志, 50 ch. Ts'ung-shu chi-shih ed., 1875.

——. *Jung-chai sui-pi* 容齋隨筆, 74 ch. Hsin-feng Hung shih ed., 1875.

Kao Ming-shih 高明士. 'T'ang-tai ti kuan-hsüeh hsing-cheng 唐代的官學行政.' *Ta-lu tsa-chih* 大陸雜誌 37, no. 11 (1968):39–53.

Kao Ssu-te 高斯得. *Ch'ih-t'ang ts'un-kao* 恥堂存稿 8 ch. Ts'ung-shu chi-ch'eng ed.

Ko Sheng-chung 葛脞仲. *Tan-yang chi* 丹陽集, 24 ch. Ch'ang-chou hsien-che i-shu ed.

Kuan-tsu 管子, 24 ch. Ssu-pu pei-yao ed.

Kung Ming-hih 龔明之. *Chung Wu chi-wen* 中吳紀聞, 1 ch. Ts'ung-shu chi-ch'eng ed.

Kuo Mo-jo 郭沫若. 'P'u T'ien-shou *Lun-yü* ch'iao-pen hou ti shih-tz'u chiu-lu 卜天壽論語抄本后的詩詞雜錄.' *K'ao-ku* 考古 no. 1 (1972):5–7.

Kuo-yü 國語, 21 ch. Ssu-pu pei-yao ed.

Li-chi 禮記. 1815 ed.

Li Hsin-ch'uan 李心傳. *Chien-yen i-lai ch'ao-yeh tsa-chi* 建炎以來朝野雜記, 40 ch. Ts'ung-shu chi-ch'eng ed.

———. *Chien-yen i-lai hsi-nien yao-lu* 建炎以來繫年要錄, 200 ch. Taipei: wen-hai ch'u-pan-she, 1968.

———. *Tao-ming lu* 道命錄. Ts'ung-shu chi-ch'eng ed.

Li Hung-chi 李弘祺 [Thomas H. C. Lee]. 'Sung-ch'ao chiao-yü chi k'o-chü san-lun chien p'ing san pen yu-kuan Sung-tai chiao-yü chi k'o-chü ti shu 宋朝教育及科學散論兼評三本有關宋代教育與科學的書.' *Ssu yü yen* 思與言 13 (1975):15–27.

———. *Sung-tai chiao-yü san-lun* 宋代教育散論. Taipei: Tung-sheng ch'u-pan shih-yeh yu-hsien kung-ssu, 1980.

Li T'ao 李燾. *Hsü Tzu-chih t'ung-chien ch'ang-pien* 續資治通鑑長編, 520 ch. Taipei: Shih-chieh shu-chü, 1967.

Li Yu 李攸. *Sung-ch'ao shih-shih* 宋朝事實, 20 ch. Taipei: Commercial Press, 1975.

Li Yu-chieh 李幼傑. *P'u-yang pi-shih* 莆陽比事, 7 ch. Wan-wei pieh-ts'ang ed.

Li Yüan-pi 李元弼. *Tso-i tzu-chen* 作邑自箴, 10 ch. Shanghai: Commercial Press, 1934.

Lin T'ien-wei 林天蔚. 'Nan-Sung shih Ssu-ch'uan t'e-shu hua chih fen-hsi 南宋時四川特殊化之分析.' *Tung-fang wen-hua* 東方文化 18 (1980):225–46.

Liu Chen 劉真. 'Sung-tai ti hsüeh-kuei ho hsiang-yüeh 宋代的學規和鄉約.' In *Sung-shih yen-chiu chi* 宋史研究集, 7 vols. Taipei: Chung-hua ts'ung-shu wei-yüan-hui, 1954–74. 1:367–92.

Liu Cheng 留正. *Huang-Sung chung-hsing liang-ch'ao sheng-cheng* 皇宋中興兩朝聖政. Yüan-wei pieh-ts'ang ed.

Liu Po-chi 劉伯驥. *Kuang-tung shu-yüan chih-tu* 廣東書院制度. Canton: Shang-wu yin-shu-kuan, 1938.

Liu Tsai 劉宰. *Man-t'ang wen-chi* 漫塘文集, 36 ch. 1604 ed.

Liu Ts'ai-shao 劉才邵. *Shan-ch'i chü-shih chi* 檆溪居士集, 12 ch. Ssu-k'u ch'üan-shu ed.

Liu Tzu-chien 劉子健 [James T. C. Liu]. 'Lüeh-lun Sung-tai ti-fang kuan-hsüeh ho ssu-hsüeh ti hsiao-chang 略論宋代地方官學和私學的消長.' *Chung-yang yen-chiu-yüan li-shih yü-yen yen-chiu-suo chi-k'an* 中央研究院歷史語言研究所集刊 36 (1965):237–48.

———. 'Sung-tai k'ao-ch'ang pi-tuan – chien lun shih-feng wen-t'i 宋代考場弊端 – 兼論士風問題' ('Misconducts at the Sung State Examinations – A Further Discussion on Literati Moral Standards'). In *Ch'ing-chu Li Chi hsien-sheng ch'i-shih sui lun-wen-chi* 慶祝李先生七十歲論文集. Taipei, 1965. 1:189–202.

Lu Chiu-yuan 陸九淵. *Hsiang-shan ch'üan-chi* 象山全集, 36 ch. Kuo-chi chi-pen ts'ung-shu chi-ch'eng ed.

Lu Yu 陸游. *Wei-nan wen-chi* 渭南文集, 41 ch. Ssu-pu ts'ung-k'an ed.

Lü Pen-chung 呂本中. *T'ung-meng hsün* 童蒙訓, 3 ch. Wan-yu wen-k'u ed.

Lü Ssu-mien 呂思勉. *Yen-shih hsu cha* 燕石續扎. Shanghai: Commercial Press, 1958.

Lü Tsu-ch'ien 呂祖謙. *Li-tai chih-tu hsiang-shuo* 歷代制度詳說, 12 ch. Ssu-k'u ch'üan-shu ed.

Ma Tuan-lin 馬端臨, *Wen-hsien t'ung-k'ao* 文獻通考, 348 ed. Taipei: Hsin-hsing shu-chü, 1964.

Mei Yao-ch'en 梅堯臣. *Wan-ling hsien-sheng chi* 宛陵先生集, 60 ch. Ssu-pu ts'ung-k'an ed.

Meng Yüan-lao 孟元老. *Tung-ching meng-hua lu* 東京夢華錄, 20 ch. Pai-pu ts'ung-k'an ed.

Min-chung chin-shih chih 閩中金石志, 14 ch. Chia-yeh-t'ang chin-shih ts'ung-shu ed.

Ou-yang Hsiu 歐陽修. *Ou-yang wen-chung kung wen-chi* 歐陽文忠公文集, 158 ch. Ssu-pu ts'ung-k'an ed.

Ou-yang Shou-tao 歐陽守道. *Sun-chai wen-chi* 巽齋文集, 27 ch. Ssu-k'u ch'üan-shu ed.

Pai-lu shu-yüan chih 白鹿書院志, 17 ch. First foreword in 1622; Ch'ing ed.

Sha-chou t'u-ching 沙州圖經. In *Ming-sha shih-shih i-shu* 鳴沙石室佚書. Edited by Lo Chen-yü 羅振玉. 1913 ed.

Shiba Yoshinobu 斯波義信. *Sōdai shogyo-shi kenkyū* 宋代商業史研究. Tokyo: Kazama-shobo, 1968.

Ssu-ma kuang 司馬光. *Wen-kuo wen-cheng Ssu-ma kung wen-chi* 溫國文正司馬公文集, 80 ch. Ssu-pu ts'ung-k'an ed.

Su Ch'e 蘇轍. *Luan-ch'eng chi* 欒城集, 50 ch. Taipei: Commercial Press, 1968.

Su Sung 蘇頌. *Su wei-kung wen-chi* 蘇魏公文集, 72 ch. Ssu-k'u ch'üan-shu ed.

Sudō Yoshiyuki 周藤吉之. *Chūgoku tochi seido shi kenkyū* 中国土地制度史研究. Tokyo: Tokyo University Press, 1954.

——. *Sōdai kanryōsei to daitochi shoyū* 宋代官僚制と大土地所有. Tokyo: Nippon Hyōronsha, 1950.

Sun Kuo-tung 孫國棟. 'T'ang Sung chih chi she-hui men-ti chih hsiao-jung 唐宋之際社會門第之消融.' *Hsin-ya hsüeh-pao* 新亞學報 4 (1959):211–304.

Sun Yen-min 孫彥民. *Sung-tai shu-yüan chih-tu chih yen-chiu* 宋代書院制度之研究. Taipei: Kuo-li Cheng-chih ta-hsüeh, 1963.

Sung hui-yao chi-kao 宋會要輯稿. *Chih-kuan* 職官, *Ch'ung-ju* 崇儒, *Hsüan-chü* 選舉, and *Shih-huo* 食貨 sections. Taipei: Shih-chieh shu-chü, 1964.

Sung Shee 宋晞. *Sung shih* 宋史, 2 vols. Taipei: Hua-kang shu-chü, 1968.

——. 'Sung-tai fu-shang ti yu shang er shih 宋代富商的由商而士.' In *Sung-shih yen-chiu lun-ts'ung* 宋史研究論叢. Taipei: Shang-te yin-shu kuan, 1962, pp. 16–17.

——. 'Sung-tai shih-ta-fu tui shang-jen ti t'ai-tu 宋代士大夫對商人的態度.' In *Sung-shih yen-chiu lun-ts'ung* 宋史研究論叢. Taipei: Shang-te yin-shu kuan, 1962, pp. 1–14.

Sung-shih hsin-pien 宋史新編. Shanghai: Commercial Press, 1974.

Sung ta-chao ling-chi 宋大詔令集, 240 ch. Peking: Chung-hua shu-chü, 1962.

Ta-Ming i-t'ung-chih 大明一統志, 90 ch. 1461 ed.

T'ang Chang-ju 唐長孺. 'Nan-pei ch'ao hou-ch'i k'o-chü chih-tu ti meng-ya 南北朝后期科舉制度的萌芽.' In *Wei Chin Nan-pei ch'ao shih lun-ts'ung* 魏晉南北朝史論叢. Peking: Hsing-chih san-lien shu-tien, 1959, pp. 124–31.

Terada Gō 寺田剛. *Sōdai kyōikushi gaisetsu* 宋代教育史概說 Tokyo: Hakubunsha, 1965.

T'o T'o 脫脫 et al. *Sung shih* 宋史, 495 ch. Taipei: I-wen yin-shu kuan, 1962.

Ts'ai T'ao 蔡絛. *T'ieh-wei-shan ts'ung-shu* 鐵圍山叢書, 6 ch. Chih-pu-tsu-chai ts'ung-shu ed.

Tseng Feng 曾丰. *Yüan-tu chi* 綠督集, 20 ch. Ssu-k'u ch'üan-shu ed.

Tseng Kung 曾鞏. *Tseng Wen-ting kung ch'üan-chi* 曾文定公全集. 1693 ed.

Umehara Kaoru 梅原郁. 'Sōsho no kùrokukan to sono shūhen: Sōdai kansei no rikai no tame ni 宋初の寄禄官とその周邊: 宋代官制の理解のために.' *Tohō gakuho* 東方學報 48 (1975):135–82.

Wang Ch'ang 王昶. *Chin-shih ts'ui-pien* 金石萃編, 160 ch. 1805 ed.

Wang Chien-ch'iu 王建秋. *Sung-tai T'ai-hsüeh yü T'ai-hsüeh-sheng* 宋代太學與太學生. Taipei: Commercial Press, 1965.

Wang P'i-chih 王闢之. *Sheng-shui yen-t'an lu* 澠水燕談錄, 10 ch. Ts'ung-shu chi-ch'eng ed.

Wang Te-i 王德毅. *Sung-tai hsien-liang fang-cheng-k'o chi tz'u-k'o k'ao* 宋代賢良方正及詞科考. Taipei: Ch'ung-wen shu-tien, 1971.

Wang Ting-pao 王庭. *T'ang chih-yen* 唐摭言, 15 ch. Shanghai: Ku-tien wen-hsüeh ch'u-pan she, 1957.

Wang T'ing-kuei 王庭桂. *Lu-ch'i wen-chi* 盧溪文集, 50 ch. Ssu-k'u ch'üan-shu ed.

Wang Yen-wu 王炎午. *Wu-wen kao* 吾汶藁, 10 ch. Ssu-pu ts'ung-k'an ed.

Wang Ying-lin 王應麟. *Yü hai* 玉海, 200 ch. Taipei: Hua-wen shu-chü, 1967.

Wang Yün-wu 王雲五. *Sung Yüan chiao-hsüeh ssu-hsiang* 宋元教學思想. Taipei: Commercial Press, 1971.

Wang Yung 王栐. *Yen-i i-mou lu* 燕翼詒謀錄, 5 ch. Ts'ung-shu chi-ch'eng ed.

Wei Liao-weng 魏了翁. *I-li yao-i* 儀禮要義, 50 ch. Ssu-k'u ch'üan-shu ed.

Wei Mei-yüeh 魏美月. 'Sōdai shinna seido ni tsuite no ichi kōsatsu: toku ni sono chokuri no enkakuhyō o chūshin ni 宋代進納制度についての一考察: 特にその敕令の沿革表を中心に.' *Makasan ronsō* 待兼山論叢 7 (1974):23–41.

Wen T'ien-hsiang 文天祥. *Wen-shan hsien-sheng ch'üan-chi* 文山先生全集, 21 ch. Taipei: Commercial Press, 1965.

Wu Tseng 吳曾. *Neng-kai-chai man lu* 能改齋漫錄, 18 ch. Pi-chi hsiao-shuo Ta-kuan hsü-pien ed.

Wu Tzu-mu 吳自牧. *Meng-liang lu* 夢粱錄, 20 ch. Pai-pu ts'ung-shu chi-ch'eng ed.

Yang Lien-sheng 楊聯陞. 'K'o-chü shih-tai ti fu k'ao lü-fei wen-t'i 科舉時代的赴考旅費問題.' *Ch'ing-hua hsüeh-pao* 清華學報 n.s. 2 (1961):116–30.

Yang Wan-li 楊邁里. *Ch'eng-chai chi* 誠齋集, 132 ch. Ssu-pu ts'ung-k'an ed.

Yen Keng-wang 嚴耕望. *Chung-kuo ti-fang hsing-cheng chih-tu shih* 中國地方行政制度史, 2 vols. Taipei: Chung-yang yen-chiu-yuan li-shih yü-yen yen-chiu-suo, 1961.

——. 'T'ang-jen tuo tu-shu shan-ssu 唐人多讀書山寺.' *Ta-lu tsa-chih* 大陸雜誌 v. 2, no. 4 (1951):5.

Yü Ying 余鍈. 'Sung-tai ju-che ti-li fen-pu ti t'ung-chi 宋代儒者地理分佈的統計.' *Yü kung* 禹貢 1 (1933):170–6.

Yüan Ts'ai 袁采. *Yüan-shih shih-fan* 袁氏世範. Chih-pu tsu-chai ts'ung-shu ed.

Yüeh K'o 岳珂. *T'ing-shih* 桯史, 15 ch. Ts'ung-shu chi-ch'eng ed.

Works in Western languages

Ahern, Emily. *Chinese Ritual and Politics*. Cambridge: Cambridge University Press, 1982.

Aoyama Sadao. 'The Newly-risen Bureaucrats in Fukien at the Five Dynasty-Sung Period with Special Reference to their Genealogies.' *Memoirs of the Research Department of the Toyo Bunko* 21 (1962):1–48.

Ariès, Philippe. *Centuries of Childhood: A Social History of Family Life*. Translator, Robert Baldick. New York: Vintage Books, 1962.

Beattie, Hilary Jane. *Land and Lineage in China: A Study of T'ung-Ch'eng County, Anhwei, in the Ming and Ch'ing Dynasties*. Cambridge and New York: Cambridge University Press, 1979.

Bielenstein, Hans. 'The Chinese Colonization of Fukien until the End of T'ang.' In *Studia Serica Bernhard Karlgren Dedicata: Sinological Studies Dedicated to Bernhard Karlgren on his Seventieth Birthday, October Fifth, 1959*. Edited by Soren Egerod and Else Glahn. Copenhagen: Ejnar Munksgaard, 1959. Pp. 98–122.

Bol, Peter Kees. 'Culture and the Way in Eleventh Century China.' Ph.D. Dissertation, Princeton University, 1982.

———. 'The *Tso-i tzu-chen*; A Twelfth Century Guide for Subprefects.' Unpublished manuscript.

Bush, Susan. *The Chinese Literati on Painting: Su Shih (1037–1101) to Tung Ch'i-ch'ang (1555–1636)*. Cambridge, Mass.: Harvard University Press, 1971.

Carter, Thomas F. *The Invention of Printing in China and Its Spread Westward*. Revised by L. C. Goodrich. New York: Ronald Press Company, 1955.

Chaffee, John W. 'Education and Examinations in Sung Society (960–1279).' Ph.D. Dissertation, University of Chicago, 1979.

———. 'To Spread One's Wings: Examinations and the Social Order in Southeastern China During the Southern Sung.' *Historical Reflections/ Réflexions Historiques* 9 (1982):305–22.

———. 'Chu Hsi and the Revival of the White Deer Grotto Academy.' Paper presented for the International Conference on Chu Hsi, University of Hawaii, July 1982.

Chang, Carson. *The Development of Neo-Confucian Thought*. New Haven, Conn.: College and University Press, 1963.

Chang Chung-li. *The Chinese Gentry: Studies on Their Role in Nineteenth Century Chinese Society*. Seattle: University of Washington Press, 1955.

Chang Fu-jui. Biography of Hung Mai in *Sung Biographies*. Edited by Herbert Franke. Wiesbaden: Franz Steiner Verlag GMBH, 1976. Pp. 469–78.

Ch'en, Kenneth. *Buddhism in China: A Historical Survey*. Princeton, N. J.: Princeton University Press, 1964.

Chi Ch'ao-ting. *Key Economic Areas in Chinese History, as Revealed in the Development of Public Works for Water Control*. London: Allen & Unwin, 1936.

Chu Hsi. *Reflections on Things at Hand: The Neo-Confucian Anthology*. Translated by Wing-tsit Chan. New York: Columbia University Press, 1967.

Ch'u T'ung-tsu. *Han Social Structure*. Edited by Jack L. Dull. Seattle: University of Washington Press, 1972.

Clark, Hugh R. 'Quanzhou (Fujian) During the Tang-Song Interregnum.' *T'oung-Pao* 68 (1982):132–49.

Cole, James. 'Shaohsing: Studies in Ch'ing Social History.' Ph.D. Dissertation, Stanford University, 1975.

Doré, Henri, S. J. *Researches Into Chinese Superstitions*, 13 vols. Translated by M. Donnelly, S. J. Shanghai: T'usewei Press, 1921.

Ebrey, Patricia Buckley. *Chinese Civilization and Bureaucracy: A Sourcebook*. New York: Macmillan Publishing Company, 1981.

———. *The Aristocratic Families of Early Imperial China.* Cambridge: Cambridge University Press, 1978.

Elvin, Mark. *The Pattern of the Chinese Past.* Stanford, Calif.: Stanford University Press, 1973.

Fei Hsiao-tung. 'Peasantry and Gentry: An Introduction to Chinese Social Structure and its Changes.' In *An American Journal of Sociology* 52 (1946):1–17.

———. *China's Gentry.* Chicago: University of Chicago Press, 1953.

Fosdick, Sidney O. 'Chinese Book Publishing during the Sung Dynasty: a Partial Translation of *Isotoriia Kitaiskoi Pechatnoi Knigi Sunskoi Epokhi* by Konstantinovich Flug with Added Notes and an Introduction.' M. A. Thesis, University of Chicago, 1968.

Geertz, Clifford. *Nagara: The Theater State in Nineteenth Century Bali.* Princeton, N. J.: Princeton University Press, 1980.

Gernet, Jacques. *Daily Life in China on the Eve of the Mongol Invasion.* Translated by H. M. Wright. Stanford, Calif.: Stanford University Press, 1962.

Graham, A. C. *Two Chinese Philosophers: Ch'eng Ming-tao and Ch'eng Yi-ch'uan.* London: Lund Humphries, 1958.

Grimm, Tilemann. 'Academies and Urban Systems in Kuangtung.' In *The City in Late Imperial China.* Edited by G. William Skinner. Stanford, Calif.: Stanford University Press, 1977. Pp. 475–498.

———. 'The Inauguration of *T'i-chü hsüeh-shih ssu* (Education Intendents) During the Northern Sung Dynasty.' In *Études Song/Institutions.* Paris: Mouton & Co., 1976. Pp. 259–74.

Haeger, John W. '1126–27: Political Crisis and the Integrity of Culture.' In *Crisis and Prosperity in Sung China.* Pp. 155–60.

Hanan, Patrick. *The Chinese Vernacular Short Story.* Cambridge, Mass.: Harvard University Press, 1981.

Hartwell, Robert M. 'Community Elites, Economic Policy-making and Material Progress in Sung China (960–1279).' Paper presented for the CISS–CSNA Workshop on the Sources of Asian History and the Generation of Quantifiable Historical Indicators. Toronto, February 1976.

———. 'Demographic, Political and Social Transformations of China, 750–1550.' *Harvard Journal of Asiatic Studies* 42 (1982):365–442.

———. 'Financial Expertise, Examinations, and the Formulation of Economic Policy in Northern Sung China.' In *Enduring Scholarship Selected from the Far Eastern Quarterly–the Journal of Asian Studies, 1941–1971.* Volume I: *China.* Edited by John A. Harrison. Tucson: University of Arizona Press, 1972. Pp. 31–64. Originally published in the *Journal of Asian Studies* 30 (1971):281–314.

———. 'Historical Analogism, Public Policy, and Social Science in Eleventh and Twelfth Century China.' *American Historical Review* 76 (1971):690–727.

———. 'Kinship, Status and Region in the Formal and Informal Organization of the Chinese Fiscal Bureaucracy, 960–1165 A.D.' Paper presented at the Annual Meeting of the Social Science History Association, Ann Arbor, October 1977.

Hatch, George. Biography of Su Shih in *Sung Biographies.* Edited by Herbert Franke. Wiesbaden: Franz Steiner Verlag GMBH, 1976: 900–68.

Hervouet, Yves. *A Sung Bibliography (Bibliographie des Sung)*. Hong Kong: The Hong Kong University Press, 1978.

Ho Ping-ti. 'An Estimate of the Total Population of Sung-Chin China.' In *Études Song/Démographie*. Paris: Mouton & Co., 1970. Pp. 33–53.

———. *The Ladder of Success in Imperial China: Aspects of Social Mobility, 1368–1911*. New York: Columbia University Press, 1962.

———. 'Reply to "The Comparative Study of Social Mobility," by Vernon Dibble.' *Comparative Studies in Societies and History* 3 (1960–1):321.

Houn, Franklin W. 'The Civil Service Recruitment System of the Han Dynasty.' *Ch'ing-hua hsüeh-pao* n.s. 1 (1956–69):138–64.

Hsu Cho-yun. *Ancient China in Transition: An Analysis of Social Mobility, 722–222 B.C.* Stanford Calif.: Stanford University Press, 1965.

Hymes, Robert. 'Doctors in Sung and Yuan China: A Local Case Study.' Paper presented to the Columbia University Seminar on Traditional China, March 1981.

———. 'Prominence and Power in Sung China.' Ph.D. Dissertation, University of Pennsylvania, 1979.

Johnson, David. 'The Last Years of a Great Clan: the Li Family of Chao-chün in the Late T'ang and Early Sung.' *Harvard Journal of Asiatic Studies* 37 (1977):51–9.

———. *The Medieval Chinese Oligarchy*. Boulder, Co.: Westview Press, 1977.

Johnson, Wallace. 'The T'ang Code: An Analysis and Translation of the Oldest Extant Penal Code.' Ph.D. Dissertation, University of Pennsylvania, 1968.

Jonker, D. R. Biography of Lü Pen-chung in *Sung Biographies*. Edited by Herbert Franke. Wiesbaden: Franz Steiner Verlag GMBH, 1976: 735–41.

Katz, Jacob. *Tradition and Crisis: Jewish Society at the End of the Middle Ages*. New York: Schocken Books, 1961.

Kracke, Edward A., Jr. *Civil Service in Sung China: 960–1067*. Cambridge, Mass.: Harvard University Press, 1953.

———. 'Family versus Merit in Chinese Civil Service Examinations under the Empire.' *Harvard Journal of Asiatic Studies* 10 (1947):103–23.

———. 'Region, Family and Individual in the Chinese Examination System.' In *Chinese Thought and Institutions*. Edited by John K. Fairbank. Chicago: University of Chicago Press, 1967. Pp. 251–68.

———. 'Sung K'ai-feng: Pragmatic Metropolis and Formalistic Capital.' In *Crisis and Prosperity in Sung China*. Edited by John W. Haeger. Tucson: University of Arizona Press, 1975.

———. 'Sung Society: Change Within Tradition.' In *Enduring Scholarship Selected from the Far Eastern Quarterly – the Journal of Asian Studies, 1941–1971*. Volume I: *China*. Edited by John A. Harrison. Tucson: University of Arizona Press, 1972. Pp. 65–9. Originally published in the *Far Eastern Quarterly* 11 (1952).

———. 'The Expansion of Educational Opportunity in the Reign of Hui-tsung of the Sung and Its Implications.' *Sung Studies Newsletter* 13 (1977):6–30.

Lee, Thomas H. C. [Li Hung-chi]. 'Education in Sung China.' Ph.D. Dissertation, Yale University, 1974.

———. 'The Schools of Sung China.' *The Journal of Asian Studies* 37 (1977):45–60.

Legge, James, trans. *The Confucian Analects*. In *The Four Books*. Shanghai:

Chinese Book Company, 1933; reprint ed. Taipei: I-shih Book Company, 1971.

——. *The Li Chi*, 2 vols. Edited by Ch'u Chai and Winberg Chai. New York: University Books, Inc., 1967.

——. *The Works of Mencius.* In *The Four Books.* Shanghai: Chinese Book Company, 1933; reprint ed. Taipei: I-shih Book Company, 1971.

Levenson, Joseph. *Confucian China and Its Modern Fate: A Trilogy.* Berkeley: University of California Press, 1968. (pb. ed.).

Li, Dun J. *The Essence of Chinese Civilization.* New York: D. Van Nostrand Company, 1967.

Lin Yu-tang. *A History of the Press and Public Opinion in China.* Chicago: University of Chicago Press, 1936.

Liu, James T. C. [Liu Tzu-chien]. 'An Early Sung Reformer: Fan Chung-yen.' In *Chinese Thought and Institutions.* Edited by John K. Fairbank. Chicago: University of Chicago Press, 1967. Pp. 105–31.

——. 'China's Imperial Power in Mid-Dynastic Crises: The Case in 1127–1130.' Paper presented to the Conference on the Exercise of Imperial Power, 10th–14th Centuries, Germany, September 1982.

——. 'How Did a Neo-Confucian School Become the State Orthodoxy?' *Philosophy East and West* 23 (1973):483–505.

——. *Ou-yang Hsiu: An Eleventh Century Confucianist.* Stanford, Calif.: Stanford University Press, 1967.

——. *Reform in Sung China: Wang An-shih (1021–1086) and his New Policies.* Cambridge, Mass.: Harvard University Press, 1959.

——. 'The Sung Views on the Control of Government Clerks.' *Journal of the Economic and Social History of the Orient* 10 (1967):317–44.

Lo Jung-pang. 'The Emergence of China as a Seapower During the Late Sung and Early Yuan Periods.' In *Enduring Scholarship Selected from the Far Eastern Quarterly – the Journal of Asian Studies, 1941–1971* Volume I: *China.* Edited by John A. Harrison. Tucson: University of Arizona Press, 1972: 91–105. Originally published in the *Far Eastern Quarterly* 11 (1952).

Ma. Laurence J. C. *Commercial Development and Urban Change in Sung China (960–1279).* Ann Arbor: Department of Geography, University of Michigan, 1971.

McKnight, Brian. 'Chu Hsi and the World He Lived In.' Paper presented to the International Conference on Chu Hsi (1130–1200), Honolulu, Hawaii, July 1982.

——. 'Fiscal Privileges and the Social Order.' In *Crisis and Prosperity in Sung China.* Edited by John W. Haeger. Tucson: University of Arizona Press, 1975. Pp. 79–100.

——. *Village Bureaucracy in Southern Sung China.* Chicago: University of Chicago Press, 1971.

Maspero, Henri. 'The Mythology of Modern China.' In *Asiatic Mythology.* Introduction by Paul-Louis Couchoud. London, 1932; reprint New York: Crescent books.

Miyakawa Hisayuki. 'An Outline of the Naito Hypothesis and Its Effects on Japanese Studies of China.' *Far Eastern Quarterly* 14 (1954–5):533–52.

Miyazaki Ichisada. *China's Examination Hell.* Translated by Conrad Shirokauer.

New York: John Weatherhill, Inc., 1976.

Munro, Donald. *The Concept of Man in Early China*. Stanford, Calif.: Stanford University Press, 1969.

Needham, Joseph. 'Science and China's Influence in the World.' In *The Legacy of China*. Edited by Raymond Dawson. Oxford: Oxford University Press, 1964. Pp. 234–308.

Nivison, David S. 'Protests Against Convention and Conventions of Protest.' In *The Confucian Persuasion*. Editor, Arthur F. Wright, Stanford, Calif.: Stanford University Press, 1960: 177–201.

Overmyer, Daniel L. *Folk Buddhist Religion: Dissenting Sects in Late Traditional China*. Cambridge, Mass.: Harvard University Press, 1976.

Rawski, Evelyn Sakakida. *Agricultural Change and the Peasant Economy of South China*. Cambridge, Mass.: Harvard University Press, 1972.

———. *Education and Popular Literacy in Ch'ing China*. Ann Arbor: University of Michigan Press, 1979.

Shiba Yoshinobu. *Commerce and Society in Sung China*. Translated by Mark Elvin. Ann Arbor: Center for Chinese Studies, University of Michigan, 1970.

———. 'Ningpo and Its Hinterland.' In *The City in Late Imperial China*. Edited by G. William Skinner. Stanford, Calif.: Stanford University Press, 1977. Pp. 391–439.

———. 'Urbanization and the Development of Markets in the Lower Yangtze valley.' In *Crisis and Prosperity in Sung China*. Edited by John W. Haeger. Tuscon: University of Arizona Press, 1975: 13–48.

Schirokauer, Conrad. 'Neo-Confucianism Under Attack: The Condemnation of *Wei hsüeh*.' In *Crisis and Prosperity in Sung China*. Edited by John W. Haeger. Tucson: University of Arizona Press, 1975. Pp. 163–98.

Skinner, G. William. 'Cities and the Hierarchy of Local Systems.' In *The City in Late Imperial China*. Edited by G. William Skinner. Stanford, Calif.: Stanford University Press, 1977. Pp. 275–351.

———. 'Introduction: Urban Development in Imperial China.' In *The City in Late Imperial China*. Edited by G. William Skinner. Stanford, Calif.: Stanford University Press, 1977. Pp. 3–31.

———. 'Mobility Strategies in Late Imperial China: a Regional Systems Analysis.' In *Regional Systems*, 2 vols. Edited by Carol A. Smith. New York: Academic Press, Inc., 1976. 1:327–64.

———. 'Regional Urbanization in Nineteenth Century China.' In *The City in Late Imperial China*. Edited by G. William Skinner. Stanford, Calif.: Stanford University Press, 1977. Pp. 211–49.

Steele, John., trans. *The I-li or Book of Etiquette and Ceremonial*. 2 vols. London: Probsthain & Co., 1917.

Stone, Lawrence. 'The Educational Revolution in England, 1560–1640.' *Past and Present* 28 (July 1964):41–80.

Tillman, Hoyt. *Utilitarian Confucianism: Ch'en Liang's Challenge to Chu Hsi*. Cambridge, Mass.: Harvard University Press, 1982.

Trexler, Richard C. *Public Life in Renaissance Florence*. New York: Academic Press, 1980.

Tu Wei-ming. 'The Confucian Perception of Adulthood.' *Daedalus* v. 105 (Spring 1976). Pp. 109–23. Reprinted in *Adulthood*. Editor Erik H. Erikson. New

York: W. W. Norton & Co., 1976. Pp. 113–20.

Twitchett, Denis. 'A Critique of Some Recent Studies of Modern Chinese Social-Economic History.' *Transactions of the International Conference of Orientalists in Japan.* 10 (1965):28–41.

——. 'The Composition of the T'ang Ruling Class: New Evidence from Tunhuang.' In *Perspectives on the T'ang.* Edited by Arthur F. Wright and Denis Twitchett, New Haven, Conn.: Yale University Press, 1973: 47–85.

——. 'Documents on Clan Administration: I. The Rules of Administration of the Charitable Estate of the Fan Clan.' *Asia Major*, n.s. 8 (1960):1–35.

——. 'The Fan Clan's Charitable Estate. 1050–1760.' In *Confucianism in Action.* Edited by David Nivison and Arthur Wright. Stanford, Calif.: Stanford University Press, 1959: 97–133.

——. 'T'ang Government Institutions: the Bureaucracy.' In *Cambridge History of China*, forthcoming.

Übelhör, Monica. 'Mr. Lu's Community Pact, With Additions and Deletions by Chu Hsi.' Paper presented to the International Conference on Chu Hsi, University of Hawaii, July 1982.

Van Gulik, R. H. 'On the Seal Representing the God of Literature on the Title Page of Old Chinese and Japanese Popular Editions.' *Monumenta Nipponica* 4 (January 1941):33–52.

Wakeman, Frederic. 'The Price of Autonomy: Intellectuals in Ming and Ch'ing Politics.' *Daedalus* 101, no. 2 (1972):35–70.

Waley, Arthur, *The Life and Times of Po Chü-i (772–846 A.D.).* London: George Allen & Unwin, Ltd., 1949.

Walton-Vargo, Linda. 'Education, Social Change, and Neo-Confucianism in Sung Yuan China.' Ph.D. Dissertation, University of Pennsylvania, 1978.

Ward, Barbara. 'Readers and Audiences: An Exploration of the Spread of Traditional Chinese Culture.' In *Text and Context: the Social Anthropology of Tradition.* Edited by Ravindra K. Jain. Philadelphia: Institute for the Study of Human Issues, Inc., 1977: 181–203.

Weber, Max. 'Bureaucracy.' *From Max Weber: Essays in Sociology.* Translated and edited by H. H. Girth and C. Wright Mills. New York: Oxford University Press 1958: 196–244.

——. *The Religion of China: Confucianism and Taoism.* Translated by Hans H. Gerth. New York: Macmillan Co., 1964.

Weng T'ung-wen. *Répertoire des dates des hommes célèbres des Song.* Paris: Mouton & Co., 1962.

Wilhelm, Hellmut. 'From Myth to Myth: The Case of Yüeh Fei's Biography.' In *Confucianism and Chinese Civilization.* Edited by Arthur F. Wright. Stanford, Calif.: Stanford University Press, 1975.

Williamson, H. R. *Wang An-shih: a Chinese Statesman and Educationalist of the Sung Dynasty*, 2 vols. London: Arthur Probsthain, 1935.

Winkleman, John H. 'The Imperial Library in Southern Sung China, 1127–1279: A Study of the Organization and Operation of the Scholarly Agencies of the Central Government.' *Transactions of the American Philosophical Society* n.s. 64, pt. 8 (1974).

Wittfogel, Karl. 'Public Office Office in the Liao and the Chinese Examination System.' *Harvard Journal of Asiatic Studies* 10 (1947):13–40.

Wolf, Arthur P. 'Gods, Ghosts, and Ancestors.' In *Religion and Ritual in Chinese Society*. Editor, Arthur P. Wolf. Stanford, Calif.: Stanford University Press, 1974. Pp. 131–82.

Wright, Arthur F. 'The Formation of Sui Ideology, 581–604.' In *Chinese Thought and Institutions*. Edited by John K. Fairbank. Chicago: University of Chicago Press, 1967. Pp. 71–104.

——. 'Symbolism and Function, Reflections on Changan and other Great Cities.' In *Journal of Asian Studies* 24 (1965):667–79.

Yang C. K. 'Some Characteristics of Chinese Bureaucratic Behavior.' In *Confucianism in Action*. Edited by David S. Nivison and Arthur F. Wright. Stanford, Calif.: Stanford University Press, 1959. Pp. 134–64.

Yang Lien-sheng. 'Buddhist Monasteries and Four Money-raising Institutions in Chinese History.' *Harvard Journal of Asiatic Studies* 13 (1950):174–91.

INDEX

Printed in the United States
55213LVS00004B/157-168

9 780791 424247